Palgrave Studies in European Political Sociology

Series Editors
Carlo Ruzza
Department of Sociology and Social Research
University of Trento
Trento, Italy

Hans-Jörg Trenz
Department of Media, Cognition and Communication
University of Copenhagen
Copenhagen, Denmark

Palgrave Studies in European Political Sociology addresses contemporary themes in the field of Political Sociology. Over recent years, attention has turned increasingly to processes of Europeanization and globalization and the social and political spaces that are opened by them. These processes comprise both institutional-constitutional change and new dynamics of social transnationalism. Europeanization and globalization are also about changing power relations as they affect people's lives, social networks and forms of mobility.

The Palgrave Studies in European Political Sociology series addresses linkages between regulation, institution building and the full range of societal repercussions at local, regional, national, European and global level, and will sharpen understanding of changing patterns of attitudes and behaviours of individuals and groups, the political use of new rights and opportunities by citizens, new conflict lines and coalitions, societal interactions and networking, and shifting loyalties and solidarity within and across the European space.

We welcome proposals from across the spectrum of Political Sociology and Political Science, on dimensions of citizenship; political attitudes and values; political communication and public spheres; states, communities, governance structure and political institutions; forms of political participation; populism and the radical right; and democracy and democratization.

More information about this series at
http://www.palgrave.com/gp/series/14630

Marco Giugni • Maria T. Grasso
Editors

Citizens and the Crisis

Experiences, Perceptions, and Responses to the Great Recession in Europe

palgrave
macmillan

Editors
Marco Giugni
University of Geneva
Geneva, Switzerland

Maria T. Grasso
University of Sheffield
Sheffield, UK

Palgrave Studies in European Political Sociology
ISBN 978-3-319-68959-3 ISBN 978-3-319-68960-9 (eBook)
https://doi.org/10.1007/978-3-319-68960-9

Library of Congress Control Number: 2017962777

Cover illustration: Stuart Minzey / GettyImages

Printed on acid-free paper

This Palgrave Macmillan imprint is published by Springer Nature
The registered company is Springer International Publishing AG
The registered company address is: Gewerbestrasse 11, 6330 Cham, Switzerland

Acknowledgments

Results presented in this book have been obtained within the project "Living with Hard Times: How Citizens React to Economic Crises and Their Social and Political Consequences" (LIVEWHAT). This project was funded by the European Commission under the 7th Framework Programme (grant agreement no. 613237). The LIVEWHAT consortium was coordinated by the University of Geneva (Marco Giugni) and was formed, additionally, by the European University Institute, later replaced by the Scuola Normale Superiore (Lorenzo Bosi); Uppsala University (Katrin Uba); the University of Sheffield (Maria Grasso); the CEVIPOF-Sciences Po, Paris (Manlio Cinalli); the University of Siegen (Christian Lahusen); the Autonomous University of Barcelona (Eva Anduiza); the University of Crete (Maria Kousis); and the University of Warsaw (Maria Theiss). We thank all the members of the LIVEWHAT research consortium for their contribution to the project.

Contents

Notes on Contributors

Eva Anduiza is Associate Professor of Political Science and ICREA (Institució Catalana de Recerca i Estudis Avançats) Academia Fellow at the Universitat Autònoma de Barcelona. Her main research interests include political participation, voting behaviour and political attitudes.

Lorenzo Bosi is Assistant Professor at the Scuola Normale Superiore (SNS) and Research Fellow within the Centre on Social Movement Studies (Cosmos). His main research interests are in political sociology and historical sociology where his studies primarily focus on qualitative research of social movements and political violence. He is mainly interested in how and when contentious political actors shift forms of action.

Didier Chabanet is Senior Researcher at IDRAC Lyon and Triangle (Ecole Normale Supérieure). He is also Associate Researcher at Sciences Po-CEVIPOF, France. His interest lies especially in the fields of social movements, social exclusion, social entrepreneurship, and European integration.

Manlio Cinalli is Research Professor at CEVIPOF (CNRS—UMR 7048) Sciences Po, in Paris. He previously delivered research and teaching in various leading universities and institutes across Europe and the USA, including Columbia University, the European University Institute (EUI) and the University of Oxford. He has published widely on citizenship and political integration.

Marco Giugni is Professor at the Department of Political Science and International Relations and Director of the Institute of Citizenship Studies (InCite) at the University of Geneva, Switzerland. His research interests include social movements and collective action, immigration and ethnic relations, unemployment and social exclusion.

Maria T. Grasso is Professor at the Department of Politics, University of Sheffield, United Kingdom. She is the author of *Generations, Political Participation and Social Change in Western Europe* (2016) and co-editor of *Austerity and Protest: Popular Contention in Times of Economic Crisis* (2015). Her research focuses on political sociology and political engagement.

Marc Guinjoan is Postdoctoral Researcher at the Department of Political Science and Public Law at Universitat Autònoma de Barcelona and visiting scholar at the Department of Political Science at University of Copenhagen. His research interests are focused on political behaviour, elections, parties, populism, electoral systems, identities and decentralisation.

Stefania Kalogeraki is Assistant Professor of Quantitative Methods in Sociology and Social Demography at the Department of Sociology, University of Crete, Greece. Her research interests include questionnaire design, quantitative comparative social research, social demographic analysis and mixed method designs.

Johannes Kiess is Researcher in Sociology at the University of Siegen. His research interests include political sociology, political attitudes and right-wing extremism, trade unions, European integration and the framing of politics and policies.

Anna Kurowska is Assistant Professor at the Institute of Social Policy, University of Warsaw. Her research focuses on family policy, employment and gender-related issues. She is an author of articles and co-author of books on mothers' employment, parental leave systems and capability approach in social policy.

Christian Lahusen is Professor of Sociology of Europe at the University of Siegen. His research is devoted to political sociology, social problems and the sociology of Europe and European integration. He is involved in international research consortia and is currently the coordinator of the TransSOL research project (Horizon 2020).

Maria M. Mexi is Scientific Collaborator at the Institute of Citizenship Studies (InCite) at the University of Geneva, Switzerland. Her research interests fall within the areas of migration, social dialogue and the future of work.

Anne Muxel is Research Professor at CEVIPOF (CNRS—UMR 7048) Sciences Po, in Paris. She studies political attitudes and behaviour in contemporary France and in European countries, focusing on youth and politics. She also works on voting, exploring electoral surveys regularly conducted at the CEVIPOF. She has written many articles on these topics.

Guillem Rico is Ramón y Cajal Research Fellow at the Department of Political Science, Universitat Autònoma de Barcelona. His research interests include political attitudes and behaviour, public opinion, political socialisation, political leadership and populism.

Luke Temple is Research Assistant in the Department of Politics and a Teaching Assistant in the Department of Geography at the University of Sheffield, UK. His research interests include the links between citizen understandings of democracy, digital engagement and political participation.

Maria Theiss is Assistant Professor at the Institute of Social Policy, Warsaw University. Her research focuses on the issues of social citizenship, social capital, civic society and the local level of social policy. She has written and co-edited books on poverty, social exclusion and governance processes at the local level in Poland.

Katrin Uba is Associate Professor at the Department of Government at the Uppsala University, Sweden. Her research focuses on social movements and trade union activism in Sweden and beyond. She is particularly interested in the role of different forms of protest activities in national and local welfare politics.

Steven M. Van Hauwaert is an Alexander von Humboldt Fellow at the University of Mainz and the principal investigator of the Global Public Opinions Project (www.gpop.eu). His primary research interests are in the fields of comparative political behaviour and public opinion, as well as populism and political extremism.

Thierry Vedel is CNRS Senior Researcher at CEVIPOF (CNRS—UMR 7048) Sciences Po, in Paris. His research interests cover the impacts of the internet on political systems and democracy, politics and communication and the regulation of media in a globalised world. He has been involved in many international projects.

Lorenzo Zamponi is a research fellow in sociology and political science at the Scuola Normale Superiore, Florence, where he is part of the COSMOS (Centre on Social Movement Studies) research team. His research interests include contentious politics, collective memory and media analysis.

List of Figures

List of Tables

CHAPTER 1

Citizens and the Crisis: Perceptions, Experiences, and Responses to the Great Recession in Nine Democracies

Marco Giugni and Maria T. Grasso

European Citizens and the Great Recession

The economic crisis starting in 2008, also known as the "Great Recession," has led to rising unemployment, shrinking growth, and, more generally, to a deterioration of macroeconomic conditions and living standards across Europe. Ten years since its onset, there is great variation in the economic conditions of different countries in Europe. As citizens still struggle to cope with the effects of the economic crisis, attention has been drawn to the implications of the recession in the social and political spheres of life. For example, the experience of economic difficulty can be understood to generate grievances which people may seek to redress through political action (Grasso and Giugni 2013; Grasso and Giugni 2016b).

M. Giugni (✉)
Department of Political Science and International Relations, University of Geneva, Geneva, Switzerland

M.T. Grasso
Department of Politics, University of Sheffield, Sheffield, UK

M. Giugni, M.T. Grasso (eds.), *Citizens and the Crisis*, Palgrave Studies in European Political Sociology, https://doi.org/10.1007/978-3-319-68960-9_1

Particularly during periods of economic challenges, macroeconomic conditions might fail to meet expectations, in turn resulting in feelings of relative deprivation and dissatisfaction. Indeed we expect that experiences of the crisis will vary depending on the political and economic context of the crisis (Giugni and Grasso 2016; Grasso and Giugni 2016a). In some countries, the economic crisis occurred in a period that was already characterized by deepening political crises (Kriesi 2014a).

As such, some of the overarching questions guiding this volume are as follows: How do citizens' perceptions and experiences of the crisis as well as their political responses to it vary between countries which have experienced much deeper and more serious economic and political crises in this period? In those countries that suffered less serious economic consequences, are the perceptions of the crisis socially differentiated between more resource-rich and more resource-poor groups? Is perceived inequality heightened in these cases? Are some social classes and more economically vulnerable and deprived groups particularly hard hit? And what about countries which experienced more mixed repercussions from the crisis, how do negative economic contexts impact on the political sphere, for example? Do these factors spur new political ruptures, critiques of neoliberalism, or newfound support for the extreme right parties as would seem to be suggested by UKIP's success in their campaign for Brexit as well as Marine Le Pen's rise in the polls or Poland's emboldened and ultraconservative Law and Justice Party?

Economic crises have historically provided opportunities through opening up new areas of contention and the restructuring of political space for the mobilization of various groups. Particularly in those countries worst hit by the crisis, large protests took place as European governments were blamed for the negative economic circumstances. Protest parties or "movement parties" (della Porta et al. 2017) such as *Syriza, Podemos* and the *Movimento 5 Stelle* have also been able to attract large proportions of electoral support across the continent. In this way, the links between economic and political crises have been further emphasized, broadening their critiques to the entire political system and fostering requests for "real democracy now" such as with Spain's *Indignados* movement or calls for more social justice and rising opposition to inequality such as with #Occupy" (della Porta 2015).

At this time where the political context is rife with diverse sources of dissatisfaction, it appears particularly important to understand how the crisis has affected the perceptions and experiences of different sectors of the public in different countries as well as the diverse types of political responses that citizens have taken in reaction (see also Giugni and Grasso 2017, Temple and Grasso 2017). Exploring these dynamics in diverse contexts is one of the key contributions of this volume. Despite the central importance of investigating these questions in the current historical juncture, the scholarly literature is fragmented and underdeveloped in key areas. There is little research on the economic correlates of populist attitudes, and the electoral and non-electoral participation literatures tend to talk past each other. The political science literature on the impact of the economy on political activity is narrowly focused on the widely tested theory of economic voting suggesting that individuals reward incumbents when the economy is doing well but punish them when the economy is doing badly. As such, the chapters in this volume aim to contribute to theorizing in these directions, attempting to push the frontiers of research on citizens' perceptions, experiences, and responses to economic crises.

This volume deals more specifically with the way in which European citizens have faced the Great Recession. It offers an informed and rich discussion of citizens' perceptions and experiences of the economic crisis as well as of their political responses to it in nine European countries: France, Germany, Greece, Italy, Poland, Spain, Sweden, Switzerland, and UK. All the chapters provide theoretically informed empirical analyses based on the survey data collected during an EU-funded collaborative research project. Each chapter focuses on one of the nine countries, but at the same time puts forward a more general argument about the impact of the crisis on citizens' perceptions, experiences, and responses to the crisis. All the chapters analyze first-hand evidence stemming from the same survey that we fielded in 2015 with a questionnaire tailor-made to answer our research questions.

Given the depth of the economic crisis that started a decade ago, it should come as no surprise that researchers have paid much attention to its impact on people's opinions, attitudes, and behaviors. Some have investigated the electoral consequences of the Great Recessions (Kriesi 2014a; Talving 2017); others its impact on collective action (Ancelovici et al. 2016; della Porta and Mattoni 2014; Giugni and Grasso 2015a), including in specific national contexts (Bernburg 2016); still others have looked at opinions about the crisis (Bermeo and Bartels 2014a). Only rarely have works dealt with all these aspects at the same time. A particularly significant volume in this regard is Bermeo's and Bartels (2014b) volume *Mass Politics in Tough Times.*

The present book takes on some of the key issues dealt with in Bermeo and Bartels' (2014b) volume but develops them in different ways. In particular, we make use of one cross-national survey fielded in all nine countries of the volume and designed specifically by the research teams and authors of the volume contributions to tackle our research questions of interest. Moreover, each chapter makes ample use of each national team's detailed knowledge of their country's politics and wider contextual conditions to discuss experiences and responses of the crisis in relation to the very specific political national developments in each country. Like the contributions in Bermeo and Bartels' volume, those in this volume are similarly interested in citizen's perceptions, experiences, and responses—namely, political responses—and we examine both electoral and institutional and extra-institutional dimensions.

The volume consists of three main parts, each focusing on a specific analytical dimension: the first part deals with citizens' political responses in the institutional realm; the second part focuses on political responses in the extra-institutional arena; finally, the third part examines variations in perceptions and experiences of the crisis across different sectors of society. Each part includes three chapters, each bearing on a given country. This introductory chapter addresses a number of issues relating to how the crisis impacts on the citizenry. More specifically, we discuss three main issues which are the focus of the three parts of the book. The first two parts deal with the ways in which citizens reacted to the crisis in two distinct political arenas, namely, the institutional arena and the extra-institutional arena, while the third part examines variations in the ways the crisis was perceived and experienced by different sectors of the population. In addition, after a brief presentation of the empirical basis of the volume, we provide a comparative overview of key indicators of perceptions, experiences, and responses to the economic crisis across the nine countries covered in the book.

Citizens, the Crisis, and Institutional Politics

Much research on the consequences of the Great Recession has focused on the impact of the crisis on institutional politics. Scholars have shown how the economic crisis led to changes in political preferences and voting patterns (Kriesi 2014a; Talving 2017). Over the past few years, the trend toward an increasing disconnection between citizens and the political system, already underway before the crisis, has accelerated dramatically.

Citizens in many—if not most—countries are more and more distrustful of politicians, whom are often seen at best as not being concerned with the public good and at worst as corrupt, disaffected from, and disenchanted with politics. Political and democratic legitimation crises plague our current times. Furthermore, economic hardship may further depress one's feelings of political efficacy. All this may lead to withdrawal from politics or entry into various forms of "protest politics" such as voting for radical right and populist parties.

Partly as a result of these dynamics, Europe has also witnessed an important decrease in electoral turnout, at least in some countries. While the causal linkages of such processes are still something in need of further analyses, these trends are most visible in those countries that have been severely struck by the crisis, such as Greece, Italy, and Spain. Those countries have also witnessed the rise of populist parties during the crisis. These have been the object of several studies (Kriesi 2014b; Kriesi and Pappas 2015; Judis 2016; Mudde 2013). So-called populist parties both from the right and from the left have either made an electoral breakthrough in the years of the crisis. Some of them were new, while others consisted in existing parties that have changed their agenda to adapt to the new political environment.

The three chapters in Part I of the book speak to these issues and deal with this connection between the economic crisis, citizens' perceptions, and experiences of the crisis, and their responses in terms of institutional politics. Luke Temple and Maria Grasso look in Chap. 2 at the relationships between the crisis, politics, and partisanship in the UK. They unpack how perceptions of economic crisis, class, and also objective economic deprivation vary across the UK's political spectrum. The UK provides a perfect test bed for this discussion as, while the country was not hit by a recession as deep as that experienced in say Greece or Spain, its close connection to the financial market and unprecedented interventions by the government in the economy mean economic management was crucial. Furthermore, the 2015 general election occurred against a backdrop of austerity and the "weakest economic recovery in recent history." However, the party that presided over the implementation of austerity policies was voted back in with a majority. Their analysis helps untangle what influences hard times may have had on voter perceptions. The results suggest that one of the most important factors in the UK context was rather existing left-right positions (see also Grasso et al. 2017).

Eva Anduiza, Marc Guinjoan, and Guillem Rico analyze in Chap. 3 the consequences of the economic recession in Spain for the development of populist attitudes and the appearance of a new, leftist populist party: *Podemos*. The chapter starts with an overview of the main elements of the Spanish political landscape between 2008 and 2016 and the evolution of key economic and political indicators. The authors then analyze the economic and political correlates of populist attitudes among the citizenry, showing that populist attitudes are relatively widespread and more likely to be present among individuals with low income, negative sociotropic perceptions of the economy, who are left-wing and politically sophisticated. Finally, they show that populist attitudes matter for electoral choice, but their effect changes depending on the characteristics of the electoral supply and the political context. In the 2015 elections populist attitudes were an important predictor of vote intention for *Podemos* and to a smaller extent for *Ciudadanos*, and had the reverse effect over the likelihood of voting for traditional parties. These attitudes are now essential to explaining electoral behavior in Spain.

Maria Theiss and Anna Kurowska deal in Chap. 4 with the legitimization divide in Poland in a context where the economic crisis had a weak impact also because of neoliberal economy and privatization of economic risk. Such an economic success, however, had political consequences and contributed to a legitimization crisis. Political narratives formulated by the conservative Law and Justice Party, which came into power, put into question most of the democratic achievements in Poland since 1989. This opened up a widespread political legitimation crisis. The authors explore this crisis at the individual level. They use the term legitimation divide for denoting a split in society between citizens perceiving the political system as legitimate and those denying political legitimation. Two broad hypotheses on the reasons for the legitimation divide are investigated. An "unfinished transformation" hypothesis assumes that the weakness of civil society and low civic skills in Poland may have resulted in the withdrawal of support for the political system. According to the second hypothesis, it has been the "neoliberal economy" in which neoliberalism may be perceived as a proactive anti-crisis measure, as well as lack of social security which contributed to the significant share of Polish society denying legitimation to the political system. The authors find that both streams of argument have their merits.

Citizens, the Crisis, and Extra-Institutional Politics

Scholarship has also looked at the impact of the economic crisis on extra-institutional engagement. Students of social movements, in particular, have paid increasing attention to movements and protests which emerged or reactivated during the Great Recession. This includes studies of the Spanish *Indignados* movement and the various Occupy movements (Ancelovici 2015; Ancelovici et al. 2016; Castells 2012; della Porta and Mattoni 2014; Flesher Fominaya and Cox 2013; Flesher Fominaya and Hayes 2017; Gamson and Sifry 2013; Giugni and Grasso 2015a; Pickerill and Krinsky 2012), the Greek situation in particular (Diani and Kousis 2014; Johnston and Seferiades 2012; Kousis 2014; Rüdig and Karyotis 2013, 2014; Sakellaropoulos 2012), but also of other countries (Bernburg 2015, 2016; Varga 2015). Again, the causal connection between the economic crisis and the rise of these movements and protests is far from being established (Cinalli and Giugni 2016). The greater amount of protests in certain countries, including those most deeply affected by the economic crisis, might result more from the specific national tradition and opportunities in those countries than to the impact of economic hardship as the grievance theory would assume. Nevertheless, studying whether and how the Great Recession has brought about new movements and protests remains important.

Just as important is the study of the relationship between the economic crisis and the propensity of people to engage in extra-institutional forms of political participation, including protest activities. As we mentioned earlier, two main hypotheses have been put forward in the literature in this regard (a third hypothesis may be advanced, namely that nothing changes): a "spurring" hypothesis, whereby economic hardship leads to an increased engagement, and a "withdrawal" hypothesis, whereby it pushes people out of politics (Grasso 2016). However, the two hypotheses could also be true at the same time, insofar as disengagement in the institutional arena might go hand in hand with increased commitment in the extra-institutional arena (Grasso 2018). Furthermore, certain forms of participation might be enhanced by the economic crisis, whereas others might be less practiced. This points to the need to study not only whether economic hardship spurs or deters extra-institutional participation but also the relationships between institutional (electoral) and extra-institutional (protest) behavior. This includes looking how certain forms of political engagement relate to each other.

The three chapters in Part II of the book speak to these issues and focus on the connection between the economic crisis, citizens' perceptions and experiences of the crisis, and their responses mainly in terms of extra-institutional politics. Didier Chabanet, Manlio Cinalli, Anne Muxel, Steven Van Hauwaert, and Thierry Vedel show in Chap. 5 that the "Contentious French" may not be that contentious anymore. The economic crisis provides a unique chance to argue that a post-contentious turning point is emerging in spite of a long-standing tradition of protest. Yet the chapter suggests that this post-contentious turning point is not bringing about acquiescence but opens space for new forms of political participation, especially in connection with resources acquired through employment and educational track. In this case, the authors find a more extensive engagement in online activism and noninstitutional forms of political participation, that is, the two forms of political participation that are less "active" and require a more modest time commitment. These findings are also put in the broader context of contemporary French politics so as to deepen interpretation of survey data at a moment when it is increasingly difficult to sustain traditionally inclusive policy-making, while electoral competition reveals growing difficulties vis-à-vis the challenges of the extreme right.

Lorenzo Zamponi and Lorenzo Bosi analyze in Chap. 6 the relationship between economic activism and political participation in Italy during the economic crisis. They investigate whether political consumerism is increasing or declining in times of economic crisis; whether it is an alternative to other forms of political participation in the current crisis, such as protest and/or voting; how "political" consumerism is in times of crisis; and whether there has been some shift in the composition of the Italian political consumerism community in times of economic crisis. Their analysis shows a visible change in the relationship between political consumerism and political participation in Italy during the economic crisis: respondents that have engaged in political consumerism in the last year are visibly less politicized than those who have engaged in buycotts or boycotts in the previous period. Furthermore, they are more likely to adopt anti-austerity stances and to express populist attitudes. This analysis suggests an ongoing process of change in the political consumerism community in Italy, with the economic crisis changing the constituency of economic activism and incentivizing the involvement of less politicized people.

Stefania Kalogeraki examines in Chap. 7 the role of volunteering in social solidarity networks during the recession in Greece. The recent global financial crisis has threatened the prosperity and economic security of the Eurozone. Greece was the epicenter of the crisis and one of the member states most severely affected. The country has experienced the most acute recession in its modern history with devastating impacts on people's lives. Despite the crisis' impacts, one positive development involves the increasing trend of citizens' volunteering in social solidarity networks such as food banks, social medical centers, exchange networks, time banks. These networks are providing alternative ways for supporting and enduring day-to-day difficulties during hard economic times. While past research has consistently shown low levels of volunteering in Greece, this chapter questions such a dominant view by presenting a picture of widespread volunteering in the prevalence of social solidarity networks.

The Social Bases of the Crisis

This volume, as a whole, highlights important cross-national variations in the ways in which citizens have apprehended the economic crisis and the policy responses to it. Comparing southern European countries with those of central and Northern Europe shows how individual perceptions and experiences of the crisis as well as political responses to it are context-dependent, how they depend both on the severity of the crisis, but also on specific nationally bounded conditions. Perceptions, experiences, and responses, however, do not only vary across countries, they also vary across different sectors of the society within a given country. The most under-privileged groups and individuals are likely to be more strongly affected by economic hardship. Thus, for example, unemployed people, migrants, and minorities as well as all the people who were already in a fragile and often marginalized situation should feel the effect of the crisis to a larger extent than people who are better off in more affluent periods. As a result, we may expect those groups and individuals to have a stronger perception as well as a more intense experience of the crisis, but also to have a more limited capacity to respond to it through various coping strategies and resilience, including political engagement.

On the other hand, however, studies have shown the strong impact of the economic crisis on the middle class raising concerns over a "middle-class squeeze" (Whelan et al. 2016). As the crisis went on, larger shares of once well-off social sectors had to put barriers to their lifestyle, reduce consumption patterns, and more generally abandon—at least temporarily—a way of life that does not to worry too much about money. All this has led to an erosion of the middle class, accelerating a process that was already under way before the crisis (Wisman 2013). Regardless of which social strata have suffered most from the Great Recession, it is important to stress that perceptions, experiences, and responses are not homogeneously distributed across the population. Quite on the contrary, they are likely to vary across social groups in important way, therefore suggesting group-specific analyses by researchers, but also more tailor-made policy measures by policy-makers to counter the negative effect of the economic crisis.

The three chapters in Part III of the book speak to these issues and examine whether and to what extent citizens' perceptions and experiences of the economic crisis as well as their political responses vary across social groups within society, in particular depending on sociodemographic and class-related characteristics. Christian Lahusen and Johannes Kiess look in Chap. 8 at perceptions and experiences of the crisis across social classes in Germany. Less than a fifth of Germans think the country is experiencing a very serious economic crisis. Encouraging labor market figures, steady growth rates, and a positive budget for consecutive years support this perception. However, in the literature there are strong claims made that despite the extension of the labor market and other positive predictors of economic and social inclusion, a considerable portion of the public is not benefitting from the relatively benign economic conditions and is rather excluded economically, socially, and politically. In this chapter the authors therefore ask which groups are especially sensitive to the crisis and what factors amplify their perceptions of the crisis. They argue that Germans feel under threat across classes because the positive economic situation is experienced as being contingent and individually precarious. Furthermore, they find that populism and dissatisfaction with government increase crisis susceptibility pointing to salient feelings of disappointment and alienation across society.

Marco Giugni and Maria Mexi deal in Chap. 9 with what they call "the silent crisis" in Switzerland. They examine whether and to what extent, in spite of Switzerland having largely been spared the negative impact of the crisis at the macroeconomic level, people have felt the negative impact of the crisis when one looks at the individual level. They focus on three main aspects: how people have perceived the economic crisis, the impact the crisis has had on their living and work conditions, and the ways in which they have dealt with it. They maintain that the effects of the economic crisis, if any, are unlikely to have been homogenous across the citizenry. They look at possible differential effects in terms of social class, income, education, and occupational status, and show that the crisis has affected in particular the most fragile and underprivileged sectors of the population. The lessons coming out of their analysis indicate that investigating links between economic crises and their impact on affluent countries means that we should rethink such an impact. The Great Recession, long seen as a problem for only the poorest, has been increasingly affecting some of the world's wealthiest nations such as Switzerland. Therefore, effective responses to counter the impact of the crisis must be informed by an awareness of how economic shocks have affected alternative strata of the population differently and how they have eroded their resilience.

Katrin Uba looks in Chap. 10 at the ways in which Swedish citizens perceived the economic crisis. Just like in Germany and Switzerland, two countries also dealt with in this section, the Great Recession of 2008 did not hit Sweden as much as it affected Greece, Italy, or Spain, for example. Yet, a majority of respondents perceived that the Swedish economy was suffering a crisis. This chapter investigates whether the perception of crisis is relatively uniform across the people with different socioeconomic backgrounds as some prior studies about crisis effect on economic mood have suggested. Such an explanation assumes that people are exposed to the same mediated representations of macroeconomic events and therefore would react to crisis in the same way, especially in the welfare states have some cushioning effect in the context of an economic downturn. The analysis demonstrates that men perceive the presence of a very serious economic crisis significantly more than women do; those with lower incomes and own experiences of crisis perceive the presence of crisis more than others; supporters of the radical right party perceive the severe crisis more often than supporters of other parties. While the analysis can only speculate on causal links, the significant support to the radical right party among those who perceive the serious crisis suggests that the perceived seriousness of crisis might be more closely related to distrust toward authorities than the real experience of economic downturn.

The Survey

All the chapters in this book are based on the analysis of survey data from the EU-funded cross-national comparative research project "Living with Hard Times: How Citizens React to Economic Crises and Their Social and Political Consequences" (LIVEWHAT).[1] In this way, the volume offers an analysis of citizens' perceptions and experiences of the crisis as well as their political responses in nine advanced industrial democracies. This improves on studies that have just focused on one country or only developing nations or have focused solely on disadvantaged communities. This set up allows us to offer an investigation into the dynamics linking economic crises, policy responses, and citizens' resilience.

The LIVEWHAT project aimed to provide evidence-based knowledge about citizens' resilience in times of economic crises. It examined in particular the ways in which European citizens have reacted to the crisis that struck Europe since 2008. The survey was developed as part of the project with the aim to analyze individual experiences and responses to the crisis. We collected data from across the nine European countries of the project. A specialized polling institute (YouGov) was subcontracted to conduct the survey in each country through the CAWI method (Computer-Assisted Web Interviewing). Each national sample contains about 2000 respondents.[2] As an Internet Panel, the survey included weights based on gender, age, region as well as education quotas. Fieldwork started on 26 May 2015 and was completed on 30 July 2015. Most of the fieldwork for all countries occurred during the period of 25 June to 30 July 2015.

The aim of the survey was to study individual perceptions, evaluations, and responses to crises by private citizens. In particular, it examined how citizens perceive and react to crises; for example, how citizens rate their living standards in relation to the past, and how hopeful they are that these will improve in the future. Moreover, it collected evidence on individuals' political attitudes and behaviors, their social relations and networks, lifestyle patterns and use of leisure time, their feelings of well-being and relative social status, and so on. It also collected classic socio-economic indicators such as gender, age, occupation, and so on in order to analyze whether there are key differences between different social groups in terms of both how they subjectively perceive and also how they objectively modify their behaviors as a result of economic hardship and the social and political ramifications of crisis. What do ordinary citizens consider as a situation of economic crisis? How do they perceive it? How do they react to crises? Who is most affected by crises? To what extent are social and political attitudes related to crises? To what extent are social and political behaviors related to crises? To what extent are the family and social life of people affected by crises? These are some of the questions that our survey was intended to answer. Additionally, a particular focus of the survey was to collect data that would enable us to evaluate citizens' views about the role of the EU in relation to crisis. Are there important differences across social groups and countries on these and other important dimensions of subjective and objective reactions to crisis?

To answer these as well as related questions, we developed our own theoretically minded questionnaire. The questionnaire includes questions measuring the material/economic dimension, the psychological/attitudinal dimension, and the behavioral dimension, as well as respondents' personal background and individual characteristics (including their embeddedness in organizational networks). Particular emphasis is put on how citizens frame economic crises and policy responses to such crises, on blame attribution, and on the potential mismatch between their views and policy responses. The questionnaire was translated in the national languages of the countries included in the project. Translation protocols were applied to ensure equivalent translations in all the languages.

Comparing Perceptions, Experiences, and Responses in Nine European Democracies

Returning to the chapters in the volume themselves, each of the chapters addresses a specific aspect relating to how citizens have faced the Great Recession in a given country: how they perceived it, how they experienced it, and how they responded politically to it. In this section we present a brief comparative assessment of citizens' attitudes toward the economic crisis. As can be seen from Table 1.1, countries tend to be differentiated in terms of their public perceptions of the crisis on the basis of whether the crisis was deeper or lighter. People in those countries where the crisis was lighter are more positive about economic conditions and less worried about the crisis. This is not surprising since they also had to suffer fewer consequences such as having to make drastic cut-

Table 1.1 Perceptions of the severity of the economic crisis (percentages)

	Fra	*Ger*	*Gre*	*Ita*	*Pol*	*Spa*	*Swe*	*Swi*	*UK*
We are suffering a very serious economic crisis	66.7	17.5	88.8	79.0	23.0	72.7	16.4	14.3	38.1
We are suffering a crisis but it is not very serious	17.2	31.4	5.1	11.5	42.0	18.2	41.3	51.3	42.6
No economic crisis	3.6	34.8	2.4	3.7	22.3	2.5	24.6	21.3	10.1

Notes: Percentages based on respondents selecting specific answer options

Q: Some say that the UK is suffering a very serious economic crisis, others say that we are suffering a crisis but it is not very serious, while others say that there isn't any economic crisis. What do you think?

backs in consumption. On the other hand, the situation is far more serious in other countries such as Greece. The extent to which citizens believe the crisis is serious maps on very clearly to the depth of the crisis in those countries. Countries with lighter experiences such as Germany, Poland, Sweden, Switzerland, and to some extent the UK show lower perceptions agreeing that the country is suffering a serious crisis. On the other end of the spectrum are Greece, Italy, and Spain. France also shows a very high proportion, even though the crisis was not as deep here (it tends to be classed with Poland and the UK as having a middle level of crisis).

People often assess their own living standard as well as their country's economy as compared to the situation in previous periods, other people, or other countries. Economic hardship has an impact on such feelings of relative deprivation. Table 1.2 gives us an indication of this in terms of current living standards as compared to one's parents (generational deprivation), in terms of one's own household as compared to the same five years earlier (pocketbook deprivation), in terms of one's country economy as compared to one year earlier (sociotropic deprivation), and in terms of one's country economy in the future (prospective deprivation). As we can see, citizens' evaluations of their relative living standards are patterned by region. Respondents tended to be more positive in countries where the crisis was lighter. The Greek result is particularly striking in this respect: only seven percent of citizens in Greece felt that their household living conditions were better than they were five years previously to when the survey took place (i.e., 2010). Similarly, the evaluation of the situation of the country's economy is also much context-dependent. Again, and quite

Table 1.2 Relative economic evaluations (percentages better)

	Fra	*Ger*	*Gre*	*Ita*	*Pol*	*Spa*	*Swe*	*Swi*	*UK*
Living standard compared to parents	37.7	56.9	32.3	39.0	51.4	49.5	64.8	61.5	59.8
Household compared to five years ago	23.8	45.2	6.8	23.4	37.7	24.0	56.5	40.7	40.7
Country economy compared to a year ago	11.8	38.4	3.7	17.2	26.6	31.5	34	21.7	49.7
Country economy in the future	15.0	31.6	18.1	25.6	25.5	41.7	32.4	26.2	47.0

Notes: Percentages based on respondents selecting points 6 through to 10 on the 0–10 scale

Q: On a scale from 0 to 10 where 0 means "much worse" and 10 means "much better" ...

understandably, Greek citizens stand out as particularly negative in this regard: four percent said their country's economy was better than one year earlier (i.e., 2014).

Table 1.3 gives us another, interesting way to assess citizens' perceptions of the economic crisis, one relating to the perceptions that Europeans have of living conditions in their own country relative to those in the other countries. First, people were asked about living conditions in their own country, then they were asked to rate them in the other countries. As we can see, some countries such as Germany, Sweden, and Switzerland tend to be rated highly by citizens of most countries, whereas others, such as Italy, Poland, Spain, but above all Greece, tend to be viewed quite poorly. Countries where the crisis was lighter are by and large also those countries that tend to be viewed more positively.

As shown in Table 1.4, the crisis has had very serious consequences for the lived experiences of European citizens. Many of them had to significantly change their consumption habits, especially so in the countries mostly affected by the crisis. In those countries where the crisis was particularly deep, citizens had to make cutbacks even in consumption of staples. For example, about two thirds said they had to reduce consumption of staple foods in Greece, and 6 respondents out of 10 said they had to postpone visits to the doctor or buying medicines. Thus, the Great Recession has not only affected the perceptions Europeans have of their own living conditions as well as of their country economy, but has had a negative impact on the very experiences of the crisis as well as on the citizens' actual living conditions.

Table 1.3 Perceptions of country living conditions relative to other countries (percentages good)

	Fra	*Ger*	*Gre*	*Ita*	*Pol*	*Spa*	*Swe*	*Swi*	*UK*
Conditions own country	42.9	70.0	9.7	19.8	24.7	33.3	75.4	75.6	70.8
France	–	62.2	71.6	70.2	74.9	79.3	62.9	48.9	73.7
Germany	71.6	–	84.7	88.4	87.7	85.2	77.5	70.6	83.8
Greece	6.7	6.9	–	8.4	21.2	5.6	9.4	5.9	14.8
Italy	24.9	37.5	39.1	–	65.7	29.4	38.1	25.6	44.4
Poland	19.5	25.6	20.2	26.2	–	21.2	23.1	16.4	24.6
Spain	27.2	31.6	35.5	48.8	48.1	–	38.9	23.2	43.3
Sweden	76.1	81.6	86.7	85.7	84.4	84.4	–	83.2	84.6
Switzerland	82.8	84.6	88.7	90.5	85.1	86.9	78.8	–	86.9
UK	64.9	63.1	81.9	83.5	85.9	80.2	64.5	57.5	–

Notes: Percentages based on respondents selecting points 6 through to 10 on the 0–10 scale

In each country, this question will be slightly different: it first asks respondents to rate the country of survey, and afterward, the other eight countries in the project, in alphabetical order

Q: The living conditions among European countries differ quite a lot today, and we would like to get your personal evaluation. Please use the scale below, where 0 means "very bad living conditions" and 10 means "very good living conditions"

All this could not but have important repercussions on citizens' political attitudes, in particular their identification of the main actors responsible for the situation and the evaluation of the government's handling of the crisis. In the perspective of retrospective and economic voting and theories, credit and blame assignment or attribution is known to be a major predictor of vote choice (Marsh and Tilley 2010; Stokes 1963). These processes might become particularly important in periods of economic downturn, as citizens would tend to rely on government policy response and assign them responsibility for the poor economic situation of the country as well as their own (Talving 2017). From Tables 1.5 and 1.6 we can see the proportion of citizens blaming different political bodies and entities for the country's economic difficulties and the rise of unemployment. As we can see, in most countries citizens tend to blame the national government, though in Germany, Switzerland, and the UK, banks and financial actors are seen as more blameworthy with respect to the country's economic difficulties, and in Switzerland the EU is blamed even more than the government for economic woes. As for the rise of unemployment, the government tends to be blamed more than banks and financial actors in all countries but Switzerland and the UK. A sizeable

Table 1.4 Reductions in consumption (percentages yes)

	Fra	*Ger*	*Gre*	*Ita*	*Pol*	*Spa*	*Swe*	*Swi*	*UK*
Reduced consumption of staple foods	36.2	18.8	65.0	42.0	34.7	27.1	16.8	24.4	20.2
Reduced recreational activities (going out, movies, theater, etc.)	62.3	39.1	90.2	69.4	56.8	68.5	31.2	48.9	46.4
Reduced use of own car	47.0	22.3	75.5	56.4	40.6	45.6	19.6	26.7	27.6
Delayed payments on utilities (gas, water, electric)	25.4	14.0	73.9	31.5	40.0	21.9	10.1	22.4	16.0
Moved home	13.7	6.7	27.3	18.3	9.0	16.2	4.8	8.6	14.6
Delayed or defaulted on a loan installment	17.0	13.3	61.0	22.2	31.2	20.9	9.6	21.2	13.3
Sell an asset (e.g., land, apt, house)	11.3	5.1	17.4	14.1	12.5	12.3	5.8	6.7	7.7
Cut TV/phone/internet service	17.6	6.9	36.7	24.4	17.5	24.0	17.0	12.2	21.0
Did not go on holiday	51.4	36.5	74.1	61.7	59.1	53.7	27.4	38.4	37.3
Reduced or postponed buying medicines/ visiting the doctor	31.1	16.6	62.5	40.4	40.0	21.0	15.0	25.2	10.9

Notes: Percentages based on respondents selecting specific answer options

Q: In the past five years, have you or anyone else in your household had to take any of the following measures for financial/economic reasons?

Table 1.5 Blame assignment for the country's economic difficulties (percentages top two)

	Fra	*Ger*	*Gre*	*Ita*	*Pol*	*Spa*	*Swe*	*Swi*	*UK*
Banks and financial actors	34.3	39.2	54.1	45.0	26.3	58.6	24.0	36.5	66.8
National government	44.6	34.0	54.3	60.5	61.5	60.0	51.9	20.9	38.2
USA	5.1	4.1	3.2	3.2	4.1	1.4	2.9	5.5	4.6
European Union	28.4	18.0	40.4	26.6	15.3	15.2	15.7	22.6	17.2
Trade unions	6.0	6.9	6.1	7.1	8.7	4.1	2.6	5.6	2.4
Migrants	11.9	5.1	5.2	9.2	4.8	4.1	17.5	13.1	12.6

Notes: Percentages based on respondents selecting specific answer options

Q: Which of the following do you think are most responsible for the UK's economic difficulties? (Please select up to two options)

Table 1.6 Blame assignment for the rise of unemployment (percentages top two)

	Fra	*Ger*	*Gre*	*Ita*	*Pol*	*Spa*	*Swe*	*Swi*	*UK*
Banks and financial actors	24.9	22.6	34.8	29.2	12.6	34.1	10.7	22.0	32.5
National government	38.8	30.4	45.2	52.9	56.2	54.1	38.4	13.6	32.6
USA	3.8	2.4	2.3	3.1	2.0	1.4	3.5	4.1	2.0
European Union	20.9	11.9	32.5	18.8	11.3	10.1	14.4	18.5	13.2
Trade unions	9.4	8.0	9.5	14.2	11.2	7.4	7.4	6.5	5.2
Migrants	17.8	8.8	21.9	18.5	17.2	11.2	19.2	25.5	26.8

Notes: Percentages based on respondents selecting specific answer options

Q: Which of the following do you think are most responsible for the rise of unemployment? (Please select up to two options)

proportion blames the EU in Greece. It is telling that in Switzerland people are more likely to blame migrants than any of the other actors and in the UK a large proportion also blames unemployment on migrants.

Blaming someone for a given situation is but one side of a broader assessment of citizens' attitudes relative to the crisis, and more specifically of the ways in which they judge responsibilities and actions by different stakeholders. What is perhaps even more important for our present purpose is the rate of approval—or disapproval—citizens have of the ways in which governments deal with the crisis. Results reported in Table 1.7 show the proportions of citizens approving different types of economic measures to deal with the economic crisis. As can be seen, increasing government control and oversight of the economy tends to be the preferred option cross-nationally, though in many countries and particularly those where the economic crisis was lighter, reducing the deficit was also popular as opposed to stimulating the economy which was more supported in countries where the crisis was deeper. On the other hand, giving financial support to the banks tends to be more unpopular as a measure.

Citizens' assessment of responsibilities and governmental responses to the economic crisis reflects more generally in their degree of satisfaction with the government's performance in different policy areas. Table 1.8 shows that satisfaction levels in government policy vary by national context—particularly in Southern Europe—to some extent but is overall very low. As can be seen, the proportion satisfied with government performance across domains is extremely low, across countries.

Table 1.7 Approval of economic measures to deal with economic crisis (percentages approve)

	Fra	*Ger*	*Gre*	*Ita*	*Pol*	*Spa*	*Swe*	*Swi*	*UK*
Giving financial support to banks in trouble	17.5	11.4	23.3	16.5	14.0	12.7	12.1	12.2	17.4
Increasing government regulation and oversight of the national economy	49.2	29.7	56.9	52.7	38.6	48.9	41.3	24.8	35.3
Significantly increasing government spending to stimulate the economy	17.9	24.9	49.3	37.4	45.9	41.3	25.7	18.8	43.9
Taking steps to reduce the government's budget deficit and debt, by cutting some spending or increasing some taxes	42.9	27.6	37.0	32.8	30.3	33.0	43.0	24.3	48.1

Notes: Percentages based on respondents selecting points 6 through to 10 on the 0–10 scale

Q: In the UK's economic conditions, do you favor or oppose the government doing each of the following? Please place yourself on a scale from 0 to 10, where 0 means "strongly disapprove" and 10 means "strongly approve"

Table 1.8 Satisfaction with government in different policy areas (percentages satisfied)

	Fra	*Ger*	*Gre*	*Ita*	*Pol*	*Spa*	*Swe*	*Swi*	*UK*
The economy	15.0	48.6	9.8	14.5	23.1	17.7	28.4	59.2	49.2
Poverty	13.0	20.5	8.8	12.2	9.2	9.2	19.2	32.3	21.2
Education	25.9	32.2	10.8	21.0	26.8	16.8	31.3	64.2	33.4
Unemployment	10.6	29.9	6.9	11.8	11.6	11.6	16.1	42.1	32.6
Healthcare	34.8	37.2	11.7	26.7	10.5	23.6	26.0	54.9	30.7
Precarious employment	14.8	20.7	8.4	14.8	9.5	10.7	22.4	36.3	21.5
Immigration	13.4	22.8	9.7	14.2	14.7	13.6	16.3	26.0	11.8
Childcare	32.5	30.8	11.2	22.2	19.6	18.4	32.6	40.3	28.0

Notes: % based on respondents selecting points 6 through to 10 on the 0–10 scale

Q: How satisfied are you with the way in which your country's government is dealing with the following on a scale from 0 to 10, where 0 means "extremely dissatisfied" and 10 means "extremely satisfied"?

Even in those countries with lighter crisis, only about half of the population—at most—are satisfied with the economic. This points to a legitimation crisis which, while already under way before the crisis (see Grasso 2011, 2014), appears to have been exacerbated by the latter. However, here patterns appear more varied than a simple matter of the severity of the crisis, and clearly national political factors are also at play.

A last aspect we would like to address, in addition to the ways in which citizens perceive the severity of the economic crisis and its consequences on living conditions as well as the country's economy, and how the assess political responsibilities and measures, resides in how they view their own role in all this. One way to do so is by referring to the concept of resilience. This refers to people's capacity of going through hard times and resisting negative changes in their life (Batty and Cole 2010; Hall and Lamont 2013). Table 1.9 reports on the resilience of European citizens. As we can see, citizens see themselves as quite resilient and active at the individual level. However, despite this silver lining, economic problems tend to have major structural implications that cannot be tackled by

Table 1.9 Citizens' resilience in times of crisis (percentages like me)

	Fra	*Ger*	*Gre*	*Ita*	*Pol*	*Spa*	*Swe*	*Swi*	*UK*
I look for creative ways to alter difficult situations	50.4	62.9	72.1	67.0	59.4	60.5	54.3	65.8	55.3
I actively look for ways to replace the losses I encounter in life	48.6	50.4	68.1	70.1	50.3	61.0	26.3	54.8	47.9
I have a hard time making it through stressful events	42.7	32.6	37.0	36.7	34.6	53.4	34.8	32.2	33.4
I keep myself active in the community where I live	47.9	35.6	35.9	41.1	40.6	35.2	24.6	45.0	32.9
I feel that I do not have much in common with the larger community in which I live	32.2	25.1	37.5	35.6	34.2	37.3	32.4	23.9	38.6

Notes: Percentages based on respondents selecting specific answer options

Q: Please rate each of the following items on a scale from 0 to 10 where 0 means "completely unlike me" and 10 means "just like me"

citizens on their own, no matter how resilient, but need effective political solutions.

Citizens not only resist, more or less tenaciously, to economic hardship; they may also react more proactively. In terms of political responses to the crisis, from Table 1.10 we can see that only in France, Greece, Italy, and Spain do the majority of citizens approve of marches and mass protest demonstrations against austerity. Only in Greece, Italy, Spain, and Sweden do a majority approve of strikes against austerity. Across the countries in our study, less than one third of people approve of indefinite occupations of squares against austerity—such as those of the *Indignados* or Occupy. Only about 15 percent or less approve of illegal actions. All in all, these cross-national variations seem more related to the specific national traditions and opportunity structures for protest than to an effect of the economic crisis (Cinalli and Giugni 2016).

In sum, this brief comparative overview suggests that the Great Recession has had a profound impact on various aspects of European citizens' lives. It points more specifically to patterns though which the long-lasting economic crisis that started out about a decade ago might have affected the perceptions, experiences, and responses by European citizens. Furthermore, it shows how such perceptions, experiences, and responses are context-dependent and vary in significant ways across countries that

Table 1.10 Approval of protest against austerity measures (percentages approve)

	Fra	*Ger*	*Gre*	*Ita*	*Pol*	*Spa*	*Swe*	*Swi*	*UK*
March through town or stage mass protest demonstrations	55.4	41.7	60.5	49.7	43.1	58.0	46.8	24.8	43.5
Take part in strikes	46.3	41.6	50.4	49.9	37.8	54.5	50.8	20.1	36.3
Occupy public squares indefinitely	26.8	24.1	22.0	32.8	24.8	26.0	20.5	16.5	24.3
Take illegal action such as blocking roads or damaging public property	11.7	6.5	6.8	11.5	14.5	10.5	9.9	6.1	7.9

Notes: Percentages based on respondents selecting points 6 through to 10 on the 0–10 scale

Q: When thinking about austerity policies and their consequences, how strongly do you approve or disapprove of the following actions? Please place yourself on a scale from 0 to 10, where 0 means "strongly disapprove" and 10 means "strongly approve"

have been struck at different degrees by the crisis. Such variations, however, while being related to the different degree of severity of the crisis, are also due to other, more country-specific features of the social and political-institutional environment (see for e.g. English et al. 2016, Giugni and Grasso 2015b, Temple et al. 2016). All this calls for more thorough analyses of the ways in which citizens have perceived, experienced, and responded to the Great Recession in the nine countries included in our study.

Notes

1. This project was funded by the European Commission under the 7th Framework Programme (grant agreement no. 613237). A more detailed description as well as various related documents and outputs are available on the project's website at http://www.livewhat.unige.ch.
2. The sample size in each country is the following: 2027 in France, 2108 in Germany, 2048 in Greece, 2040 in Italy, 2014 in Poland, 2035 in Spain, 2018 in Sweden, 2046 in Switzerland, and 2022 in the UK.

References

Ancelovici, M. (2015). Crisis and Contention in Europe: A Political Process Account of Anti-Austerity Protests. In V. Guiraudon, C. Ruzza, & H. Trenz (Eds.), *Europe's Prolonged Crisis: The Making or the Unmaking of a Political Union*. Houndmills: Palgrave.

Ancelovici, M., Dufour, P., & Nez, H. (Eds.). (2016). *Street Politics in the Age of Austerity: From the Indignad@s to Occupy*. Amsterdam: Amsterdam University Press.

Batty, E., & Cole, I. (2010). *Resilience and the Recession in Six Deprived Communities: Preparing for the Worse to Come?* (JRF Programme Paper, Poverty and Place Programme). York: Joseph Rowntree Foundation.

Bermeo, N., & Bartels, L. M. (2014a). Crisis of Confidence?: The Dynamics of Economic Opinions During the Great Recession. In N. Bermeo & L. M. Bartels (Eds.), *Mass Politics in Tough Times: Opinions, Votes and Protest in the Great Recession*. Oxford: Oxford University Press.

Bermeo, N., & Bartels, L. M. (Eds.). (2014b). *Mass Politics in Tough Times: Opinions, Votes and Protest in the Great Recession*. Oxford: Oxford University Press.

Bernburg, J. G. (2015). Economic Crisis and Popular Protest in Iceland, January 2009: The Role of Perceived Economic Loss and Political Attitudes in Protest Participation and Support. *Mobilization, 20*, 231–252.

Bernburg, J. G. (2016). *Economic Crisis and Mass Protest: The Pots and Pans Revolution in Iceland*. London: Routledge.

Castells, M. (2012). *Networks of Outrage and Hope: Social Movements in the Internet Age*. Cambridge: Polity Press.

Cinalli, M., & Giugni, M. (2016). Collective Responses to the Economic Crisis in the Public Domain: Myth or Reality? *Politics and Policy, 44*, 427–446.

della Porta, D. (2015). *Social Movements in Times of Austerity: Bringing Capitalism Back into Protest Analysis*. Cambridge: Polity Press.

della Porta, D., & Mattoni, A. (2014). *Spreading Protests in Social Movements of the Crisis*. Colchester: ECPR Press.

della Porta, D., Fernández, J., Kouki, H., & Mosca, L. (2017). *Movement Parties Against Austerity*. Cambridge: Polity.

Diani, M., & Kousis, M. (2014). The Duality of Claims and Events: The Greek Campaign Against Troika's Memoranda and Austerity, 2010–2012. *Mobilization, 19*, 387–404.

English, P., Grasso, M. T., Buraczynska, B., Karampampas, S., & Temple, L. (2016). Convergence on Crisis? Comparing Labour and Conservative Party Framing of the Economic Crisis in Britain, 2008–2014. *Politics & Policy, 44*(3), 577–603.

Flesher Fominaya, C., & Cox, L. (Eds.). (2013). *Understanding European Movements: New Social Movements, Global Justice Struggles, Anti-Austerity Protest*. London: Routledge.

Flesher Fominaya, C., & Hayes, G. (2017). Special Issue: Resisting Austerity: Collective Action in European in the Wake of the Global Financial Crisis. *Social Movement Studies, 16*, 1–151.

Gamson, W. A., & Sifry, M. L. (2013). The #Occupy Movement: An Introduction. *The Sociological Quarterly, 54*, 159–163.

Giugni, M., & Grasso, M. T. (Eds.). (2015a). *Austerity and Protest: Popular Contention in Times of Economic Crisis*. London: Routledge.

Giugni, M., & Grasso, M. T. (2015b). Environmental Movements in Advanced Industrial Democracies: Heterogeneity, Transformation, and Institutionalization. *Annual Review of Environment and Resources, 40*, 337–361.

Giugni, M., & Grasso, M. T. (2016). How Civil Society Actors Responded to the Economic Crisis: The Interaction of Material Deprivation and Perceptions of Political Opportunity Structures. *Politics & Policy, 44*(3), 447–472.

Giugni, M., & Grasso, M. T. (2017). Citizens and the Crisis: The Great Recession as Constraint and Opportunity. In M. Giugni & M. T. Grasso (Eds.), *Citizens and the Crisis: Perceptions, Experiences, and Responses to the Great Recession in Europe*. London: Palgrave Macmillan.

Grasso, M. T. (2011). *Political Participation in Western Europe*. D.Phil. Thesis, Nuffield College, University of Oxford.

Grasso, M. T. (2014). Age-Period-Cohort Analysis in a Comparative Context: Political Generations and Political Participation Repertoires. *Electoral Studies, 33*, 63–76.

Grasso, M. T. (2016). *Generations, Political Participation and Social Change in Western Europe*. London: Routledge.

Grasso, M. T. (2018). Young People's Political Participation in Times of Crisis. In S. Pickard & J. Bessant (Eds.), *Young People Regenerating Politics in Times of Crisis*. London: Palgrave.

Grasso, M. T., & Giugni, M. (2013, September 12–14). Anti-austerity Movements: Old Wine in New Vessels? In *XXVII Meeting of the Italian Political Science Association (SISP)*, University of Florence, Florence.

Grasso, M. T., & Giugni, M. (2016a). Protest Participation and Economic Crisis: The Conditioning Role of Political Opportunities. *European Journal of Political Research, 55*, 663–680.

Grasso, M. T., & Giugni, M. (2016b). Do Issues Matter? Anti-Austerity Protests' Composition, Values, and Action Repertoires Compared. *Research in Social Movements, Conflicts and Change, 39*, 31–58.

Grasso, M. T., Farrall, S., Gray, E., Hay, C., & Jennings, W. (2017). Thatcher's Children, Blair's Babies, Political Socialisation and Trickle-Down Value-Change: An Age, Period and Cohort Analysis. *British Journal of Political Science*. https://doi.org/10.1017/S0007123416000375.

Hall, P. A., & Lamont, M. (Eds.). (2013). *Social Resilience in the Neoliberal Age*. Cambridge: Cambridge University Press.

Johnston, H., & Seferiades, S. (2012). The Greek December, 2008. In S. Seferiades & H. Johnston (Eds.), *Violent Protest, Contentious Politics, and the Neoliberal State*. Burlington: Ashgate.

Judis, J. B. (2016). *The Populist Explosion: How the Great Recession Transformed American and European Politics*. New York: Columbia Global Reports.

Kousis, M. (2014). The Transnational Dimension of the Greek Protest Campaign Against Troika Memoranda and Austerity Policies 2010–2012. In D. della Porta & A. Mattoni (Eds.), *Spreading Protest: Social Movements in Times of Crisis*. Colchester: ECPR Press.

Kriesi, H. (2014a). The Political Consequences of the Economic Crises in Europe: Electoral Punishment and Popular Protest. In N. Bermeo & L. M. Bartels (Eds.), *Mass Politics in Tough Times: Opinions, Votes and Protest in the Great Recession*. Oxford: Oxford University Press.

Kriesi, H. (2014b). The Populist Challenge. *West European Politics, 37*, 361–378.

Kriesi, H., & Pappas, T. S. (Eds.). (2015). *European Populism in the Shadow of the Great Recession*. Colchester: ECPR Press.

Marsh, M., & Tilley, J. (2010). The Attribution of Credit and Blame to Governments and Its Impact on Vote Choice. *British Journal of Political Science, 40*, 115–134.

Mudde, C. (2013). Three Decades of Populist Radical Right Parties in Western Europe: So What? *European Journal of Political Research, 52*, 1–19.

Pickerill, J., & Krinsky, J. (2012). Why Does Occupy Matter? *Social Movement Studies, 11*, 279–287.

Rüdig, W., & Karyotis, G. (2013). Beyond the Usual Suspects? New Participants in Anti-Austerity Protests in Greece. *Mobilization: An International Quarterly, 18*, 313–330.

Rüdig, W., & Karyotis, G. (2014). Who Protests in Greece? Mass Opposition to Austerity. *British Journal of Political Science, 44*, 487–513.

Sakellaropoulos, S. (2012). On the Causes and Significance of the December 2008 Social Explosion in Greece. *Science & Society, 76*, 340–364.

Stokes, D. E. (1963). Spatial Models of Party Competition. *American Political Science Review, 57*, 368–377.

Talving, L. (2017). The Electoral Consequences of Austerity: Economic Policy Voting in Europe in Times of Crisis. *West European Politics, 40*, 560–583.

Temple, L., & Grasso, M. T. (2017). Austerity, Politics, and Partisanship in the UK. In M. Giugni & M. T. Grasso (Eds.), *Citizens and the Crisis: Perceptions, Experiences, and Responses to the Great Recession in Europe*. London: Palgrave Macmillan.

Temple, L., Grasso, M. T., Buraczynska, B., Karampampas, S., & English, P. (2016). Neoliberal Narrative in Times of Economic Crisis: A Political Claims Analysis of the UK Press, 2007–2014. *Politics & Policy, 44*(3), 553–576.

Varga, M. (2015). Trade Unions and Austerity in Central and Eastern Europe. *Transfer: European Review of Labour and Research, 21*, 313–326.

Whelan, C., Russell, H., & Maitre, B. (2016). Economic Stress and the Great Recession in Ireland: Polarization, Individualization or 'Middle Class Squeeze'? *Social Indicators Research, 126*, 503–526.

Wisman, J. D. (2013). Wage Stagnation, Rising Inequality and the Financial Crisis of 2008. *Cambridge Journal of Economics, 37*, 921–945.

PART I

Citizens, the Crisis, and Institutional Politics

CHAPTER 2

Austerity, Politics, and Partisanship in the UK

Luke Temple and Maria T. Grasso

The day before the 2015 general election, the UK's best-selling tabloid newspaper, *The Sun*, ran the front-page headline 'WELL HUNG'. The articled reported that 'BRITAIN faces months of political chaos after a final poll for *The Sun* revealed the Tories and Labour will both fall well short of outright victory in the General Election'. Such a result had been predicted by a glut of polls in the run-up to the election. In the event, *The Sun* and its poll were wrong: the Conservative Party won a majority of 12 seats, their first majority in 23 years.

The political chaos actually came just over a year later with the 'Brexit' referendum result, when 52% of voters chose to leave the European Union on a 72% turnout. David Cameron, the Conservative Prime Minister, resigned as a result and triggered a Conservative leadership competition. The Labour Party also saw a leadership election triggered by rebelling MPs just nine months since Jeremy Corbyn had won the leadership contest which had in turn been prompted by Ed Miliband's standing down after the general election. Nigel Farage, leader of the Eurosceptic United Kingdom Independence Party (UKIP), also stepped down, announcing that he 'couldn't possibly achieve more' and wanted his life back (Cowburn 2016).

L. Temple • M.T. Grasso (✉)
Department of Politics, University of Sheffield, Sheffield, UK

M. Giugni, M.T. Grasso (eds.), *Citizens and the Crisis*,
Palgrave Studies in European Political Sociology,
https://doi.org/10.1007/978-3-319-68960-9_2

Whilst the seeds may have been sown much earlier, it is against a backdrop of financial crisis and austerity that the historically stable UK political system has witnessed some of its most unexpected and tumultuous results. These started with the lack of a parliamentary majority in 2010—the first time such a result had occurred since 1974 and the first time that a political coalition was formed since the Second World War. The post-crisis period also witnessed the unprecedented success of minor parties such as UKIP and the Scottish National Party (SNP).

In this context, in this chapter we map out perceptions of crisis, issues of hardship, and optimistic and pessimistic understandings of the economy, to see how they relate to an individual's political alignment and voting behaviour. To do so, we examine data from a new cross-national dataset collected in 2015 in the context of the LIVEWHAT project. The survey provides a rich array of questions on voting behaviour but also on material deprivation and economic and political evaluations of government competence. This survey was carried out simultaneously in another eight European countries—France, Germany, Greece, Italy, Poland, Spain, Sweden, and Switzerland—and we discuss cross-country comparisons when they help to shed light on the UK situation. The UK provides a good test case because, whilst it was not hit by a recession as deep as that experienced in say, Spain or Greece, its close connection to the financial market and unprecedented interventions by the government in the economy provide a context where economic management, and perceptions of it, could well be crucial.

In this chapter we first provide a brief outline to the financial crisis in the UK and how it was managed by the government. We then discuss how, from 2010, the new coalition government focused on austerity politics and handling the long-term aftermath and the slump. We note the plethora of negative reports from academics, think-tanks, and economists regarding the economic and social impact of austerity. Within this discussion we touch upon theories of voting behaviour, before looking at the results of the 2015 general election. In the following sections we use results from the LIVEWHAT survey to examine perceptions of the economy, crisis and material deprivation, and economic ideology, with a focus on how these might vary by political affiliation. The final section applies regression analysis to determine which characteristics help predict who might vote for three of the UK's political parties: the Conservative Party, the Labour Party, and UKIP. We find that material deprivation and austerity-related issues have limited influence on voter choice in the 2015 general election: existing ideological perspectives and assessments of immigration are more important.

Backdrop to the 2015 General Election

The financial crisis of 2008–2009 broke under a Labour government that had been in power for just over a decade (with Tony Blair as Prime Minister from 1997 to 2007, and then Gordon Brown until 2010). The government reaction to the crisis can be simplified into two main strands: one of macroeconomic policy and one of labour market policy (see LIVEWHAT 2014). The first concerned large-scale nationalisation and recapitalisation of particular banks to prop up the financial system and ensure banks continued lending (to mitigate the credit 'crunch'). The National Audit Office (2014: 13) calculated these measures exposed the Treasury to liabilities of more than £1000 billion. Furthermore, the Bank of England injected £375 billion into the financial system and cut interest rates from 5% to a historic low 0.5%, where they remained for seven years before being cut further to 0.25%.

In terms of labour market policy, the Brown administration expanded tax credits, designed to 'top up' the wages of low earners, particularly those with families, and some employment schemes were introduced to help businesses take on the long-term unemployed (Clegg 2010). Social benefit expenditure rose by 4.1% a year between 2007–2008 and 2009–2011 during and immediately postcrisis, keenly felt because of the poor GDP growth rates in these years (Hood and Phillips 2015). After the crisis peaked, the OECD (2012: 3) concluded that 'the family payment system did what it was supposed to do and cushioned the effect of the crisis for poorer families'. Yet it has also been noted that relatively little was done to protect workers from becoming unemployed, particularly compared to other countries (Vis et al. 2011).

The Labour Party lost the 2010 general election, but, for the first time since 1974, there was no overall majority result. After some negotiation, a historic coalition of the Conservative Party and the Liberal Democrats formed a government. Their immediate concern was an 'emergency budget' introduced by the Conservative Chancellor just over a month after the election result, which proposed the general tenets of austerity, although without mentioning the word. The core of austerity focused on spending cuts for government departments and services and reducing the government deficit that had ballooned in the aftermath of the financial crisis. In the run-up to the 2010 election, there was no hiding the underlining negativity of the Conservative campaign. As Whiteley et al. (2013: 95) put it: 'Overall, the Conservative message was a gloomy one – cuts and sacrifice were the order of the day with Mr Cameron in Number 10. Bright days would be ahead, but no time soon'. Once in government, the coalition aim was to 'significantly accelerate the reduction of the structural deficit over the course of a Parliament, with the main burden of deficit reduction borne by reduced spending rather than increased taxes' (Cabinet Office 2010: 15, see discussion in Sawyer 2012: 207).

The policy approach came packaged with a number of narrative hooks that mainly emanated from the Chancellor of the Exchequer, including the fact that the austerity approach was the only approach—'there is no Plan B' (Kirkup 2010); a consistent ascribing of a large portion of the blame to pre-crisis Labour policy—'a failure to fix the roof when the sun was shining' (Holmes 2013); and perhaps the most common mantra was that the whole country was going to be making sacrifices, 'we're all in this together' (The Guardian 2009; The Telegraph 2011; Conservative Home 2015). This broader narrative was backed up with an economic narrative that married household analogies with macroeconomics, in particular the idea that the Labour government had 'maxed out the credit card' (Conservative Home 2008) and so therefore there was a desperate need to do some belt-tightening.

Swathes of academic analyses have flagged up austerity as causing social and economic impact (see Giugni and Grasso 2015a for a discussion of political effects and Lupton et al. 2016 for an overview of the social effects). Moreover, austerity policy has been suggested to have detrimental effects as wide ranging as: putting a strain on family life whilst deepening the marriage divide (Hayton 2013); heightening food insecurity (Dowler and Lambie-Mumford 2015; Lambie-Mumford and Green 2015); retracting levels of service in the field of youth justice (Yates 2012); forcing those with ill-health out of the disability benefits system (Beatty and Fothergill 2015); heightening discrimination in mental health services (Henderson et al. 2014); increasing homelessness (Communities and Local Government Committee 2016; Grice 2016); eroding the security of social housing (Hodkinson and Robbins 2013); weakening the voluntary sector (Milbourne and Cushman 2015); and undermining multiagency children's services (Ball 2014).

In terms of economic impact, a large number of prominent economists argued against the austerity approach, suggesting that a contraction in government spending and knocks to consumer confidence would lead to a weak recovery, and what was needed was further Keynesian-style stimulus and investment (see Wren-Lewis 2015 for a discussion on this general consensus). Indeed, in the early years of the coalition, growth was historically weak. In 2013 the UK suffered its first credit rating downgrade since 1978 (BBC 2016). In the same year the IMF, previously supportive of austerity policy, argued that the poor economic performance of the UK should lead to a rethink (Elliott 2013)—although this stance was changed again a year later (Armitstead 2014). By the end of 2013/2014 it seemed that growth was picking up; however in March 2015 the respected Institute for Fiscal Studies described the previous years as constituting a 'historically slow recovery in living standards' and noted, in what could be read as an implicit criticism of the austerity approach, that: 'In the long run, policies that boost productivity, and so increase real earnings, are likely to have a bigger impact on living standards than changes in tax and benefit rates' (Cribb et al. 2015). Such a view was compounded in the same month by similar findings from the government's own Office for Budget Responsibility (OBR 2015).

During this time of weak growth, individual debt peaked at £1.5 trillion in 2014, making it worth more than the value of the entire output of the economy (Davies et al. 2015). Analysis by the Trade Union Congress also suggested that between 2007 and 2015, real wages in the UK fell by 10.4%, the biggest fall amongst OECD countries, equalled only by Greece (TUC 2016). This was widely picked up in much of the media, who also reported on Chancellor George Osborne's many missed targets to tackle the deficit, including in 2012 (Wintour 2012) and 2015 (Broughton 2015) and later in 2016 (Sculthorpe 2016). He also breached his own cap on welfare spending (Alexander Shaw 2015). Perhaps crucially, what did not happen was the predicted mass rise in overall unemployment as seen in the USA; however there have been suggestions of a rise in 'zero-hour' contracts (ONS 2015).[1]

Voting Behaviour in Austere Times

As the backdrop for the 2015 election was one of generally poor economic performance, it did not look particularly positive for the incumbent government. Regarding theories of voting behaviour, Whiteley et al.'s (2013: 26–30) analysis in *Affluence, Austerity and Electoral Change in Britain* offers a useful group of interlinking approaches that try to explain the voting choices of citizens. Firstly, following Butler and Stokes (1969), sociodemographic characteristics, especially class, have been argued to influence voting behaviour with different political parties seen as better representing the needs of different sections of the population—that is, historically the Labour Party was closely linked to working class men in the industrial heartlands of Northern England. However, for many reasons—including deindustrialisation, globalisation, and rising levels of post-materialism—there has been a suggested 'dealignment' of class politics fuelled by weakening class identities (Dalton 1984; Fieldhouse 1995; Oesch 2008).

Building upon this is the idea of party identification, and in particular explanations for partisanship. Whiteley et al. (2013: 27) point to two different understandings. *Affective* attachment is a long-term socialised attachment to a party, related much more to a sense of habitus and influenced by context, family, upbringing, and so on. However, Whiteley et al. (2013) argue that evidence is much more supportive of a rational choice or 'running-tally' understanding, which emphasises citizens as individuals *choosing* to support a particular party on the back of ongoing evaluations of party performance. Therefore, the authors subsume party identification under their own broader 'valence' politics model. Valence voting is related strongly to assessments of 'performance' where voters are generally seen to undertake rational, cost-benefit analyses of how effective the government and opposition are, or would be, at carrying out policy and 'managing' the country and, in particular, the economy (Whiteley et al. 2013: 1–2). The focus is very much on the *perceived competence* of a party to handle political issues, driven by party identification (as this is already conceptualised as a 'running-tally' of performance), the image of party leaders, and, finally, on 'the capacities of competing parties to deal with the issues facing the country' (ibid.: 28).

Therefore, looking at the weight of evidence as provided by numerous academic reports, think-tanks, and also government offices themselves—which was widely reported across much of the political spectrum of UK media[2]—the valence approach, and the economic accounts of voting behaviour in particular, might arguably predict that the 2015 general election was going to be a tumultuous one for the coalition. And whilst it was for the minor partner, the Liberal Democrats, the Conservative Party went on to increase its vote share and return to government with a majority.

A last approach outlined by Whiteley et al. (2013) offers a slightly different take on voting behaviour, which could explain the return of the Conservative Party to power. Building on the rational choice approach, spatial models emphasise ideological and issue alignment between voter and party (Downs

1957). As Whiteley et al. (2013: 29) note, this approach 'contends that voters will opt for the party they consider closest to them on the position issues about which they care about most'. The idea of a left-right ideological continuum is often used as a shortcut for examining these issue positions, occasionally supplemented with more specific questions of left-right politics usually related to issues of state interventions in welfare (Enelow and Hinich 1982; Hinich and Pollard 1981). As with the sociodemographic approach, this theoretical understanding has fallen out of favour in the UK in light of what is seen as ideological convergence between the two major political parties, especially after Tony Blair's reformulation of New Labour (see also English et al. 2016; Grasso et al. 2017). In such a political landscape, many have argued that valence perceptions and economic voting become as, if not more, important than issues and ideology (Green 2007; Green and Hobolt 2008; Clarke et al. 2009; Whiteley et al. 2013). To try and get a handle on voting patterns in the UK, we look at how austerity was perceived by individuals, but we further consider their existing ideological perspectives (see also Grasso and Giugni 2016 on protest). However, before turning to this analysis, we first outline the results from the 2015 general election.

The 2015 General Election

For many, the 2015 general election was an 'austerity election' (Weeks 2015). Large-scale campaigns to end the government's, and in particular the Conservative Party's, austerity agenda were pursued by Trade Unions and oppositional parties including the SNP, Plaid Cymru, and the Green Party (People's Assembly 2015; Perraudin 2014). The election was seen by most major polling companies as too close to call, right up until the 10 pm exit poll correctly predicted the Conservative majority. The Labour Party increased their vote percentage by 1.4% (a better percentage increase than the Conservative opposition managed between both 1997–2001 and 2001–2005), but what mattered was that under the first-past-the-post system, this translated into a loss of 26 seats. In comparison, the 0.8% improvement in vote for the Conservative Party resulted in the gain of 24 seats, in particular at the expense of their Liberal Democratic coalition partners, who lost 49 seats and saw their votes slide by 15.2%.

However, this story is not complete without considering the smaller parties in the UK. In Scotland the SNP had a landslide result. They obliterated what was once a Labour stronghold and gained 56 out of the 59 seats in Scotland, up from six. This came on the back of the party *losing* an independence referendum seven months earlier (55.3% voting in, compared to 44.7% voting out, on an 84.6% turnout). The other smaller parties, the Green Party and UKIP, did historically well, but the first-past-the-post voting treated them particularly unkindly. To put the disproportionality of the UK system into perspective, the Conservative Party gained one seat for roughly every 35,000 votes, and for Labour it took around 40,000 votes per seat. In comparison, the Green Party gained just one seat on the back of 1.1 *million* votes. And yet, the ratio for UKIP is truly startling. In the 624 constituencies where UKIP stood a candidate, they came second in 120 of them, or just under a fifth. However, they came first in only one. Thus, while over 3.8 million votes were cast for UKIP (12.7% of the vote), they got just one representative in parliament to show for it.

The political opportunity structures are therefore stacked heavily against smaller parties in the UK with the first-past-the-post voting system in particular struggling with issues of fairness, representation, and accountability (Abramson et al. 2013; Quinn 2016). As John Curtice (2013: 63) presciently put it after UKIP's historic result in the 2013 local elections, when they came second in vote percentage but a rather distant fourth in seats, 'The first-past-the-post system thus insulated the traditional party system from the full force of the electoral earthquake – and could yet still play an important role in stopping the incursion from breaching the barriers at Westminster'. The experience of the SNP suggests that it takes a rather specific juncture—in this case the collapse of votes for a formerly dominant party and the rise of a popular, regionally specific party who were able to prove themselves in a devolved assembly—before a party is able to convert seats into votes at the national level. In terms of a geographic strategy to convert voters into seats more broadly, UKIP struggled.

After the election, the leader of the Labour Party, Ed Miliband, resigned, triggering a leadership competition. The election of Jeremy Corbyn (under new party rules which allowed votes to new party members who joined by paying only a very small fee) came as something of a shock to the political establishment. Corbyn was a far-left candidate who, seen as something of a rebellious back-bencher, frequently voted against his own party policy. With its history of two (and a half) party politics and unforgiving electoral system, the UK party system from the outside can appear rather stable, compared to the shifting coalitions and party lifespan in systems such as Spain, Greece, Italy, Poland, and Germany. Therefore, the election of an unknown, far-left, backbench rebel to leader of the party was yet another unexpected turn of events. Now that we have briefly discussed the UK political landscape since the financial crisis, and have highlighted various theoretical approaches towards voting behaviour, this chapter turns to addressing how it is that people in the UK have perceived austerity, and the relationship this has with their politics.

Assessing 'Hard Times' in the UK

In light of the election result, our survey data collected in 2015 can explore issues raised by austerity alongside people's political support and voting behaviour. The following section looks at this in four parts. Firstly, it maps out broad economic attitudes and assessments in the UK, looking at perceptions of crisis and also household and country-level judgements on living standards. Here, perceptions of class are used to break down the result. This focus is expanded by addressing these issues including measures of material deprivation, split by party support. The subsequent section then examines valence issues by looking at satisfaction with government performance in key areas. Finally, the last section of the analysis looks at political ideology, focusing on ideas of 'left' and 'right'.

Perceptions of the Crisis

Following the sociodemographic approach and the argued importance of class positionality (Butler and Stokes 1969), we look at the degree to which individuals think there is a crisis in the UK—when asked in July 2015, two months after the election—and broken down by self-perceived class. In the UK especially, the notion of class remains of central interest in sociological and political analysis. Since the 1980s in particular there have been unresolved debates on the changing shape of class and class voting (Dalton 1984; Fieldhouse 1995; Oesch 2008). As the economic base of the country changed over the last three decades, there have been suggestions of 'increasingly fluid' class boundaries (Clarke et al. 2004: 2) which have led some to reconceptualise the class structure completely, resulting in new categorisations, such as the NS-SEC, which can be presented as entirely devoid of any political content (Savage 2015). In this scenario, we might expect a 'dealignment' (Inglehart 1984; Dalton 1984) between class and voting, with a more complicated landscape that does not simply predict the working class would vote left but also suggests that salaried professionals in social and cultural services may support a libertarian left (see Giugni and Grasso 2015b; Grasso and Giugni 2013), whereas, if it exists, a right-wing populist party attracts disproportionate support from production workers and small business owners (see Oesch 2008).

Much of this clearly depends on the operationalisation of class (Oesch 2008; Evans 2000). Therefore, in Table 2.1, *self-perceived* class is used as a way of examining the alignment between an individual's own personal understanding of their standing in society with their assessment of the economic crisis. In total, over a third of UK respondents thought that the country was suffering from a very serious economic crisis. The largest group of respondents in the UK, 43%, believed there to be some sort of crisis but one that is not very serious. Around one in ten thought there was no crisis, and slightly less than this did not know. Only a very small amount (1.8%) thought that something 'other' was going on.

When these results are broken down by self-perceived class, a couple of patterns are notable. Firstly, there is very little difference between the perceptions of the middle and lower middle class: 35–36% see a serious economic crisis, 47–48% see one that is not serious, and 12–13% do not see a crisis. Furthermore, whilst the upper middle class is more likely to say there is no crisis compared to the two tiers below, the differences here are not large. In total, these categories make up 57% of all respondents. In contrast, those who see themselves as working class are more inclined to see a crisis: 46% see a serious one, and only 5.3% do not see one at all. Those who see themselves as lower class are also much more likely to see a serious crisis, but are more polarised on the issue, as 15.4% believe there

Table 2.1 Perceptions of economic crisis by self-perceived class (percentage agree)

	'We are suffering a very serious economic crisis'	*'We are suffering a crisis but it is not very serious'*	*'There isn't any economic crisis'*	*Other*	*Don't know*
Upper middle	28.8	48.5	16.7	4.6	1.5
Middle	34.9	48.2	12.1	1.4	3.4
Lower middle	36.0	46.9	13.1	1.1	2.9
Working	45.9	43.2	5.3	1.3	4.4
Lower	48.1	28.9	15.4	1.9	5.8
Don't know/ other	35.6	35.6	7.9	3.0	17.8
UK total	37.3	43.2	9.7	1.8	8.0

Notes: The small number of respondents who saw themselves as 'upper class' is included in the count for 'upper middle'

is no crisis (although we need to bear in mind that only a small number of respondents saw themselves as lower class). Taken together, these two tiers make up 36% of the population. For those who 'don't know' what class they see themselves in, they are also more likely not to know how to answer the question on crisis.

In addition, as we can see from Table 8.1 in Chap. 8, across nine European countries, it is the UK with the smallest difference between those who think there is a very serious crisis and those who think there is a crisis that is not serious overall (just under 6%). These are large groupings which raise the potential of quite considerable disagreements in terms of how the economy should be managed, since two rather big blocks of people think the economy is in two quite different states—and we can see that a strong dividing line between these perceptions runs through self-perceived class. Before we see how these results break down by different political alignments, we can look in further detail at perceived economic conditions in the UK by looking at household and country assessments of the past and expectations for the future. In Fig. 2.1 we see that when they think about the country—taking a broader, sociotropic analysis—respondents have a relatively optimistic outlook for the UK.[3] 55% think the country was better off compared to a year before, and the same number thought it would get better in the next year. From a more historic, but also more personal, perspective, almost two-thirds think their living conditions are better than their parents. Across these assessments around a quarter of respondents think things are worse.

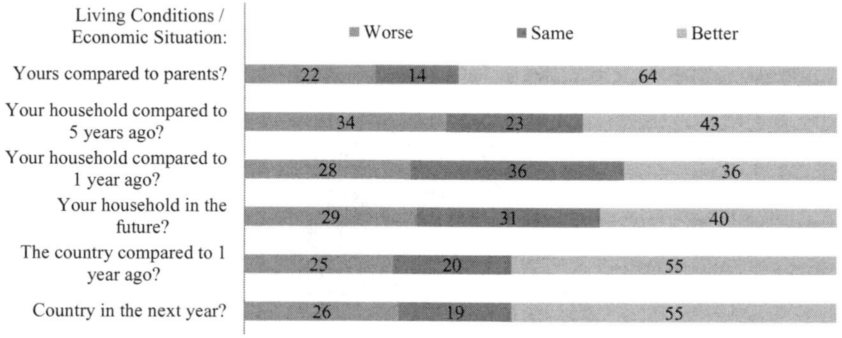

Fig. 2.1 Living conditions and economic situation in the UK—Household and country level (percentage stating worse, same, and better)

However, when thinking about their household—at the smaller, pocketbook level—this optimism diminishes slightly. At this level, people appear more likely to see things as staying the same. When respondents were asked to assess their household living conditions compared to five years ago, much closer to the time of the actual financial crash, we see that whilst 34% thought they have become worse off, 43% thought they had become better off. Only 23% thought they were the same. Whilst there is less optimism at the household level, there is still a sizeable percentage of respondents thinking that things have improved.

Hardship and Party Attachment

This section examines indicators of material deprivation and hardship, splitting survey respondents by which political party they feel closest to (Table 2.2). We can be sure that the results for the four most popular

Table 2.2 Party supporters and hard times—Party support (percentage feel closest to party) by perception of crisis, self-perceived class, outlook, and personal circumstances

	Con	*Lab*	*UKIP*	*Lib Dem*	*SNP*	*Green*	*No party*
Perception of crisis							
% severe crisis	22.7	45.4	44.1	43.4	54.5	45.1	29.5
Self-perceived class							
% working/lower	19.6	49.7	44.5	11.3	56.8	30.6	30.6
Outlook household level							
% optimist	64.1	37.9	45.0	61.7	35.8	43.0	46.2
% no change	9.3	10.8	11.9	10.4	6.2	9.9	11.6
% pessimist	26.6	51.3	43.1	27.8	58.0	47.1	42.2
Country level							
% optimist	84.2	25.3	46.8	61.8	23.5	24.0	42.8
% no change	13.5	37.0	30.3	20.9	16.1	36.4	35.8
% pessimist	2.5	37.7	22.9	17.4	60.5	39.7	21.4
Personal circumstances							
% deprived	13.5	30.2	33.1	12.7	32.5	15.6	30.0
% reduced consumption	5.3	14.4	10.7	4.9	22.6	13.7	9.5
% claiming at least one benefit	16.1	27.4	28.7	23.5	37.0	16.9	19.0
% struggling to pay bills	12.1	27.4	21.3	8.6	33.7	16.7	33.3

Q (party support): Which political party do you feel closest to?

choices—Conservative, Labour, UKIP, and 'no party'—are representationally quite robust; however, we should bear in mind that results for the smaller parties are subject to larger errors, as here the respondents' numbers are lower. When it comes to perceptions of crisis, there is a clear attitudinal split. For those who feel closest to Labour, UKIP, the Liberal Democrats, or the Green Party, around 45% think the crisis was very serious. For the SNP, this increases to 55%. However, for those who feel closest to the Conservative Party that proportion halves, to 22.7%. For those who answered that they were not close to any party (11.3% of the population) around 29.5% thought the crisis was very serious, a proportion closer to that seen in Conservative supporters than across the other political parties.

Splitting class by party, we focus on the percentage of those who perceive themselves as working or lower class. The difference between party supporters is considerable; around 10% of Liberal Democrats see themselves as working/lower class, compared to 20% of Conservatives and 50% of Labour. In terms of class alignment, UKIP and SNP voters are much closer to Labour, whilst Green and 'no party' supporters fall almost exactly in-between the two main parties. Regarding perceptions of living conditions in the UK, the categories from Fig. 2.1 have been split into household (pocketbook) and country (sociotropic) evaluations, which can be grouped into those who feel optimistic, those who feel pessimistic, and those who think nothing has changed.[4] Across all the different political parties, roughly one in ten respondents feel like there has been no real change at the household level. Therefore, the difference between various partisan supporters comes from the optimist and pessimist outlooks. Almost two-thirds of Conservative supporters feel optimistic, and just over 60% of Liberal Democrats do. The Liberal Democrat result here is somewhat surprising considering that at the time the survey was conducted they had recently suffered a large defeat and loss of seats at the general election. UKIP supporters and those supporting no party are considerably split on their outlook, whilst the gloomiest supporters are the official parliamentary opposition, Labour (37.9%), and also the SNP (35.8%). When it comes to perspectives on the country, this difference in outlook is even more acute. Only a quarter of Labour supporters are optimistic about the country's future, compared to a massive 84% of Conservative voters. And for the SNP the gloom is thicker still, with 60.5% having a pessimistic outlook on the future. This likely reflects the rather large ideological gap between the SNP and a Westminster with a Conservative Party in charge;

according to Steven et al. (2012: 72): 'Conservative politicians still do not really want to 'get' devolution – the institutional structures and wider ethos of the Scottish parliament do not sit comfortably with them'. This, we would suggest, is mutual.

When it comes to personal circumstances, we add measures on individual hardship. This is the proportion of people who answered that they had been influenced by six or more negative scenarios, such as having to meet with a social worker; having financial difficulties; not being able to go to the cinema/theatre/evening out; and unable to afford to go on holiday. In the UK (not shown in the table) the proportion is 22.9%. This is comparable to Poland and Sweden (both 22.5%), higher than Switzerland (17.3%), Spain (19.4), and Germany (20.5%), but lower than France (27%), Italy (35.4), and Greece (41.5%).[5]

The UK average split by party support shows that Conservative, Liberal Democrat, and Green supporters are the least deprived (12–15%), whereas Labour, SNP, and UKIP supporters, and those with no party affiliation, are twice as deprived (30–33%). Across UK party supporters then we see a narrower range compared to that found between countries. In terms of the reduced items measure, this is also the percentage of those who had to reduce six or more items, from a choice including consumption of staple foods, recreational activities, phone/internet, and use of a car. The UK percentage (not shown in the table) is 10%. Again as a comparison this is closest to Germany (9.1%), Sweden (9.2%), and Switzerland (14.9%), but much lower than the other countries in the survey: France (20.2%), Spain (20.6%), Poland (26.3%), Italy (28.1%), and Greece (65.9%).

A similar pattern of hardship is present between the party supporters in the UK as with the deprived measure; Conservatives (5.3%) and Liberal Democrats (4.9%) have experienced the lowest numbers of reductions in their day-to-day life. UKIP supporters (10.7%) and those with no affiliation (9.5%) are about twice as likely to have reduced six or more items, and Labour (14.4%) and Green supporters (13.7%) are around three times as likely. The SNP in comparison have 22.6% of their supporters who have had to reduce their consumption.

We see similar patterns play out across the parties when it comes to the percentage of respondents claiming at least one benefit, and the percentage struggling to pay bills. These percentages are low for the Conservatives, Liberal Democrats, and Greens in general. They're relatively higher for Labour, UKIP, and SNP. Perhaps most interesting here is the pattern for those who did not choose a party. For the non-affiliated, they are much closer to the average Conservative supporter when it comes to percentage claiming benefits, but much closer to the average Labour supporter (indeed higher) when it comes to struggling to pay the bills.

What we can see from these results is that, although levels of material deprivation measured by the deprived and reduced consumption percentages might be quite low compared to other countries who suffered severe crises, when they are felt, they are felt sharpest by supporters of UKIP and SNP, who in the run-up to the 2015 general election had been bleeding voters away from the bigger parties, and Labour in particular (see Ford and Goodwin (2014) on UKIP, and Green and Prosser (2015) and Curtice (2015) on the SNP). We can also see that this pattern holds across the issue of paying bills and claiming benefits. Indeed, the most affluent appear to be those who align with the Conservatives, Liberal Democrats, and the Green Party, whereas the Labour Party, UKIP, and SNP are in the flipside of the deprivation divide. Within these two divides we can see parties that are placed on rather different sides of the political spectrum and with rather different fortunes at the 2015 election. Tantalisingly (or frustratingly) for the larger parties, those with no party affiliation tend to sit somewhere in-between.

Government Competence and Party Attachment

In this section, we move away from issues of economic perceptions and material deprivation, and instead look at the valence theories. These take a similar rational and calculated, 'running-tally' approach to party support, but have stronger links to heuristics such as leadership qualities and competence. The LIVEWHAT survey asked, during the time that the Conservative Party had a majority in parliament, how well the government was dealing with a list of particular policy areas. In Table 2.3 these are broken down by party support.

There is no surprise that those who think the government is doing the best are Conservative supporters: eight out of ten said that the government is managing the economy competently. This falls to 53% for Liberal Democratic supporters, who may indeed still be considering that successful government measures were in some part due to their previous partnership. Almost half of UKIP supporters and a third of the non-affiliated, judge the government as competent on the economy, falling right to 23% for Labour and Greens and only 17% for the SNP. Considering their

Table 2.3 Party supporters and government competence (percentage feel closest to party by percentage choosing six or more out of ten satisfaction, by issue)

	Con	*Lab*	*UKIP*	*Lib Dem*	*SNP*	*Green*	*No party*
Economy	82.8	23.6	47.9	53.4	17.3	23.1	34.9
Unemployment	49.2	7.1	27.0	16.5	4.1	7.1	15.4
Poverty	66.4	15.6	34.7	45.6	17.7	18.2	20.4
Immigration	19.0	12.2	3.8	21.2	6.8	14.5	13.4

Q (government competence): How satisfied are you with the way in which your country's government is dealing with the following on a scale from 0 to 10, where 0 means 'extremely dissatisfied' and 10 means 'extremely satisfied'?

importance in electoral strategies for the two main parties, it is perhaps the results of UKIP supporters and the unaffiliated that are the most interesting. Whilst the percentages are not particularly high, even so, both those groups see the government as doing much better, in comparison to how Labour supporters perceive things. Compared to Labour supporters, over twice as many UKIP supporters see the government as being competent on the economy and poverty, and almost four times as many see the government as competent on dealing with poverty. For the non-affiliated the differences are not as strong, but over a third see the government as relatively competent with the economy.

As for immigration, even the government's own supporters are critical here: only a fifth judged competence in this area. In the EU referendum the topic of immigration—often connected to issues of security and employment—formed a large part of the Leave campaign rhetoric (Peers 2016; Portes 2016; Thielemann and Schade 2016) and indeed a decade before the issue was highlighted as a potentially crucial factor in EU referendums concerning further integration (de Vreese and Boomgaarden 2005). The survey results here show just how strongly people thought the government was failing on the issue—even those who supported the party in power. This will be discussed again in the final part of this chapter.

Ideology and Party Attachment

In this final section looking at differences between party supporters, we step away from issues of economic hardship and instead look to more ideological outlooks on policy issues. In Table 2.4 we outline five different approaches to

Table 2.4 Party supporters (percentage feeling closest to political party) and left-right ideology (percentage choosing 'left of centre' option, four or less on 0–10 scale)

	Con	*Lab*	*UKIP*	*Lib Dem*	*SNP*	*Green*	*No party*
(L) Incomes should be made more equal vs. (R) we need larger income differences as incentives	34.9	78.7	45.7	62.3	76.5	87.1	59.3
(L) The government should take more responsibility to ensure that everyone is provided for vs. (R) people should take more responsibility to provide for themselves	6.1	35.1	22.9	19.2	44.7	57.4	19.7
(L) People who are unemployed should have the right to refuse a job they do not want vs. (R) people who are unemployed should have to take any job available or lose their unemployment benefits	11.0	36.0	18.9	29.9	50.8	56.7	25.1
(L) Competition is harmful. It brings out the worst in people vs. (R) competition is good. It stimulates people to work hard and develop new ideas	5.5	21.7	15.4	14.7	36.2	38.4	15.8
(L) Government should increase taxes a lot and spend much more on social benefits and services vs. (R) government should decrease taxes a lot and spend much less on social benefits and services	6.7	49.6	20.8	43.6	68.1	71.0	24.2
Self-perceived left-right scale	3.0	77.9	9.5	49.3	68.7	85.3	25.2

dealing with issues on equality, government intervention, employment, competition, and social spending. In each case respondents were provided with two statements at opposite ends of a scale from 0 meaning 'left' to 10 meaning 'right (though in some cases these items were reversed in the survey). The table outlines the percentage of respondents in each scenario chosing points 0–4 (i.e. a leftist position). The final row also makes the same calculation, but based simply on the respondents' perception of how left or right-wing they thought they were when asked directly through a classic self-placement left-right scale.

Spatial theories of voting outline the importance of how voters align themselves with the ideological and policy positions of political parties, that is, the policy 'space' (Downs 1957; Enelow and Hinich 1984). Such an approach has been criticised for struggling to answer causal issues of whether individuals adapt their perspectives to match those of parties, or instead potentially convince themselves that actually their positions align, even when they might not (see Achen and Bartels 2006). Nevertheless, despite issues of causality, the results in Table 2.4 are clear—there are considerable differences in ideological outlook between party supporters and also across the different statements.

The left-wing preference for making income more equal is the most popular option, and the option where Conservatives also score the highest (over a third take the left-wing stance). However, the other options show much weaker support for the leftist options. For instance, in terms of government intervention, competition, and unemployment, only the Green Party supporters, and occasionally SNP supporters, came close to having a majority view on the left. Labour supporters hovered between a third and a fifth. The most striking difference appear in the question on taxes. Here only 6.7% of Conservative voters believe taxes should be increased to spend on social benefits and services, compared to half of Labour voters and around 70% of SNP and Green supporters.

On the self-perceived left-right scale, we see some rather stark differences, which might be of particular interest for those who label their policy interventions as 'left-wing'. Considering yourself on 'the left' is prominent for Labour, Green, and SNP supporters as might be expected, and also for almost half of Liberal Democrat supporters. However, for those who see themselves as supporting no party, only a quarter consider themselves on the left, and for UKIP supporters, this falls to only a tenth. The larger parties in opposition in England and Wales—especially Labour but also the Liberal Democrats—might consider that whilst issues of income equality chime with the public, other typically left-wing policy options present a far more mixed bag. In general, the non-affiliated and those 3.8 million UKIP voters are less sure, and, at a broader level of political discourse, do not see themselves as being 'left'.

The 2015 General Election: An Austerity Election?

Across the examined characteristics so far we see delineated camps of political supporters, especially when it comes to comparing the two biggest parties. This final part of the discussion looks at all these voter characteristics to see which are better able to explain vote choice for the 2015 general election (we use logistic regression analysis). Due to the size of the sample, the discussion focuses on the three parties with the most supporters; Labour, Conservative, and UKIP. As well as the characteristics discussed so far in this chapter—views on crisis, class, optimism/pessimism, material deprivation, government competence, party identification, and left-right ideology—the statistical models also control for classic variables such as gender, age, education, unemployment, general interest in politics, and whether the respondent has existing support for a party (descriptive statistics can be found in the Appendix, Table A.2.1). Perhaps unsurprisingly, existing party support was by far the strongest predictor of vote; for example, controlling for the other variables, a Conservative supporter in 2010 had a 0.02 probability to have voted Labour in 2015, compared to a Labour supporter in 2010. The probability of a respondent voting Labour in 2015, if they voted Labour in 2010, was a considerable 0.64: if they voted Conservative in 2010, the probability was a tiny 0.03. Because of the size of the odds ratios, and the error around the results for the smaller parties in the category, the previous party support results are not shown in Figs. 2.2, 2.3, and 2.4. However, full tables of results are provided in the Appendix, along with models that omit this variable (see Table A.2.3).

Four measures of hardship are used to try and pick up any impact that austerity might be having on a respondents' voting behaviour: reducing items, facing instances of deprivation, struggling to pay bills, and claiming benefits. However, despite the differences shown across party supporters for these measures in Table 2.2, they fail to make an impact in the regression models. The only measure to reach the standard level of statistical significance is the deprivation count for UKIP voters; for every extra count of a deprivation scenario, the respondent is 1.1 times more likely to vote UKIP ($p = 0.047$). Therefore, if we (rather artificially) hold every other variable at its mean, we can predict that the probability of a respondent with 0 instances of deprivation voting UKIP is around 0.04, whereas the probability of a respondent recording 10 instances of deprivation (the full count) is around 0.11.[6]

Degrees of optimism and pessimism concerning household and country circumstances also failed to produce any large effects. The only statistically significant effect can be seen in the Labour vote: respondents who have an optimistic outlook for the country are 0.6 times less likely to vote Labour compared to those who see things as staying the same ($p = 0.03$). So, where can we look to better explain voting behaviour? In terms of

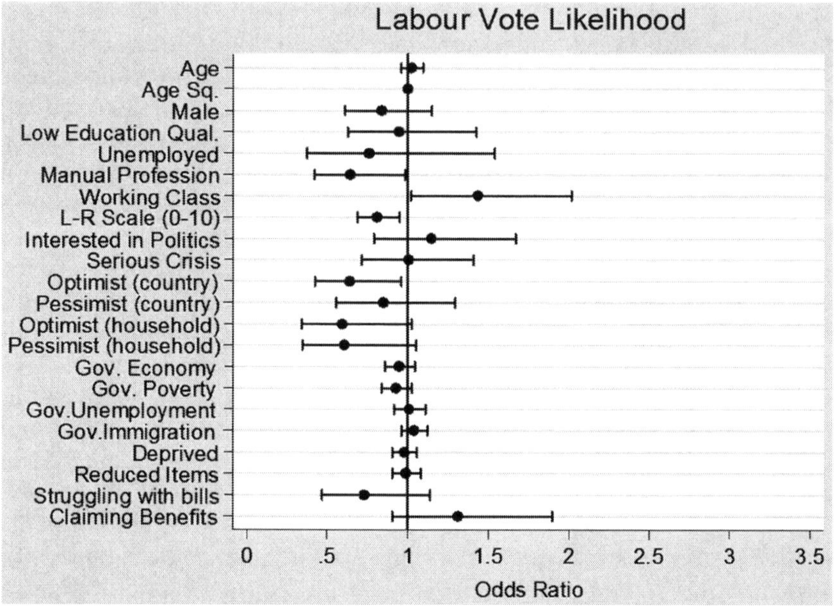

Fig. 2.2 Vote likelihood odds ratios—Labour voters in 2015

sociodemographics, gender does not predict the Labour vote; however, men are 0.5 times less likely to vote Conservative than women ($p = 0.00$) but 1.6 times more likely to vote UKIP ($p = 0.02$) (these patterns are identified and discussed elsewhere, see Annesley and Gains (2014) on the traditional, but weakening, Conservative female vote, and Ford and Goodwin (2014: 152–155), on the draw of UKIP for male voters). Perceptions of class and profession matter mostly for the Labour vote, but one element of the result is surprising; whilst those who perceive themselves as working class are 1.4 times more likely to vote Labour compared to the middle/upper classes ($p = 0.04$), those classed as being in a manual profession are 0.6 times less likely to vote Labour, compared to those who work in a white-collar profession ($p = 0.04$).[7] For the Conservative vote those who perceive themselves to be working class are 0.7 times less likely to have voted Conservative in 2015, compared to those in the middle and upper classes ($p = 0.04$). Notably, all these results for class and profession are on the margins for standard measures of statistical significance.

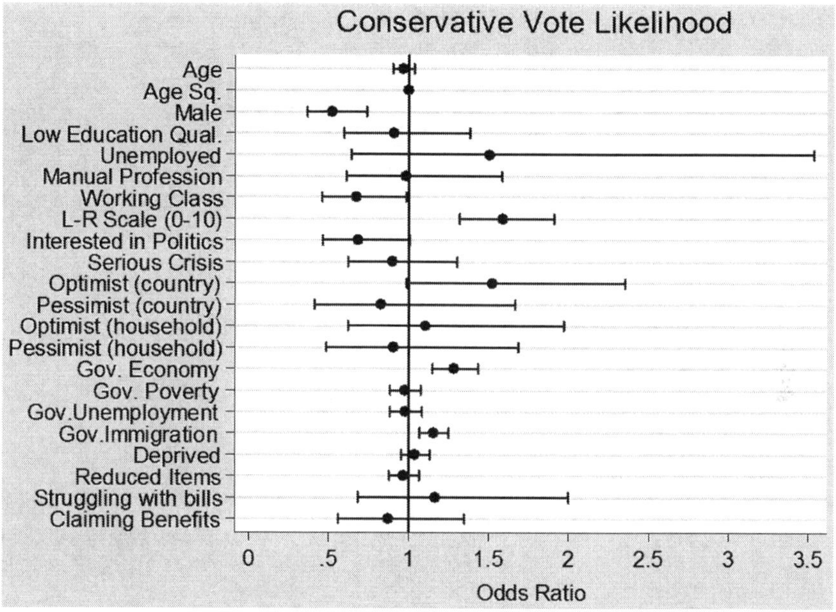

Fig. 2.3 Vote likelihood odds ratios—Conservative voters in 2015

A clearer set of results can be seen for the ideological variable. The model includes a test of left-right ideology by using an index measure built from all six questions in Table 2.4 (Cronbach's alpha = 0.9); however, the substantive pattern holds when the self-perceived left-right scale is added to the model with or without the other five specific questions. Every point move to the right on the left-right index makes a respondent 1.6 times more likely to vote Conservative ($p = 0.00$), 1.2 times more likely to vote UKIP ($p = 0.03$), and 0.8 times less likely to vote Labour ($p = 0.01$). Here then, we can see the large and important role played by ideology in vote choice. Controlling for everything else, a respondent on the very far-left of the scale has a probability of voting for Labour of 0.3, compared to only a very small 0.06 on the far-right of the scale. In comparison, a respondent on the very far-left of the scale has only a 0.03 probability of voting Conservative, but this jumps to 0.6 on the far-right. For UKIP, the pattern follows that for the Conservative vote, but the results are much more muted. A respondent on the far-left has a 0.02 probability of voting UKIP, which increases to 0.13 on the far-right. Understandings of political ideol-

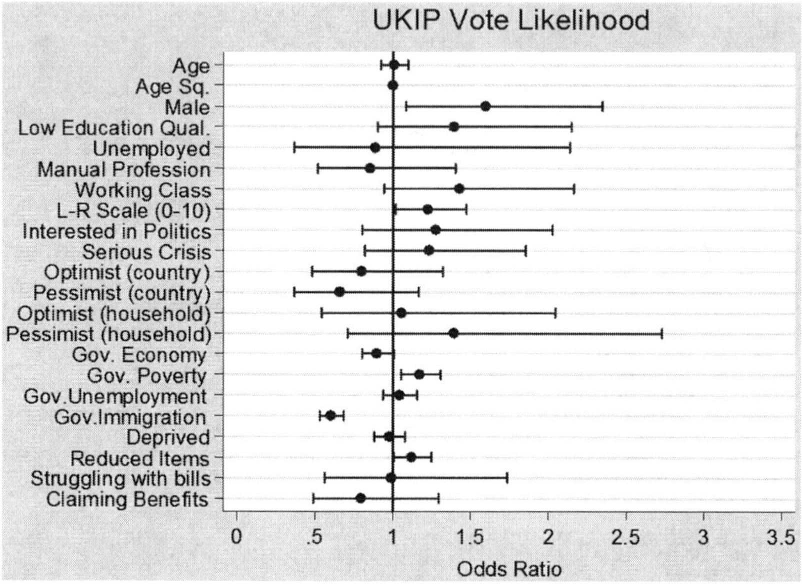

Fig. 2.4 Vote likelihood odds ratios—UKIP voters in 2015

ogy and its effects then matter much more to those who voted Labour and Conservative voters, than to those who voted UKIP, a result matching other studies that have argued that UKIP cuts across the traditional left-right scale (Curtice 2013: 65).

In terms of valence assessments of government performance, there are a number of results to consider from the figures, but also from models which did not control for previous party support (these can be seen in the Appendix, Table A.2.3). For the Labour vote, as seen in Fig. 2.2, government assessment of performance in the four policy areas did not make a difference in the models controlling for existing party support. However, when this is not controlled for, there is a negative relationship for the economy (OR = 0.89, $p = 0.01$) and for poverty (OR = 0.88, $p = 0.00$) but a positive one for immigration (OR = 1.1, $p = 0.02$). This suggests that perceived positive government performance does weaken support for opposition parties in terms of economic and hardship issues. We shall come back to the immigration result in a moment. In Fig. 2.3 we can see that when controlling for party support, believing the government is doing well on the economy and immigration increases the likelihood of voting Conservative. Immigration drops out of significance when party support is not taken into account, however. Finally for UKIP, the issue of immigration is crucial. If a respondent believes the government is doing well in terms of immigration, they are much less likely to vote UKIP.

The topic of immigration deserves some discussion. It provided a major part of the background for the 2016 Brexit vote, and has been climbing up the list of important policy areas for UK voters over the last few years. Only 0.5% of the survey sample were ten out of ten satisfied with the government on economy (and the same for nine out of ten). In comparison, 29% thought they were doing zero of ten and were *extremely dissatisfied*. Controlling for all the other factors in the models, an individual who was 10/10 happy had a probability of voting UKIP at 0.003, whereas an individual at 0/10 happiness had a probability of voting UKIP of 0.28. The scale of difference here stays the same when not controlling for existing party support and it increases when looking at how people would vote 'tomorrow' as opposed to looking at their vote in 2015.

Therefore, valence assessments of government performance matter, however, whereas in the past the key focus has been on economic and employment issues, here, we argue that immigration is becoming an issue of importance in contemporary Britain.

It is also important to note that there are questions on causality when it comes to perceptions of government competence and likelihood of voting. Building on Campbell et al.'s (1960) emphasis on partisan bias, a developing literature has outlined how existing ideology colours an individual's perception on these issues and the assessments they make of government performance (see especially Tilley and Hobolt 2011; Marsh and Tilley 2010; Cutler 2004). And indeed, we can see how important ideology and party support are from the above discussion. However, the analysis in this chapter highlights that factors such as crisis perception and assessment of household finances, plus material deprivation and reduced consumption, appear to have had no clear effect on voting behaviour when it came to the 2015 general election. Despite the negative social and economic commentary and analysis, the impact of austerity may well have not deep enough to shake up pre-existing patterns of voting (although in Scotland this may not hold, as we could not check voting for the SNP).

For the party with the big electoral gains—in vote shares, not seats—UKIP, perceptions of immigration mattered, and it appeared that the two main parties ignored this at their peril, as the Brexit EU referendum result showed a year later. Mapping these results onto the UK political landscape moving forward suggests that in many ways any economic fallout, especially in material terms, may potentially be less influential to voter consideration than we might expect. What may matter more in terms of vote winning is a credible immigration policy in the eyes of the electorate.

Conclusion

Whilst the austerity narrative has been a key part of much analysis of the UK political and social landscape, there has been less focus on the impact of austerity on voting behaviour (Giugni and Grasso 2017a). This chapter examined this topic by using a 2015 survey to look at not just perceptions of government performance but also indicators of material hardship and deprivation. In one respect, we see the expected trends for these measures across different party support groups. For example, Labour supporters are much more likely to consider themselves to be struggling to pay the bills compared to Conservative voters. Those who support opposition parties are much more likely to hold a pessimistic view on the country's economic finances, and their household finances. In this instance, we might surmise that whilst the SNP hold a majority in Scottish parliament, much of their pessimism and negative views reflect the fact that it is the Conservative Party in power in Westminster.

More interestingly, when it comes to voting behaviour, the 2015 election seems to be much better explained by issues of pre-existing support for parties, ideology, and assessment of government managing of immigration. The immigration issue was especially important for the UKIP block of supporters. Issues of hardship and material deprivation, paying the bills and claiming benefits, all failed to have any consistent or substantial effects. In many ways, then, this does not seem to be necessarily an 'austerity election', but one influenced by existing political beliefs and the issue of immigration, which had been rising in importance in the UK. Another way of understanding it can be seen in counter-narratives of austerity raised by qualitative research that uses focus groups to discuss the idea of austerity. Here, the narrative of participants suggests the idea of austerity was in fact understood as a sensible one that could legitimately close the gap in the country's finances (Stanley 2014, 2016). This is also reflected in widespread hardening of attitudes towards benefits-claimants and state spending (Taylor-Gooby 2013, Grasso et al. 2017).

This brings citizens' understandings much more in line with the Conservative message of austerity as a necessary response to profligate Labour spending before the crisis. Whilst there have been studies on the wider media narrative of austerity and crisis (Temple et al. 2016; Stronach et al. 2014) as well as the aforementioned examination of focus groups and lay narratives of hard times, it is clear more needs to be done to understand how these issues intersect for how the public have understood the last eight years (Giugni and Grasso 2017b), as well as what this means for the future political landscape in the UK.

Notes

1. This rise is difficult to quantify as there is no single definition on what a 'zero-hour' contract is. Following the ONS definition of this kind of contract—one in which there is a lack of any guaranteed hours—between May and June 2015 there were estimated to be about 744,000 contracts of this kind, around 2.4% of the employed workforce. This was a rise from the previous year although not one which is statistically significant. It is also not clear to what extent the rise was driven by people becoming more aware of the term and whether their existing contract could be classed in this way.
2. See Temple et al. (2016), for a discussion of the economic framing of the crisis and austerity in the UK, in particular how it spoke to a neoliberal narrative.
3. These questions were presented on a 0–10 scale. Here, 0–4 is classed as worse, 5 as the same, and 6–10 as better.
4. See Appendix for details on how these items were produced, Table A.2.2.
5. The result for Spain is interesting here in that out of the nine countries in our dataset it was the second-least deprived on the individual hardship scale yet one of the countries to suffer the worst economic slowdown and rising unemployment.
6. Probability calculated using the *margins* command in Stata. Furthermore, a number of other model specifications demonstrate no impact of the hardship and deprivation measures, such as trying to predict the 2010 vote, or the respondent vote intention if there was 'an election held tomorrow'. Effects were also checked for by removing the existing party preference variable from the models, but the hardship variables still all failed to come anywhere near significance. Finally, whilst multicollinearity and post-estimation checks of any variance inflation showed no concerning results, an index of deprivation was created using the Cronbach's alpha function in Stata (alpha = 0.5) to examine the effect in this way—it still failed to produce any statistically significant effects.

7. Interaction effects might help explain this result; when the manual and class-perception variables are interacted, manual falls from significance, but class perception remains significant. The interaction effect is not significant; however, it does point to a potentially interesting pattern for those who work in a white-collar capacity, yet perceive themselves as working class; these respondents make up around a third of Labour voters.

References

Abramson, P. R., et al. (2013). The British General Election of 2010 Under Different Voting Rules. *Electoral Studies, 32*(1), 134–139. Elsevier. https://doi.org/10.1016/j.electstud.2012.10.002.

Achen, C. H., & Bartels, L. M. (2006, August 30–September 3). *It Feels Like We're Thinking: The Rationalizing Voter and Electoral Democracy*. Prepared for Presentation at the Annual Meeting of the American Political Science Association, Philadelphia. https://doi.org/10.1.1.177.7498.

Annesley, C., & Gains, F. (2014). Can Cameron Capture Women's Votes? The Gendered Impediments to a Conservative Majority in 2015. *Parliamentary Affairs, 67*(4), 767–782.

Armitstead, L. (2014, June 6). IMF Accepts It Was Wrong on George Osborne's Austerity. *The Telegraph*. Available at: http://www.telegraph.co.uk/finance/economics/10881540/IMF-accepts-it-waswrong-on-George-Osbornes-austerity.html. Accessed 19 Oct 2017.

Ball, W. (2014). Providing Multi-Agency Children's Services in an Austere Climate: Professional Narratives on Parenting Support in Wales. *Families, Relationships and Societies, 3*(3), 321–337. https://doi.org/10.1332/204674313X13794304408728.

BBC. (2016, February 23). UK Loses Top AAA Credit Rating for First Time Since 1978. *BBC Business*. Available at: http://www.bbc.co.uk/news/business-21554311. Accessed 19 Oct 2017.

Beatty, C., & Fothergill, S. (2015). Disability Benefits in an Age of Austerity. *Social Policy and Administration, 49*(2), 161–181. https://doi.org/10.1111/spol.12117.

Broughton, N. (2015, July 9). Budget 2015: George Osborne Misses His Targets Again. *The New Statesman*. Available at: https://www.newstatesman.com/politics/2015/07/budget-2015-george-osbornemisses-his-targets-again. Accessed 19 Oct 2017.

Butler, D., & Stokes, D. (1969). *Political Change in Britain: Forces Shaping Electoral Change*. New York: St. Martin's Press.

Cabinet Office. (2010). The Coalition: Our Programme for Government. Available at: http://www.cabinetoffice.gov.uk/news/coalition-documents. Accessed 19 Oct 2017.

Campbell, A., et al. (1960). *The American Voter*. Chicago: University of Chicago Press.

Clarke, H., Sanders, D., Stewart, M., & Whiteley, P. (2004). *Political Choice in Britain*. Oxford: Oxford University Press.

Clarke, H. D., et al. (2009). *Performance Politics and the British Voter*. Cambridge: Cambridge University Press.

Clegg, D. (2010). Labour Market Policy in the Crisis: The UK in Comparative Perspective. *Journal of Poverty and Social Justice, 18*(1), 5–17.

Communities and Local Government Committee. (2016). Homelessness: Third Report of Session 2016–17 House of Commons. Available at: https://publications.parliament.uk/pa/cm201617/cmselect/cmcomloc/40/40.pdf. Accessed 19 Oct 2017.

Conservative Home. (2008). Labour Has Maxed Out Britain's Credit Card, Says Cameron. Conservative Home Blog. Nov 9. Available at: http://www.conservativehome.com/thetorydiary/2008/11/labourhas-maxe.html. Accessed 19 Oct 2017.

Conservative Home. (2015). George Osborne Conservative Conference Speech in Full. Available at http://www.conservativehome.com/parliament/2015/10/george-osbornes-speech-in-full.html. Accessed 19 Oct 2017.

Cowburn, A. (2016, July 4). Nigel Farage Resigns: Douglas Carswell Brands Ukip Leader 'Electorally Disastrous' After Resignation. *The Independent*. Available at: http://www.independent.co.uk/news/uk/politics/nigel-farage-resigns-as-ukip-leader-a7118626.html. Accessed 19 Oct 2017.

Cribb, J., Hood, A., & Joyce, R. (2015). *Living Standards: Recent Trends and Future Challenges*. London. Available at: https://www.ifs.org.uk/publications/7616.

Curtice, J. (2013). Never to Be Forgotten? The 2013 English Local Elections. *Juncture, 20*(1), 62–70.

Curtice, J. (2015). Ashcroft Shows Those 'Safe' Labour Seats Really Are at Risk. What Scotland Thinks Blog 4 Feb. Available at: http://blog.whatscotlandthinks.org/2015/02/ashcroft-shows-safelabour-seats-really-risk/. Accessed 19 Oct 2017.

Cutler, F. (2004). Government Responsibility and Electoral Accountability in Federations. *Publius, 34*(2), 19–38.

Dalton, R. J. (1984). Cognitive Mobilization and Partisan Dealignment in Advanced Industrial Democracies. *Journal of Politics, 46*(1), 264–284.

Davies, B. W., et al. (2015). *Financial Melancholia: Mental Health and Indebtedness*. Available at: http://www.perc.org.uk/project_posts/financial-melancholia-mental-health-and-indebtedness/.

Dowler, E., & Lambie-Mumford, H. (2015). How Can Households Eat in Austerity? Challenges for Social Policy in the UK. *Social Policy and Society, 14*(3), 417–428. https://doi.org/10.1017/S1474746415000032.

Downs, A. (1957). *An Economic Theory of Democracy*. New York: Harper.

Elliott, L. (2013, April 18). George Osborne Told by IMF Chief: Rethink Your Austerity Plan. *The Guardian*. Available at: https://www.theguardian.com/politics/2013/apr/18/george-osborne-imf-austerity. Accessed 19 Oct 2017.

Enelow, J. M., & Hinich, M. J. (1982). Ideology, Issues, and the Spatial Theory of Elections. *The American Political Science Review, 76*(3), 493–501.

Enelow, J. M., & Hinich, M. J. (1984). *The Spatial Theory of Voting: An Introduction*. Cambridge: Cambridge University Press.

English, P., Grasso, M. T., Buraczynska, B., Karampampas, S., & Temple, L. (2016). Convergence on Crisis? Comparing Labour and Conservative Party Framing of the Economic Crisis in Britain, 2008–2014. *Politics & Policy, 44*(3), 577–603.

Evans, G. (2000). The Continued Significance of Class Voting. *Annual Review of Political Science, 3*(1), 401–417.

Fieldhouse, E. (1995). Thatcherism and the Changing Geography of Political Attitudes, 1964–1987. *Political Geography, 14*(1), 3–30. https://doi.org/10.1016/0962-6298(94)P4049-D.

Ford, R., & Goodwin, M. (2014). *Revolt on the Right—Explaining Support for the Radical Right in Britain*. London: Routledge.

Giugni, M., & Grasso, M. T. (2017a). Citizens and the Crisis: Perceptions, Experiences, and Responses to the Great Recession in Nine Democracies. In M. Giugni & M. T. Grasso (Eds.), *Citizens and the Crisis: Perceptions, Experiences, and Responses to the Great Recession in Europe*. London: Palgrave Macmillan.

Giugni, M., & Grasso, M. T. (2017b). Citizens and the Crisis: The Great Recession as Constraint and Opportunity. In M. Giugni & M. T. Grasso (Eds.), *Citizens and the Crisis: Perceptions, Experiences, and Responses to the Great Recession in Europe*. London: Palgrave Macmillan.

Giugni, M. G., & Grasso, M. T. (Eds.). (2015a). *Austerity and Protest: Popular Contention in Times of Economic Crisis*. London: Routledge.

Giugni, M. G., & Grasso, M. T. (2015b). Environmental Movements in Advanced Industrial Democracies: Heterogeneity, Transformation, and Institutionalization. *Annual Review of Environment and Resources, 40*, 337–361.

Grasso, M. T., Farrall, S., Gray, E., Hay, C., & Jennings, W. (2017). Thatcher's Children, Blair's Babies, Political Socialisation and Trickle-Down Value-Change: An Age, Period and Cohort Analysis. *British Journal of Political Science*. https://doi.org/10.1017/S0007123416000375.

Grasso, M. T., & Giugni, M. (2013, September 12–14). Anti-austerity Movements: Old Wine in New Vessels? In *XXVII Meeting of the Italian Political Science Association (SISP)*, University of Florence, Florence.

Grasso, M. T., & Giugni, M. (2016). Protest Participation and Economic Crisis: The Conditioning Role of Political Opportunities. *European Journal of Political Research, 55*(4), 663–680.

Green, J. (2007). When Voters and Parties Agree: Valence Issues and Party Competition. *Political Studies, 55*(3), 629–655. https://doi.org/10.1111/j.1467-9248.2007.00671.x.

Green, J., & Hobolt, S. B. (2008). Owning the Issue Agenda: Party Strategies and Vote Choices in British Elections. *Electoral Studies, 27*(3), 460–476. https://doi.org/10.1016/j.electstud.2008.02.003.

Green, J., & Prosser, C. (2015, September 17). Learning the Right Lessons from Labour's 2015 Defeat IPPR Blog. Available at: https://www.ippr.org/juncture/learning-the-right-lessons-from-labours-2015-defeat. Accessed 19 Oct 2017.

Grice, A. (2016, August 17). Government Austerity to Blame for 30% Rise in Homelessness, Says Parliamentary Committee. *The Independent*. Available at: http://www.independent.co.uk/news/uk/politics/homelessness-austerity-government-to-blame-for-30-rise-in-homelessness-says-parliamentary-committee-a7195981.html. Accessed 19 Oct 2017.

Hayton, R. (2013). Cameronite Conservatism and the Politics of Marriage Under the UK Coalition Government. *Open Space, 4*(May), 151–156.

Henderson, R. C., et al. (2014). Viewpoint Survey of Mental Health Service Users' Experiences of Discrimination in England 2008–2012. *Social Psychiatry and Psychiatric Epidemiology, 49*(10), 1599–1608. https://doi.org/10.1007/s00127-014-0875-3.

Hinich, M. J., & Pollard, W. (1981). A New Approach to the Spatial Theory of Electoral Competition. *American Journal of Political Science, 25*(2), 323–340.

Hodkinson, S., & Robbins, G. (2013). The Return of Class War Conservatism? Housing under the UK Coalition Government. *Critical Social Policy, 33*(1), 57–77. https://doi.org/10.1177/0261018312457871.

Holmes, E. (2013). Fixing the Roof While the Sun is Shining—Osborne's New Spending Rule' Policy Exchange Blog. Available at: https://policyexchange.org.uk/fixing-the-roof-while-the-sun-is-shiningosbornes-new-spending-rule/. Accessed 19 Oct 2017.

Hood, A., & Phillips, D. (2015). Benefit Spending and Reforms: The Coalition Government's Record Institute for Fiscal Studies Briefing Note BN160. Available at: http://election2015.ifs.org.uk/uploads/publications/bns/BN160.pdf. Accessed 19 Oct 2017.

Inglehart, R. (1984). The Changing Structure of Political Cleavages in Western Society. In R. Dalton, S. Flanagan, & P. A. Beck (Eds.), *Electoral Changes in Advanced Industrial Democracies. Realignment or Dealignment?* (pp. 25–69). Princeton: Princeton University Press.

Kirkup, J. (2010, October 21). Spending Review 2010: There's No 'Plan B', Says George Osborne. *The Telegraph*. Available at: http://www.telegraph.co.uk/news/politics/spendingreview/8077541/Spending-review-2010-Theres-no-Plan- B-says-George-Osborne.html. Accessed 19 Oct 2017.

Lambie-Mumford, H., & Green, M. A. (2015). Austerity, Welfare Reform and the Rising Use of Food Banks by Children in England and Wales. *Area*, 1–7. Online Fir. https://doi.org/10.1111/area.12233.

Livewhat. (2014). Integrated Report on Policy Responses to Crises. Available at: http://www.livewhat.unige.ch/wp-content/uploads/2014/02/LIVEWHAT_D2.4.pdf. Accessed 19 Oct 2017.

Lupton, R., Burchardt, T., Hills, J., Stewart, K., & Vizard, P. (2016). *Social Policy in a Cold Climate: Policies and Their Consequences Since the Crisis*. Bristol: Policy Press.

Marsh, M., & Tilley, J. (2010). The Attribution of Credit and Blame to Governments and Its Impact on Vote Choice. *British Journal of Political Science, 40*, 115–134.

Milbourne, L., & Cushman, M. (2015). Complying, Transforming or Resisting in the New Austerity? Realigning Social Welfare and Independent Action among English Voluntary Organisations. *Journal of Social Policy, 44*(3), 463–485. https://doi.org/10.1017/S0047279414000853.

National Audit Office. (2014). The Report of the Comptroller and Auditor General to the House of Commons HM Treasury Annual Report and Accounts 2013–2014. Available at: https://www.nao.org.uk/wpcontent/uploads/2014/07/Her-Majesty-Treasury-2013-14-report-on-accounts.pdf. Accessed 19 Oct 2017.

OBR. (2015). Economic and Fiscal Outlook—March 2015 Office for Budget Responsibility. Available at: http://budgetresponsibility.org.uk/efo/economic-fiscal-outlook-march-2015/. Accessed 19 Oct 2017.

OECD. (2012). Social Spending During the Crisis: Social Expenditure (SOCX) Data Update 2012. Available at http://www.oecd.org/els/soc/OECD2012SocialSpendingDuringTheCrisis8pages.pdf. Accessed 19 Oct 2017.

Oesch, D. (2008). The Changing Shape of Class Voting. *European Societies, 10*(3), 329–355. https://doi.org/10.1080/14616690701846946.

ONS. (2015). Contracts with No Guaranteed Hours: 2015. Available at https://www.ons.gov.uk/employmentandlabourmarket/peopleinwork/earningsandworkinghours/articles/contractswithnoguaranteedhours/2015-09-02. Accessed 19 Oct 2017.

Peers, S. (2016). Migration, Internal Security and the UK's EU Membership. *The Political Quarterly, 87*(2), 247–253. https://doi.org/10.1111/1467-923X.12248.

People's Assembly. (2015, March 23). Budget 2015: Austerity Policies a Disaster for the Majority. People's Assembly Blog. Available at: http://www.thepeoplesassembly.org.uk/budget_2015_austerity_policies_a_disaster_for_majority. Accessed 19 Oct 2017.

Perraudin, F. (2014, December 16). SNP, Plaid Cymru and Greens Plan to Join Forces Against Austerity. *The Guardian*. Available at: https://www.theguardian.com/politics/2014/dec/16/snp-plaid-cymru-greensjoin-forces-austerity-election. Accessed 19 Oct 2017.

Portes, J. (2016). Immigration, Free Movement and the Eu Referendum. *National Institute Economic Review, 236*, 14–22. https://doi.org/10.1177/002795011623600103.

Quinn, T. (2016). Throwing the Rascals Out? Problems of Accountability in Two-Party Systems. *European Journal of Political Research, 55*(1), 120–137. https://doi.org/10.1111/1475-6765.12118.

Savage, M. (2015). *Social Class in the 21st century*. London: Pelican.

Sawyer, M. (2012). The Tragedy of UK Fiscal Policy in the Aftermath of the Financial Crisis. *Cambridge Journal of Economics, 36*(1), 205–221.

Sculthorpe, T. (2016, April 21). George Osborne MISSED His Borrowing Target for the Last Year by £1.8 Billion in a Fresh Blow to His Budget Plans. *The Daily Mail*. Available at: http://www.dailymail.co.uk/news/article-3551449/George-Osborne-MISSED-borrowing-target-year1-8BILLION-fresh-blow-Budget-plans.html. Accessed 19 Oct 2017.

Shaw, K. (2015, November 27). Breaching the Welfare Cap is Actually Good News for the CONSERVATIVES. LSE British Politics and Policy Blog. Available at: http://blogs.lse.ac.uk/politicsandpolicy/breaching-the-welfare-cap-is-actually-good-newsfor-the-conservatives/. Accessed 19 Oct 2017.

Stanley, L. (2014). We're Reaping What We Sowed: Everyday Crisis Narratives and Acquiescence to the Age of Austerity. *New Political Economy, 19*(6), 895–917. Taylor & Francis.

Stanley, L. (2016). Legitimacy Gaps, Taxpayer Conflict, and the Politics of Austerity in the UK. *The British Journal of Politics and International Relations, 18*(2), 389–406.

Steven, M., Llyr ap Gareth, O., & Baston, L. (2012). The Conservative Party and Devolved National Identities: Scotland and Wales Compared. *National Identities, 14*(1), 71–81. https://doi.org/10.1080/14608944.2012.657086.

Stronach, I., Clarke, J., & Frankham, J. (2014). Economic "Revelations" and the Metaphors of the Meltdown: An Educational Deconstruction. *British Educational Research Journal, 40*(2), 319–336.

Taylor-Gooby, P. (2013). Why Do People Stigmatise the Poor at a Time of Rapidly Increasing Inequality, and What Can Be Done About It? *The Political Quarterly, 84*(1), 31–42.

Temple, L., Grasso, M.T., Buraczynska, B., Karampampas, S., & English, P. (2016). Neoliberal Narrative in Times of Economic Crisis: A Political Claims Analysis of the U.K. Press, 2007–2014. *Politics and Policy, 44*(3), 553–576.

The Guardian. (2009). David Cameron Conservative Conference Speech in Full. Available at: https://www.theguardian.com/politics/2009/oct/08/david-cameron-speech-in-full. Accessed 19 Oct 2017.

The Telegraph. (2011). George Osborne Conservative Conference Speech in Full. Available at: http://www.telegraph.co.uk/news/politics/georgeosborne/8804027/Conservative-Party-Conference-2011-George-Osborne-speech-in-full.html. Accessed 19 Oct 2017.

Thielemann, E., & Schade, D. (2016). Buying into Myths: Free Movement of People and Immigration. *The Political Quarterly, 87*(2), 139–147. https://doi.org/10.1111/1467-923X.12246.

Tilley, J., & Hobolt, S. B. (2011). Is the Government to Blame? An Experimental Test of How Partisanship Shapes Perceptions of Performance and Responsibility. *The Journal of Politics, 73*(2), 316–330.

TUC. (2016). UK Workers Experienced Sharpest Wage Fall of Any Leading Economy, TUC Analysis Finds. TUC Press Release. Available at: https://www.tuc.org.uk/news/uk-workers-experienced-sharpestwage-fall-any-leading-economy-tuc-analysis-finds. Accessed 19 Oct 2017.

Vis, B., van Kersbergen, K., & Hylands, T. (2011). To What Extent Did the Financial Crisis Intensify the Pressure to Reform the Welfare State? *Social Policy & Administration, 45*(4), 338–353.

de Vreese, C. H., & Boomgaarden, H. G. (2005). Projecting EU Referendums: Fear of Immigration and Support for European Integration. *European Union Politics, 6*(1), 59–82. https://doi.org/10.1177/1465116505049608.

Weeks, J. (2015, March 12). May 2015: The Austerity Election. Talking Humanities Blog. Available at: https://talkinghumanities.blogs.sas.ac.uk/2015/03/12/may-2015-the-austerity-election/. Accessed 19 Oct 2017.

Whiteley, P., et al. (2013). *Affluence, Austerity and Electoral Change in Britain.* Cambridge: Cambridge University Press.

Wintour, P. (2012, December 3). George Osborne Prepares for Climbdown on Missed Fiscal Targets. *The Guardian*. Available at: https://www.theguardian.com/politics/2012/dec/02/osborne-climbdownfailing-fiscal-goals. Accessed 19 Oct 2017.

Wren-Lewis, S. (2015). *The Academic Consensus on the Impact of Austerity*, *Mainly Macro Blog*. Available at: https://mainlymacro.blogspot.co.uk/2015/06/the-academic-consensus-on-impact-of.html. Accessed 21 Sept 2016.

Yates, J. (2012). What Prospects Youth Justice? Children in Trouble in the Age of Austerity. *Social Policy and Administration, 46*(4), 432–447. https://doi.org/10.1111/j.1467-9515.2012.00842.x.

CHAPTER 3

Economic Crisis, Populist Attitudes, and the Birth of Podemos in Spain

Eva Anduiza, Marc Guinjoan, and Guillem Rico

Introduction

The last decade in Spain has been characterised by two extraordinary circumstances. On the one hand, Spain has suffered an economic crisis that has produced rocketing levels of unemployment, and a substantive reduction in citizens' purchasing power. As a consequence, citizens' evaluations of the economic situation have plummeted, with over 95% of the population qualifying it as bad or very bad in 2013. On the other hand, the last three years have witnessed the rise of a new, left-wing, populist party, Podemos. Founded in early 2014, Podemos obtained 8% of the votes in the European parliament elections that took place only five months later, in May 2014. In the 2015 general elections of December of that same year, Podemos obtained 21% of the popular vote. In less than two years, Podemos has consolidated as the third largest party in the Spanish political landscape, threatening (though not yet achieving) PSOE with a *sorpasso* as the main political party of the left on the June 2016 general elections.

E. Anduiza (✉) • M. Guinjoan • G. Rico
Departament de Ciència Política i Dret Públic, Universitat Autònoma de Barcelona, Cerdanyola del Vallès, Barcelona, Spain

M. Giugni, M.T. Grasso (eds.), *Citizens and the Crisis*, Palgrave Studies in European Political Sociology,
https://doi.org/10.1007/978-3-319-68960-9_3

Although Spain seems so far immune to the growth of populist radical right parties that affects other European countries (Alonso and Rovira Kaltwasser 2015), the main political consequence of the Great Recession has been the birth of a party whose discourse is structured around the constant opposition between *la gente* (the people) and *la casta* (the caste) (Gomez Reino and Llamazares 2016). Spain is hence a good case to analyse the triggering factors for the birth and rise of a populist party that has not an extreme right orientation, but that very much reflects the core elements of populism: people-centrism, anti-elitism, and the primacy of popular sovereignty (Mudde 2004; Stanley 2008).

Hence, the purpose of this chapter is to analyse the micro mechanisms that connect the economic crisis with populist electoral choices in the case of Spain. We assess the impact of economic hardship experienced at the individual level over populist attitudes, and how these attitudes are in turn associated with electoral preferences. To do so, the first section of the chapter contextualises the Spanish case in terms of political and economic circumstances, including an overview of the main elements of the Spanish political landscape between 2008 and 2016. In this section, we show that Podemos' voters are the ones that hold more populist attitudes, in contrast to the ruling conservative party PP, whose voters register the lowest value. The second section uses populist attitudes as a dependent variable to assess the extent to which economic hardship is able to explain the emergence of populist attitudes. Our findings show that the perceptions of the economic situation of the country are the main source of variation in the degree of populist attitudes. High degrees of political knowledge, lower income, not being identified with the incumbent, and being leftist are also positively related with the emergence of populist attitudes. In the third section, populist attitudes become the independent variable to explain voting behaviour and, particularly, support for Podemos. Here, we show that while in the 2011 elections the PP (at that time the main opposition party) benefitted the most from the vote of individuals with populist attitudes, in the 2015 elections it was Podemos and, to a lower degree Ciudadanos, the two parties that benefitted the most from individuals with high degrees of populist attitudes. Finally, the fourth section concludes.

An Unprecedented Economic and Political Crisis

When the economic crisis first hit Spain in 2008, the government of José Luis Rodríguez Zapatero (Partido Socialista Obrero Español, PSOE) had just been re-elected. During the previous socialist mandate (2004–2008), the level of unemployment in the country had been unprecedentedly below 10%, but the last months of the legislature showed some initial signals that the times of economic expansion were over (see Fig. 3.1). Despite this, the PSOE retained power in the 2008 elections with a discourse based on the negation of the existence of an economic crisis in Spain and the promise to make no cuts in public services. The first attempts to address the economic recession were indeed based on an expansion of public expenditure.

However, the escalation of the debt crisis and the increase in public deficit fuelled intense pressures from Brussels to Washington over Zapatero's government. He eventually gave in and introduced a U turn in his economic policy. In May 2010, the government approved a series of

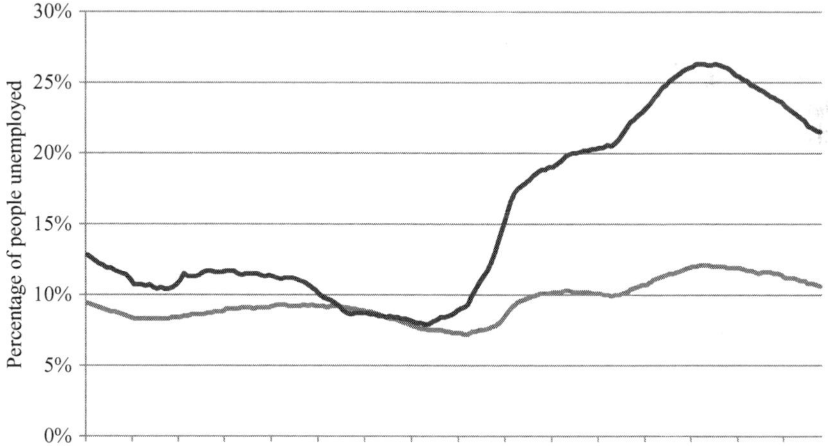

Fig. 3.1 Evolution of the unemployment rate in Spain and the EU19, 2000–2015 (Source: OECD)

measures, ranging from a 5% average reduction in the pay of public employees to severe cuts in social policies—which had been the Zapatero's main political flagship until this moment. From then on, the reduction in government spending became the main political objective. Further reforms passed by the Spanish parliament included labour regulations, a revision of the public pension scheme, cuts in public sector employment, health, social benefits, and education, to name only a few. A year later, in the summer of 2011, this process culminated in the agreement between the PSOE and the PP on a reform of the constitution to introduce a limit on future deficits with a view to win back market confidence (Rodon and Hierro 2016).

In parallel to these reforms, an intense wave of protests started with the well-known 15M or *Indignados* demonstrations of 2011 and peaked around 2013. Only a few days before the municipal elections of 2011, on the 15th of May, a demonstration was called under the motto *¡Democracia Real Ya!* (Real Democracy Now!), integrating a diverse array of social movements and networks. Although the crisis and the austerity policies were the underlying issues for these protests, it is remarkable that the main argument behind the call was political. Demonstrators protested against the two main established political parties, the PSOE and the PP, that were found to be incapable of handling the economic situation—unemployment levels were continuing in their skyrocketing trajectory—the privileges of the political class, and demanded new democratic channels for civic participation (Gómez-Reino and Llamazares 2016: 5). Traditional mobilising agents such as trade unions and political parties were absent from this protest (Anduiza et al. 2013), whereas online social networks played a crucial role mobilising thousands of people to the streets of different cities in Spain (mainly in Madrid, but also in Barcelona and Granada). The demonstration in Madrid ended up with a group of 100 individuals camping in the middle of Puerta del Sol and occupations of different public spaces followed in different cities across the country.

The protest and the electoral dynamics were at this stage still very far apart. Only one week after the demonstration and in the midst of intense protests, on the 22 of May, there were local elections and regional elections in some autonomous communities. The PP won an overwhelming majority of the local councils, as well as most of the regional elections. As a result of the poor electoral results of the PSOE in the local election, the protests on the streets, and the economic crisis, Prime Minister Zapatero

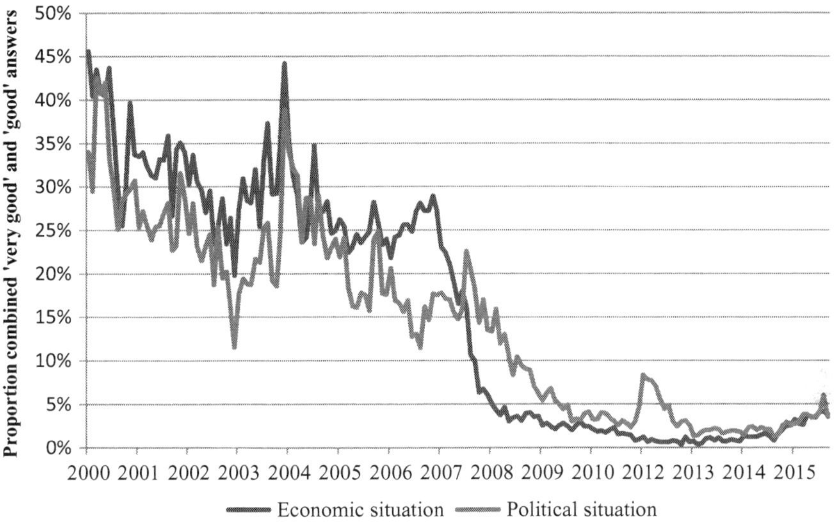

Fig. 3.2 Evaluations of the economic and political situation, 2000–2015 (Source: Centro de Investigaciones Sociológicas)

decided to call early elections by the end of 2011 and decided that he would not be running as a candidate. In this moment, the evaluation of Zapatero's political performance was at its lowest levels,[1] and the levels of satisfaction with the political and economic situation were at their historical minimum (see Fig. 3.2). In the 20th November elections, protests were still going on regularly, but this did not prevent a Partido Popular (PP) leaded by Mariano Rajoy from securing an absolute majority in the Congress and the Senate.

The harsh economic crisis with unemployment levels over 20%, but also probably the implementation of austerity policies from May 2010 (Orriols and Rico 2014; Fraile and Lewis-Beck 2014), explains the plummeting levels of confidence in Zapatero and ultimately favoured the victory of the PP. Despite the promises during the electoral campaign, the PP government raised taxes and austerity continued with additional legislation in labour regulations and pensions and an imposed reduction on regional and local public spending. On average, this reduction reached 20 percentage points between 2009 and 2013 (Lago-Peñas and Fernández Leiceaga 2013) and posed serious difficulties for the provision of education, health, and other social assistance services, for which regional governments are (financially) responsible (Rodon and Hierro 2016). Meanwhile, the level of unemployment that seemed to have stabilised by 2011 continued increasing until it reached 26% in 2013 (see Fig. 3.1).

During the PP mandate, austerity policies were combined with some pieces of legislation that were strongly contested by public opinion. In 2012 the Spanish Economy Minister Luis de Guindos obtained from the EU a bail out for banks and lending institutions. The most benefitted institutions during the years of the economic boom were now being rescued by public funding. The public sector had therefore to pay for the excesses of the banks and lending institutions. In this regard, it is not surprising that, according to the LIVEWHAT survey, 58% of the respondents in Spain claimed that banks and financial institutions were the main culprits for the global economics crisis.

In 2015, with its absolute majority in parliament, the PP approved without any difficulty the Ley de Seguridad Ciudadana, the so-called Ley Mordaza, which limited citizens' rights to protest and to demonstrate and affected fundamental civic rights.

Furthermore, between 2011 and 2015 several corruption scandals irrupted in the political landscape. The party that accumulated the larger number of cases was the PP. The main scandal, the Bárcenas affair, named after the PP treasurer, showed that PP senior officials had been receiving irregular payments in cash for almost two decades. During this period, the PP appeared in other scandals such as the Gürtel affair in Madrid, Valencia, Galicia, and Castilla y León, or the Palma Arena and Noos affairs in Illes Balears, which involved members of the royal family. Other parties also faced corruption scandals: the PSOE (involved in the ERE's affair in Andalucía regarding the use of unemployment funds for other purposes), the Catalan nationalist and conservative Convergència i Unió (CiU, with the outstanding Pujol affair, involving the family of the former regional president) or the Black Cards affair, affecting most of the delegates of the bank Caja Madrid designated by all the different parties as well as trade unions and trade associations. Eventually, the coverage of these scandals in the media influenced citizens' dissatisfaction with the political system (Villoria and Jiménez 2012; Palau and Davesa 2013; Torcal 2014) and impacted negatively on popular perceptions of traditional political parties. Corruption, on the one hand, and the political class, on the other, appear since 2008 as two increasing concerns of Spanish citizens, to an extent unprecedented in the Spanish recent democratic history.

As a synthesis, Fig. 3.2 shows the evolution of perceptions about the economic and political situation. The data report the percentage of individuals thinking that either the economic or the political situation is good or very good. The figure clearly displays that by 2013 almost nobody has a positive evaluation.

The emergence of Podemos in the political landscape cannot be understood without considering all these elements together. The economic crisis, the political crisis, and the 15M movement all bear relevance for making sense of the birth of this new party. However, the relationship between the 15M and Podemos is a complex one. The 15M was a massive, unstructured, set of events, whose demands were partially taken up by Podemos, a structured political organisation with a very clear intention to occupy institutional power.

Podemos ("We can") was launched in a press conference in Madrid in January 2014. The leadership of the party was made up by several academics from the Universidad Complutense de Madrid. The appearances of Pablo Iglesias as a TV talk show guest launched his image and his populist discourse. Iglesias' discourse has repeatedly integrated the opposition between the caste and the people, and negatively refers to the political and economic elites that built the political system represented in the 1978 constitution to their own benefit. During the first months after the foundation of the party, the anti-elitist dimension seems to prevail clearly over other political conflicts such as the opposition between left and right (Gómez Reino and Llamazares 2016), although the party's elites have their origins in leftists movements and the *Indignados*, as an anti-austerity movement, clearly support a progressive agenda.

Podemos unexpectedly achieved 8% of the vote and five seats in the 2014 European parliament elections held on May 24, only four months after the foundation of the party and with hardly any poll predicting the entrance of the party in the parliament (Cordero and Montero 2015). The months that followed saw a rapid increase in the vote intention for the party in the Spanish legislative elections. As Fig. 3.3 displays, in less than a year Podemos became the first party in terms of direct vote intention. While the rise of Ciudadanos (a centre-right Spanish nationalist party also emphatic on democratic regeneration (see Rodríguez Teruel and Barrio 2016)) may have reduced Podemos' vote intention share, it is clear that the political landscape has fundamentally changed and bears little resemblance to the electoral results of 2011. This party system change is also unprecedented since 1982, as the electoral system in Spain is extremely

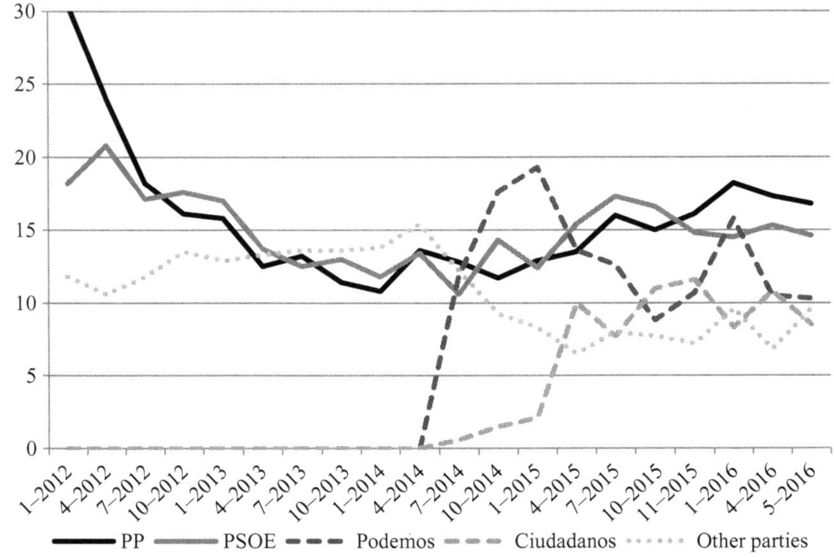

Fig. 3.3 Vote intention in the national elections (% of estimated vote intention) (Source: Centro de Investigaciones Sociologicas)

restrictive with small parties that have territorially dispersed electoral support. With a mean district magnitude of 6.7, and 54% of the districts electing five deputies or less, it is very hard for third small parties to get representation beyond large districts like Madrid or Barcelona (electing, respectively, 36 and 31 seats). This has historically helped the PP and the PSOE to remain as the main actors in the party system, and has penalised severely parties like Unión Progreso y Democracia (UPyD) who eventually managed to get a handful of seats or Izquierda Unida (IU) which has always been in parliament until the 2016 election but with a share of seats much lower than their share of votes.

In the regional elections of May 2015, Podemos performed particularly well in Aragón (21% of the votes), Asturias (19%), Madrid (19%), and the Balearic Islands (15%). Also, political confluences between Podemos and other local platforms led to mayoral victories in crucial cities such as Barcelona (where they also won the elections), Madrid, Zaragoza, Santiago de Compostela, A Coruña, and Cádiz.

In the legislative elections of 20 December 2015, Podemos obtained an overall support of 21% of the votes and 69 deputies (see Orriols and Cordero 2016). The party (with its regional partners) won the elections in Catalonia and the Basque country, and surpassed the PSOE also in Galicia and in Valencia. The socialists obtained 22% of the votes and 90 deputies, well behind the winning party, the PP (29% of the votes and 123 deputies). Ciudadanos got 14% of the vote, below the level that the polls had predicted. PP and PSOE, who in 2011 added up to 84% of the parliament 350 seats, now only received 61%. The PP was still the most voted party, but it ended up far from the absolute majority (176 deputies). Table 3.1 presents the evolution of the electoral results in the legislative elections in 2011, 2015, and 2016.

The negotiations after the 2015 elections to form a progressive government in Spain did not yield any results and early elections were automatically set for the 26 June of 2016. Podemos joined a pre-electoral coalition with the post-communist IU, which had obtained 4% of the votes in the 2015 elections but only two deputies due to the disproportional electoral system. Several surveys predicted that the new coalition, called Unidos Podemos (UP), would surpass the PSOE. However, things did not move much from December. Participation declined slowly, the PP was again the most voted party and the *sorpasso* did not eventually take place. UP obtained 21% of the votes and kept the 71 deputies that Podemos and IU

Table 3.1 The legislative election results of 2011, 2015, and 2016 (Congreso de los Diputados)

	2011		*2015*		*2016*	
	% votes	*Deputies*	*% votes*	*Deputies*	*% votes*	*Deputies*
PP	44.0%	186	28.5%	123	32.7%	137
PSOE	28.4%	110	21.9%	90	22.5%	85
Podemos	–	–	20.6%	69	20.9%	71
Ciudadanos	–	–	13.9%	40	12.9%	32
IU	6.8%	11	3.7%	2	–	–
ERC	1.0%	3	2.4%	9	2.6%	9
CiU/DL/CDC	4.1%	16	2.2%	8	2.0%	8
Other parties	15.6%	24	6.9%	9	6.4%	8
Total	100.0%	350	100.0%	350	100.0%	350

Source: Ministerio del Interior (http://www.infoelectoral.mir.es/)

got in 2015, but losing over a million voters. The party again won in Catalonia and the Basque country, and surpassed the PSOE in Valencia, but did not beat the PSOE in Galicia, as in the 2015 elections.

Notwithstanding the fact that the Popular Party won the 2015 elections and again the 2016 elections, the Spanish party system has experienced a significant political change: a new relevant actor has emerged in the left of the political landscape with distinct populist character. In the following pages, we try to disentangle the micro mechanisms that account for some of these macro changes. We start by looking in depth at the consequences of the economic crisis for populist attitudes at the individual level.

Economic Hardship and Populist Attitudes

Our initial point of departure is to assess to what extent economic hardship is related to populist attitudes among the population. Although most of existing research on the origins of populism as a mass phenomenon uses vote choice for populist parties as the dependent variable, focusing on individual populist attitudes allows to consider populism as something that can be present in various degrees and to avoid problematic categorisations. People can display different levels of populist attitudes, which are conditioned by different political and economic circumstances and which in turn may be related to specific patterns of voting behaviour.

Measuring populism is however not unproblematic. We follow Mudde (2004: 543) when arguing that populism "considers society to be separated into two relatively homogeneous and antagonistic groups, 'the pure people' versus 'the corrupt elite', and which argues that politics should be an expression of the *volonté générale* (general will) of the people". To operationalise populism as an attitude, we use a battery of indicators proposed by Akkerman et al. (2014) that build up a composite index of populism.[2] The statements are designed to tap the core ideas that make up the populist discourse, namely, people-centrism, anti-elitism, the antagonism between the people and the elite, and the primacy of popular sovereignty. Respondents' agreement with each of the statements was measured using a five-point Likert scale, coded from 0 (strongly disagree) to 4 (strongly agree). The composite index is the average score across six items, each coded from 0 to 4. Table 3.2 displays the percentage of agreeing and strongly agreeing with each of the statement in Spain.

Table 3.2 Populist attitudes in Spain (% agreeing or strongly agreeing with statement)

Statement		
1	The politicians in [country] need to follow the will of the people	83
2	The people, and not politicians, should make our most important policy decisions	65
3	The political differences between the elite and the people are larger than the differences among the people	69
4	I would rather be represented by a citizen than by a specialised politician	53
5	Elected officials talk too much and take too little action	80
6	What people call "compromise" in politics is really just selling out on one's principles	42
	Average score (0–4)	2.84

Comparative evidence shows that Spain, with a mean value of 2.84, has considerably high levels of populist attitudes. Above it, we find countries such as France, Greece, Italy, and Poland, with mean values around 3; and below Spain, Germany, Sweden, Switzerland, and the UK, with mean values ranging from 2.4 to 2.6 (Rico and Anduiza 2017). Our data would thus lend support to the claim that "a large pool of potential followers always exists" (Hawkins and Riding 2010) which populist movements can draw on.

If we look at the different items used to measure populist attitudes, we also find that in most cases a majority of people agree or strongly agree with the statements proposed, with a few exceptions. Statement 1 seems to obtain the highest levels of support: 83% of Spanish respondents think that politicians need to follow the will of the people. Statement 5 displays a similar pattern, 80% of people agreeing with the view that politicians talk too much and take too little action, a mild critical view of the political elite. Statements 2, 3, and 4 show lower levels of support, while statement 6—which reflects the rejection that populism makes of pluralist agreements—has a level of support below 50%.

Last, if we disaggregate the evidence by political parties (see Fig. 3.4), we can see that Podemos is the political party whose voters are more supportive of populist statements, with a mean value of 3.21 and almost 90% of its voters showing values above 2. Ciudadanos' voters register the second highest value in the populist scale, with a mean of 2.82, yet very close to the PSOE and non-voters (2.77). Finally, PP voters have a mean value of 2.52.

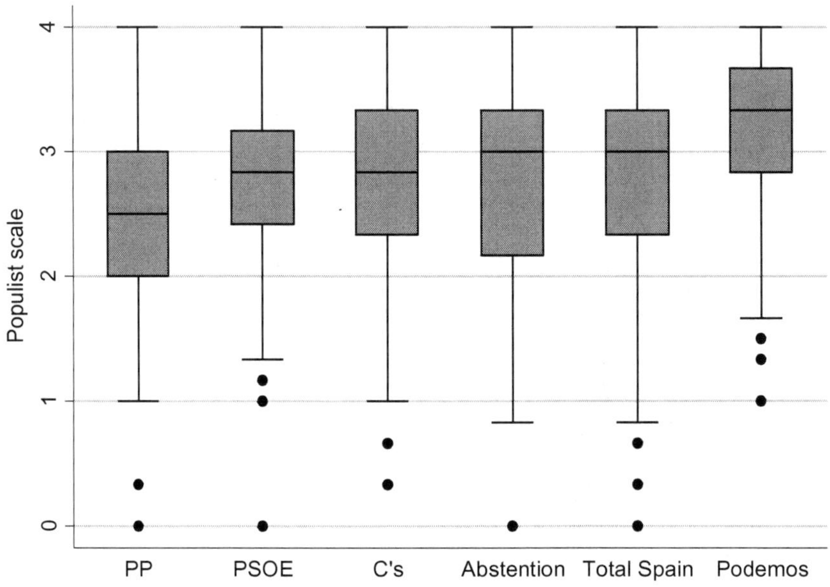

Fig. 3.4 Boxplot of the populist attitudes, by party

Once we have measured populist attitudes and we know how these are distributed across political parties in Spain, we now analyse how these are conditioned by economic and political individual circumstances. Drawing on previous works, we have a number of expectations.

First, we expect economically vulnerable individuals to show higher levels of populist attitudes. Globalisation, massive immigration flows, cultural diversity, or European integration has been interpreted to be giving rise to a new conflict opposing winners and losers of modernisation, the latter typically comprising groups with lower socioeconomic status (Kriesi et al. 2006, 2008) considered more vulnerable to the threats of these major sociopolitical changes. According to Kriesi (2014), the Great Recession would have only exacerbated the emerging cleavage, further fuelling populist radical right, while likely leading to the breakthrough of more overtly class-based, left-wing populist movements. Previous empirical research has quite consistently found that populist parties, and the populist radical right in particular, draw disproportionate support from persons with lower income, lower education, and lower occupational status (see, e.g. Lubbers et al. 2002). As a consequence, individuals with lower levels of education, manual workers, the unemployed, or people with low income levels are expected to show higher levels of populist attitudes.

Second, we expect that those individuals that have more directly suffered the consequences of economic recession will be more supportive of populist statements than their counterparts. This retrospective assessment captures the depth and pace of the deterioration that characterises economic crisis among those actually hit by it. Material strain is typically experienced as the inability to keep up with once affordable payments, the reduction in consumption of basic goods and services, worsening working conditions or loss of job. We expect higher levels of populism for individuals that have experienced such situations.

Third, we expect individual perceptions of the functioning of the economy to be related to populist attitudes. We expect sociotropic perceptions to be the relevant attitude for two reasons. First, a large body of economic voting literature has confirmed the prevalence of sociotropic perceptions, most often related to the state of the national economy, over egotropic, or pocketbook, considerations (Kinder and Kiewiet 1981). Second, people-centrism is one of the necessary components of the aforementioned definition of populism. If populism actually is the product of a "plurality of unsatisfied demands", all the more reason for the perception of grievances shared by the community identified as the people, rather than individual economic hardship, to play a paramount role in explaining citizens' degree of endorsement of populist attitudes. Indeed, Elchardus and Spruyt (2016) find that an individual's situation economic of vulnerability only indirectly affects populism, via its influence on feelings of relative group deprivation and other sociotropic considerations. Further, as just noted, above crises may be real or artificially constructed by populist leaders, but it is the subjective perceptions of crisis, rather than the picture conveyed by standard macroeconomic figures, that ultimately fuel populism. We hence expect negative perceptions of the country's economic situation to play a major role as determinant of populist attitudes.

Political attitudes are also brought into the picture. In Spain populist attitudes are expected to relate with left-wing positions in the ideological scale, because the party that has articulated a populist discourse is left wing. Unlike other cases where immigration policy grievances, mainly motivated by cultural and identity concerns (Ivarsflaten 2005, 2008; Oesch 2008), have played an important role, we do not expect this to be the case in Spain. Following Mudde (2004), political sophistication is also considered to be positively related to populism, as the more people are knowledgeable about politics the more they feel competent to be critical with the establishment and take their own decisions.

Table A.3.1 in the appendix presents the results of a series of regression models in which the three groups of variables are sequentially introduced. We include in the model standard sociodemographic controls: gender (female as a reference category), age and its square (to account for the potential curvilinear effect of age), and citizenship (non-national). We also control for attachment to the party in government.[3] The codes for all the variables are reported in the appendix. Figure 3.5 shows the coefficients of the key independent variables.

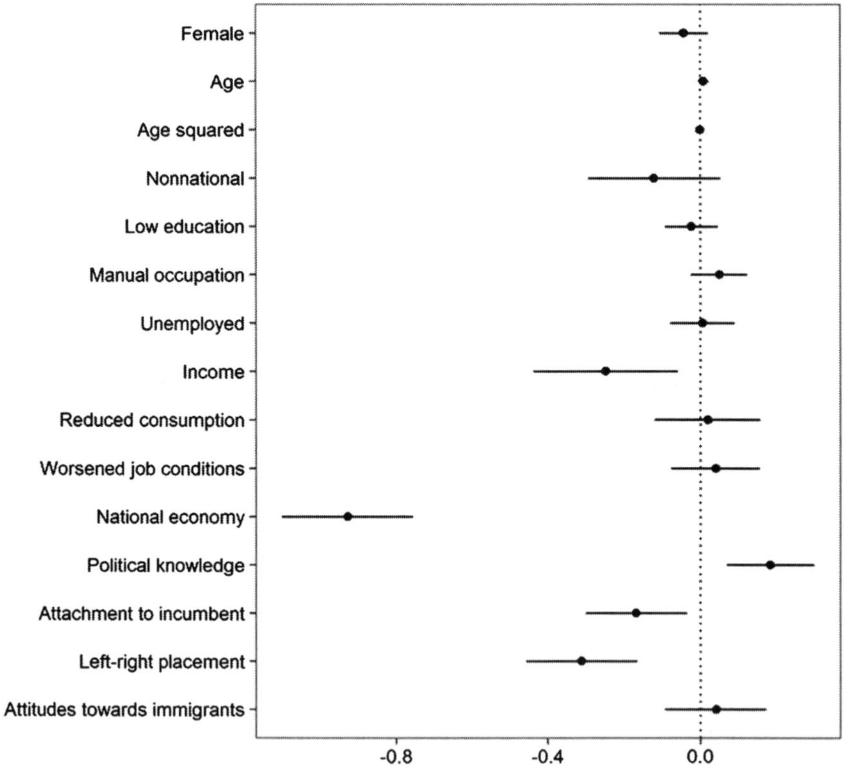

Fig. 3.5 What explains populism? (Notes: Based on the estimates in Table A.3.1 in the Appendix)

The results of the analysis show that our expectations are partially confirmed. First, income is the only variable indicating vulnerability that has a significant effect. In Spain higher income is related to lower levels of populism. However, education and occupation do not show significant effects. More surprisingly, indicators of having been personally affected by the crisis (reduced consumption, deteriorating job conditions) are not significant either. The largest effect is the one corresponding to the perceptions of the economic situation of the country, confirming our expectation that populist attitudes grow not necessarily where the crisis hits harder, but where perceptions about the crisis develop. This effect of sociotropic economic perceptions may be suspect of endogeneity: populist attitudes may induce perceptions of a crisis. Elsewhere (Rico and Anduiza 2017) it has been shown that this is not the case, and that the effect goes indeed from economic perceptions to populist attitudes.

Our political attitudes show the expected effects. Those that do not show attachment to the incumbent party (PP) are more populist, and so are those individuals that place themselves on the left of the ideological spectrum and sophisticated individuals. Among our controls, gender, age, and nationality do not seem to be related to populist attitudes in a significant way.

Do Populist Attitudes Affect Voting Behaviour?

Is vote choice affected by these populist attitudes produced by situations of economic vulnerability and by perceptions of the crisis? In this section we analyse the relationship between our index of populism and different vote choices in legislative elections. We include in the analysis the intention to vote for the main four main state-wide parties (PP, PSOE, Podemos and Ciudadanos) with abstention as the reference outcome in the models.

Our expectations are that populist attitudes will hold the strongest effect over the likelihood of voting for Podemos, a party that has endorsed an explicitly populist discourse. We also expect some positive effect over the likelihood of voting Ciudadanos, whose anti-corruption discourse may be attractive for people holding anti-establishment attitudes but do not favour the leftist agenda defended by Podemos. On the other hand, we expect populist attitudes to be negatively correlated with the likelihood of voting for mainstream parties (PP and PSOE). Finally, we expect that populist and non-populist voters will abstain to a similar degree in the 2011 elections, but that the electoral supply of a populist party in the 2015 will make the likelihood of abstaining higher among non-populist individuals than among the populist ones. Our main explanatory factor is the scale of populism. We also include a few control variables: age, gender, education, occupational status, religiosity, left-right placement, political knowledge, interest in politics, and the retrospective evaluation of the country's economic situation over the last year (see appendix for operationalisation). The result of this model is included in Table A.3.2 of the appendix.

Figure 3.6 plots the expected likelihood of voting for each of the parties as a function of the individual's degree of populism. As expected, populism is particularly related to the likelihood of voting for Podemos. Moving from the minimum to the maximum level of populism increases the likelihood of voting for this party from 4% to 36%. The effect for Ciudadanos is also positive, but far smaller (from 9% among the least populist to 19% among those with the highest score on populism). Conversely, populism reduces the chances of voting for the traditional parties (PP and PSOE).

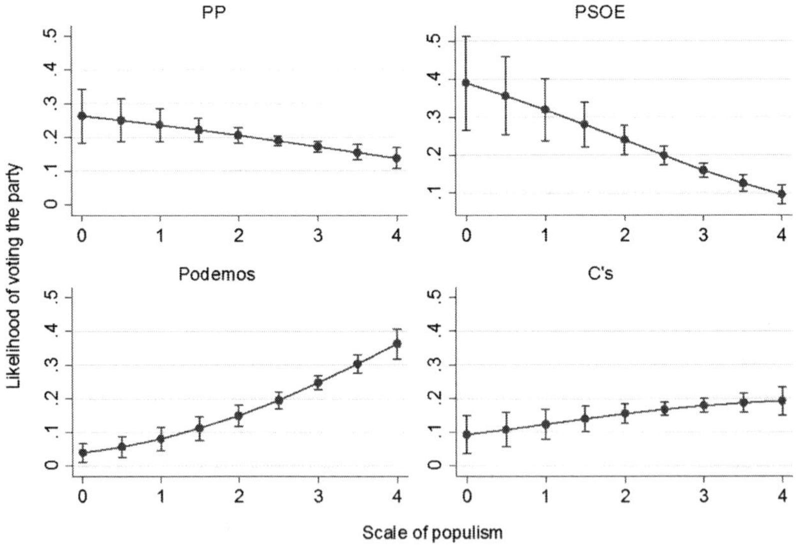

Fig. 3.6 Populism and vote intention in the 2015 general elections (Notes: Based on the estimates in Table A.3.2 in the Appendix)

The probability of voting for the PSOE drops from 39% among the least populist individuals to 10% among the most populist ones, while for the likelihood of a PP vote is reduced from 26% to 14%.

The LIVEWHAT survey also included a question of vote recall for the previous general election (held in 2011). Since Podemos did not exist at that time and Ciudadanos did not compete in this general election (for some time it was a political actor only in the Catalan arena), the comparison may be interesting to assess to what extent the supply of parties affects the relationship between populist attitudes and vote choice. We hence run the same models with the record of voting for the two main political parties (PP and PSOE) in the 2011 legislative elections.

The main difference with the 2015 legislative elections (see Fig. 3.7) is that the slope for the PP is positive, meaning that the likelihood of voting for the party increased as the individual became more populist. This is explained by the fact that in the 2011 Spanish elections the PP was the in the opposition while the PSOE was the incumbent. This may have encouraged individuals with populist attitudes to support the conservatives. On the other hand, highly populist individuals were more likely to vote for PSOE in 2011 than in 2015, when Podemos had entered the political arena.

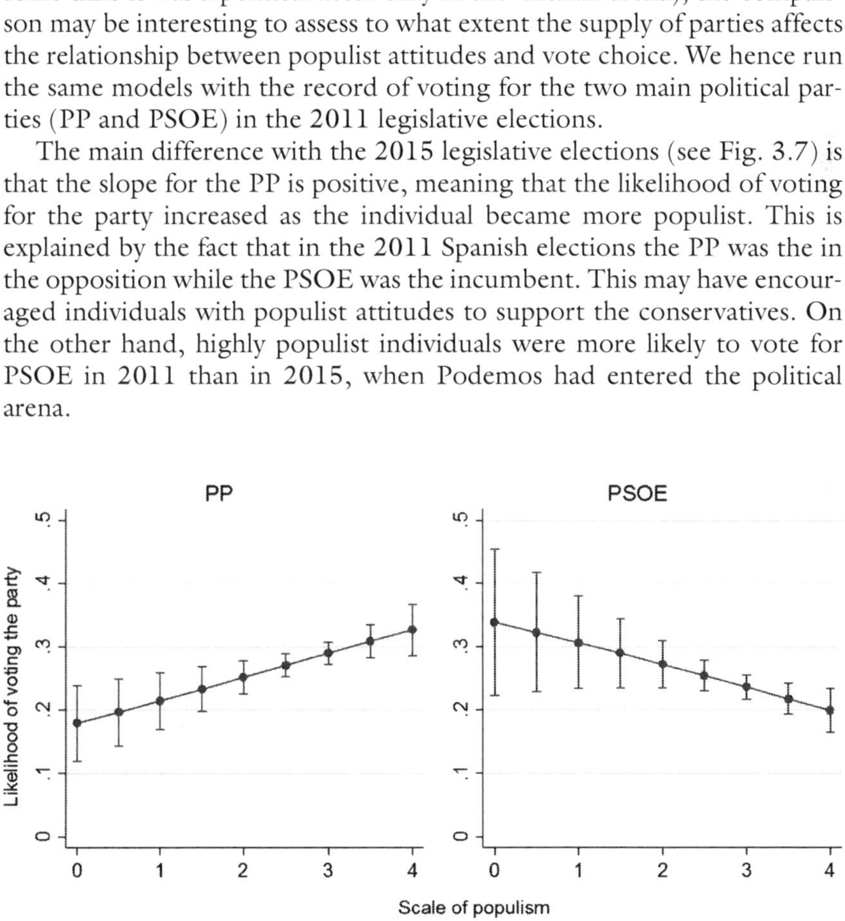

Fig. 3.7 Populism and the likelihood of voting for PP and PSOE in the 2011 legislative elections (Based on the estimates in Table A.3.3 in the Appendix)

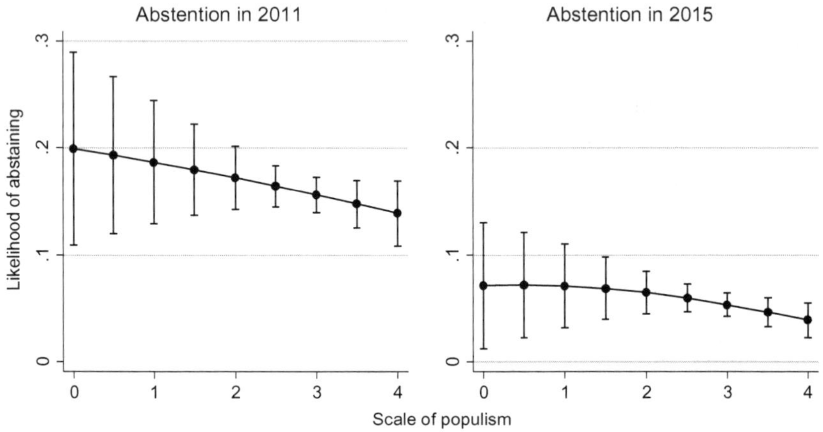

Fig. 3.8 Populism and the likelihood of abstaining in the 2011 and 2015 legislative elections (Based on the estimates in Tables A.3.2 (2015) and A.3.3 (2011) in the Appendix)

Finally, as displayed in Fig. 3.8, our results do not show any change in the relationship between populist attitudes and abstention from the 2011 to the 2015, with the likelihood of abstaining being kept reasonably constant across the populist scale in the two years.

Conclusions

The economic crisis that started in 2008 and that at 2016 was still going on in Spain has led to unprecedented levels of dissatisfaction among Spanish citizens. Negative evaluations of the political situation have been fuelled also by successive corruption scandals. After a cycle of political protests between 2011 and 2013, the party system has witnessed an important change with the irruption of Podemos, a party that has deployed a clearly populist discourse. The unfolding of political events in Spain shows how political change as a consequence of economic crisis has been first introduced through social unrest and then evolved into the electoral and institutional arena.

In this chapter, we have analysed the micro mechanisms that are behind the relationship between the economic crisis and the rise of this populist party. We have divided our empirical analysis in two different sections. First, we have addressed which individual-level factors account for a change in the populist attitudes. Our data has shown that some indicators of vulnerability (income) and particularly the perception that the economy is not going well increase the level of populist attitudes. We also show that political attitudes such as political sophistication, being left-wing oriented, or not being close to the incumbent have a positive effect. However, populist attitudes in Spain are not related to gender, age, origin, education, or employment. Unlike in other European parties, they are unrelated to attitudes towards migrants. And somewhat surprisingly are also unaffected by the personal consequences of the economic crisis such as having reduced their consumption patterns or having experienced a worsening in their working conditions.

Second, we have addressed the relationship between populist attitudes and the vote intention for the 2015 legislative elections. Our evidence supports the idea that populist attitudes are strongly correlated with the likelihood of voting for Podemos and, to a lower degree, to Ciudadanos. In contrast, populist attitudes are negatively correlated with the vote for the PP and the PSOE. By comparing the 2015 evidence with the one from 2011, when Podemos did not exist, we can assess how the changes in the electoral supply have modified the electoral behaviour of individuals with populist attitudes.

Overall, the results from this study suggest that, while it is true that populist attitudes have been affected by some aspects to the economic crisis in Spain, the relationship between populist attitudes and vote choice is more complex. In particular, the vote decision has been shown to be contingent on the characteristics of the political supply (whether or not there is a party displaying a populist discourse) and the political context (who is in government). Thus, populism and vote for the PP were positively associated in 2011 when the PP was in opposition, while they were negatively related in 2015 when the PP was in power. In contrast, in 2015 populist attitudes were associated to left-wing positions and, specifically, to Podemos vote choice. Future research will have to address the extent to which populist attitudes are contingent upon the party in government and whether the same individual in different moments in time may take on populist postulates as a function of whether its preferred party is ruling the country or not.

Notes

1. He was rated on average at 3.06 on a scale from 0 to 10 in October 2011 (Barometer 2915 from the Centro de Investigaciones Sociológicas).
2. The empirical analysis is based on an online survey conducted in Spain in June of 2015. The samples, recruited by YouGov, are quota balanced in order to match national population statistics in terms of sex, age, and education level. See the introduction for further information on the sample and appendix for operationalization details.
3. There are no substantial correlations between the different independent variables, thus discarding the possibility of facing multicollinearity problems.

References

Akkerman, A., Mudde, C., & Zaslove, A. (2014). How Populist Are the People? Measuring Populist Attitudes in Voters. *Comparative Political Studies, 47*(9), 1324–1353.

Alonso, S., & Rovira Kaltwasser, C. (2015). Spain: No Country for the Populist Radical Right? *South European Society and Politics, 20*(1), 21–45.

Anduiza, E., Cristancho, C., & Sabucedo, J. M. (2013). Mobilization Through Online Social Networks: The Political Protest of the Indignados in Spain. *Information, Communication & Society, 17*(6), 750–764. https://doi.org/10.1080/1369118X.2013.808360.

Cordero, G., & Montero, J. R. (2015). Against Bipartyism, Towards Dealignment? The 2014 European Election in Spain. *South European Society & Politics, 20*(3), 357–379.

Elchardus, M., & Spruyt, B. (2016). Populism, Persistent Republicanism and Declinism: An Empirical Analysis of Populism as a Thin Ideology. *Government and Opposition, 51*(1), 111–133.

Fraile, M., & Lewis-Beck, M. (2014). Es la economía y es la austeridad, estúpido! Las consecuencias electorales de las políticas de recesión en las elecciones de 2011. In *Las elecciones generales de 2011.* Madrid: Centro de Investigaciones Sociológicas.

Gomez Reino, M., & Llamazares, I. (2016). *From Working Class Anticapitalism to Populism.* https://doi.org/10.1017/CBO9781107415324.004.

Hawkins, K. A., & Riding, S. (2010). *Populist Attitudes and Their Correlates Among Citizens: Survey Evidence from the Americas.* Muenster. Retrieved from https://pedl.byu.edu/SiteAssets/ECPR_LAPOP/Populism_20100312.doc.

Ivarsflaten, E. (2005). The Vulnerable Populist Right Parties: No Economic Realignment Fuelling Their Electoral Success. *European Journal of Political Research, 44*(3), 465–492.

Ivarsflaten, E. (2008). What Unites Right-Wing Populists in Western Europe? *Comparative Political Studies, 41*(1), 3–23. https://doi.org/10.1177/0010414006294168.

Kinder, D. R., & Kiewiet, D. R. (1981). Sociotropic Politics: The American Case. *British Journal of Political Science, 11*(2), 129–161.

Kriesi, H. (2014). The Populist Challenge. *West European Politics, 37*(2), 361–378. https://doi.org/10.1080/01402382.2014.887879.

Kriesi, H., Grande, E., Lachat, R., Dolezal, M., Bornschier, S., & Frey, T. (2006). Globalization and the Transformation of the National Political Space: Six European Countries Compared. *European Journal of Political Research, 45*(6), 921–956.

Kriesi, H., Grande, E., Lachat, R., Dolezal, M., Bornschier, S., & Frey, T. (2008). *West European Politics in the Age of Globalization.* Cambridge: Cambridge University Press.

Lago Peñas, S., & Fernández Leiceaga, X. (2013). Las finanzas autonómicas: expansión y crisis, 2002–2012. *Papeles de Economía Española, 138*, 129–146.

Lubbers, M., Gijsberts, M., & Scheepers, P. (2002). Extreme Right-Wing Voting in Western Europe. *European Journal of Political Research, 41*(3), 345–378.

Mudde, C. (2004). The Populist Zeitgeist. *Government and Opposition, 39*(4), 542–563. https://doi.org/10.1111/j.1477-7053.2004.00135.x.

Oesch, D. (2008). Explaining Workers' Support for Right-Wing Populist Parties in Western Europe: Evidence from Austria, Belgium, France, Norway, and Switzerland. *International Political Science Review, 29*(3), 349–373.

Orriols, Ll., & Cordero, G. (2016). The Breakdown of the Spanish Two-Party System: The Upsurge of Podemos and Ciudadanos in the 2015 General Election. *South European Society and Politics, 21*(4), 469–492. Routledge.

Orriols, L., & Rico, G. (2014). El clima de opinión. In *Las elecciones generales de 2011.* Madrid: Centro de Investigaciones Sociológicas.

Palau, A., & Davesa, F. (2013). The Impact of Media Coverage of Corruption on Spanish Public Opinion. *Revista Española de Investigaciones Sociológicas, 144*, 97–124.

Rico, G., & Anduiza, E. (2017). Economic Correlates of Populist Attitudes: An Analysis of Nine European Countries. *Acta Politica*, forthcoming.

Rodon, T., & Hierro, M. J. (2016). Podemos and Ciudadanos Shake Up the Spanish Party System: The 2015 Local and Regional Elections. *South European Society and Politics, 21*(3), 339–357. https://doi.org/10.1080/13608746.2016.1151127.

Rodríguez Teruel, J., & Barrio, A. (2016). Going National: Ciudadanos from Catalonia to Spain. *South European Society and Politics, 21*(4), 587–607.

Stanley, B. (2008). The Thin Ideology of Populism. *Journal of Political Ideologies, 13*(1), 95–110.

Torcal, M. (2014). The Decline of Political Trust in Spain and Portugal: Economic Performance or Political Responsiveness. *American Behavioral Scientist, 58*(12), 1542–1567.

Villoria, M., & Jiménez, F. (2012). La corrupción en España (2004–2010): datos, percepción y efectos. *Revista Española de Investigaciones Sociológicas, 138*, 109–134.

CHAPTER 4

Unfinished Transformation or Neoliberal Economy? Exploring the Legitimisation Divide in Poland

Maria Theiss and Anna Kurowska

Introduction

The parliamentary election of October 2015 brought political change to Poland. After eight years of liberal Civic Platform rule, a right-wing party—Law and Justice—came into power. Not only has Law and Justice been the first party since 1989 to rule independently, but its position was additionally strengthened by the President Andrzej Duda being the party member. However, the meaning of its victory goes beyond mere change to Poland's ruling party. The electoral campaigns—and, more broadly, the political narratives formulated by the party—presented 1989 not so much as a moment of Polish democratic change but rather as a smokescreen that hid the transformation of capitals of former regime members. In 2015

This article is partially financed from Polish Ministry of Science and Higher Education 2014–2016 fund, granted for the international co-financed project—LIVEWHAT.

M. Theiss (✉) • A. Kurowska
Instytut Polityki Społecznej, University of Warsaw, Warsaw, Poland

M. Giugni, M.T. Grasso (eds.), *Citizens and the Crisis*,
Palgrave Studies in European Political Sociology,
https://doi.org/10.1007/978-3-319-68960-9_4

Law and Justice claimed for a far-reaching renewal of a political system, including changes in the constitution, EU-cooperation formula and the structure of courts and universities. Opposition parties emphasised the calamitous nature of the Polish political system's performance, using the slogan of Poland 'being in ruin'.

It is hence not presidential and parliamentary change per se but rather the narratives of Law and Justice and social support for the party's ideas that allow us to pose a question about political legitimisation in Poland—and its drivers. In this chapter, we start from the premise that a legitimisation crisis contributed to political change in Poland in 2015. Our goal is to explore a societal divide about the legitimisation of the political system's performance, taking into consideration the context of economic crisis in Europe and its peculiar character in Poland. We apply Schultz's (2012) notion of 'legitimation divide' to the process of citizens granting and withdrawing acceptance to the political system. *Legitimisation divide* here denotes a split in society between those citizens who perceive the performance of the political system as legitimate and those who deny this claim. We test two hypotheses concerning the delegitimisation processes: (i) the role of political socialisation typical for a post-communist country and (ii) the role of the neoliberal economy strengthened during the European economic crisis.

The first, following Giza et al. (2000), we call *the 'unfinished transformation' hypothesis*. This refers to a broad body of literature which emphasises the role of communist heritage in Polish civic culture. It is assumed that, despite the transformation of economic and political institutions after 1989, there has been insufficient change in citizens' civic and political engagement in Poland. Thus, we have seen the cumulative effect of political socialisation based on refraining from civic engagement, familialism and low levels of social capital. These, in turn, negatively affect levels of political legitimisation (Garlicki 2014; Domański 2004). However, it should be noted that we agree with recent criticisms that address this hypothesis (see, e.g. Jacobsson and Korloczuk 2017).

The second hypothesis refers to the role of the *neoliberal economy*. Its advocates stress that high levels of precarious employment, weak social mobility and the massive migration of Poles to western EU countries result in the political dissatisfaction of Polish citizens (Ost 2016; Marczewski 2016). In our chapter, this hypothesis goes beyond individuals' experiences of economic hardship. We question the Civic Platform argument that Poland has been a 'green island', the only EU country not affected by the economic crisis of 2008 (see Ministry of Foreign Affairs 2016). We interpret the proliferation of the neoliberal economy in Poland as a political means of *transferring economic risks in times of crisis in the EU to citizens and allocating them the function of potential 'shock absorbers'* (Marczewski 2016; Theiss 2016). So, we assume the economic crisis had a weak impact in Poland in part because of the neoliberal economy and privatisation of economic risk. It is plausible that this economic success had political consequences and contributed to the legitimisation crisis.

The remaining part of the chapter is structured as follows. The next two sections introduce the indicators of the legitimisation crisis in Polish public discourse and outline the framework for studying the *legitimisation divide* in Poland, respecively. The subsequent section introduces a synthetic indicator of *delegitimisation* at the individual level and shows its distribution as well as comparing the social characteristics of Poles perceiving the performance of the political system as legitimate and those who deny political legitimisation. Sections "Unfinished Societal Transformation Hypothesis" and "Neoliberal Economy Hypothesis" discuss the two hypotheses and seek to discover to what extent a legitimisation divide in Poland is parallel to differences in civic skills and individual experiences with the neoliberal economy. The fifth section reports the results of the estimated logistic regression, which confronts the role of weak individual 'civicness' and personal negative experiences with the neoliberal economy as factors explaining the propensity to delegitimising attitudes among Poles. The last section discusses the findings and concludes the paper.

Delegitimisation of the Political System: Public Discourse Manifestations

Since the fall of communism in 1989, the political landscape in Poland has undergone profound changes. Until 2016, only one parliamentary party active in 1989—the *Polskie Stronnictwo Ludowe* (PSL)—continued to exist. A multiparty system has evolved into a two-party system with Law and Justice (*Prawo i Sprawiedliwość* (PiS)) and Civic Platform (*Platforma Obywatelska* (PO)). After two terms of Civic Platform and PSL government, the parliamentary election of autumn 2015 gave the majority of seats to the conservative Law and Justice, resulting in the absence of any social democratic party in Polish parliament. These changes have been accompanied by high levels of instability in the preferences of Polish electorate, including a high level of interblock volatility (Cześnik 2014; Markowski 2007; Owen and Tucker 2010).

In this chapter, we claim that the meaning of the political rearrangement of 2015, which encompassed both the beginning of majority rule by Law and Justice and the president election won by Andrzej Duda—Law and Justice's candidate, is a part of a more in-depth change in Poland. It is worth noticing that earlier, during the 2005–2007 period, Law and Justice's government (i.e. ruled by Jarosław Kaczyński) was ruling with the conservative president (Lech Kaczyński, Jarosław's twin brother). Our argument is that the political change of 2015 had been fuelled by a far-reaching lack of legitimisation in the functioning of the Polish political system. At the macrolevel, this has meant a proliferation of political claims that Civic Platform has neither a political nor moral mandate to govern and that the performance of the political system does not serve the good of 'average citizens'. This stance has been thoroughly presented as a criticism of 'Donald Tusk's system' in the official Law and Justice's political programme of 2014 (Program Prawa i Sprawiedliwości 2014). At the individual level, a phenomenon could be observed which we label here as a legitimisation divide: a split of Polish society not into Law and Justice supporters and opponents but into those convinced the political system might be not effective but is legitimate, and those claiming its performance is fundamentally unjust and that it needs to be rebuilt from scratch.

As specified in the subsequent part of this chapter, we regard political legitimisation as a multidimensional concept which reflects people's beliefs about whether their political institutions are appropriate for their society (Lipset 1959; Beetham 1991; Garlicki 2014). Our focus is on the meso-level of these beliefs, that is, on the evaluation of the political system's performance. Although the object of our research is individuals' assessments of the how the political system in Poland operates, we contextualise our exploratory analysis by shedding light on the discursive context of what we term the 'legitimisation divide'. As noted, we assume that specific narratives present in Polish politics before the autumn of 2015, and more broadly the *Weltanschauung* (worldview) politics of the biggest parties, mirrored the growing legitimisation divide in Poland and further contributed to the political polarisation of society.

Four arguments, present in public discourse before the presidential and parliamentary elections of 2015, formed the narrative that Poland's political system was illegitimate. The first claimed that Civic Platform (which had ruled Poland for eight years) served its own particularistic goals and was deliberately harmful to the country. This was based on a leak of party officials' secret recordings to the public media (so-called Waitergate). In the summer of 2014, a leading Polish journal published typescripts of private conversations between leading Civic Platform politicians. There were quotations of officials saying that, for example, 'Only a fool would work for six thousands złoty', which is 150% of the average salary in Poland, or that the 'Polish country is just a (explicit words) and a pile of stones'. This provoked public outrage but not the dismissal of any representatives (Miller 2015; Arak and Żakowiecki 2016). The leak included long hours of recordings and conversations of dozens of people involved in politics as well as businessmen and journalists. Eating octopus and drinking expensive wine became a symbol of a vain, immoral and corrupted political elite. Law and Justice referred to these recordings in the parliamentary election to a high extent (e.g. the party's website banner included a posh restaurant picture with a list of scandals attributed to Civic Platform placed on a virtual menu). Experts commenting on events are unanimous that they brought about a political legitimisation crisis and contributed to the failure of Civic Platform in the parliamentary election of 2015 (see Wybory 2015).

According to second, more general and longer-lasting argument, the political change of 1989 did not represent the cessation of communism in Poland but instead served as a smokescreen for transforming the political capital of former regime elites into financial capital. It has been claimed that a 'shadow network' or 'square card table' of players govern Poland. Such an 'iron square' consists of some politicians, some businessman, some criminals and some secret service officers (Żukowski quoted in: Raport o stanie Rzeczpospolitej 2011). This narrative included the claim that Lech Wałęsa was a secret service informer and Donald Tusk secretly served German interests, whereas President Bronisław Komorowski was in fact a Russian ally. A radical version of the argument includes the conviction that former Polish President Lech Kaczyński and 86 other officials were assassinated in 2010 during a plane crash in Smoleńsk, Russia. The idea that a shadow network rules the country was intertwined with the assumption that Poland lacked sovereignty, being politically and economically dependent on both the EU and Russia.

The third argument focused on the low possibility of citizens influencing politics. A new party, stemming from the Kukiz social movement (and then the Kukiz '15 political party), underlined the need to change the electoral system from proportional into majoritarian in order to increase the people's influence on politics and 'renew political elites' in the country. In a similar vein, it was argued that recent social reforms introduced by Civic Platform deprived the parents from deciding about their children's education and, as such, needed to be reverted. In a broader sense, the meaning of these claims was a critique of too weak input legitimacy—it was argued that the political system did not allow for the translation of citizens' needs and choices into political decisions.

Lastly, it was argued that on the contrary to macroeconomic indicators that suggested Poland was almost immune to the economic crisis of 2008 (see Ministry of Foreign Affairs 2016), the majority of 'average citizens' were in fact gradually falling into poverty. In the context of Europe's refugee issue, a rhetoric was present in public discourse that the country could not accept refugees since there was an urgent need to take care of 'hungry Polish children' first. The figure of 'hungry Polish children' draws public attention in particular to a few cases of families deprived of parental rights, allegedly due to poverty. A political slogan of a 'good change' (*dobra zmiana*), under which Law and Justice led its 2015 electoral campaign, referred in particular to promises to undo unjust social inequalities, that is, by additional taxes on chain markets and banks in order to finance generous family benefits (see *Program Prawa i Sprawiedliwości* 2014).

The four claims presented may be regarded as an aspect of a *Weltanschauung* politics in Poland, fuelling a legitimisation divide. Simultaneously to the rhetoric concerning Poland's 'illegitimate' political system, discursive practices of group identity and antagonisation were also present. These ranged from officially used labelling into 'solidaristic Poland' and 'liberal Poland' to 'mohair berets' versus 'lemmings', the former being a group of average, relatively poor citizens, often practicing Catholics, whereas the latter being relatively well-off citizens, focused on their routine work. Oversimplistic as these labels might be, they seem to connote some aspects of a political cleavage present in Poland when our study was conducted. The idea that the Polish political system and its functioning lack legitimacy translates into set of beliefs at the individual level. However, we claim that such beliefs are held by a part of Polish society, which allows us to speak both of political polarisation and a legitimisation divide in Poland.

Researching the Legitimisation Divide

Our insight into political legitimisation in Poland is based on the outcomes of an individual survey conducted within the LIVEWHAT project. The survey was conducted on a representative sample of adult Poles three months before the 2015 parliamentary election. As noted, we look for manifestations of support for political institutions and the political regime's performance. Contrary to approaches which assume that legitimisation needs to be anchored in the external, objective, moral or rational features of a political system (Beetham 1991), our understanding of legitimisation is 'sociological'. Following Weber, we regard legitimisation as people's subjective belief in the rightfulness of institutions and their actions. We acknowledge that legitimacy and legitimisation are multidimensional concepts, whose various aspects may be pointed to as, for example, support for a regime's principles or main values, support for how the political system works and support for specific institutions, including governing elites (Norris 1999; Mider 2014a; Garlicki 2014). Other classifications point to substantive and procedural legitimisation (Wesołowski 1988). Our approach to legitimisation is based on the notion developed by Lipset (1959) with a focus on people's perceptions of a political system's performance. At the operational level, we try to measure the strength of citizens' assumptions that the Polish political system serves individual and social needs and that the main political institutions are reliable. This distinguishes our definiendum from the satisfaction of, for example, public social services or the way in which the government deals with societal problems—and it allows us to speak of the legitimisation of regime performance. We also use the categories of *input legitimisation* and *output legitimisation* to distinguish between the perceptions of the responsiveness of the system and its policy-related effects. Thus, we focus on following four aspects (dimensions) of citizens' evaluation of a political system:

1) *Input legitimisation*, which we understand as the consent of citizens and results from including their preferences in the decision-making processes; a perception political system is based on a democratic participation and representation (Scharpf 1999). We operationalise this dimension with two survey questions on external political efficacy: (a) *To what extent do you agree or disagree with the following statement: 'Public officials don't care much what people like me think'* and (b) *To what extent do you agree or disagree with the following statement: 'People like me don't have any say about what government does'*.

2) The *level of trust of national parliament and government*, which we operationalised with a question: *On a score of 0–10, how much, if at all, do you personally trust each of the following institutions where 0 means 'do not trust an institution at all', and 10 means 'completely trust this institution'? (a) National parliament and (b) national government*. Such an operationalisation uses standard measures of specific support (Norris 1999; Mider 2014b) of certain political institutions.
3) *Satisfaction with democracy* in Poland, measured by the question: *On the whole, how satisfied or dissatisfied are you with the way democracy works in your country? 0—meaning extremely dissatisfied and 10—meaning extremely satisfied*. This question has already been used as a typical indicator of support for regime performance (Norris 1999; Gjefsen 2012; Mider 2014b).
4) *Output legitimisation* which we understand as citizens' approval of how government deals with major societal problems. We measured this dimension by the use of three questions: *How satisfied or dissatisfied are you with the way in which your country's government is dealing with the following—(a) poverty, (b) unemployment, (c) precarious employment on a scale from 0 to 10, where 0 means 'extremely dissatisfied' and 10 means 'extremely satisfied'*? Similar operationalisation has been used to assess political legitimisation in international comparative studies (Domański 2004).

The complexity of political legitimisation not only refers to various aspects of what is legitimised but also the nuances of peoples' support, which tends to be partial and unstable. Mider (2014c) proposes to distinguish individuals' attitudes by the degree of legitimisation they reflect: full legitimisation; partial legitimisation, which might correspond with political apathy or detachment; 'critical legitimisation', being specific to the Polish context; political alienation, which he interprets as a partial delegitimisation; and full legitimisation. This classification helps us to explore the nature of the legitimisation divide in Poland; we aim to distinguish those citizens who fully or partially legitimise the performance of the political system from those who delegitimise it. Setting this goal, we take into account the findings of recent research on political legitimisation in post-communist countries, and on Poland specifically, which prove a relatively low level of legitimisation in the countries in the region and a particularly low level of legitimisation of the political system and its performance in

Poland (Domański 2004). We assume that the cleavage between Polish citizens who legitimise and those who do not legitimise the political system in 2015 does not result from a high level of political conflict in this specific moment but is a relatively persistent phenomenon in Polish society. However, low legitimisation level at the time of our study allows us to hypothesise a legitimisation crisis.

In order to explore the political legitimisation divide in Poland and further explore its roots, we identify those individuals who comprehensively deny any legitimisation to the political system, that is, who 'score low' in at least three of the four identified dimensions above. Scoring low in the first aspect—*input legitimisation*—meant that the respondent had 'agreed' or 'agreed strongly' with at least one of the sentences mentioned above (see point 1). Scoring low in the second aspect—*level of trust* to national parliament or government—meant that the respondent indicated that he/she, for example, agrees that public officials don't care much about what people like me think or he/she doesn't trust the parliament or the government or both.[1] Scoring low in the other two aspects—*satisfaction with democracy* and *output legitimisation*—meant that the respondent had chosen one of the five lowest values on the satisfaction scale from 0 to 10, where 0 was 'completely dissatisfied' and 10 'completely satisfied'. Such a distinction might be regarded as arbitrary, but it helps us to distinguish between the categories of full legitimisation and partial legitimisation on the one hand and full delegitimisation together with partial delegitimisation on the other hand. The great majority of respondents, that is, 63.6%, scored highly in at least three of the aspects identified above, providing support for the hypothesis that there is a widespread legitimisation crisis in Poland at the individual level. The low level of political legitimisation in our study is consistent with earlier findings, for example, the comparative research conducted by Domański, who observed in Poland the lowest level of political legitimisation among the researched 21 European countries (Domański 2004; Mider 2014a).

Broad scholarship on the individual features contributing to the legitimising of a political system proves the relevance of socioeconomic position (see Mider 2014b; Domański 2004, 2010). To what extent do we see systemic differences in education, gender or age among those denying legitimisation and legitimising the Polish political system? Table 4.1 shows the characteristics of both subgroups.

As shown in Table 4.1, Polish citizens who partially or fully delegitimise the functioning of the political system are statistically older than those

Table 4.1 Comparison of social characteristics of the respondents (a) fully or partially legitimising and (b) fully or partially delegitimising the functioning of a political system in Poland

		Fully or partially legitimising political system (N = 736)	*Fully or partially delegitimising political system (N = 1288)*
Age	Average	42	44.8
	Median	42	46
		Per cent	*Per cent*
Gender	Male	48.3	47.8
	Female	51.7	52.2
Education	Primary	3.2	2.2
	Secondary	75.8	78.4
	Tertiary	20.9	19.4
Which of the following best describes the area in which you live?	A big city	38.9	42.7
	Suburbs or outskirts of big city	8.3	6.6
	Town or small city	34.2	35.8
	Country village or a farm	18.6	14.9
Which of the following classes you feel you belong to?	Upper class	1.2	0.8
	Upper middle class	3.8	3.6
	Middle class	38.0	25.3
	Lower middle class	17.9	21.1
	Working class	23.8	33.0
	Lower class	4.9	8.6
	Other class/don't know	10.3	7.6
Religiosity	From 0 (not at all religious) to 3	23.9	27.8
	From 4 to 7	44.2	41.9
	From 8 to 10 (extremely religious)	29.2	29.3
	Don't know	2.8	1.0

who tend to legitimise it. This is consistent with a previous study of Mider (2014b), which showed that relatively younger generations tend to be more supportive of the political system performance in Poland. Although no significant differences may be observed in regard to the gender composition of the two subgroups, similarly to the aforementioned study, we observe a slight overrepresentation of men accepting the political system in Poland (ibid.). On the contrary to previous studies showing a slight overrepresentation of respondents living in the city who contribute to a diffuse legitimisation (ibid.), in our study, those citizens who accept how the political system works tend to live in rural areas.

The education level of individuals in both compared subsamples mirrors a pattern which has been proven in the studies on political legitimisation (Domański 2004). Political competences acquired with formal education positively correlate with higher support for the political system. Similarly, in our study the subgroup of citizens accepting how the political system operates is composed of those from relatively higher social strata (it consists of 43% of respondents seeing themselves as upper class, upper middle class or middle class comparing to 29.7% of respondents from these classes in the subpopulation denying political legitimisation of the system). As noted, these are the citizens who are seen in the scholarly literature as generally benefiting from the political system. Thus, a positive correlation between SES and being supportive of the political system performance may be observed.

A citizen who denies the legitimisation of the Polish political system's performance is usually an inhabitant of the city in her late forties, seeing herself as a member of the working and—paradoxically as it may seem—relatively less religious than those citizens who accept the political system. The observed pattern of supporting the political system is consistent with general regularities found both in the Polish and the aforementioned international comparative studies. In terms of the social composition of the citizens who do not accept the performance of the political system, Polish society resembles other European societies.

Unfinished Societal Transformation Hypothesis

The socioeconomic characteristics of that subpopulation which does not legitimise the Polish political system's performance do not explain the negative evaluation of the political system nor allow us to understand why, after 25 years of allegedly exemplary social transformation, 'Polish success' has begun to be widely questioned by Polish citizens. A hypothesis broadly suggested by political scientists and sociologists, both in Poland and abroad, pointed to the weak civic traditions in Poland. Following Giza et al. (2000), we call this argumentation the *unfinished transformation hypothesis*. According to this reasoning, both in the economy and the main political institutions in Poland, the transformation which took place after

1989 has been completed. However, the third dimension—that is, civil society—has remained relatively underdeveloped.

In a more general manner, a broad stream of literature on the post-communist legacy points to the stability of patterns of political attitudes and behaviours which crystallised in Poland before 1989 (Cześnik 2007). Two well-rooted categories of Polish sociology contribute to such an understanding. These are the concept of a 'sociological void', coined by Polish sociologist Stefan Nowak (1979), which denotes a lack of meso-level society organisation structures between the state and the family in communist Poland, as well as the term *homo sovieticus*. The latter is borrowed by Tischner (1992) from Zinowiew to depict a labile person, self-interested, opportunistic, escaping responsibility for others and likely to build their own economic position on private connections. It is emphasised that the historical patterns of political attitudes gained a new meaning after the political change. Thus, for example, Sztompka (2000) underlines that the clash between pre-transition models of social and political behaviour and the new political and economic reality led in Poland to a collective trauma, resulting in ritualistic strategies in the political sphere. A parallel interpretation is offered by Grabowska (2004), who proposes the idea of post-communist cleavage. Political preferences, behaviours, collective and individual identities and political institutions are polarised in Poland in regard to attitudes about the meaning of communism.

Although the hypothesis that there is an unfinished societal transformation—or more generally, that the legacy of communism has negatively affected political legitimisation—has been criticised (e.g. Domański (2004) shows how it does not explain vast differences in legitimisation among the counties from post-soviet bloc) and applies to the macrolevel, we regard it as an argument related to individuals' political socialisation. According to the mentioned body of literature, it may be hypothesised that a significant share of Polish society may be characterised by a low level of 'civicness', low levels of social capital understood in a manner proposed by Putnam (Żukowski and Theiss 2009) and shallow and ritualistic political engagement. This is accompanied by a low level of civic education, poor political knowledge and lack of understanding of public matters, which make Polish citizens easy to manipulate, antagonise and be prone to populist narratives (Cześnik et al. 2016). Thus, finding a strong correlation between low levels of social capital, low political engagement[2] and delegitimisation of political system performance in our study would be supportive of this hypothesis.

Although the reasoning which underpins the hypothesis concerning the role of communist heritage and unfinished transformation is well-rooted in the scholarly literature, it requires caution. On the one hand, a persistence of attitudes towards the public sphere derived from communism needs to be taken into account when exploring legitimisation in Poland. On the other hand, the notion of an 'all-explaining' thesis of communist heritage and low 'civicness' in Poland has faced far-reaching criticism recently. Low levels of social capital in Poland have been questioned (Rychard 2010), methodological Occidentalism in research on political activism in Poland has been emphasised (Jacobsson and Korolczuk 2017), and the evidence on low-key and informal civic activities proliferating in Poland and contributing to a vibrant civil society has been presented (ibid.). Simultaneously, scholars have argued that concepts such as *homo sovieticus* tend to be rather a cliché than part of good academic explanation (Tyszka 2009; Pawlak 2015).

In order to investigate the explanatory potential of the 'unfinished transformation' argument for the legitimisation divide in Poland, we have selected five measures of political attitudes and behaviours which may indicate different aspects of individual social capital understood in a manner proposed by Putnam. They include attitudes and formal as well as informal civic and political engagement. We try to find whether Poles who perceive the functioning of the political system as legitimate differ significantly and systematically in respect to different aspects of individual 'civicness' from those Polish citizens who deny its legitimisation. In the first step, we compare two subgroups of Polish society according to such attitudes as support for democracy in general, generalised trust level and interest in politics as measured by frequency of political discussion. Secondly, we compare the two subpopulations according to civic and political engagement, measured by membership of various civil society organisations and experiences of taking part in various formal and informal political actions.

Differences in attitude towards democracy are significant between both subgroups, although small. Surprisingly, Polish citizens who delegitimise the political system's performance are in general more supportive of democracy. Over 4% points more respondents from the subgroup delegitimising political system's performance state they either agree or agree strongly with the sentence: *Democracy may have problems but it's better than any other form of government* than those respondents who legitimise the Polish political system (see Table 4.2). Thus, these are not respondents

Table 4.2 How strongly do you agree or disagree with the statement: 'Democracy may have problems but it's better than any other form of government'

Two subgroups of respondents	*Answers*	*Per cent*
Fully or partially legitimising political system	Disagree strongly	2.8
	Disagree	6.6
	Neither	34.4
	Agree	42.3
	Agree strongly	13.9
	Total (N = 736)	100
Fully or partially delegitimising political system	Disagree strongly	3.8
	Disagree	8.8
	Neither	27.1
	Agree	45.5
	Agree strongly	14.9
	Total (N = 1288)	100

with an anti-democratic orientation who critically evaluate the Polish political system, rather, are those who include themselves relatively often in a group of citizens who approve of democracy in general.

In order to operationalise the individual level of generalised trust, we used a standard question: *Generally speaking, would you say that most people can be trusted, or that you can't be too careful in dealing with people? Please state your answer on a scale of 0 to 10, where 0 means 'You can't be too careful' and 10 means that 'Most people can be trusted'*. It turns out that the average level of generalised social trust is significantly lower among the citizens delegitimising the functioning of Polish political system (3.11) than among the rest of citizens (4.5; $p < 0.001$). Among those refusing legitimisation, only 18.1% believe that most people (rather) can be trusted (values over 5), while among the rest of the citizens this per cent amounts to 30.7%. This finding is consistent with previous studies on legitimisation in Poland (Domański 2004).

The frequency of discussing political problems with family and friends has been chosen as an indicator of interest in politics. The indicator is based on the answers to the question: *When you get together with friends and/or family, how frequently would you say that you discuss political matters on a scale where 0 means 'Never' and 10 means 'Frequently'*? The mean value for each group has been calculated and no statistically significant difference between both subgroups has been found (4.96 vs 5.05).

Looking at individuals' experiences with civil society organisations, we have found significant differences between both subgroups. This information was derived from the question: *Please look carefully at the following list of organisations. For each of them, please say which, if any, you belong to and which, if any, you are currently doing unpaid work for?* Twelve categories included political party, labour or trade union, human rights organisation, civil rights organisation, anti-racist organisation and so on. The average number of memberships in the listed types of organisation among the citizens denying legitimisation was significantly lower (0.76) than the average number of memberships among the rest of the citizens (1.61; $p < 0.001$). Among the delegitimising citizens, only 14% are members of at least two types of organisation, while among the rest of the citizens this per cent amounts to 21.6%. Table 4.3 clearly shows that citizens denying legitimisation are less engaged in all forms of civic organisation. It is worth noticing that neither the hypothesis of positive correlation between political participation in conventional forms and political legitimisation level, present in scholarly literature (Mider 2014a), nor the hypothesis of negative correlation between political protest and legitimisation finds support in our study. On the one hand, these are respondents who tend

Table 4.3 Percentage of members (active and passive) in organisations among people perceiving political system as legitimate and those denying legitimisation

Type/theme of an organisation/ movement	*Fully or partially legitimising political system (N = 736)*	*Fully or partially delegitimising political system (N = 1288)*
Political party	12.5	4.4
Labour/trade union	23.7	16.9
Development/human rights	15.1	8.2
Civil rights/civil liberties	13.9	7.7
Environment anti-nuclear or animal rights	15.4	8.5
Women's/feminist	10.8	3.8
Lesbian/gay/transgender rights (LGBT)	10	2.5
Peace/anti-war	11	3.2
Occupy/anti-austerity or anti-cuts	11.5	5.0
Anti-capitalist, global justice or anti-globalisation	9.8	3.9
Anti-racist or migrant rights	9.8	2.8
Social solidarity networks	17.9	9.3

Table 4.4 Percentage of people reporting participation in the previous year in each political action among people perceiving political system as legitimate and those denying legitimisation

Form of political participation	*Fully or partially legitimising political system (N = 736)*	*Fully or partially delegitimising political system (N = 1288)*
Contacting or visiting politician/government official	13.8	15.6
Donated money to a political organisation/party/action group	13.9	9.8
Displayed a political or campaign logo/sticker	7.7	5.7
Signed a petition/public letter/campaign appeal	19.3	27.2
Boycotted products for political/ethical/environmental reason	11.7	15.1
Attending a meeting of a political party/organisation/group	10.0	8.4
Attended demonstration, march or rally	7.5	6.0
Joined a strike	3.9	1.5
Joined an occupation, sit-in or blockade	4.2	1.4
Damaged things like breaking windows, removing road signs	4.0	0.9
Discussed or shared opinion on politics on social network	20.6	27.7
Joined, started or followed a political group on Facebook	13.1	13.7
Visited the website of political party or a politician	29.6	35.3
Searched for information about politics online	40.4	47.1

to delegitimise the political system and exchange political opinions more often; on the other hand, joining a strike or demonstration is reported more often by those who positively evaluate the political system.

Participation in different political actions has slightly different patterns in both compared groups. Table 4.4 presents the share of respondents in both groups who reported having participated in a particular form of political action in the past 12 months (before the date of the survey). These included 16 various forms of political participation, such as contacting or visiting a politician, donating money to a political organisation, displaying a political or campaign logo, signing a petition, boycotting certain products, attending a meeting and so on. Although the share of politically inactive citizens is higher among the group of respondents who legitimise the political system (26.4% vs 32.8%), the average number of forms of political participation used within past 12 months does not differ significantly between both groups (it amounts to 3.6 in the group of those legitimising the system compared to 3.3 among the other group).

We find mixed evidence on the relation between 'civicness' and the legitimisation of the performance of the political system in Poland. Support for democracy in general turns out to be higher among the respondents who delegitimise the functioning of the Polish political system. We observed no significant differences in regard to interest in politics measured by informal discussions on political issues between both subgroups. Similarly, only small differences are present between both subgroups in regard to various forms of political participation. However, two classic measures of social capital—that is, the level of generalised trust and membership in civil society organisations—differentiate to a high extent the group of citizens fully or partially legitimising the performance of the political system from those who fully or partially delegitimise it. The hypothesis of a legitimisation divide anchored in diverse political socialisation finds partial support at this level of our analysis.

Neoliberal Economy Hypothesis

The 'unfinished transformation' hypothesis has been accompanied in the scholarly literature—and more recently, in media discourse—by emphasis on the neoliberal economy's role in triggering the Polish legitimisation crisis. It is beyond the scope of this chapter to discuss the relation between neoliberalism and political legitimisation in a comprehensive manner. However, three mechanisms have been suggested relatively often in regard to the recent situation in Poland. The first assumes a mechanism of neoliberal institutions 'crowding out' the social sphere and the decisive role of contradictory (welfare-oriented and merit-oriented) values in Polish society. Since the early 1990s, the liberalisation of the labour market or pensions system has led to a welfare state model named by Księżopolski (2004) as 'a paternalistic-market hybrid'. The latter part of the model has been gradually developing during recent years. The social consequences of this process are emphasised by Ost, who notes that in case of Poland *too much reliance on the market, and a dismissive approach to social concerns, unions, work and contracts, pushes people to look for alternatives* [...], *too much economic liberalism threatens political liberalism* (Ost 2016). In regard to values conflict, Dawson and Hanley (2016) (see also: Domański 2010; Karpiński 2010) suggest the dominant social values in Poland have always been relatively pro-statist, claiming a high level of social protection. Thus, neoliberal political rules must in some social groups inevitably lead to dissonances and even an outrage.

Secondly, it has been argued that the sociopolitical order in Poland has simply led in recent years to the material deprivation of citizens (Shields 2015, see also: White et al. 2013). As Orenstein suggests, *although Poland's economy has enjoyed massive growth in recent years and convergence with the West, many Poles feel that they have been left out* (Orenstein 2015). Other political commentators claim that *despite its growing wealth, the Polish government has failed to meet basic needs of its citizens, according to a 2014 index* (Noack 2015). Social indicators are contradictory in this regard, showing that neither poverty level nor inequality level have risen during the eight years of Civic Platform rule. What has worsened, though, and has been exceptional among the EU countries, is the level of precarious employment, in particular among the youth (Pilc 2015). As Ost emphasises, under the tenure of Civic Platform, *Poland became Europe's leader in having part-time, so-called "junk" contracts for workers, while the government was so wary of trade unions that the Tripartite Commission* [...] *ground to a complete halt* (Ost 2016). Such interpretations are confirmed by Civic Platform officials, for example, in an interview of its leading politician and minister of social affairs, who revealed that the government after conducting analysis on youth situation was terrified about its foreseen political consequences, but nevertheless there was no political will to combat this situation (Boni 2016).

Thirdly, researchers claim it is not necessarily unmet basic needs or poverty itself but rather a combination of feeling relative deprivation and a lack of social security that has been an experience of a significant share of Polish citizens during very recent years. On the one hand, the income of these citizens has not risen for a long time, and their situation has often been worse than their parents (which is a more general, meaningful trend, as shown recently in a McKinsey study 2016). On the other hand, these *are those who feel insecure and excluded by post-communist neoliberal capitalism*, as Ost describes them and those who may *support Law and Justice for its economic promises to combat the insecurity and inequality of Poland's peripheral capitalism* (Ost 2016). This mechanism may in particular negatively affect the legitimisation of the political system's performance, as experiencing neoliberalism encompasses here possible feelings of the 'state's broken promises' and social injustice.

In this part of the chapter, our goal is to investigate to what extent the legitimisation divide is parallel to the divide in experiences of the neoliberal economy. Are those 'successful' at the Polish neoliberal market less prone to deny the legitimisation of the political system's performance? We explore this issue with the use of indicators on: reduced consumption, having difficulties keeping one's job, relative economic deprivation and the feeling of being discriminated against because of socioeconomic status.

The experience of being forced to reduce consumption level has been operationalised with the use of a question: *In the past five years, have you or anyone else in your household had to take reduce or postpone medical treatment/visiting the doctor/buying medicines for financial/ economic reasons?* As shown in Table 4.5, there is a vast discrepancy in this regard between both compared groups of respondents. Almost every second Pole in the group that denies legitimisation to the political system's performance says he/or she couldn't afford medicines or medical treatment in the previous five years. Among those legitimising the political system, 31% of respondents report such an experience.

Significant differences between both groups refer to their situation in the labour market, as well. Firstly, in the group of respondents who deny legitimisation to the system's performance, the share of the employed is slightly lower (57.9%) than in the other group (62.5%). Secondly, among those working, the majority of respondents who deny legitimisation admit that they do not feel confident in their ability to keep their job (65%). In the other group, this share amounts to 44.4% (see Table 4.6).

Relative economic deprivation was operationalised by two indicators, based on respondents' subjective comparison of his/her present living

Table 4.5 Reducing or postponing buying medicines/visiting the doctor

Two subgroups	*Answers*	*Per cent*
Fully or partially legitimising political system	Yes	31.0
	No	69.0
	Total ($N = 736$)	100.0
Fully or partially delegitimising political system	Yes	47.7
	No	52.3
	Total ($N = 1288$)	100.0

Table 4.6 How confident, if at all, are you in your ability to keep your job in the next 12 months?

Two subgroups	*Answers*	*Per cent*
Fully or partially legitimising political system	Not at all confident	14.5
	Not very confident	29.9
	Fairly confident	36.0
	Very confident	19.6
	Total ($N = 460$)	100.0
Fully or partially delegitimising political system	Not at all confident	20.3
	Not very confident	36.4
	Fairly confident	29.6
	Very confident	13.7
	Total ($N = 746$)	

conditions: (1) with his/her own living conditions one year before the survey and (2) with the living conditions of his/her parents when they were at his/her age. Both variables are based on responses given using a 0–10 scale, where 0-meant 'much worse' and 10 'much better'. Although in the first dimension, the differences between both groups are relatively small, the respondents denying legitimisation to the political system tend to experience worsening living conditions more frequently than those legitimising the system; the average score is 4.25 in the former group and 5.35 in the latter ($p < 0.001$).

Respondents classified in our analysis as fully or partially delegitimising political system more often report living in worse conditions than their parents than the other group. Almost every fourth respondent (24.8%) questioning the legitimacy of the political system in Poland finds his/her living conditions drastically worse than his/her parents (choosing values from 0 to 2). In the other group, this share is only 8.7%. Furthermore, it must be noted that the median score in this group is equal to six points, which means that a feeling of social advancement prevails in this subpopulation. The average score for Poles denying legitimisation is significantly lower than for the rest of population (2.62 vs 3.11; $p < 001$).

There is also a chasm between the two compared groups' subjective feelings of exclusion. Among respondents who legitimise the Polish system, 19.9% feel they belong to a group that is discriminated against in Poland (they answered positively to the question: *Do you feel that you belong to a group that is discriminated against in this country?*), while

Table 4.7 Do you feel that you belong to a group that is discriminated against in this country? Do you feel discriminated against due to your socioeconomic status?

Two subgroups	*Answers*	*Per cent*
Fully or partially legitimising political system	Do not feel discriminated	81.1
	Do feel discriminated due to socioeconomic status	8.3
	Do feel discriminated due to other reasons	10.6
	Total ($N = 736$)	100
Fully or partially delegitimising political system	Do not feel discriminated	66.8
	Do feel discriminated due to socioeconomic status	21
	Do feel discriminated due to other reasons	12.2
	Total ($N = 1288$)	100

among these who deny legitimisation to the political system, this share amounts to 33.2%. As shown in Table 4.7, as much as 21% points from those who feel discriminated against in the latter group do feel discriminated against due to socioeconomic status (the mentioned question was followed by: *If so, on what basis? (Please tick all that apply): colour/race, nationality, religion, language, ethnic group, age, gender, sexuality, disability, socioeconomic status, political views, others*). Among the 'discriminated' respondents in the group of those perceiving political system as legitimate, only 8.3% points feel discriminated due to such/this status.

As shown in this part of the chapter, there is evidence that individual experiences with the neoliberal economy differentiate to a large extent those respondents who legitimise the political system's performance and those who delegitimise it. This refers to experiences of not being able to meet basic needs, for example, medical treatment, to the feeling of insecurity at the labour market, a feeling of social degradation if compared to parents and—above all—to subjective feelings of being excluded or even discriminated against in the society. These findings support our hypothesis that difficult experiences resulting from the neoliberal economy parallel a legitimisation divide. The respondents who delegitimise the functioning of the political system relatively often feel excluded and report difficulties in the realisation of social needs. It is highly probable that public discourse narratives presented in the previous part of this chapter are a way of reasoning which corresponds closely with the experiences of those Poles who deny political legitimisation to the system. In particular, the contradiction between the narrative of Poland economically developing and being immune to financial crisis and the experiences of downward social mobility and insecurity may lead to withdrawal from supporting the political order by a significant share of Polish society.

Low Levels of Bridging Social Capital, the Experience of the Neoliberal Economy or Both? What Makes Poles Delegitimise the Performance of the Political System

In order to measure the impact of the variables which differ significantly in both researched subpopulations on the legitimisation of political system performance, we estimated a logistic regression model (see Table 4.8). The binary indicator of (de)legitimisation of the political system's performance has been set as a dependent variable. The explanatory variables included membership in civic organisations and social trust, as well as various aspects of the experience with liberal economy: social mobility (living conditions compared to those of one's parents at

Table 4.8 Logistic regression results for legitimisation denial

Explanatory variables	*Odds ratios*
Bridging social capital:	
Social capital membership in organisations (ref. in two or more organisations)	
In one organisation	2.08***
In no organisation	2.39***
Social trust (ref. trust; 1-no trust)	1.87***
Neoliberal economy:	
Living conditions compared to parents (ref. the same or higher; 1, lower)	1.62***
Change in living conditions in the previous 12 months (ref. the same or higher; 1, lower)	1.66***
Not meeting basic need of medical treatment (ref. no; 1, yes)	1.49***
Situation at the labour market (ref. stable job)	
Subjective feeling of unsecure job	1.05
Lack of job (unemployment or inactivity)	1.24
Feeling of being discriminated (ref. not feeling discriminated)	
Feeling discriminated due to socioeconomic status	2.54***
Feeling discriminated due to other reasons	1.32
Constant	−1.203***

Notes: $\alpha = 0.05$, $\alpha = 0.01$, ***$\alpha = 0.001$

his/her age, i.e. during the communist period), short-term experience of change in living conditions, present experience of healthcare needs deprivation and an individual's position in the labour market and subjective feelings of being discriminated against, particularly due to socioeconomic status. We did not include sociodemographic variables discussed in the second part of this chapter in the final version of the model as these prove not to have significant independent effect when explanatory variables are tested.

The results of the estimations are presented in Table 4.8. Low levels of bridging social capital measured in an approach proposed by Putnam retain significant impact on the propensity to delegitimise the performance of the political system when the impact of experiences with neoliberal economy is controlled for. Estimations show that no membership or only one membership in broadly understood civil society organisations (including political parties and labour unions) increases the propensity to delegitimise the political system over two times. Similarly, those who do not trust or rather do not trust others (choosing values below 5 on 10 points scale) have almost twice as high a propensity to delegitimise the political system's performance than the other group (of the respondents who scored at least 6 on the trust scale). These findings support our hypothesis that political socialisation understood in a Tocqueville's school of thought positively contributes to the legitimisation of the political system's performance. Strong involvement in civic networks, practical knowledge about the meaning of cooperation with other citizens in social organisations, engagement in pursuing collective or common goals and a trusting approach results in a propensity to generally accept the manner in which political system operates.

Various indicators of individual experiences with the neoliberal economy proved to have significant effect on legitimisation, too. The respondents who judge their situation as worse than that of their parents when they were the respondents' age have by over 60% higher chances to deny legitimisation. The same occurred for those who experienced deterioration of their living conditions during the past year. Similarly, the experience of not meeting the basic needs of medical treatment increases the propensity to delegitimise the political system's performance on average by approximately 40%. What is particularly striking is the effect of the reported feeling of being discriminated against due to socioeconomic status, which increases the probability of a delegitimising attitude by more than 2.5 times. Only an individual's week position at the labour market—neither having unemployment/inactivity status nor insecure employment—did not significantly increase the propensity of delegitimisation (comparing to employed persons, who perceive their situation in their jobs as stable).

To sum up, we have found that both arguments—the first based on the assumption that low social capital and the associative level contribute to delegitimisation and the second underlining the role of individual experiences of hardship caused by the neoliberal economy, that is, relative deprivation and feelings of discrimination due to socioeconomic status—are supported by our study.

The legitimisation divide in Poland is parallel to some extent to a 'civicness divide' and—above all—to differences in experiences with the neoliberal economy. It may be hypothesised that those people who negatively evaluate the functioning of the political system are to some extent victims of economic transformation in Poland. Resentment may be caused both by comparing their own situation to parents who were better off under communism and the lack of chance of finding a stable job, which was relatively easy for generations born in the early 1970s and entering labour market at the beginning of economic transformation. However, since age turned out to have no significant effect on delegitimisation, it seems that both experiences of hardship caused by neoliberal economy and feelings of being discriminated against are not limited to certain generations; critical self-evaluation of a person's own social standing seems to be at least partly influenced by public political narratives.

Discussion and Conclusion

Both hypotheses on the role of 'civicness' and the neoliberal economy influencing the legitimisation of the political system's performance in Poland have found partial support in our study. The number of memberships in civil society organisations turns out to be the strongest inhibitor of political delegitimisation. A similar mechanism may be observed in regard to generalised trust level: the more an individual is prone to trust others, the less she or he is critical of the political system's functioning. On the contrary, the more various forms of political participation used by a respondent in the previous year, the less she or he tends to support the political system. It must be noticed though, in regard to the unfinished transformation hypothesis, that the share of Poles who are members of at least two social organisations (including parties and labour unions) is only

16.7%. Although it is significantly lower than in other European countries, as emphasised in the argument presented about 'communist heritage', we share the criticism applied to this explanation. It might be true that those people who have less civic skills and weaker political socialisation are more prone to the described narratives which suggest that Polish political system is fundamentally unjust. However, the level of multiple membership in social organisations is too low to justify legitimisation and too stable to explain the delegitimisation crisis in Poland.

Experiences of the neoliberal economy turn out to have a significant impact on the legitimisation of the political system's performance. Objective measures, such as being unemployed or inactive at the labour market, the necessity of postponing medical treatment, subjective measures of having an insecure job, relative measures of downward social mobility (in relation to the past and in relation to parents' social position), as well as self-evaluation ofbeing discriminated against due to socioeconomic status, negatively affect the legitimisation of the political system. The impact of the last variable is particularly high. Feelings of discrimination due to sociopolitical status are reported by a surprisingly high share of Polish society: 8.3% of those who legitimise and 21% of those delegitimising the performance of the political system. We interpret this variable as a disappointment or even frustration caused both by an assessment that one unjustly receives less than she or he deserves and her or his access to crucial social instructions is limited or denied. This assessment is made both in relation to other citizens and to external norms of social equity.

It needs to be noticed that such assessments do not emerge in a sociopolitical vacuum. We find them closely related to the political narratives described in the first part of this chapter. Although we can propose only a sketchy mechanism of 'political economy of social frustration' in Poland in the context of European economic crisis, in our view, the following process took place. As Ost describes, the proliferation of the neoliberal economy has led to instability, insecurity and deprivation of a significant share of Polish households. Not necessarily sole low income, but bad working conditions and missing social security caused hardship to many, in particular younger Poles. Such experiences were in clear contradiction with the dominating political narratives of Civic Platform, claiming the country is a 'green island' in the EU, free of economic crisis and with an ever-developing economy. It is meaningful that so-called anti-crisis packages introduced in Poland implemented further employment flexibilisation measures, giving support to employers, to some extent at the expense of employees (see Duszczyk 2014). Both dismissing social concerns by former governing party (Civic Platform) and some populist narratives developed by their political opponents (Kukiz'15 and Law and Justice) fuelled the perception of being denied access to profits from their own work.

Thus, reflecting on the leading topic of this collective volume, our analysis sheds light on two implicit roles of economic crisis in triggering a legitimisation divide in Poland. Firstly, a share of Polish society was obliged to carry the burdens of a vibrant Polish economy in the times of crisis. On the one hand, neoliberal measures have contributed to the Polish economy being relatively resistant to economic shocks; on the other hand, some (further) flexibility at the labour market and instability threat was transferred to citizens. Secondly, both the (arguably) arrogant political narratives of Civic Platform, which dismissed social problems, and the discursive strategies of Law and Justice which mobilised constituencies by emphasis on social threat and injustice, enhanced a negative assessment of their own situation. It needs to be noticed that, as the bulk of literature on political legitimisation in Poland shows, legitimisation has been traditionally very low in Poland, and some authors argue Polish governments are structurally not able to retain high levels of support (Pańków 2010; Rychard 2010; Domański 2004), whereas Polish citizens judge politics in very critically and the associative levels and trust levels are low. Against this backdrop, these are experiences of economic instability and feelings of discrimination, alleviated by political narratives, which contributed to the legitimisation divide in Poland. Both neoliberal rules in the economy and the overlooking of social problems when emphasising the country's economic success are hidden economic crisis-related mechanisms which undermine political legitimisation.

Notes

1. Not trusting means providing one of the five lowest: *On a score of 0–10, how much, if at all, do you personally trust each of the following institutions where 0 means 'Do not trust an institution at all', and 10 means 'Completely trust this institution'?*
2. It needs to be noticed that in various studies on political legitimization, political participation is regarded to be its effect. Other stream of literature emphasises political socialisation and practices of political engagement as a cause of legitimization. Finally, there is an evidence of mutual relation between those features. This refers to generalised trust level, as well, for

example, Domański claims that high correlation level between trust and political legitimization is based on mutual influence (Domański 2004: 90).

References

Arak, P., & Żakowiecki, P. (2016). Poland 2016. *Nations in Transit* (Freedom House). https://freedomhouse.org/report/nations-transit/2016/poland. Date 24 Nov 2016.

Beetham, D. (1991). *The Legitimization of Power*. Basingstoke: Macmillan.

Cześnik, M. (2007). *Partycypacja wyborcza w Polsce. Perspektywa porównawcza*. Warszawa: Scholar.

Cześnik, M. (2014). In the Shadow of the Smoleńsk Catastrophe—The 2010 Presidential Election in Poland. *East European Politics and Societies and Cultures, 28*(3), 518–539.

Cześnik, M., Kwiatkowska, A., & Markowski, R. (2016, April 26). Co Polacy wiedzą o polityce? Niewiele. Między namiignorantami. *Polityka*.

Dawson, J., & Hanley, S. (2016). What's Wrong with East–Central Europe? The Fading Mirage of the 'Liberal Consensus'. *Journal of Democracy, 27*, 20–34.

Domański, H. (2004). Czynniki legitymizacji w 21 krajach. *Nauka, 4/2004*, 65–98.

Domański, H. (2010). Legitymizacja nierówności. *Nauka, 1/2010*, 49–66.

Duszczyk, M. (2014). Poland Under Economic Crisis Conditions. *Perspectives on European Politics and Society, 15*(3), 370–384.

Garlicki, J. (2014). Legitymizacja systemu politycznego—poziomy, płaszczyzny i dylematy. In J. Garlicki (Ed.), *Legitymizacja transformacji i systemu politycznego w Polsce*. Warszawa: Elipsa.

Giza, A., Marody, M., & Rychard, A. (2000). *Strategie i system. Polacy w obliczu zmiany społecznej*. Warszawa: IFiS PAN.

Gjefsen, T. (2012). *Sources of Regime Legitimacy. Quality of Government in Electoral Democracy*. Oslo: University of Oslo.

Grabowska, M. (2004). *Podział postkomunistyczny: społeczne podstawy polityki w Polsce po 1989 roku*. Warszawa: Scholar.

Jacobsson, K., & Korolczuk, E. (2017). *Civil Society Revisited. Lessons from Poland*. New York: Berghahn Books.

Karpiński, Z. (2010). Legitymizacja nierówności dochodowych w Polsce, 1988–1999. In H. Domański & A. Rychard (Eds.), *Legitymizacja w Polsce. Niustajacy kryzys w zmieniających się warunkach?* Warszawa: IFiS PAN.

Księżopolski, M. (2004). Co dalej z polityką społeczną w Polsce? Od socjalistycznych gwarancji do paternalistyczno-rynkowej hybrydy. In M. Rymsza (Ed.), *Reformy społeczne. Bilans dekady*. Warszawa: Instytut Spraw Publicznych.

Lipset, S. (1959). Some Social Requisites of Democracy: Economic Development and Political Legitimacy. *The American Political Science Review, 53*(1), 69–105.

Marczewski, P. (2016, July 25). Poland's Turn to the Right. On the Limitations of the 'Liberal Consensus'. *Eurozine*, pp. 1–6.
Markowski, R. (2007). System partyjny czy zbiorowisko partii? O stabilnym rozchwianiu polskiej polityki. In M. Marody (Ed.), *Wymiary życia społecznego*. Scholar: Warszawa.
McKinsey Global Institute. (2016). *Poorer than Their Parents? Flat or Falling Incomes in Advanced Economies*. http://www.mckinsey.com/global-themes/employment-and-growth/poorer-than-their-parents-a-new-perspective-on-income-inequality. Date 24 Nov 2016.
"Michał Boni: byliśmy głusi". (2016, April 2). *Gazeta Wyborcza*. http://wyborcza.pl/magazyn/1,124059,19853739,michal-boni-bylismy-glusi.html. Date 24 Nov 2016.
Mider, D. (2014a). Uczestnictwo w polityce jako korelat legitymizacji systemu politycznego w procesie transformacji ustrojowej—ilościowa analiza związków. In J. Garlicki (Ed.), *Legitymizacja transformacji i systemu politycznego w Polsce*. Warszawa: Elipsa.
Mider, D. (2014b). Determinanty socjodemograficzne legitymizacji systemu politycznego w Polsce. In J. Garlicki (Ed.), *Legitymizacja transformacji i systemu politycznego w Polsce*. Warszawa: Elipsa.
Mider, D. (2014c). Wymiar społeczny konsolidacji demokracji w Polsce. Typologia postaw wobec systemu politycznego. In J. Garlicki (Ed.), *Legitymizacja transformacji i systemu politycznego w Polsce*. Warszawa: Elipsa.
Miller, E. M. (2015, June 11). Secret Recordings, Posh Restaurants, Cuban Cigars and Intrigue Finally Catch Up to Polish government. *The Washington Post*. https://www.washingtonpost.com/news/morning-mix/wp/2015/06/11/sex-lies-and-audio-tape-secret-recordings-finally-catch-up-to-polish-government/. Date 26 Nov 2016.
Ministry of Foreign Affairs. (2016). *Poland in the EU: The Green Island*. http://www.msz.gov.pl/en/foreign_policy/europe/european_union/poland_ineu/poland_in_eu/poland_in_eu. Date 24 Nov 2016.
Noack, R. (2015, October 27). Why Europeans Should Care About the Return of Poland's Right. *The Washington Post*. https://www.washingtonpost.com/news/worldviews/wp/2015/10/27/why-europeans-should-care-about-the-return-of-polands-right/?utm_term=.d7a16088f2d9. Date 24 Nov 2016.
Norris, P. (1999). Introduction. The Growth of Critical Citizens. In P. Norris (Ed.), *Critical Citizens. Global Support for Democratic Governance*. New York: Oxford University Press.
Nowak, S. (1979). System wartości społeczeństwa polskiego. *Studia Socjologiczne, 4*(75), 155–173.
Orenstein, M. (2015, November 1). Paranoid in Poland. How Worried Should the West Be About the Law and Justice Party's Victory? *Foreign Affairs*.

https://www.foreignaffairs.com/articles/poland/2015-11-01/paranoid-poland. Date 24 Nov 2016.
Ost, D. (2016, January 8). Regime Change in Poland, Carried Out from Within. *The Nation*. https://www.thenation.com/article/regime-change-in-poland-carried-out-from-within/. Date 24 Nov 2016.
Owen, A., & Tucker, J. (2010). Past Is Still Present: Micro-Level Comparisons of Conventional Vs. Transitional Economic Voting in Three Polish Elections. *Electoral Studies, 29*(1), 25–39.
Pańków, W. (2010). Dylematy i pułapki legitymizacji porządku społecznego PRL i III Rzeczpospolitej. In H. Domański & A. Rychard (Eds.), *Legitymizacja w Polsce. Niustajacy kryzys w zmieniających się warunkach?* Warszawa: IFiS PAN.
Pawlak, M. (2015). From Sociological Vacuum to Horror Vacui: How Stefan Nowak's Thesis Is Used in Analyses of Polish Society. *Polish Sociological Review, 2015*(1), 5–27.
Pilc, M. (2015). The Temporary Employed in Poland: Beneficiaries or Victims of the Liberal Labour Market? *Economic and Industrial Democracy, 38*(3), 400–424.
Program Prawa i Sprawiedliwości. (2014). *Law and Justice's Programme of 2014*. http://pis.org.pl/dokumenty?page=1. Date 26 Nov 2016.
Raport o stanie Rzeczpospolitej. (2011). *Uchwała Prawa i Sprawiedliwości*. http://www.rodaknet.com/raport_o_stanie_rzeczypospolitej.pdf. Date 26 Nov 2016.
Rychard, A. (2010). Stare i nowe hipotezy o legitymizacji i zaufaniu. In H. Domański & A. Rychard (Eds.), *Legitymizacja w Polsce. Niustajacy kryzys w zmieniających się warunkach?* Warszawa: IFiS PAN.
Scharpf, F. (1999). *Governing in Europe: Effective and Democratic?* Oxford: Oxford University Press.
Schultz, J. (2012). Talk of Work: Transatlantic Divergences in Justifications for Hard Work Among French, Norwegian, and American Professionals. *Theory and Society, 41*(6), 603–634.
Shields, S. (2015). Neoliberalism Redux: Poland's Recombinant Populism and Its Alternatives. *Critical Sociology, 41*(45), 659–678.
Sztompka, P. (2000). *Trauma wielkiej zmiany. Społeczne koszty transformacji*. Warszawa: ISP PAN.
Theiss, M. (2016). Poland. In *LIVEWHAT Living with Hard Times How Citizens React to Economic Crises and Their Social and Political Consequences—Integrated Report on Alternative Forms of Resilience in Times of Crises (Deliverable: 6.4—WP6: Alternative Forms of Resilience in Times of Crises*. http://www.livewhat.unige.ch/?p=452. Date 26 Nov 2016.
Tischner, J. (1992). *Etyka solidarności i homo sovieticus*. Kraków: Społeczny Instytut Wydawniczy Znak.

Tyszka, K. (2009). Homo Sovieticus Two Decades Later. *Polish Sociological Review, 4*(168), 507–522.
Wesołowski, W. (1988). Weberowska koncepcja legitymizacji—ograniczenia I kontynuacje. In A. Rychard & A. Sułek (Eds.), *Legitymizacja. Klasyczne teorie i polskie doświadczenia*. Warszawa: Wyd PTS.
White, S., Lewis, P., & Batt, J. (Eds.). (2013). *Developments in Central and East European Politics*. Basingstoke: Palgrave Macmillan.
Wybory. (2015, October 25). Smolar: PiS będzie dążył do uzyskania większości konstytucyjnej. *Gazeta Wyborcza*.http://wyborcza.pl/1,75398,19087710,wybory-2015-smolar-pis-bedzie-dazyl-do-uzyskania-wiekszosci.html. Date 26 Nov 2016.
Żukowski, T., & Theiss, M. (2009). Islands of Civic Engagement. Differences in the Level of Civic-Associational Social Capital. *International Journal of Sociology, 39*(4), 65–87.

PART II

Citizens, the Crisis, and Extra-Institutional Politics

CHAPTER 5

A Post-contentious Turning Point for the Contentious French? Crisis Without Protest in France

Didier Chabanet, Manlio Cinalli, Anne Muxel, Steven M. Van Hauwaert, and Thierry Vedel

Introduction

The main argument of this chapter is to show that France no longer fits the typical portrait of a contentious country, as suggested by traditional scholarship of protest about the country (Kitschelt 1986; Kriesi et al. 1995). The economic crisis, which has had a strong impact in France, provides an opportunity to explore that French citizens are breaking with their secular history of being the 'contentious French' (Tilly 1986). Yet, the chapter also suggests that this 'post-contentious' turning point does

D. Chabanet (✉)
CEVIPOF, Sciences Po, Paris, France

IDRAC Lyon and Triangle (Ecole Normale Supérieure), Lyon, France

M. Cinalli • A. Muxel • T. Vedel
CEVIPOF, Sciences Po, Paris, France

S. M. Van Hauwaert
University of Mainz, Mainz, Germany

M. Giugni, M.T. Grasso (eds.), *Citizens and the Crisis*,
Palgrave Studies in European Political Sociology,
https://doi.org/10.1007/978-3-319-68960-9_5

not necessarily amount to a broader process of acquiescence, as found elsewhere in Europe (Cinalli 2004, 2007; Cinalli and Giugni 2016). In fact, a process of substituting protest with other forms of political participation is identified as an ongoing trend, thus opening space for further research on how collective action may look like in future decades. The argument about a post-contentious France, which so counter-intuitively sits in the background of the economic crisis, draws upon the main French findings from the LIVEWHAT survey. In particular, we focus on a large volume of different forms of participation with a view to weigh the specific importance of protest. Naturally, we also look into the main variables usually associated with variations of political participation, focusing in particular on the usual suspects of age, gender education, and labour market position. These findings are then placed in the broader context of contemporary French politics—including the presidential election campaign of 2012 and policy implications of the economic crisis—so as to open more room for their interpretation.

Political Participation in France at the Time of the Economic Crisis

Following Teorell et al. (2007) and Brady (1999: 737), it is possible to define political participation as 'action[s] by ordinary citizens directed toward influencing some political outcomes'. This somewhat broad conceptualisation goes well beyond electoral participation and includes more private and informal actions. In what follows, we systematically exclude electoral participation, as it is still the most widespread form of participation and high numbers of electoral participants would overshadow information from other forms of participation. In fact, some scholars have also argued that voting is qualitatively different from all other forms of political participation (Verba et al. 1995). Most of the commonly used datasets include a limited number of items that can serve as proxies for political participation. However, using the LIVEWHAT dataset, we can identify no less than 16 separate survey items that can serve as indicators of non-electoral political participation. In what follows, we provide a twofold descriptive overview of these variables in the French context. First, we individually discuss these items. Second, we harmonise these different items into distinct dimensions to provide further analysis, leading to interpretation.

Starting with the discussion of 16 items, they all indicate some form of political participation such as contacting a politician, donating money, wearing a badge, signing a petition, boycotting a product, buying a product, attending a political meeting, attending a demonstration, joining a strike, joining an occupation, damaging things, using personal violence, discussing or sharing an opinion (online), joining/starting group or following politician (online), visiting a political website (online), and searching for political information (online). Table 5.1 provides an overview of the percentage of French respondents who have (and have not) participated in each of these political activities in the past 12 months. We provide both weighted and unweighted percentages.

This leads to a number of interesting observations regarding the principal activities of French respondents. First and foremost, we notice that more French respondents participate in online forms of political participation than in offline forms, at least relatively speaking. In line with a high rate of internet users,[1] almost one third of French respondents in our sample indicate that they have searched online for political information. Furthermore, about 15 per cent of respondents indicate they have either discussed or shared their opinion online or visited a political website. Second, as some of the most common forms of offline political participation, we can identify signing a petition (18.1 per cent) and boycotting a product (17.1 per cent).

Table 5.1 Percentage distribution of individual participation items

	Unweighted		*Weighted*	
	Yes (%)	*No (%)*	*Yes (%)*	*No (%)*
Contacted a politician	7.70	92.30	8.27	91.73
Donated money	4.88	95.12	5.46	94.54
Wore a badge	3.85	96.15	4.33	95.67
Signed a petition	18.11	81.89	19.21	80.79
Boycotted a product	17.07	82.93	17.61	82.69
Bought a product	11.89	88.11	12.55	87.45
Attended a political meeting	5.28	94.72	5.80	94.20
Attended a demonstration	13.76	86.24	14.43	85.57
Joined a strike	5.33	94.67	5.49	94.51
Joined an occupation	1.73	98.27	1.89	98.11
Damaged things	0.99	99.01	1.11	98.89
Used personal violence	0.94	99.06	1.12	98.88
Discussed or shared opinion (online)	15.79	84.21	16.82	83.18
Joined/started group, followed politician (online)	5.82	94.18	6.37	93.63
Visited political website (online)	17.91	82.09	19.38	80.62
Searched for information (online)	29.50	70.50	31.49	68.51

Combined, these first two observations would indicate that French respondents are not showing signs of acquiescence at the time of economic crisis.

However, some of the more direct or 'active' forms of participation continue to be marginal among French respondents in line with a traditional political culture that avoids open display of political preferences in the same way that one finds, for example, in Anglo-Saxon countries (Kuhn 2004; Pélabay 2014). Accordingly, contacting a politician (7.7 per cent), attending a political meeting (5.3 per cent), donating money (4.9 per cent), and wearing a badge (3.9 per cent) display in our sample only limited appeal, since none of these activities manage to mobilise more than 10 per cent of French respondents.[2] If we combine this observation with the discussion above, we find some initial support for our argument that some of the initially nontraditional forms of participation by the 'contentious French' are now becoming more popular or 'mainstream'. This is consistent with the finding that some of the 'harsher' (and inadvertently, also more active) forms of political participation, like damaging things or using violence, remain quite uncommon.

These initial distributions allow us to make some preliminary observations. However, if we want to provide a more holistic and inferential account of political participation, our analysis needs to construct one or more measures that allow us to harmonise some of the information discussed above. Here, the measures used for different forms of political participation are diverse. They range from simple dichotomous variables to different indices, either aggregate or scaled. Despite the diversity of measurements, many of them have an important resemblance. They are made—or better, constructed—in support of underlying theoretical dimension/s, most often with little connection between theory and method. To account for such an anomaly, as well as the original conjecture that political participation is a latent (continuous) variable constructed from a number of individual activities (Verba et al. 1978), we use confirmatory factor analysis (CFA) to confirm any underlying dimensions. Not only can CFA validate the dependent variable's proposed dimensionality, it also allows for the estimation of the variation alongside the latent dimensions into separate dependent variables.

Since van Deth (2014) upholds it is unlikely that different dimensions of political participation are independent, this study accounts for clustering by not compelling the reference axes of the CFA to be orthogonal. Table 5.2 illustrates the result of our factor analysis of 16 different items (total Cronbach's alpha = 0.83). It brings forward four distinct latent dimensions: institutional (contacted a politician, donated money, wore a

Table 5.2 Factor loadings of CFA

Indicators of political participation		*Factor 1*	*Factor 2*	*Factor 3*	*Factor 4*
		Factor loadings			
polpart1	Contacted a politician	**0.3846**	0.2555	0.1448	−0.0281
polpart2	Donated money	**0.5882**	0.0853	0.1552	0.1680
polpart3	Wore a badge	**0.5358**	0.1447	0.1252	0.0521
polpart4	Signed a petition	0.1572	0.0931	−0.1610	**0.3268**
polpart5	Boycotted a product	−0.0818	0.0449	0.0364	**0.8182**
polpart6	Bought a product	0.0447	0.0581	0.0946	**0.8221**
polpart7	Attended a political meeting	**0.6224**	0.2024	0.0874	−0.1448
polpart8	*Attended a demonstration*	*0.1881*	*0.0333*	*0.1303*	***0.0500***
polpart9	Joined a strike	−0.1414	0.0274	**0.4294**	−0.0397
polpart10	Joined an occupation	−0.0134	0.0235	**0.6521**	0.0448
polpart11	Damaged things	0.0408	−0.0350	**0.8837**	0.0736
polpart12	Used personal violence	0.0933	−0.0001	**0.8063**	−0.0084
polpart13	Discussed or shared an opinion (online)	−0.0560	**0.4885**	0.0109	0.0074
polpart14	Joined/started group or followed politician (online)	0.0158	**0.5085**	0.2001	−0.0692
polpart15	Visited a political website (online)	0.1346	**0.7889**	0.0245	0.0180
polpart16	Searched for political information (online)	−0.0329	**0.7590**	−0.1140	0.1898

Note: Kaiser-Meyer-Olkin measure (sampling adequacy) = 0.9140; factor loadings larger than 0.30 are listed in bold. Factor analysis based on polychoric (tetrachoric) correlations

Note: For the item 'attended a demonstration', we relied on theoretical accounts to include this in the non-institutional factor (factor 4), even though it does not particularly load on any of the factors we find

badge, attended a political meeting), non-institutional (signed a petition, boycotted a product, bought a product, demonstration), direct action or protest (joined a strike, joined an occupation, damaged things, used personal violence), and online (discussed or shared an opinion, joined/started group or followed politician, visited a political website, searched for political information). Overall, given out wealth of survey items (16 items, as opposed to 6–8 items in most large-scale surveys), it should not be surprising we can offer a more detailed and multidimensional picture of political participation.

If we plot the average position of the French respondent when it comes to their participation in politics, we can gain further insights into both the

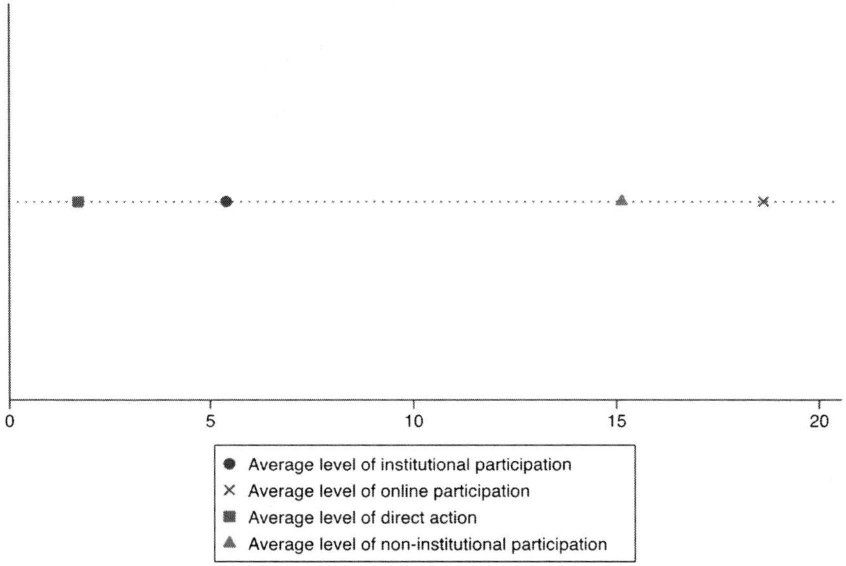

Fig. 5.1 Average levels of different forms of political participation

relative levels and frequency of the different forms of political participation. Figure 5.1 provides such a general perspective of our four dimensions of political participation. The first crucial result is that factor three—that is, direct action or protest—stands out as the most marginal, both in relative and absolute terms. Considering this factor consists of joining a strike, joining an occupation, damaging things, and using personal violence, it is not surprising it is in line with observations made above regarding some of the 'harsher' forms of participation (cf. Table 5.1). Moreover, this falls in line with some of the general observations throughout the literature that indicate such protest activism is only practised by a small proportion of individuals (Fillieule 1997; Fillieule and Tartakowsky 2008; Chabanet and Lacheret 2016). The main point to emphasise in the context of our argument here is that this trend is not that different among the no longer contentious French, even at the time of deepest economic grievances.

Yet the 'post-contentious French' systematically resort to forms of political participation other than protest, thus showing hardly any acquiescence and apathetic withdrawal from politics. Traditional forms of individual political engagement (under the form of institutional participation), collective not disruptive forms of mobilisation (under the form of non-institutional participation), together with newer forms of online activism show that respondents are hardly acquiescent at the time of the economic crisis. Figure 5.1 also enables us to observe that institutional participation is much less common in France than non-institutional mobilisation and online activism. This supports the initial observations made in Table 5.1 regarding the individual items. At the same time, this also confirms some of the hypotheses in the literature that suggest non-institutional participation might be the 'new' normal form of political participation (Mayer 2010; Ion 2012; Rosanvallon 2015).

In particular, the study of online forms of participation stands out as something new. Given our initial observations in Table 5.1, it is not surprising that we find some online activities among the most common forms of political participation in France. Whereas recent studies present similar findings in other countries (e.g. Best and Krueger 2005; Gibson et al. 2005, 2014; Chadwick and Howard 2010), the French context presents some specific features. The internet has mainly developed in France as an alternative means of information and discussion space, tightly connected to the mainstream media space. During the 2005 referendum about the draft European Constitution, activist groups used the internet to oppose mainstream media and established political parties that were largely in favour of the YES vote (Fouetillou 2008; Cardon and Granjon 2014). This was somewhat a turning point in the development of this form of participation (Mabi and Theviot 2014). This campaign and online dynamics more generally opened a more participatory space and allowed for the inclusion of (i) themes of precariousness and exclusion and (ii) the precarious and excluded citizens themselves (Blondeau and Allard 2007). Afterwards, in subsequent elections, the internet has become a battlefield ancillary to the medias and public meetings; political parties as well as interest groups and NGOs have developed strategies to gain digital presence and visibility, especially on social networks (Greffet 2011; Greffet et al. 2014; Gibson et al. 2014). One may thus wonder why our sample does not show a stronger weight of online participation, since the internet is more broadly changing how many French people become informed (Jouet et al. 2011; Le Hay et al. 2011) and has become an important tool for public expression (Wojcik and Greffet 2008). Yet it should be emphasised that only a minority of citizens is involved in intensive forms of online political participation, while experiences in using the internet as a participative tool for policy-making have generally had a very low audience and impact (Monnoyer-Smith and Wojcik 2012). This is in line with the fact that active online political participation mainly concerns highly politicised citizens (Michalska et al. 2015), and the internet might well appear as the 'weapon of the strong' (Schlozman et al. 2010), giving still more political resources and power to those who already have them.

Figure 5.1 and its subsequent discussion are particularly useful to gauge the relative levels and forms of political participation. However, it does not tell us anything about absolute levels of political participation. We know from the literature that overall participation continues to decrease in most industrial countries (Mair 2002, 2013; Wattenberg 2002; Franklin 2004; Delwit 2013). Even further, in France, absolute levels of political participation are far below European averages and French citizens are typically fairly limited when it comes to general political involvement (cf. Lijphart 1997; Melo and Stockemer 2014). Figure 5.2 illustrates this for the different forms of political participation. The vast majority of French respondents score extremely low on the respective

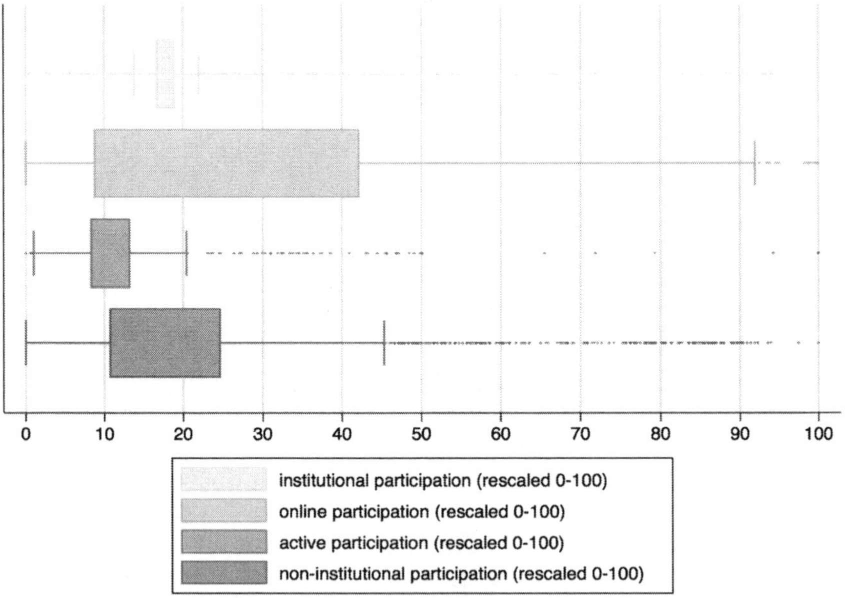

Fig. 5.2 Distributions of the different forms of political participation

participation dimensions. While this largely confirms the low percentages we found in Table 5.1, it does provide a unique perspective because it confirms this finding for the underlying participatory dimensions as well and already indicates that it is quite possible that within the same dimension of participation, it is actually the same people who systematically participate in different participatory acts.

Who Are the Post-contentious French?

So far, evidence from the LIVEWHAT survey shows that protest has not been a central form of participation through the hard times of economic crisis. While this observation is accurate, there is a need to add some comments that mitigate its scope. Most crucially, the sense of surprise about low levels of protest is based on the idea that France is traditionally a country with a high level of social and political contention. This belief seems to be borne out by statistical analysis, in any case throughout the 1990s, that is, a period of time during which France was the European country that experienced the highest levels of protest (Kriesi et al. 1995; Nam 2007). Nevertheless this capacity for protest was rarely linear and often led to extremely intensive peaks.[3] Accordingly, the first wave of protest against the economic crisis took place under the Occupy frame in May 2011, spreading from Paris to the provinces, particularly in Lyon, Marseille, Poitiers, Toulouse, and several towns in the southwest of the country. In all, 20 or so towns were involved. Yet protests were rare or of short duration,[4] and involved a few hundred people, except in Paris where a few demonstrations brought together a few thousand protestors.[5] Of course, it is possible that the overall propensity of the French to protest has undergone a momentary slump or is following a temporality of its own, without this prefiguring its future development. One may add that the density of civil society in France, especially its associative and trade union sectors (Béroud et al. 2008), is notably weak (Balme and Chabanet 2008), which may partly explain the somewhat eruptive and unpredictable nature of protest. Overall, the situation is at once complex and relatively paradoxical, combining a high level of protest with a decline in the structures that were for a long time the main channel of expression of popular discontent (Fillieule 1997).

Accordingly, the study of political discontent in France at the time of crisis tells us straight away about the need to look beyond protest. Surprisingly, yet interestingly, France as the most contentious country among its European neighbours seems to have entered a new post-contentious phase, where direct action and disruptive forms of mobilisation give way (possibly) to alternative ways of revealing political discontent. The potential route from contentious to post-contentious participation, however, is identified in a number of parallel developments, showing that the fall of protest is not coterminous with true political abstentionism and withdrawal. In fact, political abstentionism may well grow in situations of social exclusion, more so than (electoral) protest (Lancelot 1968; Pierru 2005; Braconnier and Mayer 2015). Furthermore, it is essential to reflect on the specific position of youngest generations, with an eye on a widespread, more critical model redefining the relationships to politics. In this case, research can focus on signs of 'negative politicisation' (Missika 1992) to see whether political identification is less at play than contest and systematic opposition to institutional politics. Among these signs, one can look for growing political abstention used as a protest tool to express dissatisfaction towards political parties and politicians, increasing protest voting for populist leaders or the nonmainstream parties, as well as trivialisation and legitimisation of demonstrations (Davezies and Guilluy 2013). We also need to check for the role of education, owing to the traditional division between people with and without qualifications. So, we want to see if those who are more educated are more deeply involved along this potential route (moving from contentious to post-contentious politics), or are more simply marginalised vis-à-vis all forms of political participation, including those which are replacing traditional protesting.

Shifting our attention to some of the underlying factors that can help explain both the levels and the diversity of political participation in France, emphasis must be placed on who participates and according to which different forms. In this case, a set of four models including the main socio-demographic variables can help us identify those who participate in different forms of political participation (Table 5.3).

Education is a significant contributor throughout our different forms of participation. This indicates that as French people become higher educated, they are more likely to participate in the different forms of participation, possibly even political participation in general. This would support some of the claims throughout the literature that political participation results from (cognitive) resources acquired throughout, for example, an educational track (Converse 1972; Gaxie 2007). Furthermore, it is important to emphasise the crucial role that education plays in France with reference to online political participation (Michalska et al. 2015). In a similar

Table 5.3 Impact of socio-demographic variables

	Different forms of political participation			
	Institutional	*Non-institutional*	*Direct action*	*Online*
Age				
Between 26 and 35 years old	0.0022359 (0.913)	0.0210758 (0.554)	**0.0330249 (0.002)**	**−0.0956995 (0.015)**
Between 36 and 45 years old	0.0175012 (0.484)	−0.0042174 (0.923)	0.0238658 (0.065)	−0.0666239 (0.169)
Between 46 and 55 years old	0.0149064 (0.663)	−0.0180712 (0.762)	0.0287157 (0.104)	−0.0804588 (0.225)
Between 56 and 65 years old	0.0041564 (0.927)	−0.0253779 (0.748)	0.0239396 (0.305)	−0.0543973 (0.534)
Older than 65 years old	0.0039247 (0.947)	−0.0521736 (0.613)	0.029309 (0.336)	−0.0388934 (0.734)
Age squared	−1.44e–07 (0.992)	0.0000117 (0.632)	−8.92e–06 (0.219)	8.35e–06 (0.759)
Education groups				
Completed secondary education	0.0151692 (0.124)	**0.0639769 (0.000)**	**−0.0105786 (0.038)**	**0.0575189 (0.003)**
University and above	**0.0215344 (0.046)**	**0.1044906 (0.000)**	**−0.0124684 (0.025)**	**0.0878048 (0.000)**
Employment status				
In school	0.0065682 (0.824)	0.0460496 (0.372)	0.0249141 (0.103)	−0.0188621 (0.742)
Employed	−0.0195717 (0.078)	−0.0187803 (0.334)	0.0092271 (0.108)	−0.0395345 (0.067)
Retired	−0.0039588 (0.816)	0.0092764 (0.755)	0.0013192 (0.881)	0.0061711 (0.851)
Subjective domicile				
Suburbs or outskirts of big city	−0.0183434 (0.174)	−0.0074337 (0.753)	0.007561 (0.279)	−0.0437512 (0.095)
Town or small city	−0.0076765 (0.493)	−0.0222113 (0.256)	0.0049151 (0.395)	**−0.0640148 (0.003)**
Country village	**−0.0296614 (0.012)**	−0.0401454 (0.053)	0.0101183 (0.098)	**−0.0921487 (0.000)**
Farm or home in countryside	−0.011958 (0.532)	−0.0275673 (0.410)	0.0045166 (0.648)	**−0.0788189 (0.034)**

(*continued*)

Table 5.3 (continued)

	Different forms of political participation			
	Institutional	*Non-institutional*	*Direct action*	*Online*
Income	0.0005393 (0.758)	−0.0004003 (0.896)	−0.0008049 (0.373)	0.001117 (0.742)
Gender	**−0.0468463** **(0.000)**	**−0.0429272** **(0.002)**	−0.0032276 (0.437)	**−0.1278201** **(0.000)**
Size of household	−0.0043057 (0.209)	−0.0060852 (0.310)	0.0012229 (0.490)	**−0.0142284** **(0.032)**
Constant	**0.0886027** **(0.000)**	**0.1672267** **(0.000)**	−0.0190053 (0.126)	**0.3813877** **(0.000)**
Number of observations	1789	1789	1789	1789
R^2	0.0308	0.0307	0.0328	0.0806
Adjusted R^2	0.0209	0.0208	0.0229	0.0712
Root MSE	0.16608	0.29033	0.08581	0.32194

Note: In bold if p-value < 0.05

vein, we do find that when a respondent is employed, s/he is more likely to engage in online activism, thereby strengthening the virtuous triangulation going on between education, employment, and online activism. Employment also goes together with non-institutional forms of political participation, in line with the fact that non-institutional political participation (just as online political participation) stands out for being less 'active' as well as requiring a more modest time commitment.

More surprisingly, however, we do not find evidence that age has a strong impact on the decision to participate in specific forms of political participation. There is only some initial evidence that the 26–35-year-olds are more likely to engage in direct action and online activism, particularly compared to younger cohorts. Of course, we were surprised by the finding that age is not a strong predictor either when focusing on online political participation, since young people are almost all regularly connected to the internet and more active users than older people. Yet we are also aware that political participation in general is linked to interest in politics, which is traditionally lower among young people (Quintelier 2007).

It is quite remarkable that gender appears to be significant throughout our models (with the exception of direct action), indicating that men are actually more likely to participate than women, regardless of the form of participation. While—with time—women have expanded their resources through education, higher levels of employment, and so on, resource mobilisation scholars typically argue this expanded set of resources (further) develop women's civic skills, which provide them with more assets and opportunities to participate politically (e.g. Gallego 2007; Coffé and Bolzendahl 2010). However, in France, this argument does not appear to hold, and gender differences are not significant predictors for the different forms of political participation (Allwood et al. 2000).

To complement our initial analysis of who participates in France, we further engage in a behavioural analysis of those same voters, while accounting for their socio-demographic profiles. To comprehensively do so, we include several variables that gauge political positions and socio-political attitudes, as well as different perceptions of political actors (Table 5.4).[6]

Most generally, individuals have certain positions alongside an economic and a more cultural axis and often are perceived as the principal drivers of political decisions. Therefore, it is quite surprising to see that an individual's economic left-right position is only a significant predictor for some of the more active forms of participation, namely, direct action and non-institutional participation. As an individual increasingly favours redistribution, s/he will participate more in those forms of political participation. At the same time, we find that cultural positioning does play a substantial role across the board (except for direct action). More specifically, we find significant evidence that as people are more culturally progressive (libertarian), they tend to engage in different forms of political participation more systematically. So, together, we could argue that a left-wing position, whether economic or cultural, proves to be more advantageous for political participation.

Most consistently, between the different forms of participation, we find that internal efficacy has an effect on political participation. Generally speaking, we find evidence that the more respondents actually understand politics, they also increase their political participation. However, for more active form of political participation, like political violence, the relationship is reversed. We find that an increased understanding of politics actually decreases this particular form of participation. This would indicate that direct action might be more prominent among those who do not fully understand politics. Furthermore, we also find a negative impact of external efficacy on political participation for online and non-institutional participation. In other words, those who do not particularly believe the

Table 5.4 Impact of political positions, attitudes, perceptions

	Different forms of political participation			
	Institutional	*Non-institutional*	*Direct action*	*Online*
Age				
Between 26 and 35 years old	0.0075139 (0.803)	0.0430097 (0.373)	**0.0320444 (0.049)**	−0.0981499 (0.066)
Between 36 and 45 years old	0.0255093 (0.464)	−0.017864 (0.749)	0.0325554 (0.084)	−0.1048427 (0.089)
Between 46 and 55 years old	0.0237782 (0.604)	−0.0278758 (0.704)	0.0422133 (0.088)	−0.1429874 (0.078)
Between 56 and 65 years old	0.0076201 (0.897)	−0.0526645 (0.577)	0.0476716 (0.134)	−0.1395853 (0.180)
Older than 65 years old	0.0103688 (0.891)	−0.0688063 (0.570)	0.059902 (0.143)	−0.1163643 (0.385)
Age squared	4.02e−06 (0.822)	9.36e−06 (0.744)	−0.0000155 (0.109)	0.0000307 (0.332)
Education groups				
Completed secondary education	0.0089202 (0.484)	0.0378457 (0.064)	−0.0087486 (0.204)	0.021311 (0.344)
University and above	0.0175334 (0.207)	**0.0477689 (0.032)**	−0.0014507 (0.847)	0.020708 (0.400)
Employment status				
In school	0.0346208 (0.449)	0.0173017 (0.813)	**0.0510207 (0.039)**	−0.1027403 (0.205)
Employed	−0.0123909 (0.393)	−0.0138279 (0.552)	0.0112636 (0.151)	−0.0321629 (0.211)
Retired	−0.015222 (0.467)	−0.0052795 (0.875)	0.0074189 (0.512)	−0.0428895 (0.247)
Subjective domicile				
Suburbs or outskirts of big city	−0.006171 (0.725)	0.0337632 (0.230)	0.0163788 (0.084)	−0.0114549 (0.712)
Town or small city	−0.0025218 (0.862)	0.0014879 (0.949)	0.0081031 (0.300)	**−0.0518537 (0.043)**
Country village	−0.0261985 (0.086)	−0.0206687 (0.398)	0.0151806 (0.066)	**−0.0665383 (0.014)**
Farm or home in countryside	−0.0084234 (0.722)	−0.018006 (0.635)	0.0112207 (0.381)	−0.0800129 (0.056)
Income	0.0000421 (0.986)	−0.00639 (0.097)	0.0004456 (0.731)	−0.0075646 (0.075)
Gender	**−0.0278436 (0.008)**	0.0101528 (0.544)	−0.0098887 (0.080)	**−0.0694366 (0.000)**

(*continued*)

Table 5.4 (continued)

	Different forms of political participation			
	Institutional	*Non-institutional*	*Direct action*	*Online*
Size of household	−0.0029991 (0.496)	0.0030064 (0.671)	0.0001258 (0.958)	−0.0024009 (0.758)
Cultural dimension	**−0.0080054** **(0.003)**	**−0.0124762** **(0.003)**	−0.0023199 (0.105)	**−0.0095528** **(0.042)**
Economic dimension	−0.0029283 (0.248)	**−0.0103011** **(0.011)**	**−0.0027335** **(0.046)**	−0.0005436 (0.904)
Political trust	**0.0057788** **(0.027)**	−0.0051523 (0.220)	**0.0036276** **(0.010)**	0.0003612 (0.938)
Internal political efficacy	**0.0424259** **(0.000)**	**0.072996** **(0.000)**	**−0.0131876** **(0.000)**	**0.1322672** **(0.000)**
External political efficacy	−0.0088196 (0.156)	**−0.044795** **(0.000)**	0.0052133 (0.121)	**−0.0535023** **(0.000)**
Satisfaction w/ democracy	**−0.006933** **(0.006)**	−0.0045699 (0.259)	**−0.002838** **(0.038)**	−0.0086828 (0.052)
Populism	**−0.016819** **(0.027)**	**0.0376943** **(0.002)**	−0.0023257 (0.572)	−0.0088977 (0.510)
Relative deprivation	−0.0136875 (0.370)	**0.0694839** **(0.005)**	−0.0155363 (0.060)	0.0486784 (0.072)
Subjective deprivation	0.0036072 (0.238)	0.0026015 (0.595)	−0.0002805 (0.865)	0.0077933 (0.150)
Dissatisfaction w/ employment policy	−0.0024059 (0.487)	−0.0055278 (0.319)	−0.0024561 (0.190)	0.0024953 (0.684)
Dissatisfaction w/ precarious employment policy	0.0028465 (0.381)	**0.0108987** **(0.036)**	−0.0021493 (0.221)	0.0047131 (0.412)
Dissatisfaction w/ economic policy	0.0055145 (0.093)	0.0015027 (0.775)	0.0010468 (0.555)	0.0078874 (0.175)
Dissatisfaction w/ immigration policy	−0.001116 (0.691)	−0.0045224 (0.315)	0.0009779 (0.519)	−0.003883 (0.435)
Blame attribution: banks	0.0058128 (0.605)	**0.0906882** **(0.000)**	**−0.0125195** **(0.039)**	**0.0589905** **(0.003)**
Blame attribution: government	0.0077826 (0.537)	−0.0170824 (0.398)	−0.0059378 (0.384)	0.0043998 (0.844)
Blame attribution: US	0.0207967 (0.156)	**0.0764118** **(0.001)**	−0.0004205 (0.958)	**0.0643639** **(0.013)**
Blame attribution: EU	0.0175164 (0.155)	0.0198389 (0.315)	0.0022999 (0.730)	0.0247943 (0.255)

(*continued*)

Table 5.4 (continued)

	Different forms of political participation			
	Institutional	*Non-institutional*	*Direct action*	*Online*
Constant	0.0375441 (0.560)	−0.0532993 (0.606)	**0.0775413** **(0.026)**	0.0517316 (0.650)
Number of observations	1246	1246	1246	1246
R^2	0.1092	0.1918	0.1006	0.2374
Adjusted R^2	0.0834	0.1684	0.0746	0.2154
Root MSE	0.17412	0.27904	0.09413	0.30819

Note: In bold if p-value < 0.05

government will respond to their demands are more prone to engage in online and non-institutional forms of political participation.

Electoral Politics and Policy-Making: Looking Beyond the Post-contentious Route

We can now move on to consider the extent to which the route between the contentious and post-contentious French is embedded within the broader context offered by contemporary French politics, looking in particular at elections and policy-making, respectively. Starting with the consideration of electoral politics, some observers have pointed out that the anti-austerity mobilisation began to emerge on the international and European scene in the middle of 2011, at a time when the main thrust of French political activity had turned to the presidential election of May 2012. This event harnessed a large part of the social discontent at the time. With some representatives of left-wing political parties being ideologically very close to movements, the very real possibility of a left-wing victory in the elections may have convinced some French citizens to opt for change via the ballot box, or other forms of institutional, non-institutional, and online activism rather than a strategy based on the streets. It is true that, during the presidential campaign, the visibility of the Left Front and the rhetoric of the Greens and of some leaders of the Socialist Party on the necessity of 'deglobalisation' gave the impression that the ideas of anti-austerity might be translated into true political transformations had the left won the election. One could argue that the presence of influential allies supporting the mobilisation and even picking up some of its demand may have lessened its protest capacity (Tarrow 1994) and, hence, favoured the shift to other forms of political participation.

One would find here the symptoms of a strongly politicised society, even among the youth (Bréchon 1998), whose expectations would still broadly find an institutional political expression. In particular, the 2012 presidential election has captured a relevant part of protest and political dissatisfaction through their votes and also through their abstention. On the one side, among the leftist young voters, Hollande obviously represented the possibility of a concrete political change compared to Sarkozy's mandate. On the other side, among a number of young voters, especially the less educated already at work, a vote for Le Pen represented both an act of protest against the 'elite' and the possibility to express their frustration and difficulties vis-à-vis the economic crisis.[7] So mutually combined, institutional and non-institutional types of involvement have appeared as being not mutually exclusive but rather being increasingly intertwined. The range of tools used in democratic expression has diversified hugely. Last but not least, the level of the abstention at the first round of the election was highest in 2007 among the young voters. Even those more educated and usually more participative abstained (abstentions were at 32 per cent among students).

Of course, one would expect a surge of indignation in France in the event that the new left-wing government and parliamentary majority did not succeed in finding solutions to the social problems facing the country. Yet, emphasis should still be placed on the serious crisis of confidence and credibility that the left-wing government has undergone, and its incapacity to reverse the economic crisis, thus prompting the use of other types of forms of political participation. An additional factor to consider at the macro level also includes the more or less hard stance of the government. The two most recent large protest movements—against the reform of universities in 2007 and against reform of the retirement system in 2010—were marked by the intransigence of the government, which did not yield to demonstrators. Also, in this case it is possible that this intransigence prompted most of those who struggled against liberal globalisation to direct their desire to mobilise to other forms of political participation. For a long time, the French political system has no longer talked to groups at the margins, and all of this while mass unemployment and poverty are on the rise.

Although France has been facing an economic crisis nearly as harsh as that impacting on other countries badly hit in southern Europe, with poverty and unemployment on a steady rise, it is important to consider the extent to which the country could rely on the beneficial and protective impact of its welfare state for softening the adverse economic effects of crisis. The French universalist system (Esping-Andersen 1990) fulfils its role of buffer and regulator of conflicts, which is the main function of social protection in periods of recession and mass unemployment (Piven and Cloward 1971). Applied to the whole population, the explanation can be convincing, but it is weaker with regard to those under the age of 25. Certainly, the youth unemployment level in France may be much lower than in countries strongly hit by the crisis, such as Spain or Greece, but it remains significantly higher than the French national average. Above all, the main social assistance provisions in force in France remain inaccessible—in fact, if not by law—to youths under the age of 25 who are therefore particularly socially vulnerable (Chabanet and Giugni 2013). Although diplomas represent a kind of antidote against precarity and still guarantee that one will eventually be able to obtain stable employment, most recruitment of young people today takes the form of an insecure contract or one of limited duration (CEREQ 2011). In particular, the French labour market operates according to a dichotomous rationale that protects the most educated wage earners at the expense of those who leave the education system early and are often untrained (INSEE 2013). A survey carried out in 2010 among several thousand young people who completed their education in 2007 showed that 92 per cent of those holding a doctorate were employed, stable, or otherwise, just as did 88 per cent of those who had graduated from an engineering or commerce institute, and 80 per cent of those with an undergraduate degree (bachelor) (CEREQ 2011). By contrast, only 55 per cent of those with a college diploma and 48 per cent of young people leaving the school system without a diploma were employed (CEREQ 2011).

Young people do not form a homogenous group when it comes to politics (Bourdieu 1978). Level of education is an important determinant of voting behaviours and attitudes. The most highly educated members of younger generations, though highly critical of politics, are deeply attached to representative democracy. Their internalisation of universalist values, with which they interpret political issues, compensates for their scepticism of politics, and underpins their unwavering attachment to the current system of representation (Muxel 2011). As for less educated young people, although they more readily embrace universalist values than older people with the same level of education, their universalist beliefs are not sufficiently strong to compensate for their relative rejection of politics (Muxel 2010). Their trust in representative democracy has been more seriously undermined, and their estrangement from politics extends to a weakening of their belief in democracy itself (Braconnier and Dormagen 2014). When compared to their highly educated contemporaries, they are less likely to be involved in any kind of civic participation, such as voting and political protest, and more likely to view in a favourable light the kind of authoritarian regimes which rely on charismatic and populist personal leadership and are based on limiting the power of democratically elected bodies, such as Parliament. Simply put, the dangers of an increasing deficit are greatest among the less educated young.

These trends do not amount to a worrying political withdrawal, hiding some crucial evidence for some consistent developments taking place between a contentious and a post-contentious age. Suffice it to say that people at the margins have demonstrated the capacity to organise politically on the basis of many previous developments. In fact, actions of solidarity with the precarious continue at the present time. For example, some of these so-called 'Robin Hood' operations have been conducted by some of EDF employees who, against the advice of their managers, restore electricity to people who cannot pay their bills. These actions are particularly supported by the CGT. This shows the possibility of prompting a transformation of trade union action and renewed political commitment (Béroud et al. 2008). At the same time, one should observe that the suburban youth who quickly deserted the French version of the Occupy movement may have done so because the labour market was able to protect and integrate the educated youth. By forcing the terms of argument, one may go as far as saying that the educated youth has no real reason to protest or even to rally, while the excluded youth (the famous 'lost generation') has been pushed to secede from politics and for a long time. Either way, interaction with politics has been growing in complexity, since it is widely individualised and of more difficult aggregation within traditional collective forms of mobilisation of the contentious era.

Final Discussion

Known universally in the field of contentious politics as the protest country *par excellence*, France is emerging as a post-contentious country, where not even the economic crisis paralleled by a favourable political context has led to protest. Protest, as a specific form of political mobilisation, plays no relevant role at the time of crisis. By contrast, institutional politics stands out as a channel of political influence to consider side by side with non-institutional forms to express and to act. The chapter has thus analysed the intermingling between institutional and non-institutional forms of political participation and the fact that, especially among the youngest, the panoply of political expressions has been widespread. In the context of the economic crisis, French people can choose from among different types of participation the one which seems to be more relevant to what they would like to express at the moment, and also to protest. This trend has also emerged in the growing importance of online participation, even if a relevant cleavage is shaped between a virtuous triangulation combining high online participation with high education and high resources via employment on the one hand, and a vicious triangulation combining low online participation with low education and low resources via employment on the other. We acknowledged our surprise in finding that age is not relevant to explain online political participation, given that young people spend much time on the internet and are more active users than older people. Yet scholarship of political participation has put a final word on the fundamental role of political interest, which brings us to consider that this latter is traditionally lower among young people. Hence, our guess for future years is that older people will be more politically active online than younger people, especially when baby-boomers (who have used computers most of their professional life) will be retiring and will have more time to engage in various political activities.

Most crucially, the chapter has showed that a key moment of political change in France comes together with other ongoing developments, say, in terms of intermittent commitment and individualised participation. This crucial moment has been put in a longer diachronic context with a view to reflect more closely on the *question sociale* in France accounting for profound transformations of political participation. In particular, we have shed light on the opening of a route leading from contentious to post-contentious French. In so doing, we have found some evidence for deep political change, particularly in terms of the relationship between young people and politics. Engagement in traditional political institutions has declined (Faucher 2015). Partisan allegiances have become looser in the same way that social allegiances have, and the links that ordinary French have established with the political system have become more individualised than in the more recent past (Braconnier 2010). The great political narratives have faded and no longer provide a readable map of systems of belonging to which individuals can attach themselves and become involved (Rosanvallon 2006). In terms of social politicisation, experimentation has won out over identification and affiliation among the younger generations (Muxel 2015). Increasingly, political involvement takes place by means of many different types of expression and action. In this new post-contentious scenario, the civic norm linked to the duty to vote has weakened, but political abstention is by far prevailing on a number of various forms of political participation telling that the post-contentious French may still be a long way from final acquiescence.

Notes

1. This rate has reached 85 per cent in 2016. Cf. available data online at http://www.internetlivestats.com/internet-users-by-country
2. The percentage is more or less the same among the French population.
3. See, for example, the strikes in the public sector or the 2006 protest against the reform of the labour law (Lindvall 2011).
4. But see the exception of protests in Bayonne lasting over six weeks.
5. On 15 October 2011, anti-austerity mobilisation organised simultaneously in several dozen countries made it possible to measure the level of mobilisation on a world scale. In Paris and in France's main provincial towns, however, no gathering of more than 3,000 people was recorded, while in other European cities attendance was much multiplied in some cases by hundreds. Suffice it to put emphasis on numbers in Madrid (500,000), Barcelona (300,000), Rome (100,000), and Lisbon (80,000).
6. For more details about question wordings, answer categories, and descriptive statistics of these behavioural variables, we refer to the Appendix.
7. 17 per cent voted for Marine Le Pen (+11 points compared to 2007). More than a third of them (35 per cent) used the 2012 presidential election to express their discontent and vent their worries, in the process disposing of the tag of 'vote utile' (useful vote), which the two main parties in the past took for granted. To put this in perspective again, in 2007, only 20 per cent ventured from the mainstream parties (Perrineau 2014).

References

Allwood, G., Wadia, K., & Wadia, K. (2000). *Women and Politics in France 1958–2000*. London/New York: Routledge.

Balme, R., & Chabanet, D. (2008). *European Governance and Democracy*. Lanham: Rowman & Littlefield.

Béroud, S., Denis, J. M., Desage, G., Giraud, B., & Pélisse, J. (2008). *La lutte continue? Les conflits du travail dans la France contemporaine*. Broissieux: Le Croquant.

Best, S. J., & Krueger, B. S. (2005). Analyzing the Representativeness of Internet Political Participation. *Political Behavior, 27*(2), 183–216.

Blondeau, O., & Allard, L. (2007). *Devenir Média. L'activisme sur Internet, entre défection et expérimentation*. Paris: Editions Amsterdam.

Bourdieu, P. (1978). La jeunesse n'est qu'un mot. In *Les jeunes et le premier emploi* (entretien avec Anne-Marie Métailié). Paris: Association des Anges.

Braconnier, C. (2010). *Une autre sociologie du vote. Les électeurs dans leurs contextes: bilan critique et perspectives.* Paris: LGDJ.

Braconnier, C., & Dormagen, J.-Y. (2014). Une démocratie de l'abstention. Retour sur le non-vote et ses conséquences politiques lors des scrutins municipaux et européens de 2014. *Hérodote, 3*, 42–58.

Braconnier, C., & Mayer, N. (Eds.). (2015). *Les inaudibles. Sociologie politique des précaires.* Paris: Presses de Sciences Po.

Brady, H. E. (1999). Political Participation. In J. P. Robinson, P. R. Shaver, & L. S. Wrightsman (Eds.), *Measures of Political Attitudes.* San Diego: Academic Press.

Bréchon, P. (1998). Les jeunes et la politique en Europe et en France. *Agora débats/jeunesses, 12*(1), 11–22.

Cardon, D., & Granjon, F. (2014). *Médiactivistes.* Paris: Presses de Sciences Po.

Centre d'études et de recherches sur les qualifications (CEREQ). (2011). *Le diplôme, un atout gagnant pour les jeunes face à la crise. Premiers résultats de l'enquête 2010 auprès de la « génération 2007 ».* Paris: Ministère de l'Éducation nationale, de la Jeunesse et de la Vie associative, du ministère du Travail de l'Emploi et de la Santé.

Chabanet, D., & Giugni, M. (2013). Patterns of Change in Youth Unemployment Regimes: France and Switzerland Compared. *International Journal of Social Welfare, 22*, 310–318.

Chabanet, D., & Lacheret, A. (2016). The Occupy Movement in France. Why Protests Have Not Taken Off. In M. Ancelovici, P. Dufour, & H. Nez (Eds.), *Street Politics in the Age of Austerity.* Croydon: Amsterdam University Press.

Chadwick, A., & Howard, P. N. (2010). *Routledge Handbook of Internet Politics.* London: Taylor & Francis.

Cinalli, M. (2004). Horizontal Networks Vs. Vertical Networks in Multi-Organisational Alliances: A Comparative Study of the Unemployment and Asylum Issue-Fields in Britain. *EurPolCom, 8*(4), Leeds: University of Leeds.

Cinalli, M. (2007). Between Horizontal Bridging and Vertical Governance: Pro-Beneficiary Movements in New Labour Britain. In D. Purdue (Ed.), *Civil Societies and Social Movements: Potentials and Problems.* Houndmills: Routledge.

Cinalli, M., & Giugni, M. (2016). Collective Responses to the Economic Crisis in the Public Domain: Myth or Reality? *Politics and Policy, 44*(3), 427–446.

Coffé, H., & Bolzendahl, C. (2010). Same Game, Different Rules? Gender Differences in Political Participation. *Sex Roles, 62*(5–6), 318–333.

Converse, P. (1972). Change in the American Electorate. In A. Campbell & P. Converse (Eds.), *The Human Meaning of Change*. New York: Russell Sage Foundation.

Davezies, L., & Guilluy, C. (2013). La France périphérique et marginalisée: les raisons du ressentiment. *Esprit, 3*(393), 23–33.

Delwit, P. (2013). The End of Voters in Europe? Electoral Turnout in Europe Since WWII. *Open Journal of Political Science, 3*, 44–52.

Esping-Andersen, G. (1990). *The Three Worlds of Welfare Capitalism*. Princeton: Princeton University Press.

Faucher, F. (2015). New Forms of Political Participation. Changing Demands or Changing Opportunities to Participate in Political Parties? *Comparative European Politics, 13*(4), 405–429.

Fillieule, O. (1997). *Stratégies de la rue. Les manifestations en France*. Paris: Presses de Sciences Po.

Fillieule, O., & Tartakowsky, D. (2008). *La manifestation*. Paris: Presses de Sciences Po.

Fouetillou, G. (2008). Le web et le traité constitutionnel européen. Écologie d'une localité thématique compétitive. *Réseaux, 1*(147), 229–257.

Franklin, M. N. (2004). *Voter Turnout and the Dynamics of Electoral Competition in Established Democracies Since 1945*. Cambridge: Cambridge University Press.

Gallego, A. (2007). Unequal Participation in Europe. *International Journal of Sociology, 37*(4), 10–25.

Gaxie, D. (2007). Cognitions, auto-habilitation et pouvoirs des «citoyens». *Revue française de science politique, 57*, 737–757.

Gibson, R. K., Lusoli, W., & Ward, S. (2005). Online Participation in the UK: Testing a 'Contextualised' Model of Internet Effects. *The British Journal of Politics and International Relations, 7*(4), 561–583.

Gibson, R., Michalska, K., & Vedel, T. (2014). Online Campaigning in France, 2007–2012: Political Actors and Citizens in the Aftermath of the Web.2.0 Evolution. *Journal of Information Technology & Politics, 11*(2), 220–244.

Greffet, F. (Ed.). (2011). *Continuerlalutte.com. Les partis politiques sur le web*. Paris: Presses de Sciences Po.

Greffet, F., Wojcik, S., & Blanchard, G. (2014). S'engager dans la campagne présidentielle. Les formes multiples de la participation politique en ligne. *Politiques de communication, 3*, 25–58.

Institut national de la statistique et des études économiques (INSEE—Martinelli, D., & Minni, C.). (2013). Face à la crise, le diplôme protège du chômage et

favorise l'accès à la formation continue [online]. Available: http://www.insee.fr/fr/ffc/docs_ffc/FORMEMP13_a_Diplome_chomage.pdf. 30 Oct 2016.
Ion, J. (2012). *S'engager dans une société d'individus*. Paris: Armand Colin.
Jouet, J., Vedel, T., & Comby, J. B. (2011). Political Information and Interpersonal Conversations in a Multimedia Environment: A Quantitative and Qualitative Examination of Information Practices in France. *European Journal of Communication, 26*(4), 361–375.
Kitschelt, H. P. (1986). Political Opportunity Structures and Political Protest: Anti-Nuclear Movements in Four Democracies. *British Journal of Political Science, 16*(1), 57–85.
Kriesi, H., Koopmans, R., Duyvendak, J. W., & Giugni, M. (1995). *New Social Movements in Western Europe*. Minneapolis: University of Minnesota Press.
Kuhn, R. (2004). Vive la Différence' ? The Mediation of Politicians' Public Images and Private Lives in France. *Parliamentary Affairs, 57*, 24–40.
Lancelot, A. (1968). *L'abstentionnisme électoral en France*. Paris: Presses de Sciences Po.
Le Hay, V., Vedel, T., & Chanvril, F. (2011). Usages des médias et politique: une écologie des pratiques informationnelles. *Réseaux, 170*, 45–73.
Lijphart, A. (1997). Unequal Participation: Democracy's Unresolved Dilemma Presidential Address. *American Political Science Review, 91*(1), 1–14.
Lindvall, J. (2011). The Political Foundations of Trust and Distrust: Reforms and Protests in France. *West European Politics, 34*(2), 296–316.
Mabi, C., & Theviot, A. (Eds.). (2014). *S'engager sur Internet. Mobilisations numériques et pratiques politiques*. Grenoble: Presses universitaires de Grenoble.
Mair, P. (2002). In the Aggregate: Mass Electoral Behaviour in Western Europe, 1950–2000. In H. Keman (Ed.), *Comparative Democratic Politics. A Guide to Contemporary Theory and Research*. London: Sage.
Mair, P. (2013). *Ruling the Void: The Hollowing of Western Democracy*. London/New York: Verso.
Mayer, N. (2010). *Sociologie des comportements politiques*. Paris: Armand Colin.
Melo, D. F., & Stockemer, D. (2014). Age and Political Participation in Germany, France and the UK: A Comparative Analysis. *Comparative European Politics, 12*(1), 33–53.
Michalska, K., Chiche, J., & Vedel, T. (2015). Connaissances politiques et participation politique: ce que change l'internet. *Sciences de la société, 94*, 177–200.
Missika, J.-L. (1992, January–February). Les faux-semblants de la 'dépolitisation'. *Le débat*.
Monnoyer-Smith, L., & Wojcik, S. (2012). Technology and the Quality of Public Deliberation: A Comparison Between On and Offline Participation. *International Journal of Electronic Governance, 5*(1), 24–49.
Muxel, A. (2010). *Avoir 20 ans en politique*. Paris: Seuil.
Muxel, A. (2011). *La politique au fil de l'âge*. Paris: Presses de Sciences Po.

Muxel, A. (2015). Les jeunes et la politique: vers un nouveau modèle de citoyenneté dans les démocraties avancées. In *Points de vue sur la jeunesse: vol 2—Connexions et déconnexions*. Strasbourg: Conseil de l'Europe.
Nam, T. (2007). Rough Days in Democracies: Comparing Protests in Democracies. *European Journal of Political Research, 46*(1), 97–120.
Pélabay, J. (2014). Privatiser les valeurs publiques La citoyenneté comme intime conviction? In A. Muxel (Ed.), *La vie privée des convictions*. Paris: Presses de Sciences Po.
Pierru, E. (2005). *Guerre aux chômeurs ou guerre au chômage*. Broissieux: Editions du Croquant.
Piven, F. F., & Cloward, R. (1971). *Regulating the Poor: The Functions of Public Welfare*. New York: Random House.
Quintelier, E. (2007). Differences in Political Participation Between Young and Old People. *Contemporary Politics, 13*(2), 165–180.
Rosanvallon, P. (2006). *La Contre-Démocratie. La politique à l'âge de la défiance*. Paris: Seuil.
Rosanvallon, R. (2015). *Le bon gouvernement*. Paris: Seuil.
Schlozman, K. L., Verba, S., & Brady, H. E. (2010). Weapon of the Strong? Participatory Inequality and the Internet. *Perspectives on Politics, 8*(2), 487–509.
Tarrow, T. (1994). *Power in Movement*. Cambridge: Cambridge University Press.
Teorell, J., Torcal, M., & Montero, J. R. (2007). Political Participation. Mapping the Terrain. In J. W. van Deth, J. R. Montero, & A. Westholm (Eds.), *Citizenship and Involvement in European Democracies: A Comparative Analysis*. London: Routledge.
Tilly, C. (1986). *The Contentious French*. Cambridge, MA: Belknap Press.
van Deth, J. W. (2014). A Conceptual Map of Political Participation. *Acta Politica, 49*(3), 349–367.
Verba, S., Nie, N., & Kim, J.-O. (1978). *Participation and Political Equality: A Seven Nation Comparison*. New York: Cambridge University Press.
Verba, S., Schlozman, K. L., & Brady, H. E. (1995). *Voice and Equality: Civic Voluntarism in American Politics*. Cambridge, MA: Harvard University Press.
Wattenberg, M. P. (2002). *Where Have All the Voters Gone?* Cambridge, MA: Harvard University Press.
Wojcik, S., & Greffet, F. (2008). Parler politique...en ligne: une revue des travaux français et anglo-saxons. *Réseaux, 26*(150), 19–50.

CHAPTER 6

Political Consumerism and Participation in Times of Crisis in Italy

Lorenzo Zamponi and Lorenzo Bosi

Introduction

Political consumerism has been increasingly analysed in the last few years as an additional form of action that extends the traditional boundaries of conventional and unconventional political participation (Baek 2010; Newman and Bartels 2010; Stolle et al. 2005; Stolle and Micheletti 2015). Identifying economic choice and political behaviour, and politicising the market in order to empower citizens in their role as consumers, political consumerism is thought to have provided an alternative to traditional means of expressing political preferences and collective identities, through activities such as recycling, culture jamming, freecycling, the forwarding of political emails about companies' labour practices and downshifting, fair trade, anti-sweatshop purchasing, ethical banking and so on. As Stolle and her colleagues suggest:

> Political consumers choose particular producers or products because they want to change institutional or market practices. They make their choices

L. Zamponi (✉) • L. Bosi
Institute of Humanities and Social Sciences, Scuola Normale Superiore, Firenze, Italy

M. Giugni, M.T. Grasso (eds.), *Citizens and the Crisis*,
Palgrave Studies in European Political Sociology,
https://doi.org/10.1007/978-3-319-68960-9_6

> based on considerations of justice or fairness, or on an assessment of business and government practices. Regardless of whether political consumers act individually or collectively, their market choices reflect an understanding of material products as embedded in a complex social and normative context, which can be called the politics behind products. (Stolle et al. 2005: 246)

In this chapter, we analyse the relationship between political consumerism and political participation in Italy during the current phase of economic crisis. Italy has been in recession since 2009, with the consequence of a steadily increasing unemployment (LIVEWHAT 2014a). In particular, the country was significantly hit by the crisis of sovereign debt in 2011. The "spread crisis" of the summer of 2011, with the difference between the interest rates of the Italian and German public debt bonds skyrocketing from 173 to 528 points in a few months, forced then Prime Minister Silvio Berlusconi to resign and opened a phase of technocratic grand-coalition governments. Differently to other Southern European countries, Italy did not need a bailout programme and thus was not committed to a "memorandum of understanding". Nevertheless, austerity policies were implemented in the country, involving labour regulations, welfare and education, even if they did not reach the extreme levels of Greece and Spain (LIVEWHAT 2014b). The peculiarities of the Italian experience of the crisis have been analysed elsewhere: "the Italian public discourse on the crisis seems to see a consistent centrality, in relative terms, of labor-related issues and labor-related actors. This centrality, together with the tendency to see earlier references to the crisis than in the other countries, might be interpreted through the idea of Italy as a country living through a 'crisis within the crisis'" (Zamponi and Bosi 2016: 417).

The impact of the crisis on political participation has been at the core of both social movement studies and electoral studies in the last few years (Giugni and Lorenzini 2014). In particular, researchers on social movements have been investigating the role of the crisis in triggering anti-austerity protest (Giugni and Grasso 2015), claiming a comeback of materialistic issues and the analysis of structural economic factors in the field of social movement studies (Della Porta 2015; Hetland and Goodwin 2013), identifying the peculiarities of the Italian case both in terms of protest (Zamponi 2012) and of public discourse (Zamponi and Bosi 2016) and measuring the relationship between perceived economic loss and political attitudes in protest behaviour (Bernburg 2015). Conversely, much still needs to be done towards a comprehensive analysis regarding political consumerism and its relationship with the crisis. Where a growing literature on political consumerism on the Italian case exists (among others, Forno and Graziano 2014, 2016; Grasseni 2013; Graziano and Forno 2012; Lombardi et al. 2015; Pascucci et al. 2016), and some exploratory projects have partially addressed the role of the economic crisis (Bosi and Zamponi 2015; Guidi and Andretta 2015), no comprehensive work to our knowledge has investigated political consumerism in the current economic crisis. Our analysis promises to be particularly relevant because it provides us the opportunity to investigate, during a period of change in the social and economic context, shifts in political consumerism in terms of its type of politicisation and how this relates to conventional and unconventional forms of action. We believe in fact that political consumerism is possibly affected by the economic crisis. Through the analysis of survey data produced by the LIVEWHAT project on boycotting and buycotting in Italy in 2015, we are keen to investigate whether political consumerism is increasing or declining in times of economic crisis; whether it is an alternative to other forms of political participation in the current crisis, such as protest and/or voting; how "political" political consumerism is in times of crisis; and whether there has been some shift in the composition of the Italian political consumerism community in times of economic crisis.

Our analysis focuses mainly on four elements. Firstly, we aim to understand the significance of political consumerism in Italy in times of crisis. Is it a growing phenomenon or it is declining? Does economic hardship deprive citizens of the resources necessary to engage in these forms of action, or does the crisis raise the awareness of the people of their active role in the market?

Secondly, we aim to analyse the relationship between political consumerism and other forms of political participation in times of crisis. Is political consumerism alternative to other forms of political participation in the current crisis, such as protest and conventional politics, or does it go together with them?

Thirdly, we aim to investigate the political characteristics of critical consumers in Italy in times of crisis. How "political" is political consumerism in a context of economic hardship? Are the people who engage in political consumerism more or less likely than others to choose or support other forms of political participation, both conventional and conventional? Are they more or less likely than others to be members of political parties, unions and social movement organisations? Are they more or less likely than others to distrust political institutions and express populist attitudes?

Fourthly, we aim to reconstruct the ongoing evolution of the political traits of Italian critical consumers in times of economic crisis. Are there significant differences, from the political point of view, between the people that have been participating in political consumerism lately and those who did it in a previous phase?

We aim at answering our research questions by using the Italian sample of a cross-national representative web-based survey data which was collected between June and August of 2015 in nine European countries (France, Germany, Greece, Italy, Poland, Spain, Switzerland, Sweden and the UK). In particular, we refer to the questions about political consumerism (viz. boycotts and buycotts), political participation, protest approval and political attitudes.

Political Consumerism in Times of Crisis: A Growing Movement

What is the effect of the economic crisis on political consumerism? Does the crisis produce a positive or negative effect on this form of action? In this section, we aim to understand whether political consumerism in Italy during the current economic crisis has increased or declined.

These questions echo the long-standing debate on the dichotomy between grievance and resource mobilisation as the main trigger of social mobilisation (for reviews of the literature related to the two hypotheses, see Buechler 2004; Kriesi 2004). From strain and breakdown theories (Smelser 1962) to relative deprivation (Geschwender 1968) and progressive deprivation (Korpi 1974), grievances have been considered for a long time as a direct effect of economic hardship, incentivising people to participate in politics, sometimes through recourse to protest. Giugni and Grasso have investigated the role of grievances in the context of the current economic crisis in Europe, and have observed that they do matter, but they "do not so much have an unconditional effect on the responses of civil society actors in the public domain, but material deprivation interacts with perceptions of the political environment to influence the responses by civil society actors in the public domain, in terms of their presence, the use of protest actions, the targeting state actors, and the focus on socioeconomic issues" (Giugni and Grasso 2016: 463).

On the one hand, economic hardship and the strain under which it puts people's lives might be a significant incentive for participating in forms of action aiming at changing the established social and economic order. On the other hand, it might drain resources from political participation, pushing people to spend most of their resources in coping with everyday problems and making rarer and difficult the engagement in civic and political action.

Furthermore, as Giugni and Lorenzini wrote:

> citizens may and do react in a variety of ways to the experience of economic crisis, such as engaging in a wide repertoire of non-capitalist practices that involve citizens lowering their cost of living, connecting to other communities and assisting others. Alternative forms of resilience include the strengthening of social and family networks and community practices to foster solidarity, changing lifestyles towards more sustainable forms of consumption and production, developing new artistic expressions, and moving abroad for short or long durations (or on the contrary, reducing mobility). (2014: 45)

This mechanism is particularly relevant in the analysis of political consumerism and in the meaning that citizens attach to it: is it mainly an ethical gesture, an expression of post-materialistic values of altruism, or does it imply a political choice, an attempt to change society through the intervention in the market? In the former case, the effect of the economic crisis would probably be negative, while in the latter it might go in the opposite direction.

We can contribute to this debate through the analysis of survey data. If we compare the answers to the question regarding boycotts in our survey with those to the identical questions posed by the European Social Survey (ESS) in 2002, 2004 and 2012 and the question regarding buycotts with the identical question posed by the ESS in the round of 2002[1] (it was not asked in the following rounds), we observe that the increase in the engagement in political consumerism, that had already been pointed out by the existing literature (Stolle and Micheletti 2015), did not stop in the crisis. On the contrary, during the economic crisis the share of people that have chosen this form of participation in Italy has drastically increased. In fact, the percentage of people who have boycotted in the last 12 months, which was 7.57% in 2002 and 7.05% in 2004, increased to 12% in 2012 and to 18.4% in 2015.[2] Furthermore, the percentage of people who have buycotted in the last 12 months, which was 6.51% in 2002, increased to 14.96% in 2015.[3]

This increase cannot be univocally interpreted as an effect of the economic crisis: the data is not available for every year, and the growth of political consumerism in Italy might be the effect of a gradual process of education of the Italian citizens on these forms of action and the issues they address. Nevertheless, it is very unlikely that the crisis has had a significant negative effect, and we can unequivocally state that political consumerism as a movement has been significantly growing in Italy during the economic crisis.

Political Consumerism and Other Forms of Political Participation

Over recent years, scholars working on political consumerism (Stolle and Hooghe 2005) have tended to challenge those readings that suggested political participation was in a declining phase (Putnam et al. 1993). In their view, political participation is instead evolving to include other forms of action, among which political consumerism is certainly one. But such evolution has been shown not to have been at the expenses of conventional and unconventional forms of action. In fact, political consumerism has been said to show a positive relationship with other forms of political action, such as voting and protesting (Stolle et al. 2005; Strømsnes 2009; Ward and de Vreese 2011). Are these findings still valid even in periods of economic crisis?

In this section, we aim to analyse the relationship between political consumerism and other forms of political participation, including both conventional and unconventional forms of actions, in times of crisis. Is political consumerism alternative to other forms of political participation in the current crisis, such as protest and conventional politics, or does it go together with them?

Political consumerism, like other forms of direct social action, is structurally part of the repertoire of collective action (Bosi and Zamponi 2015). It is one of the forms of political participation used by citizens in times of crisis, sometimes together with other forms of action, sometimes as an alternative to them. The people engaging in political consumerism share the profile of politically active citizens, but they are also characterised by their own peculiarities, suggesting that an original type of politicisation is at work in the milieu of political consumerism.

In order to analyse the relationship between different forms of political participation, we have grouped the forms mentioned in the LIVEWHAT survey into three categories: conventional politics (including "Contacted or visited a politician or government/local government official (online or offline)"), "Donated money to a political organisation/party or action group (online or offline)", "Displayed/worn a political or campaign logo/badge/sticker (online or offline)", "Signed a petition/public letter/campaign appeal (online or offline)" and "Attended a meeting of a political organisation/party or action group", protest (including "Attended a demonstration, march or rally", "Joined a strike", "Joined an occupation, sit-in, or blockade", "Damaged things like breaking windows, removing roads signs, etc." and "Used personal violence like fighting with the police") and political consumerism (including "Boycotted certain products for political/ethical/environment reasons (online or offline)" and "Deliberately bought products for political/ethical/environment reasons (online or offline)").

As our data show, there is a strong relationship between engagement in conventional forms of political participation and political consumerism. In particular, political consumerism seems to work as a subset of conventional politics, for most people. In fact, 90.97% of those who have not participated in any form of conventional politics in the last five years have not engaged in political consumerism either, while, among those who did participate in conventional politics, half (51.33%) chose to buycott or boycott certain products and half (48.67%) did not. Furthermore, 88.88% of those who have boycotted or buycotted a product in the last five years have also participated in conventional politics in the same period, while the sample of those who have not engaged in political consumerism is almost evenly divided between those who have participated in conventional politics (45.35%) and those who have not (54.65%). From this figure, political consumerism seems a subset of conventional politics, chosen by a part of the same people that engaged in other forms of political participation, and by very few of those who did not.

The relationship with protest is less simple. In fact, the relationship is clearer on the negative side than on the positive: of those who did not participate in any form of protest in the last five years, only 23.12% engaged in political consumerism, and of those who did not boycott or buycott any product in the last five years, only 25.7% took part in at least a protest event. Among those who did protest, instead, 58.7% also engaged in political consumerism, while 41.3% did not, and among those who boycott or buycotted a product in the last five years, 62.04% participated also in protest events, while 37.96% did not. From this point of view, it seems like participation in protest and in political consumerism partially overlap but are also partially alternative to each other. While those who do not participate in one are likely not to participate in the other either (showing that both forms of action prevalently address the same audience of politicised individuals), a relevant part of those who participate in one do not participate in the other, expressing their political identity and pursuing their political goals in different ways.

The idea of political consumerism as a subset of conventional politics, partially overlapping and partially alternative to protest, is confirmed by Fig. 6.1, which illustrates the distributions of respondents who engaged in any form of political participation across the different combination of forms of participation.

The data shows very clearly that, of the respondents who participated in any kind of political action, almost all took part in conventional politics. In fact, only 3.96% of them have engaged in political consumerism as the only form of action, only 6.46% in political protest and only 1.45% in political consumerism and protest together but without conventional politics. The vast majority of the people who have engaged in any form of political participation in the last five years took part in forms of conventional politics. Both protest and political consumerism are, from this point of view, a subset of conventional politics, an addition to the repertoire. The choice of what to add to conventional politics is quite diverse: 27.55% of the politically active respondents participated only in conventional politics, 17.69% in conventional politics and protest but not in political con-

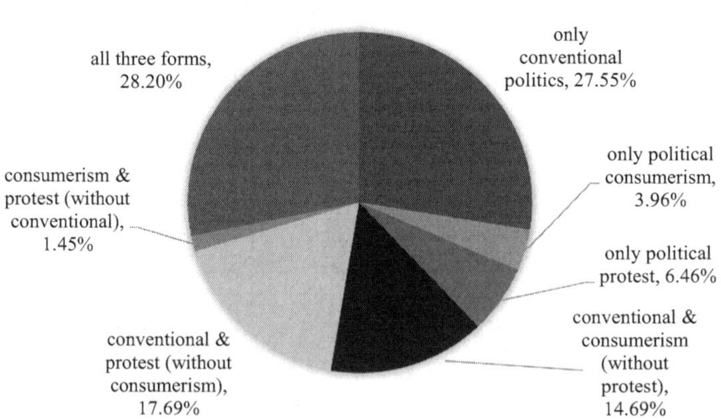

Fig. 6.1 Forms of political participation

sumerism, 14.69% in conventional politics and political consumerism but not in protest and 28.2% in the all three forms of action.

The picture that emerges is that of conventional politics as an almost all-encompassing type of political participation, with protest and political consumerism as two subsets of it, sometimes overlapping with each other and sometimes alternative to each other.

How "Political" Is Political Consumerism?

Once we have placed political consumerism within the repertoire of political participation of Italian active citizens, we will try to illustrate what is characteristic of it from the point of view of politicisation.

In this section, we aim to investigate the political characteristics of critical consumers in Italy in times of crisis. How "political" is political consumerism in a context of economic hardship? Are the people who engage in political consumerism more or less likely than others to choose or support other forms of political participation, both conventional and unconventional? Are they more or less likely than others to be members of political parties, unions and social movement organisations? Are they more or less likely than others to distrust political institutions and express populist attitudes?

Stolle and Micheletti have observed that "political consumers are among the most resourceful citizens", "they are also highly interested in politics", they "are also more trusting of the various political institutions" but "a bit more skeptical of the police and the legal systems in their respective countries", they "believe more strongly than nonpolitical consumers in the efficacy of people and other such actors", they "are by far significantly more engaged in innovative politics" but "are overall also more engaged in electoral political activities", showing that "political consumerism does not crowd out other forms of political participation; indeed, political consumerism is an additional tool of participation for those who are already active, particularly in other new types of participation" (Stolle and Micheletti 2015: 83–91). We are keen to see if these observations are valid also for the Italian case during the recent economic crisis. In order to do so, we have divided our sample of politically active citizens (those who have engaged in any form of political participation in the last five years, i.e. conventional, unconventional and consumerism) into two groups: those who have engaged in political consumerism (51.70% of the sample of politically active citizens) and those who did not (48.30%). In this way, measuring the difference, according to a series of indicators, between politically active citizens who have participated in political consumerism and politically active citizens who did not, we aim to assess, in the context of political participation, the characteristic politicisation of political consumerism, the "plus" that this form of action adds to the repertoire.

Our analysis shows a stronger level of politicisation according to all the indicators: the politically active citizens who participate in political consumerism seem to be "supermilitants": they are more likely to be active or passive members of political organisations and groups, they show higher levels of internal political efficacy, and they tend to trust political actors (a part from the police) more, to approve all the forms of anti-austerity protest more and to discuss politics with friends more often than politically active citizens who have not participated in political consumerism in the last five years.

Figure 6.2 illustrates the differences between the two groups for what regards their membership[4] in political groups and organisations. The results are rather clear: politically active citizens that have engaged in political consumerism in the last five years show higher levels of membership to all kinds of political and social organisations.

Regarding internal political efficacy, Fig. 6.3 shows how the group of politically active citizens that have engaged in political consumerism is characterised by a stronger feeling of self-empowerment in politics than the other group, according to all three indicators. A similar phenomenon is observable in Fig. 6.4 for what regards political trust: politically active citizens who have participated in political consumerism tend to trust more all political actors apart from the police and the military than the other group.

Figure 6.5 also confirms the tendency for a stronger politicisation that characterises the citizens participating in political consumerism among the politically active citizens: they tend to approve all forms of anti-austerity protest more than the other group. Finally, the same tendency is also visible with regard to the habit of discussing politics with friends, that involves 62.97% of political consumerists and only 51.59% of the citizens who are active in different forms.

An Evolving Politicisation

In the previous sections, we have illustrated the peculiarities of political consumerism in terms of politicisation, according to different indicators, in the Italian context during the economic crisis. In this section, we will

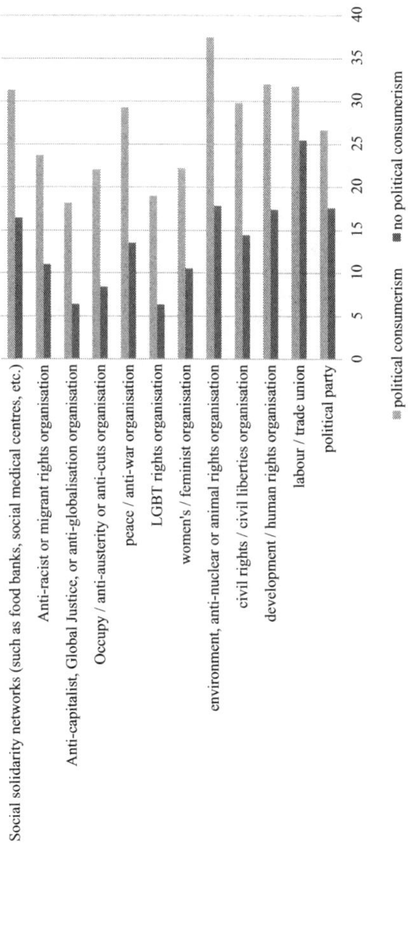

Fig. 6.2 Political consumerism and membership in political and social organisations

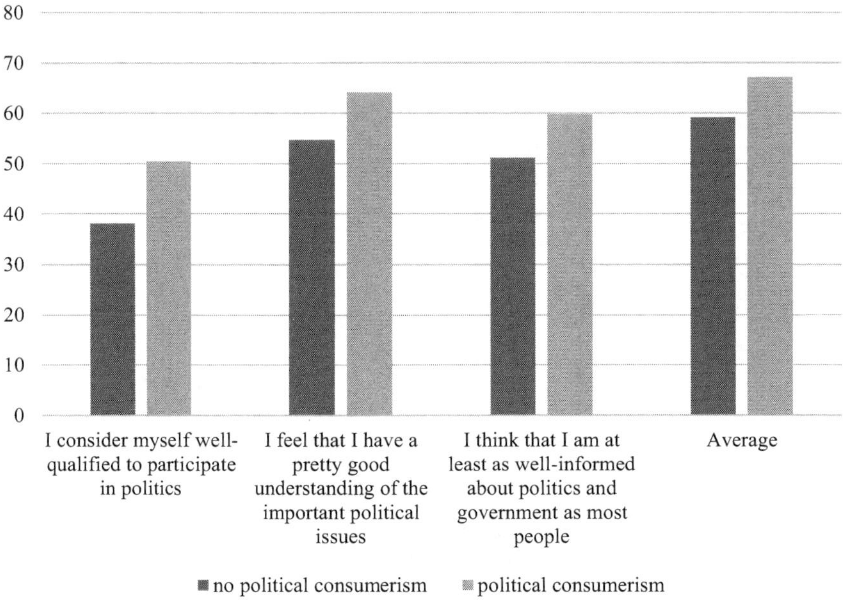

Fig. 6.3 Political consumerism and internal political efficacy (The figure shows the percentage of people that answered "Agree" of "Agree strongly" to the questions)

dig deeper in the issue diachronically, trying to analyse the evolution of the politicisation of political consumerism in Italy during the economic crisis. Is there an ongoing change in the political composition of the Italian political consumerism community in times of economic crisis?

In order to answer this question, we compare, according to different indicators, two groups: those who have engaged in at least one form of political consumerism (boycott or buycott) in the last 12 months (71.92% of those active in last five years in total) and those who have participated in these forms of action in the last five years but not in the last year (28.08%). In this way, we aim to show the changes in the political composition of the Italian political consumerism community in times of economic crisis. To be clear, we must say that the answers to our question were mutually exclusive: respondents were asked whether they had engaged in certain forms of political participation in the last 12 months or in the previous five years (but not in the last 12 months) or previously in life (but not in the last five years) or never. We chose to compare the first

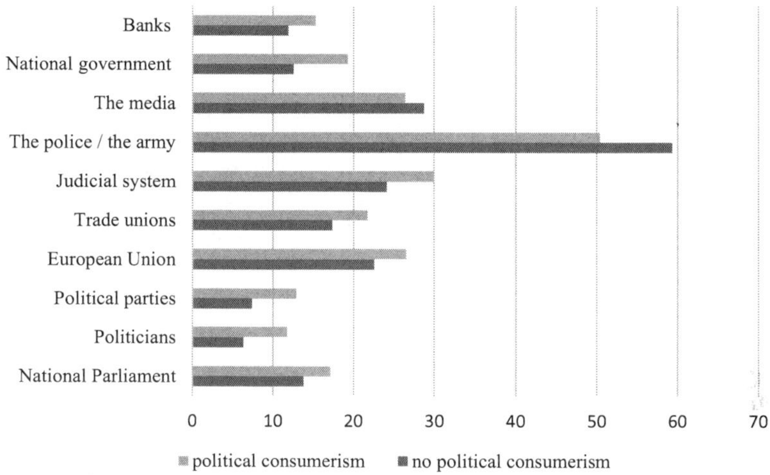

Fig. 6.4 Political consumerism and political trust (This figure shows the percentage of people that chose 6 or a higher value in response to the question "On a score of 0–10 how much, if at all, do you personally trust each of the following institutions where 0 means 'Do not trust an institution at all', and 10 means 'Completely trust this institution'?")

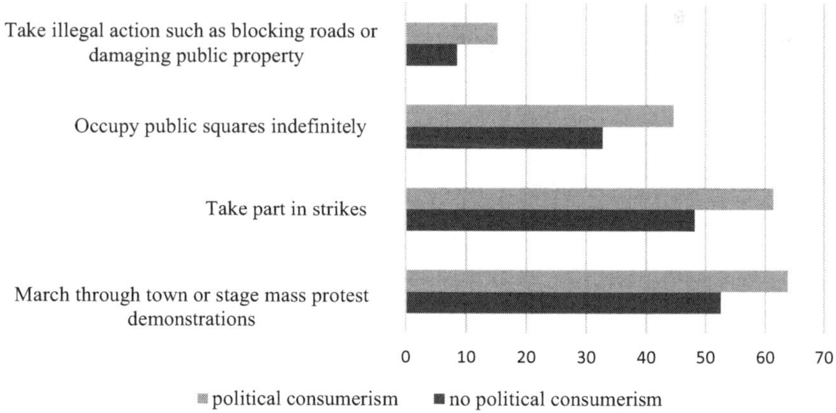

Fig. 6.5 Political consumerism and anti-austerity protest approval (This figure shows the percentage of people that chose 6 or a higher value in response to the question "When thinking about austerity policies and their consequences, how strongly do you approve or disapprove of the following actions? Please place yourself on a scale from 0 to 10, where 0 means 'Strongly disapprove' and 10 means 'Strongly approve'")

two groups, knowing that it is likely that some of the people who checked the "last 12 months" options were active in political consumerism even before, and thus we cannot treat them as newcomers in the field. Nevertheless, we consider the comparison between the two groups interesting, because, even if all the members of the first group had already been active before (and we consider this possibility rather unlikely), the difference between the two groups would show in any case a change in the composition of Italian political consumerism community as a whole.

In this way, measuring the difference, according to a series of indicators, between the political consumers that were active in the last year and those who were active in the previous period but not in the last year, we aim to assess the evolutions and changes in the politicisation of political consumerism in times of economic crisis.

Our analysis shows a visible change in the relationship between political consumerism and political participation in Italy during the economic crisis: respondents that have engaged in political consumerism in the last year show a visibly different politicisation than those who have engaged in buycotts or boycotts in the previous period: while internal political efficacy is increasing and protest approval is increasing, respondents that engaged in political consumerism in the last 12 months are less likely to be members of political organisations and show lower levels of political trust and stronger populist attitudes.

The level of politicisation of political consumers seems to increase, during the economic crisis, at least if we look at the data regarding internal political efficacy and political discussion with friends. In fact, as Fig. 6.6 shows, all the indicators of internal political efficacy show a visible increase: political consumers are increasingly convinced of their capacity to follow politics and participate in it. The same is true if we look at political discussion with friends: it is frequent in 66.17% of those who engaged in political consumerism in the last 12 months and only in 54.76% of those who were active previously and now are not.

Changes in politicisation are visible also for what regards the approval of anti-austerity protests. Coherently with what was observed regarding internal political efficacy and political discussion with friends, the politicisation of political consumer is increasing: in fact, the approval of anti-austerity protests is generally higher among those who engaged in political consumerism in the last year than in those who did it in the previous period but not in the last year. Here we see also a first sign of change in this politicisation: in fact, the only form of anti-austerity protest towards

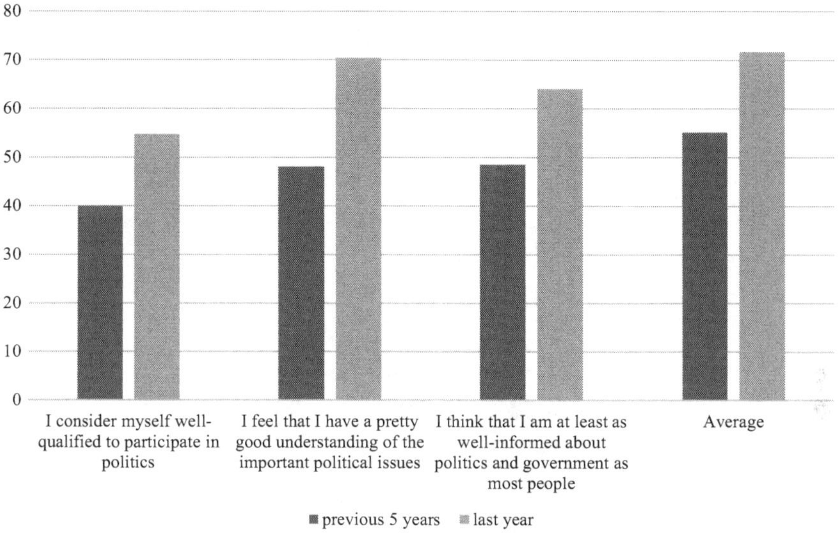

Fig. 6.6 Political consumerism and internal political efficacy across time

which the approval is decreasing is illegal action. As we will see later, the composition of political consumers seems to become more politicised but also more "legalitarian" (Fig. 6.7).

If we focus on membership in social and political organisations and on political trust instead, we see a different picture. Membership is systematically declining, with the only exception of environmental organisations. In the same vein, political trust is also significantly lower in those who were active in the last year than in those who stopped their previous commitment in political consumerism. The only exception here is the police, confirming the legalitarian attitude already mentioned (Figs. 6.8 and 6.9).

Coherently with what was observed regarding political trust, populist attitudes[5] are also stronger in political consumers who have been active in the last year than in those who were not: the average support for our battery of populist statements, in fact, is 4.14 for recent political consumerists and 3.84 for those who were active before and now are not. In the same vein, the political consumers who were most recently active tend to consider the crisis as more serious than others (Fig. 6.10).

The picture emerging from this comparison is rather interesting. In fact, while in the previous section we have observed that, in general, the Italian

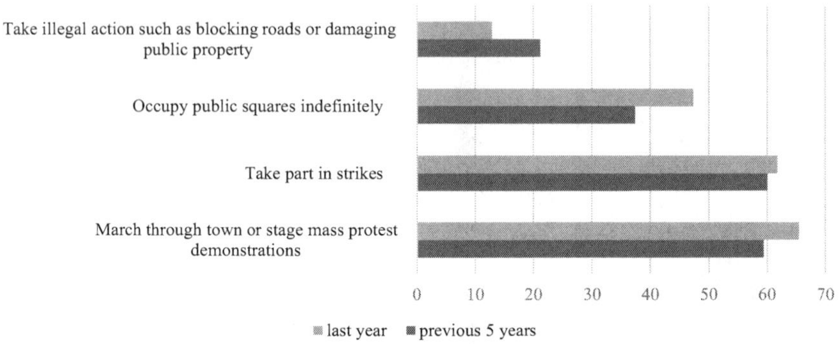

Fig. 6.7 Political consumerism and anti-austerity protest approval across time

Fig. 6.8 Political consumerism and membership in social and political organisations across time

political consumerism community is made of "supermilitants" who tend to participate in organisations, trust institutions and discuss politics more than others, in this section we have pointed out that there is the tendency towards a change in the politicisation of this community: on the one hand, the culture of discussing politics and feeling active and engaged remains

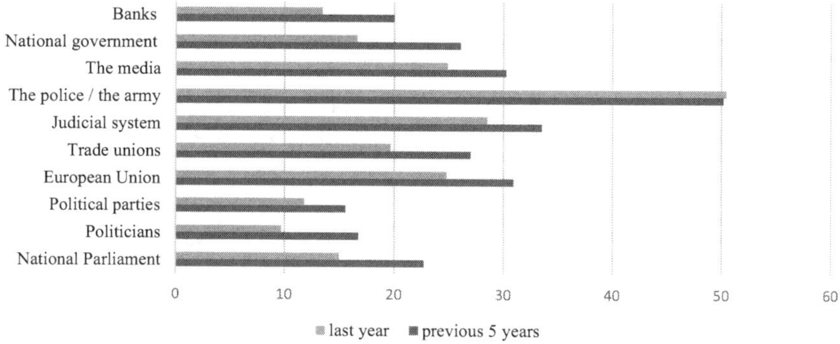

Fig. 6.9 Political consumerism and political trust across time

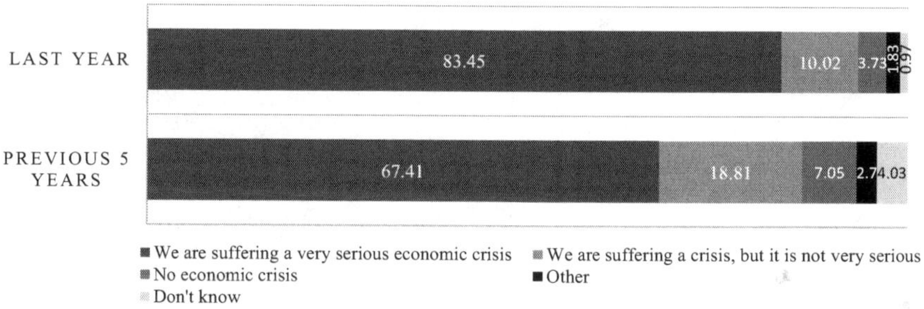

Fig. 6.10 Political consumerism and crisis assessment across time

and is even becoming stronger; on the other hand, the participation in organisations and the trust in institutions is visibly weakening, and populist attitudes are getting stronger. During the economic crisis, the politicisation of Italian political consumers has not declined, but it is changing, towards a culture of participation that focuses less on organisations and institutions than before, that is more sceptical towards power, while remaining strong.

This tendency is coherent with the literature on anti-austerity movements in Italy and in particular with the analyses of the role of the economic crisis in reshaping the repertoire of political action (Bosi and Zamponi 2015). For example, the distrust of representative institutions that characterised the Global Justice Movements has significantly increased among the participants in anti-austerity protests (Della Porta and Andretta 2013). In the same vein, attempts to take the political temperature of the anti-cuts student movement in Italy show a complete distrust of parties and a "legalitarian" attitude, with "high trust towards the judiciary, preoccupation for corruption" (Novelli 2010: 136).

More in general, the change in socioeconomic context seems to favour a change in the composition of the people who engage in political consumerism. As we have observed elsewhere,

> there appears to be a continuity in economic activism that attributes political meaning to market behaviour, but the economic crisis seems to favour a recontextualisation and reshaping of these practices. If, in the early 2000s, activists of the GJM were involved in such direct social actions partly as a way of building a collective identity through private action, now these forms address a wider audience, beyond the bounds of organized politics. Direct social actions are being reshaped, shedding some of their more "altruistic" and ideological layers, and taking on a more materialistic character. (Bosi and Zamponi 2015: 385)

Conclusions

Our analysis shows that, regarding our first research question on the significance of political consumerism in the context of the economic crisis, the increase in the engagement in political consumerism that had already been pointed out by the existing data did not stop in the crisis. On the contrary, during the economic crisis, the share of people who have chosen this form of participation in Italy has drastically increased.

Concerning our second point, whether political consumerism is an alternative to other forms of political participation in the current crisis, such as protest and/or voting, our results are consistent with the existing literature on political consumerism. Furthermore, in relation to our third point, our analysis shows that, among the politically active citizens, those who choose political consumerism as a form of political participation are "supermilitants" who show a higher level of politicisation according to all the indicators, thus confirming what observed by Stolle and Micheletti (2015). They are more likely to be active or passive members of political organisations and groups, they show higher levels of internal political efficacy, and they tend to trust political actors more, to approve all the forms of anti-austerity protest more and to discuss politics with friends more often than those that choose different forms of political participation.

For our fourth point, whether there has been some shift in the composition of the Italian political consumerism community in times of economic crisis, the diachronical analysis shows a visible change in the relationship between political consumerism and political participation in Italy during the economic crisis, consistently with the existing scholarship on the relationship between the crisis and the repertoire of action (Bosi and Zamponi 2015). Respondents who have engaged in political consumerism in the last year show a visibly different politicisation than those who have engaged in buycotts or boycotts in the previous period: while internal political efficacy is increasing and protest approval is increasing, respondents that engaged in political consumerism in the last 12 months are less likely to be members of political organisations and show lower levels of political trust and stronger populist attitudes. This analysis suggests an ongoing process of change in the political consumerism community in Italy, with the economic crisis changing the constituency of economic activism and incentivising the involvement of people that participate in politics in innovative ways.

These findings suggest further implications that require to be addressed in a comparative fashion, mainly on two points. Firstly, our finding about the increasing relevance of political consumerism in a context of economic crisis may suggest that this form of action cannot be understood as an eminently middle-class ethical gesture, an expression of post-materialistic values, typical of contexts in which socioeconomic grievances are far from urgent. Rather, the positive effect of the economic crisis on political consumerism strengthens its interpretation as a political choice, a political empowerment of people in their role of consumers, typical of contexts characterised by a significant salience of politics in the public debate. Secondly, in the same vein, the issue of the ongoing change in the politicisation of political consumers needs to be explored in a deeper way, in order to understand where new culture of participation, more sceptical towards power than before, is rooted.

Notes

1. The European Social Survey data was collected face to face, while the LIVEWHAT survey data retrieval was done through the CAWI (Computer Assisted Web Interviewing) method. The robust methodological standards that were applied, the coincidence of the questions and the application of population weights suggest that comparability is possible between the two datasets. Nevertheless, an instrument effect cannot be excluded.

2. The data on 2015 comes from the Italian sample of the LIVEWHAT survey and refers to the people who have chosen the answer "In past 12 months" to the question "There are different ways of trying to improve things or help prevent things from going wrong. When have you LAST done the following?" in correspondence of the option "Boycotted certain products for political/ethical/environment reasons (online or offline)". The data on 2002, 2004 and 2012 comes from the Italian sample of the Rounds 1, 2 and 6 of the European Social Survey, and refers to the people who have chosen the answer "Yes" to the question "There are different ways of trying to improve things in Italy or help prevent things from going wrong. During the last 12 months, have you done any of the following?" in correspondence of the option "Boycotted certain products".
3. The data on 2015 comes from the Italian sample of the LIVEWHAT survey, and refers to the people who have chosen the answer "In past 12 months" to the question "There are different ways of trying to improve things or help prevent things from going wrong. When have you LAST done the following?" in correspondence of the option "Deliberately bought products for political/ethical/environment reasons (online or offline)". The data on 2002 comes from the Italian sample of the Round 1 of the European Social Survey, and refers to the people who have chosen the answer "Yes" to the question "There are different ways of trying to improve things in Italy or help prevent things from going wrong. During the last 12 months, have you done any of the following?" in correspondence of the option "deliberately bought certain products for political, ethical or environmental reasons".
4. In this chapter we do not distinguish between active and passive membership, and, thus, we have considered all the positive answers (both "Belong to only (passive member)" and "Belong to AND do volunteer/unpaid work for (active member)") to the question "Please look carefully at the following list of organisations. For each of them, please tell which, if any, you belong to and which, if any, you are currently doing unpaid work for?"
5. Here we use as an indicator of populist attitudes, as suggested by Anduiza and Rico (2015), the average between the level of agreement shown by respondents, in a range from 1 to 5, to a battery of 8 questions: "The politicians in the Italian parliament need to follow the will of the people", "The people, and not politicians, should make our most important policy decisions", "The political differences between the elite and the people are larger than the differences among the people", "I would rather be represented by a citizen than by a specialized politician", "Elected officials talk too much and take too little action", "What people call "compromise" in politics is really just selling out on one's principles", "The particular interests of the political class negatively affect the welfare of the people", "Politicians always end up agreeing when it comes to protecting their privileges".

References

Anduiza, E., & Rico, G. (2015). *Economic Correlates of Populist Attitudes: An Analysis of Nine European Countries.* Paper presented at the LIVEWHAT International Scientific Conference, University of Geneva, October 14–16, 2015.

Baek, Y. M. (2010). To Buy or Not to Buy: Who Are Political Consumers? What Do They Think and How Do They Participate? *Political Studies, 58,* 1065–1086.

Bernburg, J. G. (2015). Economic Crisis and Popular Protest in Iceland, January 2009: The Role of Perceived Economic Loss and Political Attitudes in Protest Participation and Support. *Mobilization: An International Quarterly, 20,* 231–252.

Bosi, L., & Zamponi, L. (2015). Direct Social Actions and Economic Crises: The Relationship Between Forms of Action and Socio-Economic Context in Italy. *Partecipazione e Conflitto, 8*(2), 367–391.

Buechler, S. M. (2004). The Strange Career of Strain and Breakdown Theories of Collective Action. In D. A. Snow, S. A. Soule, & H. Kriesi (Eds.), *The Blackwell Companion to Social Movements* (pp. 47–64). Oxford: Blackwell.

Della Porta, D. (2015). *Social Movements in Times of Austerity: Bringing Capitalism Back into Protest Analysis.* Cambridge/Malden: Polity Press.

Della Porta, D., & Andretta, M. (2013). Protesting for Justice and Democracy: Italian Indignados? *Contemporary Italian Politics, 5,* 23–37.

Forno, F., & Graziano, P. R. (2014). Sustainable Community Movement Organisations. *Journal of Consumer Culture.* https://doi.org/10.1177/1469540514526225.

Forno, F., & Graziano, P. (2016). *Il consumo critico. Una relazione solidale tra chi acquista e chi produce.* Bologna: Il Mulino.

Geschwender, J. A. (1968). Explorations in the Theory of Social Movements and Revolutions. *Social Forces, 47,* 127–135.

Giugni, M., & Grasso, M. (Eds.). (2015). *Austerity and Protest: Popular Contention in Times of Economic Crisis.* Oxon: Routledge.

Giugni, M., & Grasso, M. T. (2016). How Civil Society Actors Responded to the Economic Crisis: The Interaction of Material Deprivation and Perceptions of Political Opportunity Structures: CIVIL SOCIETY ACTORS' RESPONSE TO THE ECONOMIC CRISIS. *Politics & Policy, 44,* 447–472. https://doi.org/10.1111/polp.12157.

Giugni, M., & Lorenzini, J. (2014). Hypotheses on Citizens' Political Reactions to Economic Crises. In LIVEWHAT (Ed.), *Working Paper on Definition and Identification of Crises.*

Grasseni, C. (2013). *Beyond Alternative Food Networks: Italy's Solidarity Purchase Groups.* London: A&C Black.

Graziano, P. R., & Forno, F. (2012). Political Consumerism and New Forms of Political Participation The Gruppi di Acquisto Solidale in Italy. *The Annals of the American Academy of Political and Social Science, 644*, 121–133.

Guidi, R., & Andretta, M. (2015). Between Resistance and Resilience. How Do Italian Solidarity Purchase Groups Change in Times of Crisis and Austerity? *Partecipazione e Conflitto, 8*, 443–477.

Hetland, G., & Goodwin, J. (2013). The Strange Disappearance of Capitalism from Social Movement Studies. In L. Cox, J. Krinsky, & G. Nilsen (Eds.), *Marxism and Social Movements* (pp. 82–102). Leiden: Brill.

Korpi, W. (1974). Conflict, Power and Relative Deprivation. *American Political Science Review, 68*, 1569–1578.

Kriesi, H. (2004). Political Context and Opportunity. In D. A. Snow, S. A. Soule, & H. Kriesi (Eds.), *The Blackwell Companion to Social Movements* (pp. 67–90). Oxford: Blackwell Publishing Ltd.

LIVEWHAT. (2014a). Working Paper on Definition and Identification of Crisis. *LIVEWHAT*. Available online at http://www.livewhat.unige.ch/wp-content/uploads/2014/02/LIVEWHAT_D1.2.pdf. Accessed 10 Mar 2016.

LIVEWHAT. (2014b). Integrated Report on Policy Responses to Crises. *LIVEWHAT*. Available online at http://www.livewhat.unige.ch/wp-content/uploads/2014/02/LIVEWHAT_D2.4.pdf. Accessed 10 Mar 2016.

Lombardi, A., Migliore, G., Verneau, F., Schifani, G., & Cembalo, L. (2015). Are 'Good Guys' More Likely to Participate in Local Agriculture? *Food Quality and Preference, 45*, 158–165.

Newman, B. J., & Bartels, B. L. (2010). Politics at the Checkout Line: Explaining Political Consumerism in the United States. *Political Research Quarterly, 64*(4), 803–817.

Novelli, E. (2010). L'Onda capitale. In L. Caruso, A. Giorgi, A. Mattoni, & G. Piazza (Eds.), *Alla Ricerca dell'Onda. I Nuovi Conflitti Nell'istruzione Superiore*. Milano: Franco Angeli.

Pascucci, S., Dentoni, D., Lombardi, A., & Cembalo, L. (2016). Sharing Values or Sharing Costs? Understanding Consumer Participation in Alternative Food Networks. *NJAS-Wageningen Journal of Life Sciences, 78*, 47–60.

Putnam, R. D., Leonardi, R., & Nanetti, R. Y. (1993). *Making Democracy Work: Civic Traditions in Modern Italy*. Princeton: Princeton university press.

Smelser, N. J. (1962). *Theory of Collective Behavior*. New York: Free Press.

Stolle, D., & Hooghe, M. (2005). Inaccurate, Exceptional, One-Sided or Irrelevant? The Debate About the Alleged Decline of Social Capital and Civic Engagement in Western Societies. *British Journal of Political Science, 35*, 149–167.

Stolle, D., & Micheletti, M. (2015). *Political Consumerism: Global Responsibility in Action*. New York: Cambridge University Press.

Stolle, D., Hooghe, M., & Micheletti, M. (2005). Politics in the Supermarket: Political Consumerism as a Form of Political Participation. *International Political Science Review, 26*, 245–269.

Strømsnes, K. (2009). Political Consumerism: A Substitute for or Supplement to Conventional Political Participation? *Journal of Civil Society, 5*, 303–314.

Ward, J., & de Vreese, C. (2011). Political Consumerism, Young Citizens and the Internet. *Media, Culture & Society, 33*, 399–413.

Zamponi, L. (2012). Why Don't Italians Occupy? Hypotheses on a Failed Mobilisation. *Social Movement Studies, 11*, 416–426. https://doi.org/10.1080/14742837.2012.708833.

Zamponi, L., & Bosi, L. (2016). Which Crisis? European Crisis and National Contexts in Public Discourse. *Politics & Policy, 44*, 400–426. https://doi.org/10.1111/polp.12156.

CHAPTER 7

Experiences of the Economic Crisis: Volunteering in Social Solidarity Networks During the Recession in Greece

Stefania Kalogeraki

Introduction

Since 2008 the global economic crisis has been leaving deep and long-lasting traces on economic performance and social hardships in Europe. In the context of the recent crisis, Greece has been the most severely affected country as well as the first member-state which resorted to EC-IMF-ECB bail-out mechanisms under the pressure of austerity measures and structural reforms. The austerity measures involved severe reductions in salaries, cuts in public spending on health, education and social security, extensive privatization, closures and mergers of public organizations, increases in taxes (e.g. VAT and property taxes), as well as labour market reforms which increased employment insecurity (Matsaganis and Leventi 2014).

Despite the structural adjustments and austerity policies aimed at reducing the country's fiscal deficit, the Greek economy continued to decline

S. Kalogeraki (✉)
Department of Sociology, University of Crete, Rethymno, Crete, Greece

M. Giugni, M.T. Grasso (eds.), *Citizens and the Crisis*,
Palgrave Studies in European Political Sociology,
https://doi.org/10.1007/978-3-319-68960-9_7

leading the country into a vicious circle of recession, unemployment, growing and extreme poverty, and deregulation (OECD 2014; Petmesidou and Guillén 2015). Following the first memorandum in 2010, the general government gross debt (as a percentage of GDP) increased from 146.2% to 176.9% in 2015,[1] which was the highest in the European Union-28 and the Eurozone. In 2013, Greece became the first developed nation to be downgraded from a developed to an emerging economy (MSCI 2013),[2] unveiling the failure of the implemented structural reform programmes to improve the country's fiscal position. Beyond the economic figures, Greece has faced a social and humanitarian crisis, with an increasing number of individuals facing extreme hardship and having to deal with daily financial problems, such as the inability to cover basic needs (e.g. food and clothing), lack of housing, and limited access to healthcare (Balourdos and Spyropoulou 2012).

As the economic crisis worsened and public spending for the social sector further contracted, a variety of formal and informal social solidarity initiatives have emerged, attempting to cover for the gaps in social protection left by the Greek state. These initiatives acted as alternative forms of resilience representing a shift from mainstream socio-economic practices (Kousis and Paschou 2014) and included food banks, free medical services, soup kitchens, barter networks, new cooperatives, and social economy enterprises that targeted the assistance of socio-economically deprived individuals to help improve their means of subsistence and healthcare (Garefi and Kalemaki 2013; Afouxenidis and Gardiki 2014; Rakopoulos 2014; Sotiropoulos 2014; Vathakou 2015; Kalogeraki et al. 2016).

Although the existing data on volunteering in social solidarity initiatives is rather limited and ambiguous, some preliminary indications and findings from small-scale surveys illustrate an increasing trend in Greeks' volunteering and participation in groups, networks, and organizations that provide alternative ways of enduring day-to-day difficulties under hard economic times (Sotiropoulos 2014; Clarke 2015; Jones et al. 2015). For instance, Sotiropoulos and Bourikos (2014) underline that in both formal and informal organizations, an increasing trend in volunteers participating in initiatives targeting to assist groups most severely affected by the crisis is detected. Moreover, recent qualitative empirical findings underpin the increase in volunteering specifically in informal organizations including social solidarity networks that act as emergency relief mechanisms for those in need (Clarke 2015). Similarly, Bourikos (2013: 13) argues that "there is an emerging trend towards increased public participation in informal volunteerism at neighbourhood level and in the wider local community".

Such preliminary evidence has been interpreted as an indication of strengthening social capital (Jones et al. 2015) and emergence of civil society during recessionary times (Sotiropoulos 2014; Simiti 2015). It should be noted that previous research underpins the lower levels of volunteering (e.g. European Commission 2007, 2010, 2011) and social capital (Jones et al. 2008) along with a weaker civil society in Greece (Mouzelis 1995; Lyrintzis 2002) compared to other European countries. With respect to the latter, Mouzelis (1995) argues that the "anaemic" Greek civil society can be attributed to the dominance of clientelism and patronage and the vertical, rather than horizontal, incorporation of the social spectrum to politics. Other scholars underscore additional factors, including, among others, the close church-state relationship, weak tax incentives for charitable giving, and a lack of civic education in public schools (Houliaras 2015).

Despite these arguments, others emphasize that there is a vibrant, informal, non-institutionalized, often non-registered Greek civil society sector which does not fall into the normative definitions of civil society; hence not captured in official statistics (Karamichas 2007; Loukidou 2013). This informal civil society tends to be distant from the state, more politicized and often characterized by fluid, open, and anti-hierarchical forms of relations (Rozakou 2011), whereas it primarily aims to protect vested interests in specific regions or local areas or volunteer to help people in need (Sotiropoulos 2004).

Since 2008 there has been a great proliferation of civil society initiatives traced in the plethora of social solidarity networks that target to assist vulnerable social groups to cope with crisis' detrimental impacts signifying one of the—scarce—positive outcomes of the Greek crisis. As Sotiropoulos (2014: 31) underlines:

> The emergence of civil society in the wake of the economic crisis was a positive development for Greece. Compared to the pre-crisis period, more citizens participated in collective efforts to preserve the living standards of the population and exercise their rights.... This was a turn in the evolution of civil society.

To the best of our knowledge, previous studies explore neither the prevalence of volunteering in social solidarity networks (such as food banks, social medical centres, exchange networks, time banks) nor the profiles of citizens volunteering in such networks using nationally representative data during the Greek crisis. LIVEWHAT project provides such data and a unique opportunity to explore a distinct facet of the Greek crisis reflecting some positive actions which individuals have taken up as a result of the negative conditions generated by the economic crisis.

Individual-Level Attributes of Volunteering

Volunteering is considered a complex and multidimensional phenomenon embracing different definitions, meanings, functions, and motivations developed in a variety of disciplines and theoretical approaches (Musick and Wilson 2008; Hustinx et al. 2010). Sociologists primarily inspired from Durkheim's classical work (1893) of social solidarity and social order view volunteering as a social phenomenon which involves social relations and interactions among individuals, volunteer groups/associations/organizations, and as a critical form of social solidarity and cohesion that binds society members together (Hustinx et al. 2010).

In political science, volunteering acts as a critical form of civic engagement and an expression of democratic values or as Theiss-Morse and Hibbing (2005: 230) put it a way "to instil civic values, enhance political behavior, and improve democracy and society". Psychologists focus on key psychological traits such as extraversion, agreeableness, resilience, and so on (Bekkers 2005; Matsuba et al. 2007) that impact on the predisposition of an individual to volunteer. Economic scientists adopt a rational-based approach viewing volunteering as a form of unpaid labour where volunteers undertake activity depending on the consuming resources and the rewards they may gain through volunteering (Wilson 2000; Musick and Wilson 2008; Hustinx et al. 2010; Wilson 2012).

Given the disciplinary heterogeneity as captured in the different meanings and functions of volunteering, some scholars synthesize hybrid theoretical approaches. For instance, Wilson and Musick (1997) develop a structural approach that leads to an integrated theory of human, social, and cultural capital predictors forming volunteering. Einolf and Chambre (2011) construct a hybrid theory of volunteering using similar classifications to Wilson and Musick (1997), including individual characteristics (cultural capital), resources (human capital), and social factors (social capital).[3] One of the most well-known hybrid theoretical approaches is developed by Hustinx et al. (2010) recognizing the relevance of sociological, political, economic, and psychological dimensions to the study of volunteering.

The present study draws on Hustinx et al. (2010) hybrid mapping by focusing specifically on the individual-level social and political attributes of volunteering. The main reasons for applying the specific approach are associated with methodological as well as theoretical issues. With respect to the former, the study's questionnaire includes items that could capture the social and political characteristics of volunteering. At the theoretical level, Hustinx et al. (2010) emphasize alternative streams of theorizing that enrich our knowledge beyond the conventional assumptions and match with the special features of volunteering specifically in social solidarity networks. Under such framework, as social solidarity networks represent a specific domain of volunteering (Musick and Wilson 2008) associated with specific activities (i.e. providing support to those affected by the crisis) and structure,[4] the literature review and the hypotheses formed take into account these peculiarities. Moreover, the study's approach takes into consideration the intensity of volunteering which varies from active engagement, that is, actively engaging in activities to passive involvement (or participation) including passive members who just pay their dues (Wollebaek and Selle 2002a).[5]

Sociological approaches have been primarily preoccupied with understanding who volunteers, that is, the social profiles of volunteers, and why by concentrating on the social determinants of prosocial behaviour exploring social and demographic attributes such as age, gender, and social class as well as ecological variables including community characteristics and social networks (Musick and Wilson 2008). For the rationale of the present study, of particular interest are individual-level attributes of age, gender, and socio-economic status.

With respect to age, volunteering is more common among middle-aged and elderly individuals; with an exception to high-risk volunteering activities which primarily attract younger individuals (Wilson 2000; Bekkers 2005). With respect to gender, previous research shows the different rates, patterns, and types of volunteering activities that men and women engage (Wilson 2012). Specifically about Europe, Gaskin and Smith (1997) argue that there is no clear pattern of gender differences in volunteering across different countries. However, other scholars underline that gender makes a difference to the kind of volunteering activities men and women do. For instance, women tend to have higher rates of volunteering in activities associated with more caring tasks and lower ones in political activities (Schlozman et al. 1994; Cnaan et al. 1996); a pattern which appears quite consistent across different age groups (Wuthnow

1995). Gender ideologies as well as the gendered division of labour partly explain why women tend to volunteer more in activities associated with caring and compassionate tasks (Wilson 2000).

One of the most consistent findings of volunteering research is that citizens of higher social status tend to volunteer more than those with a lower one (Wilson 2000). For instance, volunteering is more common among the higher educated as they are said to have more civic skills, advanced awareness of problems, and a stronger feeling of efficacy than lower educated citizens (Brady et al. 1995; Nie et al. 1996). Moreover, cross-national studies report that low-income earners tend to volunteer less than higher earners as well as that unemployment status is usually associated with lower levels of volunteering (Pho 2008; Wilson 2012).

Whilst various scholars consider socio-economic status as one of the most critical individual-level attributes of volunteering, others suggest that citizens of lower social status are more likely to engage in informal volunteering sectors than formal ones (Williams 2002). In line with such arguments, Omoto and Snyder (1993) find that higher education is positively correlated with activities in formal volunteering activities (such as political volunteering) but not related to informal community work. Moreover, Musick and Wilson (2008) argue that citizens who have experienced a decline in their economic resources and living standards are more likely to volunteer as a means of dealing with their own hardships and personal problems.

From a sociological perspective, volunteering can be seen as the fundamental expression of community belonging and group identity that binds society together and contributes to individuals' social integration (Wuthnow 1991). Particular emphasis has been placed on the role of feelings of community belonging and social trust as indicators of social cohesion and social capital that increase volunteering. With respect to the former, previous research has shown that citizens who feel they belong to their community are more likely to take voluntary action with others for the common good (Valle Painter 2013).

With respect to interpersonal trust cross-national studies indicate that it is positively associated with volunteering regardless of socio-economic differences (Smidt 1999; Anheier and Kendall 2002). Some scholars underline that social trust is associated with specific types of volunteering activities which primarily target to provide services to individuals in need; on the contrary trusting people are "less likely to volunteer in activities that involve confrontation with authorities or working to change the system" (Musick and Wilson 2008: 46). In line with such arguments, Greenberg (2001) argues that politically oriented volunteering associated with government-related activities, among others, is motivated by lack of interpersonal trust, whereas service-oriented volunteering including non-governmental activism is motivated by trust in others. Similarly, Kohut (1997) in an American study finds that social trust is positively correlated with volunteering in cases of civic engagement in voluntary associations such as churches or schools, whereas volunteering in governmental activities (such as working for a political candidate or campaign, contacting a public official, and attending a political meeting) is associated with lower levels of interpersonal trust. Moreover, Putnam (1993) underlines the positive correlation between social trust, as one of the critical components of social capital and volunteering. However, Putnam (1995a, b, 2000) has paid special attention to the differences between active volunteering and passive membership underlining that interpersonal trust is associated only with the former as it entails a face-to-face interaction.

Based on the above literature capturing the social attributes of volunteering as well as taking into consideration the peculiarities of social solidarity networks, the following hypotheses are formed:

i. Older citizens are more likely to volunteer in or participate to social solidarity networks than younger ones.
ii. As social solidarity networks are primarily involved in helping—in terms of food, health issues, basic material staff, and so on—those severely affected from the crisis, we hypothesize that active volunteering or membership to such networks is more prevalent among women than men.
iii. As social solidarity networks primarily involve informal volunteering that target to assist vulnerable social groups affected by the recession, we hypothesize that the "upper-class" hypothesis will not hold in our study. Instead, we expect that volunteering or membership may involve citizens of different social status. Moreover, as the current recession has severely affected broader segments of the Greek population (Balourdos and Spyropoulou 2012; OECD 2014), we hypothesize that citizens more severely affected are more likely to volunteer in or participate to social solidarity networks as a means of dealing with their own hardships.

iv. Citizens with stronger feelings of community belonging are more likely to volunteer and be members in social solidarity networks. However, taking into consideration Putnam's view on the differences between active volunteering and passive membership with respect to social trust, we would expect that the specific indicator to play a greater role for volunteering rather than membership in social solidarity networks.

The political approach to volunteering highlights its role as a form of civic engagement and as an expression of democratic values. Several studies underpin that volunteers tend to be more politically active in conventional and unconventional behaviours than non-volunteers (Dekker and Van den Broek 1998; Musick and Wilson 2008). The grounds of such an associational behaviour involve, among others, the opportunity to develop specific civic skills (such as the ability to organize a meeting) and the sharing of information as well as the fostering of general trust (Verba et al. 1995; Stolle 1998). In line with such arguments, Hodgkinson's (2003) cross-national findings underline that volunteers are more likely to be politically engaged, in terms of discussing politics and signing petitions, than non-volunteers. Similarly, citizens' interest in politics, participation in protests or demonstrations, working on a political campaign, and lobbying are correlated with volunteering (Verba et al. 1995). Based on such empirical evidence capturing the political dimension of volunteering, we hypothesize that:

v. Citizens engaging in conventional and unconventional political behaviours are more likely to be volunteers or members in social solidarity networks.

Exploring Volunteering in Social Solidarity Networks

In empirical research, commonly used indicators of volunteering involve (a) whether respondents volunteered, (b) for how many organizations, (c) in how many areas, and (d) for how much time they volunteered (Musick and Wilson 2008). In the LIVEWHAT project's questionnaire (a) and (b) are available by asking respondents whether they currently belong and do volunteer/unpaid work (active volunteering) or they just belong (membership) or do not belong (non-membership) in a variety of groups/organizations/associations including social solidarity networks (such as food

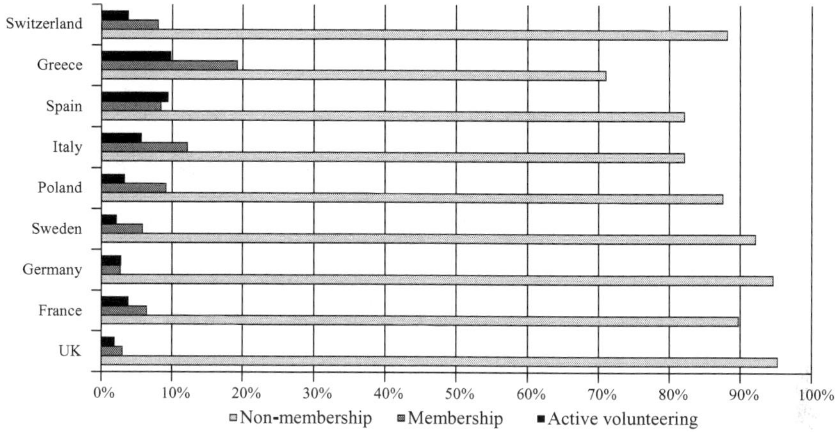

Fig. 7.1 Active volunteering, membership, and non-membership in social solidarity networks across LIVEWHAT countries, 2015

banks, social medical centres, exchange networks, time banks). The specific item measures "volunteering in social solidarity networks" and includes three categories: active volunteering, membership, and non-membership.

Figure 7.1 shows the prevalence of active volunteering, membership, and non-membership in social solidarity networks across countries participating in the LIVEWHAT project. Across all countries non-membership is most prevalent; the highest percentages are reported for the UK (95.2%), Germany (94.6%), and Sweden (92.1%). Except from Germany and Spain, in the rest countries membership is higher than volunteering in social solidarity networks. The highest prevalence of active volunteering is detected in Greece (9.8%) closely followed by Spain (9.4%), whereas membership is most prevalent among Greeks (19.2%). It should be noted that Southern European countries most severely affected by the crisis such as Greece, Spain, and Italy have the highest prevalence of both volunteering and membership compared to less affected countries such as Germany, Sweden, and the UK.

The descriptive analysis in Fig. 7.2 presents active volunteers', members', and non-members' main demographic and social class attributes. Respondents' social status is measured with: (a) main activity ("employed", "unemployed" and "other" including students, retired, doing housework, looking after children or other persons, etc.), (b) educational level ("university and above", "completed secondary education", "less than secondary

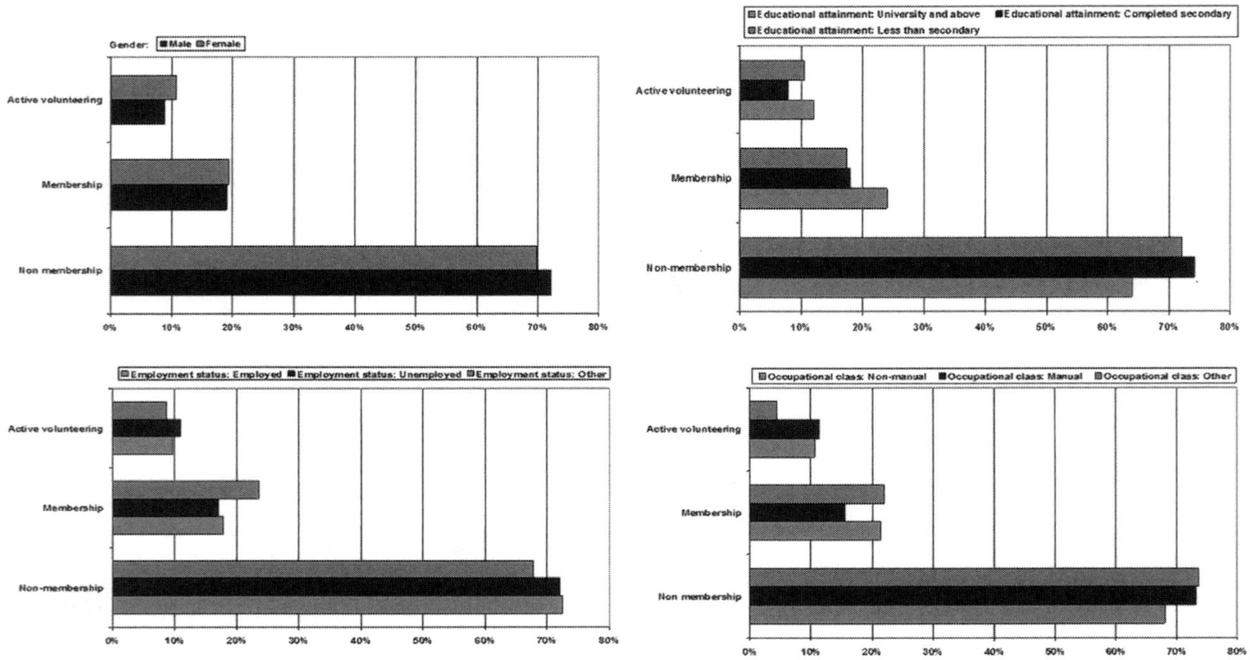

Fig. 7.2 Percentages of main demographic and social status attributes of individuals being active volunteers, members, and non-members in social solidarity networks in Greece, 2015

education"), and (c) class ("nonmanual", "manual", and "other", e.g. farming, military).

As Fig. 7.2 illustrates, slightly more women (10.7%) are volunteers and members (19.3%) in social solidarity networks than men. With respect to educational attainment, non-membership is most prevalent among respondents with completed secondary education (74.2%), and the least prevalent among individuals with higher educational attainment (i.e. university and above) (64.0%). The highest percentages for membership (24.0%) and active volunteering (12.1%) are reported for individuals with higher educational attainment. Membership is the least prevalent among respondents with lower than secondary education (17.4%) and active volunteering among those with completed secondary education (7.8%).

With respect to respondents' employment status, non-membership is most prevalent among employed individuals (72.5%), closely followed from unemployed (72.1%). The highest percentage for membership in social solidarity networks is reported for respondents with "other" employment status (including students, retired, doing housework, looking after children or other persons, etc.) (23.5%) and the lowest one for unemployed individuals (17.0%). However, unemployed have the highest prevalence of active volunteering (10.9%), whereas the lowest one is reported for "other" employment status (8.7%).

With respect to respondents' occupational class, the highest percentage for non-membership is reported for individuals with "other" occupational class (including farming, military, etc.) (73.5%), closely followed by manual workers (73.1%). Membership in social solidarity networks is most prevalent among respondents with "other" occupational class (22.0%) closely followed by nonmanual workers (21.4%). Active volunteering is most prevalent among manual workers (11.3%) and the least prevalent among "other" occupational class (4.5%).

Table 7.1 presents the results from a multinomial logistic ("logit") model using as dependent variable "volunteering in social solidarity networks". The multinomial logit model requires that one category of the dependent variable is the "base" category to serve as a comparison point for all other categories; in the present analysis the base category is "non-membership".

The independent variables include a set of items associated with the social and political approaches of volunteering as developed in the study's research hypotheses. The social approach and related hypotheses of volunteering involve the demographic and social status attributes described

Table 7.1 Multinomial logistic regression of volunteering in social solidarity networks in Greece, 2015 (n = 2048)

	Active Volunteers vs. Non-members[a]		*Members vs. Non-members*[a]	
	B	*Std. Error*	*B*	*Std. Error*
Age	−0.018*	0.007	0.010+	0.006
Male (ref. female)	−0.119	0.190	0.026	0.150
Employment status: employed (ref. unemployed)	−0.196	0.219	0.113	0.182
Employment status: other employment status (ref. unemployed)	0.342	0.253	0.764**	0.200
Educational level: university and above (ref. less than secondary)	−0.160	0.241	0.142	0.193
Educational level: completed secondary (ref. less than secondary)	−0.624**	0.217	−0.173	0.175
Occupational class: nonmanual worker (ref. manual worker)	−0.266	0.225	−0.124	0.190
Occupational class: other (ref. manual worker)	−1.134**	0.402	−0.008	0.264
Living conditions	0.075+	0.042	0.097**	0.033
Social trust	0.059+	0.032	0.037	0.026
Community belonging	0.266**	0.047	0.086*	0.036
Unconventional political behaviours	0.518**	0.072	0.171**	0.057
Intention to vote (1 = Yes, ref. No)	0.842	0.596	0.235	0.343
Intercept	−4.849**	0.797	−3.615**	0.557
Nagelkerke R^2	0.159			

Notes: Table presents multinomial regression coefficients B with standard errors

[a]Reference category is "non-membership"

+$p < 0.10$, *$p < 0.05$, **$p < 0.01$

earlier as well as respondents' living conditions, social trust, and feelings of community belonging as indicators of social cohesion. Respondents' changes in living conditions during the last five years, that is, at the context of the recent crisis, are captured with a composite index which accounts for reductions in staple foods, recreational activities, use of own car, delay of gas payments, water or electricity bills, delay or default on loans instalments, sell assets, cut of phone, TV or internet service, not going on holiday or postponing doctor visits or buying medicines. Higher scores of the composite index indicate higher levels of citizens' deterioration in their living conditions during the past five years.

Social trust is captured with an item measuring on a scale from 0 to 10 respondents' level of trustfulness to people; higher values indicate higher levels of interpersonal trust. Feelings of community belonging are captured with a composite index including the mean score of three items (on a scale from 0 "completely unlike me" to 10 "just like me") asking respondents whether they keep themselves active in the community they live, they feel they do not have much in common with the larger community they live (inversed), and they feel that no one in the community where they live seems to care much about them (inversed). Higher scores of the specific index indicate citizens' intense feelings of community belonging.

With respect to the political attributes of volunteering and the related hypotheses, two measures are used in the analysis measuring involvement in conventional and unconventional political behaviours. The former is measured with a voting intention question (*If there were a general election in your country tomorrow, would you vote?*) and the latter with a composite score including respondents' participation (in the past five years) to unconventional forms of political behaviour such as signing a petition/public letter/campaign appeal, boycotting certain products for political/ethical/environment reasons, deliberately buying products for political/ethical/environment reasons, and attending a demonstration, march, or rally. Higher scores of the specific index indicate higher levels of citizens' unconventional political engagement.

As presented in Table 7.1, the analysis indicates some similar as well as distinct attributes of citizens' active volunteering and membership compared to non-membership in social solidarity networks. With respect to the demographic characteristics, older individuals are significantly less likely to be active volunteers but more likely to be members (significant at $p < 0.10$). Whilst it is hypothesized that older individuals are more likely to be either active volunteers or members in social solidarity networks, it seems that the hypothesis is partly confirmed for membership.

Although the reported associations are non-significant, men are less likely to be active volunteers but more likely to be members than women. The results provide some preliminary support that women tend to get involved in more caring volunteering activities such as the ones included in social solidarity networks targeting to assist socio-economic vulnerable groups affected from the recent crisis.

With respect to respondents' social class characteristics and specifically their employment status most of the reported associations are non-significant. Citizens with "other" employment status (including students, retired, doing housework, looking after children or other persons, etc.) are more likely either being active volunteers or members compared to unemployed; however only the latter is significant.

Although the reported associations are non-significant, citizens with higher educational attainment, that is, university and above, are less likely to be active volunteers but more likely to be members in social solidarity networks compared to individuals with lower educational attainment (i.e. less than secondary education). Moreover, citizens with completed secondary education are significantly less likely to actively volunteer compared to those with less than secondary education; a similar association is reported for membership whilst non-significant. Whilst the associations are non-significant, nonmanual workers are less likely either to volunteer or being members in social solidarity networks compared to manual workers. Individuals of "other" occupational class (e.g. farming, military) are significantly less likely to volunteer; a similar association is reported for membership whilst non-significant.

Whilst the majority of the associations are non-significant, their direction provides some preliminary support to our hypothesis that due to the peculiarities of social solidarity networks (e.g. informal volunteering) and their key tasks to help those affected from the current crisis, volunteering and participation will not necessarily be associated with the upper class but involve citizens of different socio-economic backgrounds. In agreement with the above arguments and in line with the study's hypothesis the analysis indicates that citizens who have experienced deterioration in their living conditions during the past five years are more likely to be either active volunteers (significant at $p < 0.10$) or members in social solidarity networks.

With respect to the hypothesis related to the rest social aspects of volunteering, the findings show that the indicators of social cohesion have positive effects both on volunteering and membership compared to non-membership. More specifically, the analysis illustrates that citizens' feelings of interpersonal trust increases the likelihood of volunteering (significant at $p < 0.10$). A similar association is reported for membership; however it is non-significant. Moreover, citizens with a strong sense of community belonging are significantly more likely to actively volunteer and being members in social solidarity networks.

With respect to the political approach of volunteering, the findings partly support the study's hypothesis. Conventional political engagement such as voting intention has a positive impact both on volunteering and membership; however the reported associations are non-significant. Citizens engaged in unconventional behaviours are significantly more likely to be active volunteers and members in social solidarity networks.

Discussion

In the context of the recent global economic crisis, Greece enforced a severe austerity regime that has put enormous strain on its citizens. Greeks have experienced an unprecedented deterioration in their living and working conditions traced in wage and pension reductions, public spending cuts in health and social security, record unemployment, and poverty rates (Balourdos and Spyropoulou 2012; OECD 2014; Petmesidou and Guillén 2015). Most importantly, an increasing segment of the population has become unable to cover basic needs (such as food, clothing, education, and healthcare) that are considered essential for a decent standard of living. Under such devastating conditions, the emergence of social solidarity networks and the increasing trend of volunteers targeting to assist those in need signify the evolution of the Greek civil sector as the most positive outcomes during the recession (Sotiropoulos 2014; Clarke 2015). In line with such arguments Garefi and Kalemaki (2013: 7) argue:

> A new era for civil society organizations started in 2009 and is still developing today. Since 2009 there has been a boom in informal citizen networks and grassroots movements shaping an "alternative", "parallel" economy in Greece. Despite the poor tradition of Greece in the field, a rather stronger "informal" civil society has emerged.

It should be noted that whilst past research has consistently underpinned the lower levels of volunteering in Greece compared to other European countries (e.g. European Commission 2007, 2010, 2011), the present findings show that in the specific domain volunteering and membership is more prevalent in Greece than in the rest countries participating in LIVEWHAT project.

Drawing on Hustinx et al. (2010) hybrid mapping of volunteering, the study explores the social and political attributes of individuals being active volunteers and members in social solidarity networks during recessionary times in Greece. With respect to their demographic characteristics, although some of the reported associations are non-significant, there is some preliminary evidence that younger citizens and women are more likely to actively volunteer, whereas older citizens and men are more likely to be members in social solidarity networks.

The analysis provides some preliminary evidence which partly supports study's hypotheses that volunteering in social solidarity networks does not fit with the mainstream of theorizing about the "upper-class" involvement. According to Hustinx et al. (2010) individuals of lower social class are more likely to engage in informal volunteering rather than formal one. As argued earlier social solidarity networks primarily involve citizens' informal volunteering in order to support those severely affected from the crisis (Garefi and Kalemaki 2013). Whilst the reported associations are non-significant, their direction indicates that employed citizens, higher educated, and non-manual workers are less likely to actively volunteer; on the contrary, employed and higher educated citizens are more likely to be members. Such preliminary evidence partly rejects the "upper class" hypothesis of active volunteering and unveils the distinct individual-level attributes in forming active volunteering and membership in social solidarity networks in Greece.

Moreover, the findings show that individuals who have experienced deteriorating living conditions during the crisis are more likely to volunteer or being members in social solidarity networks. Such evidence fits with Musick and Wilson's (2008) arguments that citizens with declining economic resources and living standards are more likely to volunteer as a means of coping with their own hardships they are facing in life. Similar findings are reported from scholars conducting research on social solidarity networks during the Greek recession highlighting that:

> Volunteers are not necessarily upper- or middle-class citizens but also the unemployed who have free time, citizens who experience social isolation as a side effect of the economic crisis and employees and workers obtaining very low wages or having precarious jobs who are both participants and beneficiaries of social solidarity activities (Sotiropoulos and Bourikos 2014: 51).

Inspired from Putnam's view (1995a, b, 2000) about the differences between active volunteering and membership, we hypothesized that as the former entails a face-to-face interaction may involve citizens with greater levels of interpersonal trust. The analysis indicates that social trust has a positive significant impact on volunteering[6] and a non-significant one on membership; however community belonging significantly increases both volunteering and membership in social solidarity networks. It should be noted that Putnam's perspective has been challenged by other scholars reporting that passive membership is associated with higher levels of social capital (as captured through measured as social trust, civic engagement, and social networks) compared to non-members (Wollebæk 2000; Wollebæk and Selle 2002b; Wollebaek and Selle 2003).

In agreement with past research (Verba et al. 1995; Dekker and Van den Broek 1998; Hodgkinson 2003; Musick and Wilson 2008), volunteers and members are more likely to be politically engaged than non-members, such finding holds specifically for unconventional political behaviours where significant associations are reported.

Despite the potential merits of the study, there are a few limitations that need to be addressed. A primary limitation of the analysis is that the data applied are cross-sectional; hence we are unable to determine the direction of causal relationships. For example, does political engagement or interpersonal trust lead to volunteering/membership in social solidarity networks or does volunteering/membership in such networks increases citizens' political engagement and social trust?[7] Similar concerns over selections bias have consistently plagued the volunteering empirical research (Wilson 2000). Another limitation of the present study is that due to the lack of relevant items in the project's questionnaire information about the time volunteers devote and their specific tasks could not be measured. Such information could shed more light on the intensity of volunteering as well as on specific activities volunteers engage in to assist those severely affected from the crisis.

Nevertheless, the study provides some preliminary evidence on one of the positive outcomes of the Greek recession and questions the dominant view of the anaemic volunteering tradition in Greece. The present findings could be further enriched with qualitative approaches including in-depth interviews with volunteers that would allow a deeper understanding of how they frame their activities in social solidarity networks during recessionary times.

Notes

1. Eurostat, General government gross debt—annual data. Available from: http://epp.eurostat.ec.europa.eu/tgm/table.do?tab=table&plugin=1&language=en&pcode=teina225 [Last accessed: 7/7/2016].
2. MSCI (2013). *MSCI Announces the Results of the 2013 Annual Market Classification Review*. Geneva, NYSE:MSCI. Retrieved from http://www.msci.com/eqb/pressreleases/archive/2013_Mkt_Class_PR.pdf.
3. Einolf and Chambre (2011) disaggregated the social factors into social context, social roles, and social integration to gain more insights about their relationship with volunteering.
4. As argued earlier, social solidarity networks primarily involve informal volunteering.
5. It should be noted that patterns of intensity of membership are not always dichotomous, they should be perceived as a spectrum ranging from entirely passive at one extreme and extremely active volunteering at the other; however in between there are different levels of active and passive participation (Wollebaek and Selle 2002a).
6. Significant at $p < 0.10$.
7. Several studies explore the reciprocal effects of volunteering and social trust (see Stolle 1998; Bekkers 2012).

References

Afouxenidis, A., & Gardiki, M. (2014). Mapping Civil Society in Contemporary Greece: Problems and Perspectives (in Greek). *The Greek Review of Social Research, 143B*, 33–53.

Anheier, H., & Kendall, J. (2002). Interpersonal Trust and Voluntary Associations. *British Journal of Sociology, 53*, 343–362.

Balourdos, D., & Spyropoulou, N. (2012). Portraits of Poverty in Crisis Ridden Greece. In A. Mouriki et al. (Eds.), *The Social Portrait of Greece: Facets of the Crisis (in Greek)*. Athens: National Centre of Social Research.

Bekkers, R. (2005). Participation in Voluntary Associations: Relations with Resources, Personality, and Political Values. *Political Psychology, 26*, 439–454.

Bekkers, R. (2012). Trust and Volunteering: Selection or Causation? Evidence from a 4 Year Panel Study. *Political Behavior, 34*, 225–247.

Bourikos, D. (2013). *Social Solidarity in Greek Crisis: A New Wave of Civil Society Growth or a Consolidation of Fragmented Social Citizenship? (in Greek)*. Athens: Hellenic Foundation for European and Foreign Policy.

Brady, H., Verba, S., & Schlozman, K. (1995). Beyond SES: A Resource Model of Political Participation. *American Political Science Review, 89*, 269–295.

Clarke, J. (2015). Solidarity and Survival: A Multidisciplinary Exploration of Volunteering During the Greek Crisis. In J. Clarke, A. Huliaras, & D. Sotiropoulos (Eds.), *Austerity and the Third Sector in Greece: Civil Society at the European Frontline*. London: Ashgate.

Cnaan, R., Handy, F., & Wadsworth, M. (1996). Defining Who Is a Volunteer: Conceptual and Empirical Considerations. *Nonprofit and Voluntary Sector Quarterly, 25*, 364–383.

Dekker, P., & Van den Broek, A. (1998). Civil Society in Comparative Perspective. *VOLUNTAS: International Journal of Voluntary and Nonprofit Organizations, 9*(1), 11–38.

Durkheim, É. (1893). *De la Division du Travail Social*. Paris: Alcan.

Einolf, C., & Chambre, S. (2011). Who Volunteers? Constructing a Hybrid Theory. *International Journal of Nonprofit and Voluntary Sector Marketing, 16*, 298–310.

European Commission. (2007). *Special Eurobarometer 273/Wave 66.3. European Social Reality*. Brussels: European Commission.

European Commission. (2010). *Volunteering in the European Union*. Brussels: European Commission, Educational Audiovisual & Culture Executive Agency.

European Commission. (2011). *Special Eurobarometer Wave 75.2. Volunteering and Intergenerational Solidarity*. Brussels: European Commission.

Garefi, I., & Kalemaki, E. (2013). *Informal Citizen Networks: The Case of Greece*. A Deliverable of the Project: "The Theoretical, Empirical and Policy Foundations for Building Social Innovation in Europe" (TEPSIE), European Commission-7th Framework Programme. Brussels: European Commission, DG Research.

Gaskin, K., & Smith, J. (1997). *A New Civic Europe? A Study of the Extent and Role of Volunteering*. London: National Center for Volunteering.

Greenberg, M. (2001). Elements and Test of a Theory of Neighborhood Civic Participation. *Research in Human Ecology, 8*, 40–51.

Hodgkinson, V. (2003). Volunteering in Global Perspective. In P. Dekker & L. Halman (Eds.), *The Values of Volunteering: Cross-Cultural Perspectives*. New York: Kluwer Academic.

Houliaras, A. (2015). Greek Civil Society: The Neglected Causes of Weakness. In J. Clarke, A. Huliaras, & D. Sotiropoulos (Eds.), *Austerity and the Third Sector in Greece: Civil Society at the European Frontline*. London: Ashgate.

Hustinx, L., Cnaan, A., & Handy, F. (2010). Navigating Theories of Volunteering: A Hybrid Map for a Complex Phenomenon. *Journal for the Theory of Social Behaviour, 40*(4), 410–434.

Jones, N., Malesios, C., Iosifides, T., & Sofoulis, C. M. (2008). Social Capital in Greece: Measurement and Comparative Perspectives. *South European Society & Politics, 13*(2), 175–193.

Jones, N., Proikaki, M., & Roumeliotis, S. (2015). Social Capital Levels in Greece in Times of Crisis. In J. Clarke, A. Huliaras, & D. Sotiropoulos (Eds.), *Austerity and the Third Sector in Greece: Civil Society at the European Frontline*. London: Ashgate.

Kalogeraki, S., Velonaki, M., & Papadaki, M. (2016, June 18–19). *Exploring Alternative Forms of Resistance to the Greek Economic Crisis' Impacts*. Paper Presented at ISCAR Conference "Cultural-Historical Activity and Socio-cultural Research at Times of the Contemporary Crisis: Implications for Education and Human Development", University of Crete, Rethymno, Greece.

Karamichas, J. (2007). The Impact of the Summer 2007 Forest Fires in Greece: Recent Environmental Mobilizations, Cyber-activism and Electoral Performance. *South European Society and Politics, 12*(4), 521–533.

Kohut, A. (1997). *Trust and Citizen Engagement in Metropolitan Philadelphia: A Case Study*. Philadelphia: Pew Research Center for the People and the Press.

Kousis, M., & Paschou, M. (2014, September 3–6). *Portraying Alternative Forms of Resilience in Hard Economic Times: Theoretical and Methodological Considerations*. Paper Presented at the ECPR General Conference, Glasgow.

Loukidou, K. (2013). *Formal and Informal Civil Society Associations in Greece: Two Sides of the Same Coin?* (Greek Politics Specialist Group (GPSG) Working Paper No. 13). Available at: http://www.gpsg.org.uk/wp-content/uploads/2013/07/Working_Paper_13.pdf. Accessed 5 Oct 2016.

Lyrintzis, C. (2002). Greek Civil Society in the 21st Century. In P. C. Ioakimidis (Ed.), *Greece in the European Union: The New Role and the New Agenda*. Athens: Ministry of Press and Mass Media.

Matsaganis, M., & Leventi, C. (2014). Poverty and Inequality During the Great Recession in Greece. *Political Studies Review, 12*(2), 209–223.

Matsuba, M., Hart, D., & Atkins, R. (2007). Psychological and Social-structural Influences on Commitment to Volunteering. *Journal of Research in Personality, 41*, 889–907.

Mouzelis, N. (1995). Modernity, Late Development and Civil Society. In J. A. Hall (Ed.), *Civil Society: Theory, History, Comparison*. Cambridge: Polity Press.

Musick, M., & Wilson, J. (2008). *Volunteers: A Social Profile*. Bloomington: Indiana University Press.

Nie, N., Junn, J., & Stehlik-Barry, K. (1996). *Education and Democratic Citizenship in America*. Chicago: University of Chicago Press.

OECD. (2014). *Society at a Glance 2014, Highlights: GREECE, The Crisis and Its Aftermath*. Paris: OECD Publishing.

Omoto, A., & Snyder, M. (1993). Volunteers and Their Motivations: Theoretical Issues and Practical Concerns. *Nonprofit Management & Leadership, 4*, 157–176.

Petmesidou, M., & Guillén, A. (Eds.) (2015). *Economic Crisis and Austerity in Southern Europe: Threat or Opportunity for a Sustainable Welfare State* (OSE Paper Series Research Paper No. 18). Available at http://www.ose.be/files/

publication/OSEPaperSeries/Petmesidou_Guillen_2015_OseResearchPaper18.pdf. Accessed 2 Oct 2016.

Pho, Y. (2008). The Value of Volunteer Labor and the Factors Influencing Participation: Evidence for the United States from 2002 Through 2005. *Review of Income and Wealth, 54*(2), 220–236.

Putnam, R. (1993). *Making Democracy Work. Civic Traditions in Modern Italy.* Princeton: Princeton University Press.

Putnam, R. (1995a). Bowling Alone: America's Declining Social Capital. *Journal of Democracy, 6*(1), 65–78.

Putnam, R. (1995b). Tuning In, Tuning Out: The Strange Disappearance of Social Capital in America. *Political Science and Politics, 28*(4), 664–683.

Putnam, R. (2000). *Bowling Alone: The Collapse and Revival of American Community.* New York: Simon and Schuster.

Rakopoulos, T. (2014). The Crisis Seen from Below, Within, and Against: From Solidarity Economy to Food Distribution Cooperatives in Greece. *Dialectical Anthropology, 38*(2), 189–207.

Rozakou, K. (2011). The Pitfalls of Volunteerism: The Production of the New, European Citizen in Greece. *European Institute for Progressive Cultural Policies.* Available at http://eipcp.net/policies/rozakou/en. Accessed 1 Oct 2016.

Schlozman, K., Burns, N., & Verba, S. (1994). Gender and the Pathways to Participation: The Role of Resources. *The Journal of Politics, 56*, 963–990.

Simiti, M. (2015). *'Social Need' or 'Choice'? Greek Civil Society During the Economic Crisis* (Hellenic Observatory Papers on Greece and Southeast Europe, Paper No. 95). The London School of Economics and Social Science.

Smidt, C. (1999). Religion and Civic Engagement: A Comparative Analysis. *The Annals of the American Academy of Political and Social Science, 565*, 176–192.

Sotiropoulos, D. (2004). *Formal Weakness and Informal Strength: Civil Society in Contemporary Greece* (Discussion Paper No. 16). London: Hellenic Observatory.

Sotiropoulos, D. (2014). *Civil Society in Greece in the Wake of the Economic Crisis.* Athens: ELIAMEP foundation and the Konrad Adenauer Stiftung.

Sotiropoulos, D., & Bourikos, D. (2014). Economic Crisis, Social Solidarity and the Voluntary Sector in Greece. *Journal of Power, Politics and Governance, 2*(2), 33–53.

Stolle, D. (1998). Bowling Together, Bowling Alone: The Development of Generalized Trust in Voluntary Associations. *Political Psychology, 19*, 497–525.

Theiss-Morse, E., & Hibbing, J. (2005). Citizenship and Civic Engagement. *Annual Review of Political Science, 8*, 227–249.

Valle Painter, C. (2013). *Sense of Belonging: Literature Review.* Ottawa: Citizenship and Immigration Canada.

Vathakou, E. (2015). Citizens' Solidarity Initiatives in Greece During the Financial Crisis. In J. Clarke, A. Huliaras, & D. Sotiropoulos (Eds.), *Austerity and the Third Sector in Greece: Civil Society at the European Frontline.* London: Ashgate.

Verba, S., Schlozman, K., & Brady, H. (1995). *Voice and Equality: Civic Voluntarism in American Politics*. Cambridge, MA: Harvard University Press.
Williams, C. (2002). Harnessing Voluntary Work: A Fourth Sector Approach. *Policy Studies, 23*(3/4), 247–260.
Wilson, J. (2000). Volunteering. *Annual Review of Sociology, 26*, 215–240.
Wilson, J. (2012). Volunteerism Research: A Review Essay. *Nonprofit and Voluntary Sector Quarterly, 41*, 176–212.
Wilson, J., & Musick, M. (1997). Who Cares? Towards an Integrated Theory of Volunteer Work. *American Sociological Review, 62*, 694–713.
Wollebæk, D. (2000). *Participation in Voluntary Associations and the Formation of Social Capital*. Bergen: LOS Centre.
Wollebaek, D., & Selle, P. (2002a). Does Participation in Voluntary Associations Contribute to Social Capital: The Impact of Intensity, Scope and Type. *Nonprofit and Voluntary Sector Quarterly, 31*(1), 32–61.
Wollebæk, D., & Selle, P. (2002b). Passive Support: No Support at All? *Nonprofit Management and Leadership, 13*(2), 187–203.
Wollebaek, D., & Selle, P. (2003). The Importance of Passive Membership. In M. Hooghe & D. Stolle (Eds.), *Generating Social Capital: Civil Society and Institutions in Comparative Perspective*. New York: Palgrave Macmillan.
Wuthnow, R. (1991). *Acts of Compassion*. Princeton: Princeton University Press.
Wuthnow, R. (1995). *Learning to Care*. New York: Oxford University Press.

PART III

The Social Bases of the Crisis

CHAPTER 8

An Island of Bliss—For Everyone? Perceptions and Experiences of the Crisis Across Social Classes in Germany

Johannes Kiess and Christian Lahusen

Introduction

In public debates and the literature, Germany is often pictured as a net beneficiary of the crisis. While experiencing a dramatic demand shock in 2009, which mostly hit the export-led industrial sectors, mechanisms of internal flexibility and the effects of targeted growth packages buffered the external shock. In the following years, the German economy was able to recover fast, building on stable employment and skilled personnel, robust domestic demand, as well as increasing demand for capital goods from world markets. Furthermore, state finances benefitted from low (or often even negative) interest rates due to the state debt crisis in Southern Europe and the resulting safe harbor effect for German state bonds. This allowed for budget consolidation without (more) pressure on welfare spending. However, at closer examination, all that glitters is not gold. After incisive labor market reforms in the 2000s, inequalities and insecurities were rising

J. Kiess (✉) • C. Lahusen
Fakultät I: Seminar für Sozialwissenschaften, University of Siegen, Siegen, Germany

M. Giugni, M.T. Grasso (eds.), *Citizens and the Crisis*, Palgrave Studies in European Political Sociology, https://doi.org/10.1007/978-3-319-68960-9_8

in Germany and the shock of the economic crisis was certainly not helping the middle classes to resolve their "status panic" (Goebel et al. 2010). Thus, while Germany as a whole may have "emerged stronger from the crisis" (Angela Merkel),[1] this optimistic picture potentially papers over the crisis experiences of many, especially in the middle and lower classes. Even without the crisis, the literature provides many findings of economic, social, and political exclusion of considerable proportions within the German public (e.g. Bude 2014; Decker et al. 2012; Schäfer 2015). These consequences are not only felt by those excluded, the lower classes, but also those feeling threatened by exclusion, that is, the (lower) middle classes, and the experience of the economic crisis 2008–2009 has added to this.

Clearly, there have been noticeable consequences of the crisis, both in terms of subjective experience and in terms of objective exposure. This is true, first and foremost, for experiences in the labor market. Admittedly, actual labor market numbers were kept relatively stable throughout the first phase of the crisis 2008–2009 and even improved in the subsequent phase. However, the exhaustive impact on the core industries with, at peak times, 1.5 million workers in short-time schemes (or 5.2% of the total working population, see Brenke et al. (2011); plus those working lesser hours within other internal flexibility measures) did have substantial psychological effects: this had simply not been experienced before in the industrial cores. It must also be kept in mind that the continuing dualization of the German labor market in objective terms, too, means increasingly less protection for growing numbers of workers. Furthermore, even in the recovery period since 2010 where pressures on job security declined, the pressure on working conditions and performances rose (Detje et al. 2013). Thus, we argue that in Germany, too, crisis experiences are part of people's day-to-day lives.

Moreover, we expect these experiences of crisis to be stratified by class. Indeed, the middle classes might feel the pressure because they have, compared to the lower classes, "something to lose" without the economic security of the upper classes. While middle class is a contested and woolly concept, higher levels of income, education, and social capital, predominantly service sector employment, political self-efficacy, and certain types of values are considered to be characterizing (Nolte and Hilpert 2007: 31–33). These resources come with expectations of status. The middle classes are in a position in between (Simmel 1908: 451–452) on the one hand, but have in Germany's postwar history always been the center of attention and national self-assurance. Thus, potentially, the experience of (permanent) crisis touching the middle classes goes to the core of the self-understanding of a vast majority of the Germans—according to our data, 43.5% of the Germans consider themselves as middle class, another 22% as lower middle class (see below).

In this chapter, we aim to examine the experience and perception of crisis in Germany with an analytical focus on social classes. Our general research questions read as follows: which social groups and classes in Germany are particularly crisis sensitive and what factors amplify perceptions of crisis? Are the middle classes more susceptible to the crisis, when compared to the perceptions of other social classes? Or are other factors that cross class boundaries, for example, specific forms of individual deprivation or political attitudes, the driver for crisis susceptibility? To this end, in this chapter, we first review the literature on social vulnerability, precarity, and risks of social degradation in order to develop our research hypotheses. We proceed then with the presentation of our data and method. In what follows, we will present and discuss our findings. Finally we conclude with a contextualization of these findings.

Pressure on German Social Classes in Times of Crisis

We start this section with a summary of the history of the crisis in Germany to provide contextual knowledge as basis for our argument. We then review the state of the art on precarization in Germany, including insecurities in the middle classes and the effects of the continuing dualization of the German labor market. We will mainly limit ourselves to the German case and rely on mostly German literature which, however, should be to the benefit of the reader since we discuss it in English. Finally, we will develop our hypotheses at the end of this section leading to our empirical assessment of the perception of crisis in Germany.

The common depiction of Germany as a beneficiary of the crisis often overlooks the historical slump that the German economy went through in 2009. German GDP dropped by 5.6% in 2009 (EU 28: 4.4%) which was by far the sharpest decrease of GDP since World War II. Following the institutional legacy of the "German model" of a coordinated market economy (Hall and Soskice 2001) with strong industrial relations and a focus (at least in the export-led chemical as well as metal, automobile, and electronic industries) on high-skill, high-wage labor, external flexibility was used only on the fringes of the labor market. The unemployment rate went up only slightly, mostly due to the dismissal of temporary workers, a relatively new phenomenon in the German labor market. The bulk of employment, however, was secured by measures of internal flexibility like working-time accounts and then short-time work schemes. It is reported that alone by granting short-time allowances for 1.5 million workers during the peak period in 2009, more than 300,000 full-time equivalents were secured (Brenke et al. 2011). Respectively, the stabilization of the labor market arguably also stabilized domestic demand and thus had further economic and labor market effects. Still, the thorough use of short-time work schemes and the exceptional growth packages also evince the pressure for action on policy makers. While the slump was dramatic, with 4.1% in 2010 and 3.7% GDP growth in 2011, the recovery was fast and strong as well and by 2011 the economy had compensated its losses.

Compared to other European countries and specifically the countries participating in LIVEWHAT the German crisis was over fast. While growth was restored in most countries by 2010, the discourse shifted from financial and economic crisis to state debt crisis. The high fiscal effort to rescue European banks unloaded in pressure on the state finances especially in Ireland, Spain, Portugal, Italy, and Greece. This corresponded in Germany with the discursive externalization of the crisis (cf. Kiess 2015a). The German budget was, in the light of revitalized export industries, not considered problematic while financial markets now targeted the weaker economies. More importantly, in the debate, the origin of the crisis as a financial market crisis—strongly connected to the changing German model of capitalism from Teilhabekapitalismus (participatory capitalism) to competitive capitalism embedded in global financial capitalism (Busch and Land 2012)—was not a major subject anymore. The crisis, we argue, hit Germany in a phase where it consolidated its changed model of capitalism. This included most specifically a radicalization of its export orientation (export surplus increasing from 1.36% of GDP in 1998 to 7% in 2007, see Busch and Land 2012: 129) which at least partly was the result of strict wage restraints, liberalization of the labor market, and further pressures on labor like restrictions on welfare benefits and lower pensions (Agenda 2010 reforms).

Our analysis in this chapter builds on the assumption that the crisis did have an impact in German society, even though these effects are linked also to broader and long-standing transformations. The crisis seems to have amplified or accelerated the abovementioned changes in the structure of capitalism and its implications for labor markets and living conditions. Scholarly writing helps us to specify more clearly the type of consequences this situation implies. Two strands of research in particular will be employed to identify competing research assumptions and hypotheses: studies addressing the transformations of the class structures, in particular the position of the middle classes therein, and research on social exclusion, vulnerability, and precarity, which, in its concern for social degradation, move beyond established class structure analysis.

A first important research strand is that related to the themes of the potential destabilization and fragmentation of the German middle classes. This research interest emanates from the traditional picture of German postwar society as a "leveled middle-class society" (nivellierte Mittelstandsgesellschaft, cf. Schelsky 1954). Even though it is not entirely clear what exactly "middle class" includes, ever since the postwar era, the notion is still cherished as a social norm. This is illustrated by the fact that in the 1990s 58% of the Germans considered themselves to be middle class (Noll 1996: 492). In 2008, this number only slightly changed to 56% (Noll and Weick 2011: 3). If we take income as reference point for social class position, we can see that in 2005 only 35.2% of the German population had between 100% and 200% of the median income and were statistically counted as "middle class" (Nolte and Hilpert 2007: 31). This suggests that considerably more people see themselves as belonging to the middle class than we might think of when looking at "hard" criteria. In this sense, self-proclaimed class-affiliation indicates also a sense of being placed in the middle of society, economically, socially, culturally, and politically.

This observation helps to identify the implications of crisis-driven transformations: if belonging to the middle class is a social norm, we might expect that the inability to fulfill this norm and to find a place in the middle of society will result in "status panic" (Bude 2014; Schimank et al. 2014). This follows from the specific situation of the middle class, having "an upper and a lower edge, in the sense of continuously giving and taking individuals to and from both the upper and lower classes", which has long been a topic in sociology (Simmel 1908: 451f, own translation). Other authors speak of the "exhausted" middle class (Heinze 2011; Mau 2012) in order to highlight that these strata are not necessarily confronted directly with downward social mobility, but experience growing challenges and try to keep their position and adequate future perspectives for their children. What is more, with the growing uncertainty and destabilization, also the (peer) pressure to comply with the norm increases (Koppetsch 2013).

This research strand builds on a growing literature that is particularly interested in the economic situation of households and the growing precarity of living conditions as well as that on the hollowing out of the middle class (Geiling et al. 2001; Bude and Willisch 2006; Lessenich 2009; Vogel 2009). The most apparent result of this process is the polarization of incomes, which is characterized particularly by a decrease of middle-range households with a simultaneous increase of the groups with lowest and highest incomes. Following the German Institute for Economic Research (DIW), this trend is definitely to be interpreted as shrinkage of the middle class (Grabka and Frick 2008), since the polarization of incomes results in the losing of middle-class members (Goebel et al. 2010). Similar findings have been presented in comparative studies (Mau 2014; Pressman 2007).

Even though some studies do not agree with the outright polarization hypothesis, they still acknowledge the explosive nature of such growing pressures in the center of society (Vogel 2010; Marg 2014). Apparently, in the most recent economic upswing the size of the middle class is not increasing again (Bosch and Kalina 2015). And even the number of the poor is not going down after the crisis: in 2014, 15.4% of the population was considered poor compared to 14.7% in 2005 (Wohlfahrtsverband 2016: 14). This is connected to what has been discussed as dualization of the labor market, of industrial relations and of social security, all of which tend to serve insiders and disadvantage outsiders (Jackson and Sorge 2012; Palier 2012; Palier and Thelen 2010). As Haug and Stoy (2015) argue, the crisis management and changes in welfare policies continued to follow the path of dualization. Consequently, some authors speak of the crisis of a model of society (Heinze 2011: 8), even more so in the light of globalization and the re-measurement of inequality (Beck 2008). Globalization, many observers argue, produces a new cleavage between winners and losers (Kriesi et al. 2012; Teney et al. 2014; Kiess et al. 2017).

A second research strand focuses more intensively on risks of social exclusion and degradation, which are not necessarily restricted to income structures and social classes. Scholars argue that ongoing transformations of modern societies are increasing the social vulnerability of large parts of the population: they augment hardships and contribute to the social exclusion of less privileged strata (Kronauer 1998; Kieselbach 2003), but they generalize risks also by subjecting more settled strata of the population to status instabilities and uncertain biographic transitions (Ranci 2010). In fact, the range of groups affected by risks of social exclusion increases and comprises, for instance, single parents, young adults in transition from school to work, families in cities with a tight housing market, women and men in caregiving responsibilities, migrants, aged employees threatened by dismissals, old-age pensioners, and citizens living in deprived neighborhoods or regions. Research has highlighted a number of reasons for this development: most importantly transformations of work and employment, of informal networks and social capital, and of welfare state benefits (Esping-Anderson 1999; Castel 2002; Ranci 2010).

In regard to work and employment more specifically, we see a continuous deregulation and flexibilization of labor markets (Countouris 2007) that increase the instability of employment and enlarge the range of atypical and precarious jobs. The "zone of precariousness" has severely expanded into the general population (Ehrenreich 1989; Furlong 2007) and has increased the experiences of instability and insecurity among the middle classes as well (Burzan 2008; Castel and Dörre 2009). Risks of social degradation and exclusion increase also through a potential weakening of informal networks of sociability and support. In fact, research has shown that social isolation and the perception of being left out of society is stronger among those groups with a more vulnerable social position, for example, the poor and the jobless, single parents and households, sick and disabled people (Böhnke 2006, 2008 2015). Moreover, the transformation of gender roles, family models, and household structures also affects patterns of sociability, for example, by putting family-based networks under strain and placing more emphasis on peers and friends (Baas 2008). This might well lead to social isolation and solitude across various social classes and groups (e.g. among single households, men, and single partners), thus increasing fears about social degradation and the susceptibility to economic shocks. Finally, scholarly writing has insisted that the reform of the welfare state is boosting uncertainties and instabilities (Clayton and Pontusson 1998; Steijn et al. 1998; Wacquant 2010). In this regard, we can point to the retrenchment of social rights and benefits, the increased conditionality of services and provisions, and the growing importance of private pension and insurance schemes to the detriment of state-led redistribution. Also in this regard, we might expect that these retrenchments increase the susceptibility for economic threats among recipients of social benefits across various social classes.

The political implications of this increased vulnerability have moved to the center stage in scholarly writing, particularly because increased anxieties and frustrations now also affect what are understood as "the middle classes" (Heitmeyer and Anhut 2008; Burzan 2008; Castel and Dörre 2009; Decker et al. 2012). This is especially true of (perceived) downward mobility. Consequently, perceived deprivation is repeatedly found to increase authoritarian, anti-democratic, and anti-immigrant attitudes (Pettigrew 2002; Rippl and Baier 2005; Decker and Brähler 2006; Buraczynska et al. in press). Furthermore, polarization can, combined with decreasing experiences of alienation, lead to general societal disintegration (Heitmeyer and Anhut 2008). In this context, new forms of political protest, including "occupy", mobilization against infrastructure projects, but also right-wing extremist protests against immigration, have made their appearance (Geiges et al. 2015; Butzlaff 2016; Kiess 2015b). These political implications are of particular relevance for our study, because they also might entail a stronger sensitivity for economic shocks. In particular, crisis susceptibility may be a question of political attitudes rather than social factors. Those who already are critical toward the government and the political system might as well be more critical about the economic situation, regardless of social background and across classes.

In sum, previous research has assembled enough evidence in order to corroborate the assumption that the crisis has affected German society in a more substantial manner than we might expect when looking at macroeconomic indicators. The crisis might accentuate the sensitivity to economic shocks, because they reinforce ongoing transformations of social reality in the "middle" of German society. Before this backdrop, we wish to approach the public perception of the economic crisis. Building on the literature addressing the precarious state of the middle classes in Germany, we ask: which groups and classes in Germany are particularly crisis sensitive, and what factors amplify perceptions of crisis? In order to answer these questions, we propose to test a number of research assumptions and hypotheses, which are directly linked to the previous description of available scientific evidence. Overall, we suggest distinguishing between three sets of assumptions with related factors.

First, it is plausible to assume that the social-structural position of respondents will be a determinant of crisis perceptions. In this regard, we propose to distinguish between objective and subjective components of class positions. On the one hand, we argue that crisis perceptions might be determined by objective class position in three different ways: crisis sensitivity will be distributed in a curvilinear pattern along the social ladder, when focusing on occupational status groups, income, and education. The guiding hypothesis resides on the notion that middle classes might have a stronger feeling of having something to lose in times of crisis when compared to the underprivileged classes. Additionally, this feeling may also be stronger among the middle classes when compared to the upper strata, which might be at levels that prevent them from worrying about economic shocks. On the other hand, we suggest that crisis sensitivity is not directly linked to objective class positions, but rather to the subjective perception of class alignments. Hence, it is not the specific amount of income or education that matters for crisis sensitivity, but rather if respondents feel themselves to be a member of society's core, that is, the middle class, that is threatened by economic shocks. In this respect, it is probable that the class background of the family might play an important role, because parents' social class and the social habitus transmitted by them will shape subjective class affiliation.

Second, we argue that social vulnerability will impact on crisis perceptions, too. Here, we wish to add those factors that are not linked to social class in the strict sense, but might increase the risks of social degradation and exclusion, namely, economic and social deprivation. In the first instance, it might not be the professional status and income that matter, but the objective employment status in general and perceived employment stability in particular. In other words: precarity is the factor to be taken into consideration. This includes relative deprivation, that is, the feeling of being worse off compared to other reference groups or compared to earlier times. Moreover, we assume that social isolation will increase crisis susceptibility, because it deprives people from the material or emotional support of informal networks and increases the feeling of being exposed directly to economic shocks. In this sense, household structure, family constellations, and social contact networks will be decisive factors.

Finally, it is necessary to address also the political dimension of crisis perceptions. On the one hand, this political dimension has to do with political institutions and their public perceptions. As we have seen before, studies have put an emphasis on welfare retrenchment and the contribution of these reforms to the growing anxieties about social degradation within the public sphere. Therefore, we can assume that the confidence with the performance of the welfare state will be directly linked to the trust in its ability to buffer off economic shocks and collective harms.

Consequently, we assume that respondents being less confident with the performance of the state in policy fields directly linked to social security might also be those citizens more sensitive to the crisis. On the other hand, we need to be aware that crisis perceptions are mediated by political ideas and preferences. Economic threats, social risks, and increased vulnerabilities might not determine the crisis susceptibility, because it is rather the frustration with the political establishment in its willingness and ability to respond to the needs of the affected population that increases the worries of living in times of (uncontrolled and harmful) crisis. Crisis perceptions should consequently be higher among supporters of populist or right-wing ideologies.

A number of control variables will be included into the analysis, because crisis perceptions might vary also by other sociodemographic and contextual factors, such as age, gender, religion, migrant background, and residency.

Measuring Crisis Perception and Class Affiliation

We use a unique data set prepared within the EU project LIVEWHAT across nine European countries. For each country, an online survey was conducted (for more details, see Chap. 1 to this volume) including more than 2000 cases in each country. In Germany, 2.108 persons participated in the survey.

In order to test our hypothesis, we employ multinominal and binominal logistic regression models. Our dependent variable is a measure of whether people think that there is an economic crisis in their country. The original question reads as follows: "Some say that Germany is suffering a very serious economic crisis, others say that we are suffering a crisis but it is not very serious, while others say that there isn't any economic crisis. What do you think?" The variable includes four categories (plus "don't know") and Table 8.1 shows the distribution of answers across nine countries. In comparison, it strikes that German respondents have among the lowest sensitivity to crisis. Only 16.7% think that their country suffers a severe crisis and another 32.2% thinks there is a crisis but that it is not severe. Together, less people in Germany think that there is a crisis at all, even compared to Swedish and Swiss respondents, which have in many respects a similar perception of the crisis. However, if we consider that the question is on the national economy, not about the European economic situation, and that the German economy has not only compensated for the

Table 8.1 Is your country suffering an economic crisis?

Country	*Suffering severe crisis*	*Crisis but not severe*	*No economic crisis*	*Others*	*DN*
UK	37.3%	43.2%	9.7%	1.8%	8%
France	66.9%	16.8%	3.5%	3%	9.8%
Germany	**16.7%**	**32.2%**	**35.3%**	**2.5%**	**13.2%**
Sweden	16.2%	41.8%	24.4%	1.6%	16%
Poland	23.6%	41.7%	22.9%	1.7%	10.1%
Italy	79%	11.8%	3.5%	1.9%	3.8%
Spain	73.6%	17.4%	2.5%	3.8%	2.8%
Greece	88.1%	5.4%	2.5%	2.8%	1.2%
Switzerland	15.3%	51.9%	21.1%	3%	8.7%
Total	46.2%	29.1%	14%	2.5%	8.2%

losses in 2009 but has since been booming, crisis sensitivity still seems quite high. We take this as reason to proceed with our investigation.

As proposed above, we first focus on subjective and objective class belonging as independent variables. Our first variable is occupational class and is based on a range of occupations for self-placement. We assume that occupational status is an important measure for social stratification (Erikson and Goldthorpe 1992; Faunce 1990) and that it affects the way in which individuals cope with change (Hooghe and Marks 2007). Furthermore, occupational status is key for accounting for class-specific fears (Kiess et al. 2017), especially if they are related to job security (Lengfeld and Hirschle 2009) which, we assume, is highly relevant for individuals in times of economic crisis. We recoded this variable into four categories from upper to lower class. Second, we include income class as an independent variable. The original variable used in the survey allowed for self-placement along income deciles. We recoded this in order to have four groups, higher net household incomes exceeding 3.160 €, middle incomes between 2.160 and 3.160 €, lower middle incomes between 1.240 and 2.160 €, and lower incomes below 1.240 € (for distribution see Table 8.2 below). Third, we use education as measure for class belonging. We recoded an inclusive list of educational degrees to three categories, namely, less than secondary education, secondary education, and higher education.

In addition to these objective measures of class belonging, we propose to include a variable measuring subjective association to class on a scale including “upper class”, “upper middle class”, “middle class”, “lower

Table 8.2 Perceived class belonging in nine European countries

Country	*Upper class*	*Middle class*	*Lower middle class*	*Lower middle class*	*Total*
UK	4.1%	36.3%	22.6	37.0	100.0%
France	2.1%	42.5	4.2%	51.3%	100.0%
Germany	**10.4%**	**47.7%**	**24.1%**	**17.8%**	**100.0%**
Sweden	12.3%	46.9%	12.2%	28.5%	100.0%
Poland	6.4%	33.7%	22.0%	38.0%	100.0%
Italy	1.0%	14.8%	30.7%	53.5%	100.0%
Spain	6.4%	37.8%	20.2%	35.6%	100.0%
Greece	3.2%	37.9%	30.4%	28.5%	100.0%
Switzerland	10.7%	43.9%	23.0%	22.5%	100.0%
Total	6.3%	38.1%	21.1%	34.5%	100.0%

middle class", "working class", "lower class", and "other class". Only 0.6% of the respondents placed themselves in the category of "upper class", so we had to combine this one with the next category, namely, "upper middle class" (8.9% of the German cases). This seems justified since both groups should not feel subjected to polarization processes, as assumed for the (lower) middle classes in the section above. In line with findings in the literature, the biggest group places itself as being "middle class" (43.5%), which is more than in all other countries participating in the LIVEWHAT project (see Table 8.2). Another 22% consider themselves "lower middle class", which we keep as category. We combined the 10.4% of the respondents choosing "working class" with the 5.7% choosing "lower class". The remaining answered "other class" (1.7%) or "don't know" (7.2%). Additionally, we propose to consider that the class background of the respondent's family might influence the subjective class affiliation as well. For this purpose, we include a variable measuring the education of the respondent's father (same recoding as education variable above) into the model as a control.

Another set of hypotheses relates to social, economic, and especially job-related deprivation in order to test whether vulnerabilities might be more relevant, when compared to objective and subjective class belonging in a strict sense. Thus, we include a scale measuring relative economic deprivation compiled of five items ($r^2 = 0.75$). To measure social deprivation, we include variables measuring living alone (single item, dummy), frequency of meeting friends (single item, dummy), life satisfaction (ordinal), social trust (single item, ordinal), and social deprivation (two single items, ordinal, reading "If I have difficulties, someone could take care of me" and "If I have difficulties, someone could take care of me financially").

Finally, we include a number of variables measuring the political dimension of crisis susceptibility, namely, a scale measuring political institutional trust ($r^2 = 0.96$), a left-right scale ($r^2 = 0.67$), left-right self-placement (single item, ordinal), satisfaction with democracy (single item, ordinal), an index measuring support of democracy ($r^2 = 0.75$), libertarian-authoritarian scale (aggregate index), a populism scale ($r^2 = 0.88$), political interest (single item, ordinal), political knowledge (dummies), scales for internal ($r^2 = 0.85$) and external political efficacy ($r^2 = 0.55$), and satisfaction with government performance on various topics (eight single items, ordinal).

As sociodemographic controls, we included age (ordinal), gender (dummy), father's educational attainment (dummy), migrant background (dummy), religion (dummy), religiosity (ordinal), and residency (two single items, dummy). All variables were standardized in order to allow for comparison of coefficients in the models.

What Affects People's Perception of Crisis?

We start this further analytical section with a brief look at the relation between the four dimensions of class (occupation, income, education, and perceived belonging) and crisis perception. The simple cross-tabulation shows expected results in all four dimensions. In the occupational dimension, we see stronger support of the "severe crisis" narrative among the middle classes. This supports the claim that it is the middle classes that fear crises even if they have higher status employment than the unskilled workers. Furthermore, the descriptive findings suggest that there is an interrelation between income and crisis susceptibility, that is, the lower the income class, the more people see a severe economic crisis. In regard to education, there is a clear distinction between those holding no or a degree less than secondary education and the higher groups. Finally, people that perceive they belong to the higher and to the middle classes are less eager to think that there is a severe crisis.

Multinominal regression analysis revealed that there are no big differences between the answer categories "no crisis" and "crisis but not severe". Thus, we decided to recode the dependent variable for the subsequent analyses, by merging the two categories. Moreover, it seems advisable to center our focus on differences between the respondents opting for "severe crisis" and the groups being less alarmed by the current situation. For this purpose, we conducted four binominal logistic regression analyses, the findings being summarized in Table 8.4.

Model 1a consists only of the variables measuring social class affiliation. The findings restate the results of Table 8.3. It supports the interpretation that lower classes are more crisis sensitive, at least if we concentrate on subjective class affiliation: the more we move down the social ladder, the stronger the opinion that we are experiencing a severe crisis.[2] It is interesting to note, however, that these effects decrease and are not statistically significant anymore, once we include a set of variables measuring different forms of deprivation (Model 2a): the model gives us an improved picture as relative deprivation and social trust show significant effects along what we have hypothesized above: higher social trust seems to imply lower crisis sensitivity, though with a comparatively low coefficient, and higher relative deprivation seems to imply higher crisis sensitivity.

In Model 3a we included political attitudes as well as items for satisfaction with government performance in various policy fields. General satis-

Table 8.3 Class belonging along three dimensions and perception of crisis (without "other" and "don't know")

Class dimension	*Class belonging*	*Suffering severe crisis*	*Crisis but not severe*	*No economic crisis*	*Total*
Occupational class	Higher class	19.3%	35.8%	44.9%	100.0%
	Service class	20.4%	39.2%	40.4%	100.0%
	Skilled manual	23%	36.4%	40.7%	100.0%
	Unskilled	16.3%	43.1%	40.6%	100.0%
Income class	Upper class	14.7%	35.1%	50.2%	100.0%
	Middle class	16%	37.1%	47%	100.0%
	Lower middle	21.5%	36%	42.6%	100.0%
	Lower class	23.1%	41%	35.9%	100.0%
Educational class	Higher education	18.2%	38%	43.9%	100.0%
	Secondary	18.7%	38.8%	42.3%	100.0%
	Less than secondary	36.8%	36.8%	26.3%	100.0%
Perceived class	Higher class	14.4%	38.7%	47%	100.0%
	Middle class	14.1%	38.4%	47.6%	100.0%
	Lower middle	24%	39.5%	36.5%	100.0%
	Lower class	29.6%	36.8%	33.7%	100.0%

Table 8.4 Logistic regression Models 1a to 4a with upper class as base

	Model 1a $R^2 = 0.0347$	*Model 2a* $R^2 = 0.1281$	*Model 3a* $R^2 = 0.2405$	*Model 4a* $R^2 = 0.254$
Middle class	0.135	0.062	0.009	0.011
Lower middle class	0.735*	0.371	0.269	0.262
Lower class	1.252**	0.656	0.274	0.260
Lower service class	−0.359	−0.421	−0.538	−0.702**
Skilled manual worker	−0.479	−0.472	−0.510	−0.504
Unskilled worker	−0.839*	−0.772*	−0.654	−0.824
Middle income	0.001	−0.162	−0.283	−0.335
Lower middle income	0.200	−0.059	−0.301	−0.343
Lower income	0.092	−0.352	−0.562	−0.633
Secondary education	0.182	0.265	0.472*	0.587*
Less than secondary	0.441	0.388	0.384	0.490
Relative deprivation		0.791**	0.532**	0.514**
Living alone		−0.068	−0.109	−0.079
Social trust		−0.245**	−0.119	−0.133
Friends regularly		0.058	0.105	0.099
Life satisfaction		−0.023	0.107	0.082
Confident in assistance		−0.145	−0.164	−0.127
Financial assistance		0.081	0.140	0.138
More right wing			0.015	0.012
High political trust			0.031	−0.025
Satisfied w/ democracy			−0.325**	−0.330**
Less support for democracy			0.053	0.033
Culturally left wing			−0.130	−0.139
Economically right wing			−0.218*	−0.225*
Higher populism			0.452**	0.437**
Politically interested			−0.057	−0.027
Higher internal efficacy			−0.138	−0.098
Higher external efficacy			0.009	0.027
Political knowledge			−0.250*	−0.190
Satisfied how government deals with economy			−0.519**	−0.539**
Satisfied how government deals with poverty			0.023	0.019
Satisfied how government deals with education			−0.086	−0.073
Satisfied how government deals with unemployment			−0.338	−0.316
Satisfied how government deals with healthcare			0.156	0.167

(*continued*)

Table 8.4 (continued)

	Model 1a $R^2 = 0.0347$	*Model 2a* $R^2 = 0.1281$	*Model 3a* $R^2 = 0.2405$	*Model 4a* $R^2 = 0.254$
Satisfied how government deals with precemployment			0.114	0.113
Satisfied how government deals with immigration			0.031	0.047
Satisfied how government deals with childcare			0.057	0.050
Father secondary education				−0.153
Father less educated				0.163
Female				0.284**
Older				−0.057
Living in East Germany				0.124
Living in rural area				0.087
Migrant background				−0.001
More religious				0.186
Member of any religion				−0.060
_cons	−1.997**	−1.659**	−1.685**	−1.592**
N	1060	1060	1060	1060

Notes: *$p < 0.05$; **$p < 0.01$

faction with democracy decreases crisis sensitivity, which may imply that if people perceive democracy as working and problem solving they are less troubled by crises. Furthermore, interest in politics shows no significant effect but political knowledge, right-wing economic attitudes (both weak effect), satisfaction with democracy, populism, and at least one item measuring satisfaction with government performance (with stronger effects) do as expected. Holding populist opinions on politics increases and satisfaction with how the government deals with economic issues and with democracy overall decreases the perception of a severe crisis. This shows how crisis perception is dependent on the perception of government to act and to handle crisis and nicely fits with the observation we made regarding satisfaction with democracy. If people have the impression that the government is acting, for example, only on behalf of the elites and not for the common good, or just isn't doing a good job on economic issues, they perceive crisis as more severe and frightening. Other policy fields, including poverty and immigration, do not have a significant effect, which may imply that these issues are not connected to a severe economic crisis in the perception of people.[3] Interestingly, political interest and internal and external political efficacy have no significant effect and the (weak) effect of political knowledge disappears when we include controls (see Model 4a). Secondary education (base, tertiary education) and lower service class occupation (base, higher service class) are significant now on the 0.05 level. The coefficients suggest that lower service class workers are less crisis sensitive but that people with middle class education are more crisis sensitive—more than the less educated (see also Model 4b). Compared to Model 2a, all other significant effects disappeared.

Last but not least, in Model 4a we included a number of socioeconomic control variables. Only gender has a significant effect in our model: women are more likely to see a crisis. Especially the effects of political variables stay stable (populism, satisfaction with democracy, and satisfaction with government dealing with economy), strengthening this core finding of Model 3a. In sum, the explained variance of the models leads us to conclude that deprivation (variables added in Model 2a) and political attitudes (variables added in Model 3a) contribute strongly to crisis susceptibility. Also, the relative stability of the non-importance of class (with the exception of lower service class and secondary education, see paragraph above) leads us to believe that crisis susceptibility is something we can find throughout the social strata, explicitly including the idealized middle classes.

We also conducted a number of binominal regressions varying the respective class reference category to shed light not only on linear effects in the class dimension but also on the relation between them. Since one of our main interests lies on the crisis perceptions by German social classes, and one may expect the lower middle classes to feel under pressure the most, we now turn to a series of models in which we set the lower middle classes (instead of upper class in Table 8.4) as the reference categories for the first set of independent variables (i.e. class belonging along the four dimensions). The results are shown in Table 8.5 and hold some interesting findings.

We observe that subjective affiliation to the saturated middle class instead of the lower middle class decreases the likelihood of seeing a severe economic crisis in Germany (Model 1b). Interestingly, this effect can be observed, to a lesser extent, in Models 2b and 3b, but not if socioeconomic variables are employed. We thus conclude that it is relatively stable. Class along educational attainment is again significant in Model 4b, and we can, combining the Models 4 and 4b with varying reference categories, conclude that there is a linear (and significant) effect. However, both the other class variables do not generate significant effects. Hence, other

Table 8.5 Logistic regression Models 1b to 4b with lower middle class as base

	Model 1b $R^2 = 0.0347$	*Model 2b* $R^2 = 0.1281$	*Model 3b* $R^2 = 0.2405$	*Model 4b* $R^2 = 0.254$
Upper middle class	−0.735*	−0.371	−0.269	−0.262
Middle class	−0.601**	−0.309	−0.260	−0.251
Lower class	0.517*	0.285	0.006	−0.002
Higher service class	0.479	0.472	0.510	0.504
Lower service class	0.119	0.050	−0.028	−0.198
Unskilled worker	−0.361	−0.300	−0.144	−0.319
Higher income	−0.200	0.059	0.301	0.343
Middle income	−0.199	−0.103	0.019	0.008
Lower income	−0.108	−0.293	−0.261	−0.290
Higher education	−0.182	−0.265	−0.472*	−0.587*
Less than secondary	0.259	0.123	−0.089	−0.097
Relative deprivation		0.791**	0.532**	0.514**
Living alone		−0.068	−0.109	−0.079
Social trust		−0.245**	−0.119	−0.133
Friends regularly		0.058	0.105	0.099
Life satisfaction		−0.023	0.107	0.082
Confident in assistance		−0.145	−0.164	−0.127
Financial assistance		0.081	0.140	0.138
More right wing			0.015	0.012
High political trust			0.031	−0.025
Satisfied w/ democracy			−0.325**	−0.330**
Less support for democracy			0.053	0.033
Culturally left wing			−0.130	−0.139
Economically right wing			−0.218*	−0.225*
Higher populism			0.452**	0.437**
Politically interested			−0.057	−0.027
Higher internal efficacy			−0.138	−0.098
Higher external efficacy			0.009	0.027
Political knowledge			−0.250*	−0.190
Satisfied how government deals with economy			−0.519**	−0.539**
Satisfied how government deals with poverty			0.023	0.019
Satisfied how government deals with education			−0.086	−0.073
Satisfied how government deals with unemployment			−0.338	−0.316
Satisfied how government deals with healthcare			0.156	0.167

(*continued*)

Table 8.5 (continued)

	Model 1b $R^2 = 0.0347$	*Model 2b* $R^2 = 0.1281$	*Model 3b* $R^2 = 0.2405$	*Model 4b* $R^2 = 0.254$
Satisfied how government deals with precarious employment			0.114	0.113
Satisfied how government deals with immigration			0.031	0.047
Satisfied how government deals with childcare			0.057	0.050
Father secondary education				−0.153
Father less educated				0.163
Female				0.284**
Older				−0.057
Living in East Germany				0.124
Living in rural area				0.087
Migrant background				−0.001
More religious				0.186
Member of any religion				−0.060
cons	−1.359**	−1.553**	−1.755**	−1.591**
N	1060	1060	1060	1060

Notes: $*p < 0.05$; $**p < 0.01$

objective indicators (income, occupation) of social class do not seem to determine crisis sensitivity alone—and we may argue that education aligns here more closely with subjective affiliation with class than with "objective" class. We are not including the other variables employed in the different models in our further discussion since their effects stay more or less the same.

In sum, we found some evidence to support the claim that the lower the social status of a person is and, thus, the more he or she experiences economic pressure, the more will this person perceive of a severe economic crisis in Germany. However, this evidence is only partly viable, because when we include different measures for class, it is mostly subjective class affiliation that matters. In fact, those who perceive themselves to belong to the lower middle class are more crisis sensitive. It is obviously more important to see oneself in a certain societal position (viz. lower middle class) and to perceive deprivation than actually being part of the lower middle class in terms of the "objective" dimensions we applied. Thus, we reject our first hypothesis. But the findings support our claim that parts of the middle classes, more specifically: those who place themselves on the lower fringe, are more crisis sensitive. This could be explained by the continuing dualization of the German model of capitalism, including its labor market and welfare system (Jackson and Sorge 2012; Palier 2012; Palier and Thelen 2010).

A second finding, however, seems to deliver more exhaustive explanations for crisis sensitivity. Regardless which reference group we choose, three variables came out significant, namely, satisfaction with democracy, populism, and satisfaction with government performance regarding the economy (see Models 4a and 4b). Including these measures (with and without the variables added in Model 2) led to class variables becoming insignificant. People who are satisfied with democracy in general and particularly how the government deals with economic issues are less likely to see a crisis. In return, people holding populist attitudes and who are not convinced by crisis solving capacities of democratic government have higher odds of seeing a "severe economic crisis". Hence, we confirm hypotheses 5 and 6. If we think of recent developments in German politics, this finding seems to be very plausible. The new right-wing populist party "Alternative für Deutschland" is benefiting not only from the currently heated debate about refugees but also from a more substantial frustration with the established parties and alienation from democratic politics (Kiess et al. 2015; Decker et al. 2016). Accordingly, Detje et al. (2013), among others, argue that most political actors continued to lose trust after the crisis, even though many aspects of the actual crisis management are perceived as being successful. We would even argue that the narrative of crisis plays an important role as catalyst for developments that have their origin in the pre-crisis period. Furthermore, relative deprivation does indeed increase crisis susceptibility, though we could not find clear indications for factors of resilience (e.g. social ties).

Finally, while our findings regarding differences between classes seem not very strong at first sight, our claim that crisis is perceived not only by the lowest status groups because they are the ones subjected to economic hardship is actually supported quite firmly: crisis sensitivity is not something we just find among the lower classes. Quite the opposite, the more saturated classes, too, may perceive of a "severe crisis" in the country, depending, among others, on their political views. This goes along with findings in the literature of "status panic" even among the (upper) middle classes (Bude 2014; Ehrenreich 1989; Furlong 2007; Koppetsch 2013;

Schimank et al. 2014) including experiences of instability and insecurity (Burzan 2008; Castel and Dörre 2009).

Conclusion

We set out to investigate whether social status has an effect on the way people perceive the current situation and define the severity of economic crisis in Germany. We started from the observation that a considerable proportion of German respondents testify that they are living a "severe crisis". This fact raises questions about the factors determining crisis sensitivity among the German population. With reference to scholarly writing, we proposed three complementary readings: the susceptibility for economic threats is determined by social class affiliation, and here in particular concerns about social degradation among the middle classes; by exposure to precarity, vulnerabilities, and instabilities in the respondents living conditions; and/or by the political orientations toward the political system and its performance.

Our findings corroborate that class belonging has an effect but that the effect is to be attributed to subjective class affiliations rather than to objective indicators of social status. Perceived class belonging has the expected effect, that is, those seeing themselves as lower middle class are more likely to see a severe crisis. The importance of social class, however, is qualified substantially, because our analysis uncovered, along with previous findings in the literature, that it is other and at least to some part even independent factors that make the difference. The clearest factor seems to be political positions and attitudes—in particular populist orientations and the evaluation of government performance regarding the economy. Furthermore, another important factor seems to be perceived relative economic deprivation. People who feel worse off compared to the past or others are more susceptible to crisis.

However, in our view, this reading of the role of class would be underestimating our findings. The fact that we find a linear effect only for perceived class belonging (and educational attainment) suggests that crisis sensitivity is spread through income groups and occupational classes. Depending on indicators of social status, our descriptive findings underlined that a considerable minority of respondents is sensitive for the threat of economic crisis, with at least 15% of the sample. While the economic situation was stable and promising in Germany during 2015 (the year of our survey), the feeling that something might be wrong is vivid in all layers of society. This crisis susceptibility is stronger among the disappointed and alienated (Decker et al. 2016). Our results suggest that these feelings have reached the core of German society. Feelings of disappointment and alienation have become more salient and maybe even widespread with the crisis which urges us not to downplay the long-term implications of the crisis.

Notes

1. Speech at the German Bundestag, September 8th 2009, https://www.bundesregierung.de/Content/DE/Bulletin/2009/09/93-4-bk-bt.html
2. If we test the class dimensions separately, only income and perceived class show significant effects.
3. The only policy field significant when all others are excluded is unemployment. We can assume collinearity between economy and unemployment here.

References

Baas, S. (2008). Soziale Netzwerke verschiedener Lebensformen im Längsschnitt – Kontinuität oder Wandel? In W. Bien & J. H. Marbach (Eds.), *Familiale Beziehungen, Familienalltag und soziale Netzwerke* (pp. 147–183). Wiesbaden: VS Verlag.

Beck, U. (2008). *Die Neuvermessung der Ungleichheit unter den Menschen: Soziologische Aufklärung im 21. Jahrhundert; Eröffnungsvortrag zum Soziologentag "Unsichere Zeiten" am 6. Oktober 2008 in Jena*. Frankfurt am Main: Suhrkamp.

Böhnke, P. (2006). Einkommensarm, aber beziehungsreich? In J. Alber and W. Merkel (Hg.), *Europas Osterweiterung* (p. 107). Berlin: WZB.

Böhnke, P. (2008). Are the Poor Socially Integrated? The Link Between Poverty and Social Support in Different Welfare Regimes. *Journal of European Social Policy, 18*(2), 133–150.

Böhnke, P. (2015). Wahrnehmung sozialer Ausgrenzung. *Aus Politik und Zeitgeschichte, 67*, 18–25.

Bosch, G., & Kalina, T. (2015). *Die Mittelschicht in Deutschland unter Druck* (IAQ-Report). Duisburg-Essen: Institut Arbeit und Qualifikation.

Brenke, K., Rinne U., & Zimmermann, K. F. (2011). *Short-Time Work: The German Answer to the Great Recession* (IZA DP 5780). Bonn: Institute for the Study of Labor (IZA).

Bude, H. (2014). *Gesellschaft der Angst*. Hamburg: Hamburger Edition.

Bude, H., & Willisch, A. (2006). *Das Problem der Exklusion. Ausgegrenzte, Entbehrliche, Überflüssige*. Hamburg: Hamburger Edition.

Buraczynska, B., Van Hauwaert, S. M., & Kiess, J. (in press). Picking on Immigration. A Cross-National Analysis of Individual-Level Relative Deprivation and Authoritarianism as Predictors of Anti-Foreign Prejudice. *Acta Politica*.

Burzan, N. (2008). Die Absteiger: Verunsicherung in der Mitte der Gesellschaft. *Aus Politik und Zeitgeschichte, 33–34*, 6–12.

Busch, U., & Land, R. (2012). Teilhabekapitalismus. In P. Bartelheimer, S. Fromm, J. Kädtler, & Forschungsverbund Sozioökonomische Berichterstattung (Eds.), *Berichterstattung zur sozioökonomischen Entwicklung in Deutschland* (pp. 111–151). Wiesbaden: VS Verlag für Sozialwissenschaften.

Butzlaff, F. (2016). *Die neuen Bürgerproteste in Deutschland. Organisatoren – Erwartungen – Demokratiebilder*. Bielefeld: Transcript.

Castel, R. (2002). *From Manual Workers to Wage Laborers: Transformation of the Social Question*. New Brunswick: Transaction.

Castel, R., & Dörre, K. (Eds.). (2009). *Prekarität, Abstieg, Ausgrenzung. Die soziale Frage am Beginn des 21. Jahrhunderts*. Frankfurt am Main/New York: Campus.

Clayton, R., & Pontusson, J. (1998). Welfare-State Retrenchment Revisited: Entitlement Cuts, Public Sector Restructuring, and Inegalitarian Trends in Advanced Capitalist Societies. *World Politics, 51*(1), 67–98.

Countouris, N. (2007). *The Changing Law of the Employment Relationship. Comparative Analysis in the European Context*. Aldershot: Ashgate.

Decker, O., & Brähler, E. (2006). *Vom Rand Zur Mitte. Rechtsextreme Einstellungen in Deutschland 2006*. Berlin: Friedrich-Ebert-Stiftung.

Decker, O., Weißmann, M., Kiess, J., & Brähler, E. (2012). *Die Mitte in Der Krise: Rechtsextreme Einstellungen in Deutschland* (2nd ed.). Springe: Zu Klampen.

Decker, O., Weißmann, M., Kiess, J., & Brähler, E. (2016). *Die enthemmte Mitte: Autoritäre und rechtsextreme Einstellungen in Deutschland*. Die Leipziger Mitte-Studie 2016. Gießen: Psychosozial.

Detje, R., Menz, W., Nies, S., Sauer, D., & Bischoff, J. (Eds.). (2013). *Krisenerfahrungen und politische Orientierungen: der Blick von unten auf Betrieb, Gewerkschaft und Staat*. Hamburg: VSA Verl.

Deutscher Paritätischer Wohlfahrtsverband. (2016). *Zeit Zu Handeln. Bericht Zur Armutsentwicklung in Deutschland 2016*. Berlin: Deutscher Paritätischer Wohlfahrtsverband.

Ehrenreich, B. (1989). *Fear of Falling: The Inner Life of the Middle Class*. New York: Pantheon.

Erikson, R., & Goldthorpe, J. H. (1992). *The Constant Flux: A Study of Class Mobility in Industrial Societies*. Oxford: Clarendon Press.

Esping-Anderson, G. (1999). *Social Foundations of Post-industrial Economies*. Oxford: Oxford University Press.

Faunce, W. A. (1990). On the Meaning of Occupational Status: Implications for Stratification Theory and Research. *Sociological Focus, 23*(4), 267–285.

Furlong, A. (2007). The Zone of Precarity and Discourses of Vulnerability. *Journal of Social Sciences and Humanities, 381*, 101–121.

Geiges, L., Marg, S., & Walter, F. (2015). *Pegida. Die schmutzige Seite der Zivilgesellschaft?* Bielefeld: Transcript.

Geiling, H., Hermann, T., Müller, D., von Oertzen, P., & Vester, M. (2001). *Soziale Milieus im gesellschaftlichen Strukturwandel. Zwischen Integration und Ausgrenzung*. Frankfurt: Suhrkamp Verlag.

Goebel, J., Gornig, M., & Häußermann, H. (2010). Polarisierung der Einkommen: Die Mittelschicht verliert. *Wochenbericht des DIW, 2010*(24), 2–8.

Grabka, M. K., & Frick, J. R. (2008). Schrumpfende Mittelschicht – Anzeichen einer Dauerhaften Polarisierung der Verfügbaren Einkommen? *Wochenbericht des DIW, 2008*(10), 101–108.

Hall, P. A., & Soskice, D. (2001). *Varieties of Capitalism: The Institutional Foundations of Comparative Advantage*. Oxford/New York: Oxford University Press.

Haug, L., & Stoy, V. (2015). Deutschland: Mit Kontinuität durch die Krise. In H.-J. Bieling & D. Buhr (Eds.), *Europäische Welten in der Krise: Arbeitsbeziehungen und Wohlfahrtsstaaten im Vergleich* (pp. 31–56). Frankfurt: Campus.

Heinze, R. G. (2011). *Die erschöpfte Mitte. Zwischen marktbestimmten Soziallagen, politischer Stagnation und der Chance auf Gestaltung*. Weinheim: Juventa.

Heitmeyer, W., & Anhut, R. (2008). Disintegration, Recognition, and Violence: A Theoretical Perspective. *New Directions for Youth Development, 2008*(119), 25–37, 8.

Hooghe, L., & Marks, G. (2007). Sources of Euroscepticism. *Acta Politica, 42*(2–3), 119–127.

Jackson, G., & Sorge, A. (2012). The Trajectory of Institutional Change in Germany, 1979–2009. *Journal of European Public Policy, 19*(8), 1146–1167.

Kieselbach, T. (2003). Long-Term Unemployment Among Young People: The Risk of Social Exclusion. *American Journal of Community Psychology, 32*(1/2), 69–76.

Kiess, J. (2015a). Konfligierende Krisenframings deutscher Gewerkschaften und Arbeitgeberverbände. In J. Preunkert & G. Vobruba (Eds.), *Krise und Integration. Gesellschaftsbildung in der Eurokrise* (pp. 21–46). Wiesbaden: Springer.

Kiess, J. (2015b). 50 Shades of Brown: Pegida und der Wunsch nach Autorität. *Jahrbuch Für Öffentliche Sicherheit*, 2014/2015, 205–219.

Kiess, J., Brähler, E., & Decker, O. (2015). Die Wählerinnen und Wähler von AfD und NPD – Gemeinsamkeiten und Unterschiede. In O. Decker, J. Kiess, & E. Brähler (Eds.), *Rechtsextremismus der Mitte und sekundärer Autoritarismus* (pp. 83–104). Gießen: Psychosozial.

Kiess, J., Brähler, E., Schmutzer, G., & Decker, O. (2017). Euroscepticism and Right-Wing Extremist Attitudes in Germany: A Result of the 'Dialectic Nature of Progress'? *German Politics, 26*(2), 235–254.

Koppetsch, C. (2013). *Die Wiederkehr der Konformität: Streifzüge durch die gefährdete Mitte*. Frankfurt am Main/New York: Campus Verlag.

Kriesi, H., Grande, E., Dolezal, M., Helbing, M., Höglinger, D., Hutter, S., & Wüest, B. (2012). *Political Conflict in Western Europe*. Cambridge: Cambridge University Press.

Kronauer, M. (1998). 'Social Exclusion' and 'Underclass'. New Concepts for the Analysis of Poverty. In H.-J. Andress (Ed.), *Empirical Poverty Research in a Comparative Perspective* (pp. 51–75). Aldershot: Ashgate.

Lengfeld, H., & Hirschle, J. (2009). Die Angst der Mittelschicht vor dem sozialen Abstieg. Eine Längsschnittanalyse 1984–2007. *Zeitschrift für Soziologie, 38*(5), 379–398.

Lessenich, S. (2009). 'Neue Mitte'. Das Ende der Planwirtschaft Campus. In R. Castel & K. Dörre (Eds.), *Prekarität, Abstieg, Ausgrenzung. Die Soziale Frage Am Beginn Des 21. Jahrhunderts* (pp. 259–268). Frankfurt/New York: Campus.

Marg, S. (2014). *Mitte in Deutschland: Zur Vermessung eines politischen Ortes*. Bielefeld: Transcript.

Mau, S. (2012). *Lebenschancen: Wohin Driftet Die Mittelschicht?* Berlin: Suhrkamp.

Mau, S. (2014). Transformation und Krise der europäischen Mittelschichten. In M. Heidenreich (Ed.), *Krise der europäischen Vergesellschaftung?* (pp. 253–279). Wiesbaden: Springer.

Noll, H.-H. (1996). Ungleichheit der Lebenslagen und ihre Legitimation im Transformationsprozeß: Fakten, Perzeptionen und Bewertungen. In L. Clausen (Ed.), *Gesellschaften im Umbruch: Verhandlungen des 27. Kongresses der Deutschen Gesellschaft für Soziologie* (pp. 488–504). Frankfurt am Main: Campus.

Noll, H.-H, & Weick, S. (2011). Schichtzugehörigkeit nicht nur vom Einkommen bestimmt. In *Informationsdienst Soziale Indikatoren* 45. Mannheim: Gesis.

Nolte, P., & Hilpert, D. (2007). Wandel und Selbstbehauptung. Die gesellschaftliche Mitte in historischer Perspektive. In S. Hradil & H. Quandt-Stiftung (Eds.), *Zwischen Erosion und Erneuerung: Die gesellschaftliche Mitte in Deutschland. Ein Lagebericht* (pp. 11–103). Frankfurt: Societäts-Verlag.

Palier, B. (2012). Turning Vice Into Vice. In G. Bonoli & D. Natali (Eds.), *The Politics of the New Welfare State* (pp. 232–255). Oxford: Oxford University Press.

Palier, B., & Thelen, K. (2010). Institutionalizing Dualism: Complementarities and Change in France and Germany. *Politics & Society, 38*(1), 119–148.

Pettigrew, T. F. (2002). Summing Up: Relative Deprivation as a Key Social Psychological Concept. In I. Walker & H. J. Smith (Eds.), *Relative Deprivation. Specification, Development, and Integration* (pp. 351–374). Cambridge: Cambridge University Press.

Pressman, S. (2007). The Decline of the Middle Class: An International Perspective. *Journal of Economic Issues, 41*(1), 181–200.

Ranci, C. (2010). *Social Vulnerability in Europe: The New Configuration of Social Risks*. Basingstoke: Palgrave.

Rippl, S., & Baier, D. (2005). Das Deprivationskonzept in der Rechtsextremismusforschung. *KZfSS Kölner Zeitschrift für Soziologie und Sozialpsychologie, 57*(4), 644–666.

Schäfer, A. (2015). *Der Verlust politischer Gleichheit. Warum sinkende Wahlbeteiligung der Demokratie schadet*. Frankfurt am Main: Campus.

Schelsky, H. (1954). *Wandlungen der deutschen Familie in der Gegenwart: Darstellung und Deutung einer empirisch-soziologischen Tatbestandsaufnahme*. Stuttgart: Ferdinand Enke.

Schimank, U., Mau, S., & Groh-Samberg, O. (2014). *Statusarbeit unter Druck? Zur Lebensführung der Mittelschichten*. Weinheim: Beltz Juventa.

Simmel, G. (1908). *Soziologie. Untersuchungen über die Formen der Vergesellschaftung* (1st ed.). Berlin: Duncker & Humblot.

Steijn, B., Berting, J., & de Jong, M.-J. (Eds.). (1998). *Economic Restructuring and the Growing Uncertainty of the Middle Class*. Boston: Kluwer Academic Publishers.

Teney, C., Lacewell, O., & De Wilde, P. (2014). Winners and Losers of Globalization in Europe: Attitudes and Ideologies. *European Political Science Review, 6*(4), 575–595.

Vogel, B. (2009). *Wohlstandskonflikte: Soziale Fragen, die aus der Mitte Kommen* (1. Aufl). Hamburg: Hamburger Edition.

Vogel, B. (2010). Wohlstandspanik und Statusbeflissenheit. Perspektiven auf die nervöse Mitte der Gesellschaft. In N. Burzan & P. A. Berger (Eds.), *Dynamiken (in) der Gesellschaftlichen Mitte* (pp. 23–41). Wiesbaden: VS Verlag für Sozialwissenschaften.

Wacquant, L. (2010). Crafting the Neoliberal State: Workfare, Prisonfare, and Social Insecurity. *Sociological Forum, 25*(2), 197–220.

CHAPTER 9

The Silent Crisis: Perceptions and Experiences of the Economic Crisis in Switzerland

Marco Giugni and Maria M. Mexi

Introduction

Switzerland is known as a peaceful and prosperous country with low unemployment and a per capita GDP among the highest in Europe. Its economy is one of the most stable in the world. As such, while other European countries—most notably South European countries such as Greece, Italy, and Spain—fell into a deep economic downturn which has come to be known as the "Great Recession," Switzerland has largely been spared from the most dramatic consequences of the economic crisis. This can be seen in some key macroeconomic indicators such as economic growth, national debt, and unemployment, which have remained rather stable during the crisis.

Yet, things were perhaps not so rosy as they seem at first glance. Although it never reached the depth encountered by other European

M. Giugni (✉) • M.M. Mexi
Department of Political Science and International Relations, University of Geneva, Geneva, Switzerland

M. Giugni, M.T. Grasso (eds.), *Citizens and the Crisis*, Palgrave Studies in European Political Sociology,
https://doi.org/10.1007/978-3-319-68960-9_9

countries, the economic crisis has been felt in Switzerland too, including at the macroeconomic level. For example, the per capita GDP decreased in 2009, an unusual situation for Switzerland for a long time. Similarly, while remaining at relative lower levels in international perspective, the unemployment rate boosted between 2008 and 2010, accompanied by a decrease in the percentage of the population belonging to the middle-income group over the period 2009–2013 (Federal Statistical Office 2016). Thus, while the Swiss situation cannot be compared to that of other European countries, there are signs that this "economic heaven" has become less attractive since the start of the Great Recession.

Swiss authorities—specifically the Swiss central bank—were in fact well aware of the risks for the country relating to what was happening in the Eurozone as well as of the fact that the Swiss franc's strength had made Swiss exports less competitive and weakened the country's growth outlook. So, they made a bold move when they pegged the Swiss franc against the euro in September 2011 in an attempt to protect its economy from the European debt crisis. This move introduced a cap in the value of the Swiss franc against the euro, effectively devaluating the former vis-à-vis the latter. This move, however, was reverted in January 2016 when the central bank abolished the Swiss franc cap. According to several observers, the latter move in a way decreed the "import" of the euro crisis in Switzerland.

Our discussion so far has dealt with decisions by political and economic elites as well as the macroeconomic consequences of such decisions. What about the ordinary citizens? How have they perceived the economic situation of their country and, most importantly, their own? Have they felt the crisis (provided one can speak of a crisis in this case)? Have they experienced a deterioration of their "objective" conditions? If so, have the negative consequences of the crisis perceived differently across groups? This chapter tries to provide some answers to these and related questions. We do so with the help of the LIVEWHAT survey data, which include a wealth of variables pertaining to how citizens have perceived and experienced the economic crisis.

Our analysis has an exploratory aim. We examine whether and to what extent, in spite of Switzerland having largely been spared the negative impact of the crisis at the macroeconomic level, people have felt the negative impact of the crisis when one looks at the individual level. Furthermore, given that the population is not a homogeneous entity, we assume that the effects of the economic crisis, if any, are unlikely to have been homogenous across the citizenry. Therefore, we look whether and to what extent this applies for the most fragile and underprivileged sectors of the population such as the working classes, the poorest layers of society, the less educated, and the unemployed. Accordingly, we look at possible differential effects in terms of social class, income, education, and occupational status. These are all aspects determining the socioeconomic status of individuals and which provide key resources for political engagement (Brady et al. 1995; Verba et al. 1995), but they are also more generally related to the ways in which people view their social and political environment.

Concerning social class, we compare manual workers (skilled, semi-skilled, or unskilled) to all other classes. In addition, we examine the role of income and education. The former contrasts those whose income is lower than 4125 Swiss francs to those whose income is higher. The latter opposes those who have less than secondary occupation to those who have completed secondary education or university and above. Finally, looking at occupational status, we consider whether unemployed people have a different perception and experience of the economic crisis than the other people. Overall, we focus on three main aspects: how people have perceived the economic crisis (perceptions of the crisis), the impact the crisis has had on their living and work conditions (impact of the crisis on living and work conditions), and the ways in which they have dealt with it (citizens' resilience in dealing with the crisis). Before we move to the analysis of our survey data, however, we discuss the impact of the Great Recession on European citizens more generally, both in the light of the existing literature and of the evidence found within the LIVEWHAT project.

The Losers of the Great Recession

The economic crisis that hit Europe since 2008 without doubt has been the most important international event in post-war economic history, bearing serious implications for the growth potential of Europe and the Eurozone (De Grauwe and Ji 2013). As happened in the 1930s, the 2008 crisis' impact has not been confined to the economic field but extended to the social field, while implications for nation states globally have depended on the specifics of their domestic contexts. In fact, the literature on the crisis' effects has become abundant. Scholars in sociology, political science, and economics, as well as from other disciplines, have written extensively on the impact of the crisis on a variety of aspects such as the labor market through greater flexibilization of, and reduction of, labor law provisions, as well as to the depletion of minimum labor protection standards (Clauwaert and Schomann 2012), and through a rise in unemployment and underemployment, as well as a dramatic impact on most vulnerable groups (Seguino 2010; Stiglitz Commission 2009). Massive unemployment, in particular among the younger population groups, or in-work poverty, have resulted in the emergence of new populist parties and the rise of anti-austerity protest movements (Bermeo and Bartels 2014; Giugni and Grasso 2015; Goodwin and Ford 2014; Kriesi and Pappas 2015). Across countries, these adverse effects have been more evident in rising inequalities and deprivation, a decline in well-being, but also in the increasing clash between the winners and the losers of economic globalization and the global economic crisis (Kriesi et al. 2008, 2012).

Recent years have seen a growth in studies on inequality as a consequence of exogenous dynamics of globalization, technological development, and changing patterns of labor relations at global level, but also as endogenous responses to successive crises through the implementation of stringent austerity measures, including cuts to welfare states (Atkinson 2015; Beatty and Fothergill 2013; Dabla-Norris et al. 2015; Dorling 2014; Crouch 2015; Musterd and Ostendorf 2014; Nolan et al. 2014; Piketty 2013; Standing 2009). While in most Western capitalist economies, jobs have been shrinking and unemployment rates have been rising, globally, there has been an increasing amount of people available for a decreasing amount of jobs. Jobless recoveries "in which economic growth returns after a crisis but job growth remains anaemic" are now more regular than ever before (Srnicek and Williams 2015: 94). With the ongoing job crisis has come the rise of precarity which involves "social positionings of insecurity" (Lorey 2015). Increasingly, the arrangements of work have been changing more and more to flexible, short-term, and insecure labor relations. This has created the precariat (Standing 2011, 2014), that is, workers who live in permanent uncertainty because they lack the safety and stability that long-term labor contracts used to offer. The shift from Fordist, long-term, stable jobs to flexibility raises many questions about traditional class distinctions, as the precariat cuts across classes and consists "of many millions around the world without an anchor of stability" (Standing 2011: 1). Hence, the precariat as a distinct socioeconomic group could be understood as those who "have minimal trust relationship with capital or the state" (Standing 2011: 8) and live under permanent socioeconomic insecurity.

The combined effects of flexibilization and precarity have privileged labor market insiders (those with permanent jobs) at the expense of outsiders (precarious employees) and led to greater labor earning inequality (Bonesmo Fredriksen 2012). Indeed, as stressed by many international organizations, wage and income inequality has been widening within many G20 countries. According to the OECD (2015), income inequality is at its highest level for the past half century, posing a threat to future equity and growth, and intensifying long-term social disadvantage for both the middle and lower classes, which traditional welfare regimes have rarely addressed (Jenson 2012). For many in Europe, this seems to necessitate a structural recalibration of the welfare state and the transition to a different model of welfare capitalism, which will hardly be straight forward (Carlin 2012; Diamond and Lodge 2013; Morel et al. 2012).

Work on inequalities has mostly concentrated on the differences between the top and the bottom (European Parliament 2015). The standpoint that the middle classes are financially converging toward the lower classes, leading to higher social inequality and polarization, has become widespread. (Foster and Wolfson 2010; Petmesidou and Guillén 2015; Pressman 2010; Pressman and Scott 2011). At the same time, a sort of vicious circle has developed with downside risks in the foreseeable future: the crisis has weakened the middle class, which in turn has reduced aggregate demand, thereby deepening and prolonging economic downturn. Moreover, as expected, the consequences of the crisis on population groups experiencing social vulnerability have been harshest. In particular, Eurostat (2016) data shows that migrants were highly affected by the economic crisis, being among the first to lose their jobs. In 2015, the employment rate of non-EU nationals aged 20–64 was 13.3 percent below the total employment rate and 13.9 percent below that of EU nationals. This is a significant widening of the gap since the onset of the crisis in 2008, when the difference in the employment rates between non-EU citizens and the total population was only 7.8 percent. Furthermore, the economic recession has hit younger workers especially hard. Since the onset of the crisis in 2008, the employment rate of young people aged 20 to 29 has dropped by 4.2 percent, from 65.6 percent in 2008 to 61.4 percent in 2015. People with the lowest education levels not only had the lowest employment rate but were also hit hardest by the crisis, experiencing a 4.3 percent fall in their employment rate between 2007 and 2015. The negative impact of the economic crisis on European countries' financial and labor markets was the most likely cause of the rise in the amount of people at risk of poverty or social exclusion from 2009 to 2012. Despite the slight reduction in poverty figures between 2012 and 2014, a little over 122 million people—24.1 percent of the European Union population—were still at risk of poverty or social exclusion in 2014. This means almost one in four people in the European Union experienced at least one of the three forms of poverty or social exclusion. Of all groups examined, the unemployed faced the greatest risk of poverty or social exclusion, while more than 30 percent of young people aged 18 to 24 and 27.8 percent of children aged less than 18 were at risk in 2014. At 17.8 percent, this rate was considerably lower among the elderly aged 65 or over. More generally, the deterioration of economic and social conditions as a result of the crisis exhibits an increased polarization between the young and the old. Intergenerational unfairness is creating a "lost generation" of young people, while young people are increasingly missing out on perks enjoyed by their parents, such as free university education and generous, defined-benefit pension schemes (Bell and Blanchflower 2011; Glover et al. 2011; Hur 2016).

In such a context of heightening social vulnerability, there is a growing emphasis on the individual's resilience and responsibility to bounce back and stand against economic hardship—both as a worker and as a citizen—and a decreasing attention to social solidarity as an institution (Clegg and Clasen 2011; Hemerijck 2012). In times of crisis, diminishing solidarity (as an element of policy measures or institutional welfare) is associated with the emergence of new divides between weaker and better-off social groups and broader adverse social situations. Simultaneously, the notions of social inequality and social stratification are becoming even more important, as the distance between the winners and the losers of in the global economy becomes greater and conventional wisdom about when and why economic growth fails to trickle down and help the most vulnerable is challenged (Kenworthy 2011).

Taking a comparative perspective reveals that, while the effects of the crisis on middle class and on weaker, less privileged groups have been observed in several European countries; its impact has been uneven across Europe. The deep recession and the harsh austerity policies taken since the onset of the crisis have influenced particularly Southern Europe, where large parts of the population have suffered great losses in their income and they have been living in a climate of rising unemployment, poverty, insecurity, fear, anger, and pessimism regarding the future (European

Parliament 2016). At the same time, some countries like Germany have been largely resilient, although one has to be aware of the uneven distribution of the effects across social groups and the capacity of affluent economies to absorb the shocks and limits their impact on labor markets and people's incomes. Underpinning this evidence is a deep-seated economic divide between the fiscally pious nations above of the Alps and the profligate countries in the South.

Our cross-national survey data show that the North-South divide is more evident in four key areas. First, when citizens were asked to report their satisfaction with governmental policies in four fields: poverty, unemployment, precarious employment, and immigration. Results show that satisfaction levels in all four policy fields are particularly low in Southern European countries as opposed to satisfaction levels reported in the Continental, Scandinavian, and Anglo-Saxon countries. Second, when citizens were asked to compare their living standards to those of their parents: most citizens in Continental, Scandinavian, and Anglo-Saxon countries believe their living standards were better vis-à-vis a third of respondents in the Mediterranean and Southern countries. Third, when citizens were asked to rate living conditions in their own country and then those in the other countries in the project. Results show once again that a small-to-moderate proportion of citizens in Mediterranean and Southern countries rate living conditions in their own country as good vis-à-vis an overwhelming majority in Continental, Scandinavian, and in Anglo-Saxon countries. Fourth, when the proportion of individuals in various countries having to make reductions in consumption as a result of the crisis' impact. Results show again that reductions were more widespread in Southern European countries as opposed to the Continental, Scandinavian, and Anglo-Saxon countries.

Within this matrix, the most commonly held assumption is that Switzerland was not hit by the crisis in the same way as most European countries. Just as Germany or Sweden, this country is generally considered to have been largely spared by the negative effects of the Great Recession. Yet, while this might be true at the aggregate level, we argue that the economic crisis was also felt there and, above all, that its impact has been unevenly felt between worse-off and better-off groups exposing dimensions of inequalities which underpin individual perceptions, lived experiences, and modes of social resilience.

Perceptions of the Crisis

Since the onset of the economic crisis, Switzerland has been shown on the surface and at the macro level to have weathered the crisis well, at least in comparative terms. What does the Swiss population think about this? What is the perception of Swiss residents of the crisis at the micro level? Moreover, does such a perception vary in terms of social class, income, education, and occupational status?

Table 9.1 provides a first, general indicator of how the Swiss residents have viewed the economic crisis. It shows the perceptions of the severity of the crisis. This allows us to see to what extent the view that the impact of the crisis in Switzerland was rather marginal reflects on individual views. Looking first at the full sample in the last row, we can see that most of the respondents consider that Switzerland was undergoing an economic crisis. Thus, while the country was largely able to escape the most negative consequences of the Great Recession, still people had the

Table 9.1 Perceptions of the severity of the economic crisis in Switzerland (percentages)

	Very serious crisis	*Not very serious crisis*	*No crisis*	*Total*	*N*	*Statistical test*
Social class						
Manual workers	13.5	64.0	22.5	100%	347	Chi2 = 5.680
Other classes	18.2	57.7	24.1	100%	1433	$p = 0.058$ Cramer's V = 0.057
Income						
Lower income	21.1	58.0	20.9	100%	469	Chi2 = 10.289
Higher income	14.8	59.9	25.3	100%	1006	$p = 0.006$ Cramer's V = 0.084
Education						
Lower education	21.0	57.0	22.0	100%	328	Chi2 = 4.045
Higher education	16.5	59.2	24.3	100%	1479	$p = 0.132$ Cramer's V = 0.047
Occupational status						
Unemployed	17.4	60.0	22.6	100%	115	Chi2 = 0.119
Employed	17.3	58.7	24.0	100%	1692	$p = 0.942$
Full sample	17.3	58.8	23.9	100%	1807	Cramer's V = 0.008

feeling that the situation had worsened. Most of them, however, consider that the crisis was not very serious, while about one fourth of the respondents consider that there was no crisis at all.

In this chapter, however, rather than looking at perceptions and experiences of the economic crisis per se, we are more interested in examining who has had the strongest perceptions and experiences so as to capture inequality in the way the crisis was felt by different strata of the population. Just like the following ones, therefore, this table breaks down the data according to the criteria mentioned earlier. While not all variables reach the canonical 95-percent significance level, we do observe some differences suggesting that the economic crisis was not felt homogeneously across the population. Specifically, among those who consider themselves as belonging to the lower strata of the society, those who have lower income and those who have a lower education, there is a higher share of respondents who believe that the crisis was very serious. The differences, however, are not very strong, which explains why the significance level reaches 95 percent only for the income variable. In contrast, manual workers do not have a stronger perception of the economic crisis than the other social classes, quite on the contrary. Similarly, there is no difference between unemployed people and the rest of the population as both groups show virtually the same distribution.

This first indicator of the evaluation of the economic crisis suggests, firstly, that a large part of the Swiss residents believe that there was indeed an economic crisis—whether severe or, most often, not so severe—secondly that such an evaluation varies to some extent across sectors of the population, with less privileged people being in general more aware of the crisis, and thirdly that the differences with the rest of the population are not very large. This indicator makes explicit reference to the economic crisis, which might be difficult for people to say insofar as what qualifies as a crisis to someone might not be so for someone else.

Another, more concrete way to grasp the perceptions of the crisis consists in asking people to assess the state of the economy in the country over, for example, the past year. Table 9.2 shows the results relating to this question. This table, like the following ones, compares means rather than percentages as the measure consists of a scale. The lower scores on the scale refer to the evaluation that the economy is worse than one year earlier, while the higher scores means that respondents believe that the economy is better. Those who have a lower income, and unemployed people score significantly lower on the scale, meaning that they are more inclined

Table 9.2 Evaluation of the state of the economy in Switzerland over the past year (means)

	Mean	*Standard deviation*	*N*	*Statistical test*
Social class				$p = 0.701$
Manual workers	4.73	1.47	361	
Other classes	4.70	1.66	1484	
Income				$p = 0.000$
Lower income	4.47	1.65	493	
Higher income	4.85	1.58	1027	
Education				$p = 0.485$
Lower education	4.65	1.82	339	
Higher education	4.72	1.58	1535	
Occupational status				$p = 0.003$
Unemployed	4.28	1.71	117	
Employed	4.74	1.62	1757	
Full sample	4.71	1.63	1874	

Notes: 0–10 scale, whereby 0 stands for "much worse" and 10 for "much better"

to believe that the Swiss economy has worsened during the year prior to the interview.

The first two indicators of how Swiss residents perceive the economic crisis refer to the crisis as such, with no reference to the role or responsibility of the government therein. As economic voting theories have shown, however, people—voters—most often link the state of the economy with the performance of the government in dealing with it. More specifically, these theories suggest that citizens will punish incumbents in times of economic downturn for their poor economic performances (see Lewis-Beck and Stegmaier 2000 for a review). Table 9.3 thus shows a third way to grasp people's perceptions of the economic crisis, one that looks at the degree of satisfaction with the way the government is dealing with the economy. People dissatisfied gave low scores, while people satisfied gave higher scores. The findings suggest that manual workers, the lower income groups, and jobless people (but only at the 90-percent level) tend to be less satisfied with the way the Swiss government is dealing with the economy.

In sum, this first assessment of the perception of the economic crisis by Swiss residents yields two main findings. Firstly, in spite of Switzerland having been largely spared by the deepest negative effects of the Great Recession—at least in the way the situation has been depicted in the

Table 9.3 Satisfaction with the way the Swiss government is dealing with the economy (means)

	Mean	*Standard deviation*	*N*	*Statistical test*
Social class				$p = 0.041$
Manual workers	55.75	2.28	379	
Other classes	6.01	2.17	1538	
Income				$p = 0.000$
Lower income	5.51	2.35	493	
Higher income	6.26	2.11	1069	
Education				$p = 0.580$
Lower education	5.91	2.30	359	
Higher education	5.98	2.17	1591	
Occupational status				$p = 0.062$
Unemployed	5.62	2.24	129	
Employed	5.99	2.19	1821	
Full sample	5.97	2.19	1950	

Note: 0–10 scale, whereby 0 stands for "extremely dissatisfied" and 10 for "extremely satisfied"

media—when it comes to individual perceptions, Swiss residents felt indeed that there was a crisis, albeit not necessarily a very serious one. Secondly, such a perception is not homogeneously distributed across the population, and, although the differences observed are not always statistically significant, the most unprivileged strata of the population often have a stronger perception of the crisis as well as of the way in which the government has dealt with it, perhaps with the exception of people belonging to the working class.

Impact of the Crisis on Living Conditions

Next we turn to the ways in which the economic crisis has impacted on the living conditions or Swiss residents and how this varies according to our four criteria (social class, income, education, and occupational status). While the previous section referred to people's perceptions of the economic crisis, this one speaks about how they experience it.

Looking at how people assess their own economic situation rather than that of the country in which they live is a standard way to grasp people's experiences of economic downturn and to relate them to relative deprivation theories (Gurr 1970; Runciman 1966). In the language of economic voting theories, this reflects so-called "egocentric" or "pocketbook"

Table 9.4 Evaluation of own household's economic situation as compared to 12 months earlier (means)

	Mean	*Standard deviation*	*N*	*Statistical test*
Social class				$p = 0.224$
Manual workers	4.99	1.98	385	
Other classes	5.12	1.91	1550	
Income				$p = 0.000$
Lower income	4.57	2.02	511	
Higher income	5.35	1.89	1064	
Education				$p = 0.111$
Lower education	4.95	2.12	358	
Higher education	5.13	1.87	1609	
Occupational status				$p = 0.000$
Unemployed	4.32	2.23	124	
Employed	5.15	1.89	1853	
Full sample	5.10	1.92	1967	

Note: 0–10 scale, whereby 0 stands for "much worse" and 10 for "much better"

evaluations, as opposed to "sociotropic" evaluations which refer to the state of the economy as we did in the previous section (Lewis-Beck 1988). Such an assessment can be absolute or relative. If relative, one might compare the current situation with that of other people or other social groups, or with one's own situation in the past. Here we follow the latter route. Table 9.4 shows the evaluation of the respondents' household economic situation as compared to 12 months earlier. Lower scores on the scale indicate that respondents view their situation as worse, while higher scores mean that they think it is better.

The comparisons of the average evaluations show a trend which is consistent with what we found earlier: those with a lower income and jobless people are more inclined to believe that their household's economic situation has worsened in the past 12 months. Clearly, these sectors of the population have felt the crisis in a stronger way as compared to the rest of the population. Moreover, here the differences across groups are larger than in the case of "sociotropic" evaluations, suggesting that what really matters for people is not how the economy in general is going but rather how their own situation changes—at least in their perception—for the good or for the better.

One year is a relatively short period of time to assess changes in one's economic conditions. Perhaps a longer time frame can better capture improving or deteriorating conditions. Table 9.5 looks, on a similar scale,

Table 9.5 Evaluation of own household's economic situation as compared to five years earlier (means)

	Mean	*Standard deviation*	*N*	*Statistical test*
Social class				$p = 0.015$
Manual workers	4.97	2.40	384	
Other classes	5.29	2.31	1575	
Income				$p = 0.000$
Lower income	4.15	2.48	523	
Higher income	5.73	2.12	1073	
Education				$p = 0.246$
Lower education	5.10	2.46	365	
Higher education	5.26	2.30	1627	
Occupational status				$p = 0.000$
Unemployed	4.09	2.55	128	
Employed	5.31	2.30	1864	
Full sample	5.23	2.33	1992	

Notes: 0–10 scale, whereby 0 stands for "much worse" and 10 for "much better"

at the evaluation of the respondents' household economic situation as compared to five years earlier. Incidentally, this time frame more or less corresponds to the start of the economic crisis, or at least of its more visible consequences in Europe. With the exception of education, all other criteria show statistically significant differences. More specifically, manual workers, lower income, and jobless people display a significantly lower score on the scale, meaning that they are more inclined to believe that their household's economic situation has worsened in the past five years.

Whether in terms of 12 months or 5 years, the last two indicators refer to retrospective evaluations. We can also look at prospective evaluations of one's own economic situation. Table 9.6 shows how respondents' evaluation of their household economic situation in the near future varies across groups according to our four criteria. Three out of four of the differences tested are statistically significant and in the expected direction. Specifically, manual workers, people with lower income, people with lower education are all more inclined to expect that the financial situation of their household will get worse, as compared to the other groups. We also see that unemployed score lower on the scale, but here the difference if not significant. Thus, not only have the most fragile and underprivileged sectors of the population a more grim view when one looks back in the past, but this also applies to how one sees the future.

Table 9.6 Evaluation of own household's economic situation in the near future (means)

	Mean	*Standard deviation*	*N*	*Statistical test*
Social class				$p = 0.001$
Manual workers	5.22	2.09	378	
Other classes	5.60	2.08	1547	
Income				$p = 0.000$
Lower income	5.00	2.27	510	
Higher income	5.82	2.00	1067	
Education				$p = 0.007$
Lower education	5.26	2.34	356	
Higher education	5.59	2.04	1600	
Occupational status				$p = 0.124$
Unemployed	5.25	2.36	123	
Employed	5.55	2.08	1833	
Full sample	5.53	2.10	1956	

Notes: 0–10 scale, whereby 0 stands for "much worse" and 10 for "much better"

Feelings of relative deprivation—in this case, individual assessments of changes in one's own economic situation over time—get closer to actual living conditions, but they still are strongly dependent on subjective perceptions. Another way to do so, but anchored on more "objective" indicators, consists in asking about restrictions for financial or economic reasons that respondents or someone else in their household had to go through in terms of reduced consumption or other. Table 9.7 shows the results of this indicator. Here the specific measure is a 0–1 scale based on a number of items, whereby 0 stands for no restrictions and 1 for restrictions on all counts.

All the criteria display statistically significant differences, pointing to an important effect of the economic crisis in particular on the less privileged sectors of the society. We observe particularly large differences for the criteria of income and occupational status: people with a lower income and unemployed people had to go through more restrictions than the rest of the population, suggesting that they have suffered much more than the latter from the crisis. Moreover, manual workers and people with lower education are also worse off in this respect, but the differences with the counterpart are smaller.

A last indicator that we use to grasp the impact of the economic crisis looks at a number of negative things that happened to respondents on the

Table 9.7 Restrictions for financial or economic reasons during the past five years (means)

	Mean	*Standard deviation*	*N*	*Statistical test*
Social class				$p = 0.000$
Manual workers	0.29	0.26	400	
Other classes	0.23	0.25	1611	
Income				$p = 0.000$
Lower income	0.37	0.27	530	
Higher income	0.19	0.22	1093	
Education				$p = 0.011$
Lower education	0.27	0.26	386	
Higher education	0.23	0.25	1660	
Occupational status				$p = 0.000$
Unemployed	0.39	0.28	133	
Employed	0.23	0.25	1913	
Full sample	0.24	0.25	2046	

Notes: 0–1 scale, whereby 0 stands for no restrictions and 1 for restrictions on all counts. The scale is based on the following items: reduced consumption of staple foods, reduced recreational activities, reduced use of own car, relayed payments on utilities, forced to move home, relayed or defaulted on a loan installment, sell an asset, cut TV/phone/internet service, did not go on holiday, reduced or postponed buying medicines/visiting the doctor. Cronbach's alpha = 0.82

workplace during the last five years. This measure is more specific than the previous one as it focuses on the working situation. The workplace may be a particularly good place to assess the negative effects of the crisis as the latter often bears directly on it, either through losing the job or through worsening working conditions. Table 9.8 shows the results, which rely on a 0–1 scale based on a number of items going from a reduction in pay to a worsening working environment and so forth, whereby 0 stands for no negative things and 1 for negative things on all counts.

We find that the manual workers, those with a lower income, and especially jobless people had to undergo a number of negative things on their workplace, significantly more so than the rest of the population. Thus, once again, the less privileged groups seem to have suffered more from the economic crisis than other groups also when it comes to working conditions in particular.

In sum, our assessment of the impact of the Great Recession on Swiss residents' living conditions suggest that, just as for individual perceptions, the experience of the economic crisis was not homogenously distributed among the population. There are, sometimes quite large, differences

Table 9.8 Negative things that happened on the workplace in the last five years (means)

	Mean	*Standard deviation*	*N*	*Statistical test*
Social class				$p = 0.023$
Manual workers	0.29	0.23	400	
Other classes	0.27	0.23	1611	
Income				$p = 0.000$
Lower income	0.33	0.24	523	
Higher income	0.26	0.22	1078	
Education				$p = 0.320$
Lower education	0.26	0.24	372	
Higher education	0.27	0.22	1639	
Occupational status				$p = 0.000$
Unemployed	0.39	0.24	127	
Employed	0.26	0.22	1884	
Full sample	0.27	0.23	2011	

Notes: 0–1 scale, whereby 0 stands for no negative things and 1 for negative things on all counts. The scale is based on the following items: I took a reduction in pay; I had to take a job I was overqualified for; I had to work extra unpaid overtime hours; I had to work shorter hours; I had to take or look for an additional job; my work load increased; the working environment deteriorated; I had less security in my job; I had to accept less convenient working hours; employees were dismissed in the organization for which I work; I was forced to take undeclared payments. Cronbach's alpha = 0.75

across social groups and sectors of the society, both in terms of "subjective" aspects such as the evaluation of changes in the respondents' household economic situation and in terms of "objective" aspects such as restrictions for financial or economic reasons or negative things that happened to respondents during the years of the crisis.

Citizens' Resilience in Dealing with the Crisis

The previous two sections have addressed the perceptions Swiss residents, and more specifically certain particularly exposed groups, have of the economic crisis as well as the impact that the latter has had on their living conditions in spite of its limited scope in Switzerland. The picture we obtain is one of a real impact, especially so on certain sectors of the society and, more specifically, on the less privileged social groups. This picture, however, yields the image of a passive subject who endures the negative effects of the crisis without being able to do anything against them. Here we look at how people have dealt with the crisis in more proactive terms by looking at strategies of citizens' resilience. By that we mean their capacity of going through hard times and resist negative changes in their life (Batty and Cole 2010; Hall and Lamont 2013), hence adding the agentic dimension to our analysis.

To capture this aspect we have created a measure of resilience based on a question asking respondents to position themselves on a number of items concerning their capacity for resilience and their ties to the community where they live. Our measure combines the following two items: "I look for creative ways to alter difficult situations" and "I actively look for ways to replace the losses I encounter in life." The resulting indicator is a 0–10 scale, whereby 0 stands for weak capacity for resilience and 10 for strong capacity for resilience. Table 9.9 shows the results of this analysis, again focusing on group differences according to our five criteria.

Here the findings are less conclusive than the previous ones, at least as far as statistical significance is concerned. Only one of the five differences is statistically significant, plus another one at the 90-percent level. The most important effect is found for social class, insofar as manual workers have a significantly a weaker capacity for resilience than other classes. To some extent, education also play a role, as people with lower education are less resilient than people with higher education. The other criteria do not seem to matter, at least in statistical terms.

Table 9.9 Capacity for resilience (means)

	Mean	*Standard deviation*	*N*	*Statistical test*
Social class				$p = 0.038$
Manual workers	6.05	1.96	382	
Other classes	6.30	2.15	1562	
Income				$p = 0.115$
Lower income	6.41	2.10	517	
Higher income	6.24	2.07	1070	
Education				$p = 0.078$
Lower education	6.07	2.10	362	
Higher education	6.28	2.12	1616	
Occupational status				$p = 0.420$
Unemployed	6.39	2.03	127	
Employed	6.23	2.12	1851	
Full sample	6.24	2.11	1978	

Note: 0–10 scale, whereby 0 stands for weak capacity for resilience and 10 for strong capacity for resilience. The scale is based on the following items: I look for creative ways to alter difficult situations; I actively look for ways to replace the losses I encounter in life. Cronbach's alpha = 0.62

Table 9.10 Effects of selected variables on the capacity for resilience (standardized regression coefficients)

Perception of the severity of the economic crisis (ref.: no crisis)	
Very serious crisis	0.29
	(0.18)
Not very serious crisis	0.10
	(0.13)
Evaluation of the state of the economy over the past year	−0.10*
	(0.04)
Satisfaction with the way government is dealing with economy	0.07**
	(0.03)
Evaluation of own household's economic situation (12 months)	0.01
	(0.03)
Evaluation of own household's economic situation (five years)	−0.10***
	(0.03)
Evaluation of own household's economic situation (future)	0.14***
Restrictions for financial or economic reasons during the past five years	0.95***
	(0.25)
Negative things on the workplace in the last five years	0.67**
	(0.25)
Constant	5.61***
	(0.29)
Adjusted R-squared	0.06
N	1602

Notes: Standard errors in parentheses. $*p < 0.05$, $**p < 0.01$, $***p < 0.001$

Our last analysis inquires some of the correlates of the resilience shown by our respondents—all of them, not only the less privileged, since we did not find a significantly stronger capacity for resilience by the latter. Table 9.10 shows the results of an OLS regression on our resiliency scale where all the other aspects considered so far are entered as predictors. This analysis is by no means intended to explain resilience, but rather to look if and to what extent the latter is associated with the various perceptions and experiences of the economic crisis examined so far, net of all other aspects.

The capacity for resilience appears to be negatively associated with the evaluation of the state of the economy in Switzerland over the past year and positively associated with the degree of satisfaction with the way the Swiss government is dealing with the economy. In other words, the more one believes that the economy today is better than it was one year earlier, the less their capacity for resilience. However, the more one is satisfied with the way the government is dealing with the economy, the more their capacity for resilience.

We also observe a significant relationship with two of the indicators of relative deprivation, namely, the five-year retrospective evaluation and the future evaluation of one's own household economic situation. The two variables, however, point in different directions. On the one hand, viewing the own economic situation as having improved in the past five years is associated to a weaker capacity for resilience. On the other hand, however, believing that the situation is likely to improve in the near future is correlated with a stronger capacity for resilience. While the former result is not easy to interpret, the latter might suggest that resilience impact on how one looks into the future. In other words, those who have a stronger capacity for resilience are more likely to project themselves positively in the future.

Finally, we can see a significant effect of the two "objective" indicators of the impact of the economic crisis on living conditions, namely, restrictions for financial or economic reasons and negative things. Both have an important and positive effect on the capacity for resilience. Thus, resilience seems related to the way people assess the overall state of the economy (sociotropic evaluations) as well as to how they assess their own economic situation (pocketbook evaluations)—at least in prospective terms, but also to how they relate to changes in one's living conditions. More specifically, a deterioration in the latter leads to a stronger capacity for resilience.

Conclusion

The global financial crisis has rocked the world's economies since late 2008. To various degrees and in different contexts, many countries have experienced a protracted economic downturn unparalleled since the Great Depression of the 1930s. As a result, many governments have been struggling to balance their budgets while also assuming a greater role in stimulating the economy. Although Switzerland has dealt with the crisis better than other European countries, the vulnerability of particular segments of its society has largely gone unnoticed.

What lies behind the Swiss case is a story about the Great Recession's uneven effects on society and the labor market as some groups have been affected more than others. Certainly, this is not one of the most talked about crisis; it is a silent crisis—a neglected area of research, as academic and policy attention has been heavily focused on overall country performance and outcomes. Middle class apart, the more vulnerable and the poor seem to be more affected by the recession than other groups. It also appears that the burden of coping has been borne disproportionately by them. These groups, who were already struggling with financial, social, and employment difficulties before the 2008 economic crisis, have been found to feel further disadvantaged but more resilient when their living conditions are threatened.

As shown by our analysis, the most unprivileged segments of the Swiss population often have a stronger perception of the crisis as well as of the way in which the government has responded to it. Manual workers, lower income, and jobless people seem (variably) to have suffered more from the economic crisis than other groups with regard to their working conditions and to have resorted to more financial restrictions (e.g. in terms of reductions in consumption) than the rest of the population. They are also more likely to be pessimistic about their future financial situation. Interestingly, education seems to play a role in triggering resilience, as people with lower education are less resilient than people with higher education. Social class seems to play a role as well—manual workers seem to have a lower capacity for resilience than other classes—pointing to the fact that in times of crisis people with less material and presumably relational resources maintain their disadvantage in terms of the "conversion capabilities" of any (perceived or objective) opportunities (Nussbaum 2011; Sen 1985) over those with more resources.

What is noteworthy, though, is that the capacity of unprivileged groups for resilience seems to be contingent upon the general state of the economy and government responses. Our analysis suggests that there is a negative relationship with the evaluation of the state of the economy and a positive one with the evaluation of how the government deals with it. These findings add another perspective to recent literature on the post-2008 crisis' effects and resilience. While in less affluent countries individual resilience is enhanced in the face of diminishing public resources and state responses (Dalakoglou 2012; Kousis 2014; Pautz and Kominou 2013), in affluent country contexts individuals may become more resilient even when problems are properly addressed by the state and/or public policy interventions. More generally, this might further suggest that individual resilience is more closely related to micro-level agency—that is, individual capacity to mobilize resources and fulfill their own needs—than to macro-level (institutional) structures. It seems thus to be more related to one's own evaluations of the (present and future) situation of their own household within a general economic context and to a lesser extent to the capacity of state institutions—and other macro-level structures—to solve problems.

The lessons coming out of our analysis indicate that investigating links between economic crises and their impact on affluent countries means that we rethink such an impact. The Great Recession, long seen as a problem of only the poorest, has been increasingly affecting some of the world's wealthiest nations such as Switzerland. Overall, assessments of macroeconomic resilience tell us little about the impacts of the crisis on the poor and other vulnerable populations. Our analysis suggests that we need to shape our responses and refine our perspective on what seems to have been overlooked in current debates on widening inequalities and crises effects within affluent countries. That is to say that the resilience of national economies praised by many observers is fueled in large part by the coping strategies that individuals had to adopt, and that this coping has not come without a cost. To be effective, responses to counter the impact of the crisis must be informed by an awareness of how economic shocks have affected different strata of the population differently, how they have eroded these strata's resilience, what exactly has changed, and which interventions have "trickled down" to meet the immediate needs of the less privileged and most vulnerable groups in society.

References

Atkinson, A. B. (2015). *Inequality: What Can be Done?* Cambridge, MA: Harvard University Press.

Batty, E., & Cole I. (2010). *Resilience and the Recession in Six Deprived Communities: Preparing for the Worse to Come?* (JRF Programme Paper, Poverty and Place Programme). York: Joseph Rowntree Foundation.

Beatty, C., & Fothergill, S. (2013). *Hitting the Poorest Places Hardest: The Local and Regional Impact of Welfare Reform.* CRESR: Sheffield Hallam University.

Bell, D. N., & Blanchflower, D. G. (2011). Young People and the Great Recession. *Oxford Review of Economic Policy, 27*, 241–267.

Bermeo, N., & Bartels, L. M. (2014). Mass Politics in Tough Times. In N. Bermeo & L. M. Bartels (Eds.), *Mass Politics in Tough Times: Opinions, Votes and Protest in the Great Recession.* Oxford: Oxford University Press.

Bonesmo Fredriksen, K. (2012). *Income Inequality in the European Union* (OECD Working Paper No. 952). Paris: OECD Publishing.

Brady, H. E., Verba, S., & Lehman Schlozman, K. (1995). Beyond SES? A Resource Model of Political Participation. *American Political Science Review, 89*, 271–294.

Carlin, W. (2012). *A Progressive Economic Strategy: Innovation, Redistribution and Labour-Absorbing Services*. London: Policy Network.

Clauwaert, S., & Schömann I. (2012). *The Crisis and National Labour Law Reforms: A Mapping Exercise* (ETUI Working Paper 2012/04). Brussels: ETUI.

Clegg, D., & Clasen, J. (2011). The Transformation of Unemployment Protection in Europe. In J. Clasen & D. Clegg (Eds.), *Regulating the Risk of Unemployment: National Adaptations to Post-Industrial Labour Markets in Europe*. Oxford: Oxford University Press.

Crouch, C. (2015). Class Politics and the Social Investment Welfare State. In M. Keating & D. McCrone (Eds.), *The Crisis of Social Democracy in Europe*. Edinburgh: Edinburgh University Press.

Dabla-Norris, E., Ji Y., Townsend R. M., & Filiz Unsal D. (2015). *Distinguishing Constraints of Financial Inclusion and Their Impact on GDP and Inequality* (NBER Working Paper 20821). Cambridge, MA: National Bureau of Economic Research.

Dalakoglou, D. (2012). Beyond Spontaneity: Crisis, Violence and Collective Action in Athens. *City, 16*, 535–545.

De Grauwe, P., & Ji, Y. (2013). From Panic-Driven Austerity to Symmetric Macroeconomic Policies in the Eurozone. *Journal of Common Market Studies, 51*, 31–41.

Diamond, P., & Lodge, G. (2013). *European Welfare States After the Crisis*. London: Policy Network.

Dorling, D. (2014). *Inequality and the 1%*. London: Verso.

European Parliament (2015). *Wages and Income Inequality in the European Union* (Study for the EMPL Committee. IP/A/EMPL/2013-05). Brussels: Policy Department A: Economic and Scientific Policy, European Parliament.

European Parliament (2016). *Poverty in the European Union: The Crisis and its Aftermath*. EPRS - European Parliamentary Research Service. PE 579.099.

Federal Statistical Office (2016). *Labour Market Indicators for 2016: Comments on Findings for the Period 2010–2016*. Neuchâtel, July.

Foster, J. E., & Wolfson, M. C. (2010). Polarization and the Decline of the Middle Class: Canada and the U.S. *Journal of Economic Inequality, 8*, 247–273.

Giugni, M., & Grasso, M. T. (Eds.). (2015). *Austerity and Protest: Popular Contention in Times of Economic Crisis*. London: Routledge.

Glover, A., Heathcote, J., Krueger, D., and Ríos-Rull, J. (2011). *Intergenerational Redistribution in the Great Recession* (NBER Working Paper w16924).

Goodwin, M., & Ford, R. (2014). *Revolt on the Right: Explaining Public Support for the Radical Right in Britain*. London: Routledge.

Gurr, T. (1970). *Why Men Rebel*. Princeton: Princeton University Press.

Hall, P. A., & Lamont, M. (Eds.). (2013). *Social Resilience in the Neoliberal Age*. Cambridge: Cambridge University Press.

Hemerijck, A. (2012). *Changing Welfare States*. Oxford: Oxford University Press.

Hur, S. (2016, February 9). *The Lost Generation of the Great Recession*. University of Pittsburg. Available at http://www.pitt.edu/~sewonhur/papers/Hur2012.pdf

Jenson, J. (2012). Redesigning Citizenship Regimes After Neoliberalism: Moving Towards Social Investment. In N. Morel, B. Palier, & J. Palme (Eds.), *Towards a Social Investment Welfare State? Ideas, Policies and Challenges*. Bristol: Policy Press.

Kenworthy, L. (2011). *Progress for the Poor*. Oxford: Oxford University Press.

Kousis, M. (2014). The Transnational Dimension of the Greek Protest Campaign Against Troika Memoranda and Austerity Policies, 2010–12. In D. della Porta & A. Mattoni (Eds.), *Spreading Protests in Social Movements of the Crisis*. Colchester: ECPR Press.

Kriesi, H., & Pappas, T. S. (Eds.). (2015). *European Populism in the Shadow of the Great Recession*. Colchester: ECPR Press.

Kriesi, H., Grande, E., Lachat, R., Dolezal, M., Bornschier, S., & Frey, T. (2008). *West European Politics in the Age of Globalization*. Cambridge: Cambridge University Press.

Kriesi, H., Grande, E., Dolezal, M., Helbling, M., Hutter, S., Höglinger, D., & Wüest, B. (2012). *Political Conflict in Western Europe*. Cambridge: Cambridge University Press.

Lewis-Beck, M. S. (1988). *Economics and Elections: The Major Western Democracies*. Ann Arbor: University of Michigan Press.

Lewis-Beck, M. S., & Stegmaier, M. (2000). Economic Determinants of Electoral Outcomes. *Annual Review of Political Science, 3*, 183–219.

Lorey, I. (2015). *State of Insecurity: Government of the Precarious*. London: Verso Books.

Morel, N., Palier, B., & Palme, J. (Eds.). (2012). *Towards a Social Investment Welfare State: Ideas, Policies and Challenges*. Bristol: The Policy Press.

Musterd, S., & Ostendorf, W. (2014). *Urban Segregation and the Welfare State*. London: Routledge.

Nolan, B., Salverda, W., Checchi, D., Marx, I., McKnight, A., György Tóth, I., & Van de Werfhorst, H. (Eds.). (2014). *Changing Inequalities and Societal Impacts in Rich Countries: Thirty Countries' Experiences*. Oxford: Oxford University Press.

Nussbaum, M. C. (2011). *Creating Capabilities. The Human Development Approach*. Cambridge, MA: The Belknap Press of Harvard University Press.

OECD (2015). *In It Together: Why Less Inequality Benefits All*. Paris: OECD Publishing.

Pautz, H., & Kominou, M. (2013). Reacting to 'Austerity Politics': The Tactic of Collective Expropriation in Greece. *Social Movement Studies, 12*, 103–110.

Petmesidou, M., and Guillén, A. (2015). *Economic Crisis and Austerity in Southern Europe: Threat or Opportunity for a Sustainable Welfare State?* OSE Research Paper Nr. 18O. Bruxelles: European Social Observatory.

Piketty, T. (2013). *Capital in the 21st Century*. Harvard: Harvard University Press.

Pressman, S. (2010). Public Policy and the Middle Class Throughout the World in the Mid 2000s. *Journal of Economic Issues, 44*, 243–262.

Pressman, S., & Scott, R. H. (2011). A Double Squeeze on the Middle Class. *Journal of Economic Issues, 45*, 333–342.

Runciman, W. G. (1966). *Relative Deprivation and Social Justice: A Study of Attitudes to Social Inequality in Twentieth-Century England*. Berkeley: University of California Press.

Seguino, S. (2010). The Global Economic Crisis, Its Gender and Ethnic Implications, and Policy Responses. *Gender and Development, 18*, 179–199.

Sen, A. (1985). *Commodities and Capabilities*. Amsterdam: North-Holland.

Srnicek, N., & Williams, A. (2015). *Inventing the Future: Postcapitalism and a World Without Work*. London: Verso Books.

Standing, G. (2009). *Work After Globalization: Building Occupational Citizenship*. Cheltenham: Elgar.

Standing, G. (2011). *The Precariat: The New Dangerous Class*. London: Bloomsbury Press.

Standing, G. (2014). *A Precariat Charter: From Denizens to Citizens*. London: Bloomsbury.

Stiglitz Commission. (2009). *Report by the Commission on the Measurement of Economic Performance and Social Progress*. Paris: Commission on the Measurement of Economic Performance and Social Progress.

Verba, S., Lehman Schlozman, K., & Brady, H. E. (1995). *Voice and Equality: Civic Voluntarism in American Politics*. Cambridge, MA: Harvard University Press.

CHAPTER 10

Critical Men? Perceptions of Crisis Without Crisis in Sweden

Katrin Uba

Introduction

It is well known that the Great Recession of 2008 did not hit all countries in Western Europe equally. In Sweden, the GDP per capita did not drop as much as in Greece and the unemployment rate did not increase as much as in Spain; in general, the economic situation looked quite similar to that of Germany or Switzerland (Livewhat D1.2 2014). Swedish economic growth did decline for a while and unemployment among young people—that is, people between 15 and 24 years old—increased from 20% in 2008 to 25% in 2009 (SCB 2016). Still, the economic situation had already improved by 2011, when the governor of the Swedish national bank officially stated that the financial crisis was over for Sweden (*Svenska Dagbladet* 04.03.2011). According to the media, the government had handled the crisis very well. *Financial Times* ranked the Swedish finance minister Anders Borg as the best finance minister in Europe—"the wizard behind one of Europe's best-performing economies" (*Financial Times* 22.11.2011).

K. Uba (✉)
Department of Government, Uppsala University, Uppsala, Sweden

M. Giugni, M.T. Grasso (eds.), *Citizens and the Crisis*,
Palgrave Studies in European Political Sociology,
https://doi.org/10.1007/978-3-319-68960-9_10

In the context of this "success story", it is somewhat surprising that when a representative sample of the Swedish population was surveyed in June 2015, five years after the economic crisis peaked and just before the "refugee crisis" started in August of 2015, 16% of the respondents noted that Sweden was suffering *a very serious economic crisis*. With the addition of those who noted that *we are suffering a crisis but it is not a serious one*, the pessimists formed a clear majority (58%) of the respondents. These numbers are obviously low in comparison with the respective numbers in crisis-affected Greece, where 88% of respondents perceived the country to be suffering a very serious crisis, or those in Italy, where 90% of respondents perceived that the Italian economy was suffering some crisis. The perceptions of crisis in Sweden are more comparable to those in Germany, where 17% of respondents noted that there was a very serious crisis and a total of 49% of respondents perceived the presence of some economic crisis. Although the Swedish public appears to be somewhat more pessimistic than the German one, this picture resembles the situation even before the Great Recession of 2008, when northern European countries had a more positive economic mood than the countries in Southern Europe did (Anderson and Hecht 2014).

While some people always have pessimistic economic perceptions, the numbers in Sweden are still somewhat striking, especially considering that welfare states such as Sweden are expected to provide some cushioning effect in the context of an economic downturn. Thus, it would be interesting to know whether those who perceive Sweden to be suffering a very serious economic crisis are people who have suffered from the crisis, or if real economic experience plays little role here. In this chapter, I investigate which socioeconomic groups are more likely to express a negative economic mood in Sweden, by testing two general hypotheses. Some prior studies about public economic mood suggest that people react negatively to a macroeconomic downturn (Anderson and Hecht 2014) and that this reaction is relatively uniform across different income groups. Thus, personal exposure to economic crisis would not decrease their economic mood (Duch et al. 2014). Rich and poor have similar perceptions of macroeconomic circumstances since they are exposed to the same mediated representations of macroeconomic events (Duch et al. 2014: 252). In contrast, other studies argue that the effect of macroeconomic changes on individual satisfaction with the state of the economy is conditioned by the objective personal economic situation. Citizens with higher income and higher socioeconomic status are more affected by economic crisis and therefore have different levels of satisfaction with the state of the economy than those with lower levels of income (Fraile and Pardos-Prado 2014). Although satisfaction with the state of the economy is somewhat different from the perception that the national economy is suffering a crisis, these perceptions are generally comparable. Hence, the analysis presented in this chapter tests which of these two approaches about the variation of economic mood is supported by the recent survey data for Sweden. In addition to the effects of personal experience and income, I focus on the specific roles of age and gender, for two reasons. First, the cushioning effect for youth has decreased in Sweden because the coverage of unemployment benefits for young unemployed persons has significantly decreased since 2006 (Lorentzen et al. 2014). Second, women report a lower health status more often than men in times of economic downturn (Hammarström et al. 2011), and women with low socioeconomic status were more affected than their male counterparts by the severe economic crisis that hit Sweden in the early 1990s (Burström et al. 2012). During the years of welfare retrenchment in Sweden (2006–2010), mental distress increased among women in the labour market as well as among unemployed women (Blomqvist et al. 2014). It is likely that these groups also had more negative perceptions of the Swedish state of economy after the Great Recession.

The following analysis does not aim to provide a causal explanation of which factors explain the development of individuals' economic perceptions. The cross-sectional character of the survey data only permits a finding regarding which socioeconomic groups are more likely to have a more negative economic mood. While prior studies usually make large cross-national comparisons of economies that suffered crises of various degrees, focusing on one country that is (almost) without a crisis allows us to take a closer look at specific individual factors. This study could also be helpful for future research on economic voting and political preferences, which are often related to public economic opinion (e.g., Niemi et al. 1999; Pardos-Prado and Sagarzazu 2014).

Economic Mood and the (Lack of) Crisis in a Comparative Perspective

In order to better understand the perceptions of crisis among Swedish respondents in 2015, it is useful to take a short look at the changes in the economic situation and examine how individuals' economic mood in Sweden has changed during recent years. In the autumn of 2007, 43% of respondents noted that the Swedish economy had improved during the last 12 months. However, a year later, that number was down to 11%; and in 2009, only 3% of survey respondents saw any improvements in the Swedish economy (Shehata and Falasca 2014). This decline seems to reflect the economic situation, as the Swedish real GDP fell drastically in 2009 (as it did in many other countries) and the unemployment rate peaked to 25% in 2009–2010 (SCB 2016).[1] On the other hand, major political reforms, such as the restructuring of state subsidies for unemployment insurance, had already taken place before the Great Recession in 2007—just after the centre-right government came to power in 2006. Restrictions in sickness benefits were implemented in 2008 (Livewhat D2.4 2014). Despite these reforms, trust in the ruling centre-right coalition increased from 33% in 2007 to 52% in 2010 (Nord and Shehata 2013), and the coalition did not lose its power until the 2014 elections.

Data from the Eurobarometer's survey (Fig 10.1) demonstrates further fluctuations and shows how pessimism towards the economic situation in Sweden dominated perspectives from mid-2011 until mid-2013. This is not surprising, considering the intensive media coverage of the economic crisis that occurred during these years (Asp 2011; Färm et al. 2012). The media mainly focused on the consequences of the crisis in Southern Europe; however, local events such as the closure of the famous Swedish automobile producer SAAB were also widely covered. On the other hand, it has been noted that the media framing of the Swedish economy and unemployment trends became increasingly positive in the second half of 2010 (Asp 2011).

The presented numbers align with prior research about the changing public economic mood, in that economic mood is expected to reflect changes in the economic situation and media coverage; however, this is an aggregate picture. A more detailed picture is obtained by comparing the Swedish numbers with those of the other countries examined in the survey, and by taking a particular look at how the perceptions of crisis vary across gender (Table 10.1). Regardless of general differences in economic

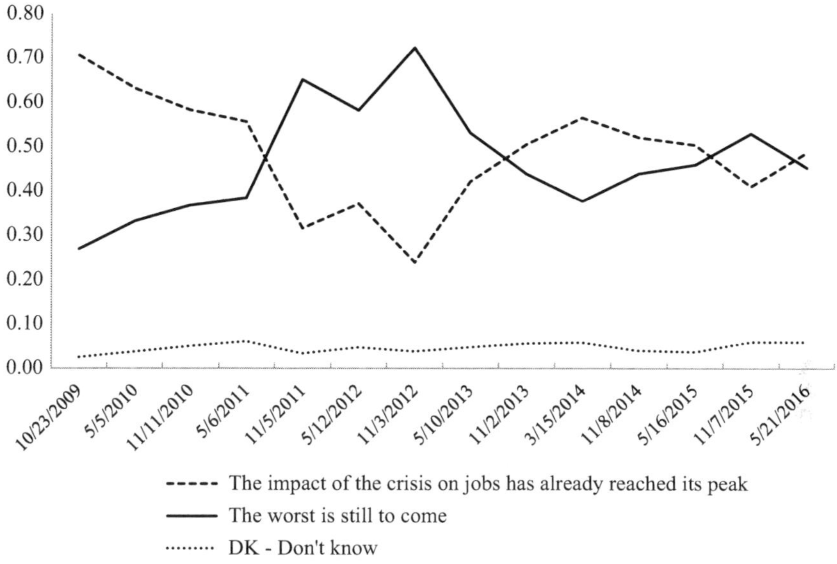

Fig. 10.1 Individuals' perceptions of economic crisis in Sweden from 2009 to 2016 (Source: Eurobarometer)

mood, the difference between male and female respondents is very similar across all examined countries except Sweden. While women are generally more critical towards the state of the economy in their country, Swedish male respondents have *significantly more negative perceptions* of their country's state of economy than female respondents.

Examining the reasons behind these very interesting differences across countries goes beyond the scope of this chapter, but it is likely that the effect of a crisis does not explain the difference as well as some other factors do (e.g., gender equality or the character of the welfare state). I focus only on the case of Sweden, and examine whether this gender difference disappears when I account for factors that explain the variance of citizens' economic mood according to prior studies.

Explaining the Varying Perceptions of Crisis

Individuals' assessments of their country's state of economy are much discussed by scholars of economic voting, who tend to treat assessment as an independent variable in their analyses (e.g., Lewis-Beck and Paldam

Table 10.1 Perceptions of crisis by gender across nine countries

Country	*% "a very serious crisis"*		*t-test*	*N*
	Women		*Men*	
France	57.0	43.0	0.520	2027
Germany	54.7	45.3	2.239*	2108
Greece	54.0	46.0	2.447**	2048
Italy	53.6	46.4	2.133*	2040
Poland	59.3	40.7	1.835	2024
Spain	51.6	48.7	2.280*	2035
Sweden	**42.8**	**57.2**	**4.723*** **	**2018**
Switzerland	55.3	44.7	0.825	2046
UK	53.0	47.0	0.041	2022
Total	53.8	46.2		18,368

Note: The t-test is based on a comparisons of means, where answers of "very serious crisis" were coded as 1 and the rest of the answers were coded as 0

***$p<0.01$; **$p<0.05$; *$p<0.1$

2000). More recent studies have shifted towards investigating factors that explain the varying economic moods, as well as the mechanism that might explain the effect of these various factors (Duch and Stevenson 2010; Fraile and Pardos-Prado 2014; Pardos-Prado and Sagarzazu 2014). Many of these studies note, for example, that varying economic assessment is closely related to context-specific factors, such as the media coverage of the issue or the real economic situation of the country, and to micro-level factors such as the individuals' own experience of an economic downturn, income and individuals' political attitudes, and self-interest (Duch et al. 2000; Duch and Sagarzazu 2014; Fraile and Pardos-Prado 2014; Niemi et al. 1999; Pardos-Prado and Sagarzazu 2014).

The effects of macro-level factors are not much disputed, and it has been shown that economic decline has a generally negative impact on individuals' economic mood (Duch and Sagarzazu 2014). Similarly, negative media coverage of economic news is shown to play an important role in individuals' evaluation of government economic policies (Kalogeropoulos et al. 2017).[2] These arguments also align with studies in psychology, which report how the anticipation and experience of economic hardship influence the development of poor mental and physical health (Sargent-Cox et al. 2011; Smith and Huo 2014). The major disagreements in prior research are rather about the group-level effects: whether all groups are equally affected by a crisis and the negative media coverage or whether there are significant differences across socioeconomic groups.

The first approach argues that people react negatively to a macroeconomic downturn, and that this reaction is relatively uniform across different socioeconomic groups (Anderson and Hecht 2014). Due to their similar exposure to negative media coverage and economic crisis, perceptions regarding macroeconomic circumstances or the status of a crisis in the country should not differ between rich and poor (Duch and Sagarzazu 2014). Rather, economic perceptions and expectations are mainly related to the political position of the individual and to the party they support (Duch and Stevenson 2011). People tend to be more optimistic about the economy when they are partisans of the incumbent than when they are partisans of the opposition (Duch and Stevenson 2011:18). This approach might work well for economic expectations, but it is unreasonable to suggest that citizens' economic mood or evaluation of the state of the economy changes as soon as a new party or governing coalition comes into power. This approach leads to two hypotheses to be tested: first, that there will be no significant differences in perception of crisis between those who have experienced economic downturn and those who have not. Here, experience will be measured as restricted consumption. The second hypothesis focuses on the support for non-incumbent political parties. Considering that Sweden was ruled by the centre-right coalition during the crisis, and that during the survey there was already a left-wing government, the only party that has been in opposition throughout the entire period is the populist right-wing Sweden Democrats party. The party won 29 new seats in the 2014 elections and became the third largest party in parliament (Berg and Oscarsson 2015). Thus, following Duch and Stevenson (2011), I would expect the electorate of the Sweden Democrats to be more critical towards the economic situation in Sweden than voters for other parties.

The second approach for explaining the different economic moods among citizens claims that individuals are affected by the economic crisis by different degrees, and that they would therefore perceive the severity of a crisis in their country differently (Fraile and Pardos-Prado 2014). People with higher socioeconomic status have more to lose and would therefore be more vulnerable and disappointed. This perspective aligns with studies about relative deprivation, which find that a perceived reduction in the standard of living has a strong emotional effect by increasing individuals' anger and perceptions of subjective injustice (Ragnarsdóttir et al. 2013).

While Fraile and Pardos-Prado (2014) focused mainly on the difference between income groups, it is likely that in countries with relatively small income differences, such as Sweden, the effect of a crisis on the economic mood of people from different income groups is not as strong. Similar to several prior studies, I suggest that two other factors might play a more important role here—the status of being employed or unemployed (cf. Anderson 2007; Fraile and Pardos-Prado 2014), and the sector in which one has existing employment—that is, the public versus the private sector (cf. Singer 2011).

Employment status is particularly relevant in the context of an economic crisis, when many people might lose their jobs, particularly since the cushioning effect of the welfare state is limited due to retrenchments. For example, youth unemployment in Sweden increased directly in relation to the financial crisis (8.6% in 2009). Even though unemployment among women before the crisis in Sweden was higher than that of men, the situation has changed since 2008; the unemployment rate among men is now higher than that of women (SCB 2016). The unemployed are expected to be more likely than the employed to perceive that there is a severe economic crisis in Sweden.

The expected difference between public- and private-sector workers is also motivated by the character of the recent crisis because public-sector workers suffered the most from retrenchments in many countries (Livewhat D2.3 2014). This was not the case in Sweden, where the crisis affected several industries, including the automobile industry (SAAB). The share of employment in the public sector, out of total employment, did not change much in Sweden during the crisis, remaining at around 5% for the central government and 24% for the local government (Mailand and Hansen 2016). Thus, public-sector workers are expected to be less likely to perceive that Sweden is suffering a very serious economic crisis.

Finally, as already suggested above, it is reasonable to expect that gender and age affect perceptions of the national state of the economy in Sweden. It is not just personal experience that might influence a negative mood; a certain group identity might play a role here. When the media reports on increasing unemployment among youth, it might have a spillover effect on the attitudes of employed young people as well. For example, a medical study found that, regardless of employment status, young people reported poorer health during a recession than during a boom; this effect was particularly significant for women (Novo et al. 2001). Hence, it is likely that young people and women are more pessimistic in their evaluation of the economic situation, regardless of their employment status.

Data and Operationalization

I used the same dataset described in the introduction of this book—the nine-country survey focusing on questions of economic crisis, political attitudes and behaviour. I analysed only the data about Sweden, which initially yielded about 2000 respondents with relatively representative social backgrounds. As all the respondents did not answer every question of interest in this chapter, the final analysis used only the responses from 1375 individuals (descriptive details about the data are in the Appendix).

The survey captures the economic mood of the respondents by the following statement: "Some say that Sweden is suffering a very serious economic crisis, others that there is a crisis but not a serious one or that there is no economic crisis. What do you think?" The dependent variable for this analysis is the binary variable, which measures whether or not the respondent notes that "We are suffering a very serious economic crisis". After omitting all those who did not answer the question at all or who stated *Do not know*, 19.7% of the respondents perceived the presence of a serious crisis (the rest stated that "We are suffering a crisis but it is not very serious" or "No economic crisis"). Figure 10.2 demonstrates the clear difference between the responses of male and female respondents across age: young men seem to be much more pessimistic than young women about the Swedish economic status. The analysis below will demonstrate whether this difference remains once personal experience of crisis, political party support, and employment status have been controlled for, along with several control variables.

Personal experience of crisis could be measured in various ways, but in this context, reported experience regarding reduced consumption over the past five years seems to be a more appropriate measure than that of relative deprivation, such as estimated household situation.[3] Reduced consumption measure is an index of reported reductions of consumption, composed of ten different variables referring to reducing consumption of staple foods, reducing IT services or entertainment, delaying payments for gas or water, reducing or postponing the buying of medicines, reducing car use, skipping holidays, and moving to live with parents. Descriptive information of all variables are presented in Appendix; here, it suffices to

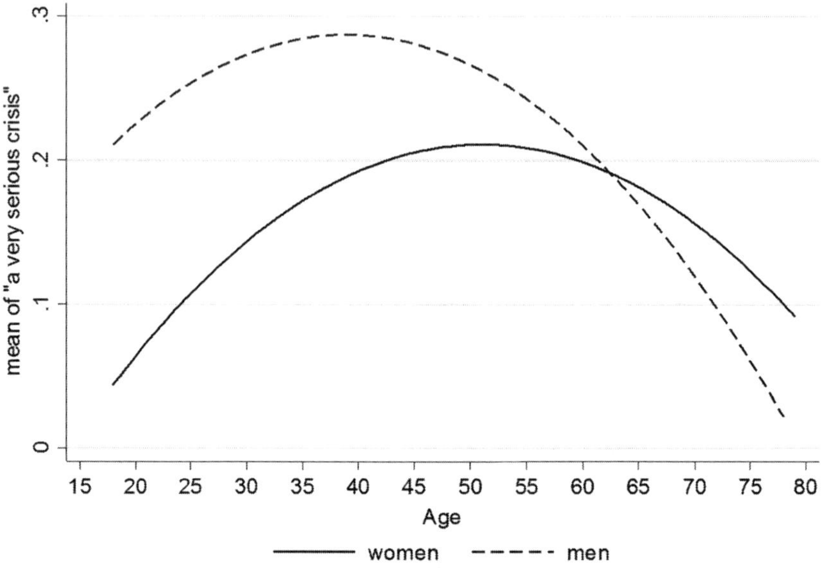

Fig. 10.2 Perceptions of crisis across age and gender in Sweden

note that more than half of the Swedish respondents did not reduce their consumption of any of the listed items.

The second independent variable of interest is the electoral support for the Sweden Democrats party in the last national election in 2014 (coded as 1 if the respondent voted for the Sweden Democrats party and zero if not). Of the respondents, 19.4% reported that they voted for this party; this is an overestimation, as the party actually won only 12.9% of the votes. It is likely that the sample includes slightly more supporters of the party than in reality, but it might also reflect the tendency of people to over-report their electoral participation.

Next, there are two employment-related variables—being unemployed at the time of the survey (5.4%) and working in the public sector (34%). The last variable refers only to those who are active in the labour market; therefore, the effect of this variable will be analysed separately from the effect of unemployment.

There are also several control variables that might be correlated to the perception of crisis in addition to the listed independent variables. Such controls are income on a ten-step scale from low (£760) to high (more than £4200); level of education measured in three categories (upper, middle, lower); and an index of reported newspaper readership, which refers to the number of different newspapers the respondent reads. The last is an important variable because of the theoretical idea that the perception of a crisis, or individuals' economic mood, is strongly related to media presentation of the issue (Duch and Sagarzazu 2014).

What Matters: Crisis Experience, Party Support, or Gender?

To examine which factors correlate with the perceptions of serious economic crisis, I use a simple logistic analysis. The results are presented in Table 10.2. In addition to the variables discussed above, the analysis also includes the measure of squared age, in order to account for the curvilinear relationship between crisis perception and age (as shown in Fig. 10.2). Also relying on Fig. 10.2, the models include interaction variables for gender and age. Young male respondents seem to hold more pessimistic views than young female respondents, while at the age of 60, there was no clear gender difference in respondents' perception of crisis. Thus, it is reasonable to account for these interaction effects in the statistical analysis as well.

The results (Table 10.2) do not support the first hypothesis, which suggested that there would be no differences in economic mood between people who experienced a crisis to different degrees. Swedish data shows a slightly positive effect of reduced consumption on perceptions of a serious crisis. The effect of this variable is significant, even when other independent variables are included along with the control variables (Models 3 and 4). Based on the results in Model 3, the predicted probability of perceiving a very serious crisis can be calculated: of those who have not reduced their consumption at all (55% of respondents), the probability is 14%; and of those who reduced their consumption of almost all the items listed in the survey (3% of respondents), the probability is 38% (holding all other variables at their mean). These results provide more support for the so-called pocketbook perspective, which suggests that personal experiences play a role in economic predictions (Niemi et al. 1999), than for those who argue that a crisis affects all groups equally and that there should not be much difference between the crisis perceptions of different socioeconomic groups.

The importance of economic situation in the perception of a crisis is also visible when the effect of individuals' reported income is examined: those with higher income are significantly less likely to perceive

Table 10.2 The probability of perceiving that Sweden is suffering a very serious economic crisis (log coefficients)

Variables	*Model 1*	*Model 2*	*Model 3*	*Model 4*	*Model 5*
Age	0.101***	0.093**	0.093**	0.089**	0.090**
	(0.034)	(0.037)	(0.037)	(0.038)	(0.037)
Age^2	−0.001***	−0.001***	−0.001***	−0.001***	−0.001***
	(0.0003)	(0.0003)	(0.0003)	(0.0003)	(0.0003)
Female	−1.851***	−1.579***	−1.578***	−1.563***	−1.529**
	(0.517)	(0.548)	(0.548)	(0.560)	(0.554)
Age*Female	0.026**	0.025**	0.025**	0.024**	0.023**
	(0.010)	(0.011)	(0.011)	(0.011)	(0.011)
Reduced consumption	0.143***	0.149***	0.149***	0.148***	0.153***
	(0.030)	(0.033)	(0.033)	(0.034)	(0.033)
Voted Sweden Democrats		1.903***	1.904***	1.857***	1.838***
		(0.163)	(0.163)	(0.168)	(0.164)
Unemployed			−0.0575		-0.021
			(0.345)		(0.345)
Public sector				−0.0520	
				(0.180)	
Trust in media					-1.054***
					(0.277)
Controls					
University education (baseline)					
Completed secondary	0.280	0.146	0.145	0.147	0.113
	(0.186)	(0.197)	(0.197)	(0.206)	(0.199)
Below secondary	0.582***	0.228	0.226	0.237	0.197
	(0.190)	(0.207)	(0.207)	(0.217)	(0.208)
Income	−0.064**	−0.061**	−0.062**	−0.059*	−0.063**
	(0.028)	(0.030)	(0.031)	(0.032)	(0.0325)
News readership	1.144	0.913	0.909	0.896	0.912
	(0.659)	(0.705)	(0.706)	(0.719)	(0.713)
Constant	−3.089***	−3.478***	−3.480***	−3.362***	−3.227***
	(0.817)	(0.888)	(0.888)	(0.918)	(0.897)
Pseudo R^2	0.08	0.181	0.181	0.174	0.193
Observations	1357	1375	1375	1311	1375

Notes: Standard errors in parentheses ***p<0.01; **p<0.05; *p<0.1

that Sweden is suffering a very serious economic crisis, although this effect is actually very small. It is possible that the crisis in Sweden was too small to have any large effect on individuals' income and consumption; in that case, the correlations presented in this study might not actually reflect the effects of economic crisis, but might rather describe which socioeconomic groups tend to have a more pessimistic perception of the Swedish economic state, regardless of the objective situation.

The second hypothesis suggests that political party support will have an effect on individuals' perception of a crisis, and Model 2 in Table 10.2 demonstrates clear support of this. Those who reported voting for the Sweden Democrats party in 2014 are significantly more likely to perceive that Sweden is suffering a very serious economic crisis. The probability of seeing a crisis is 45% among Sweden Democrats voters, while it is 11% among voters for other parties. This effect, however, is not consistent across all age groups. As Fig. 10.3 demonstrates, the difference in the per-

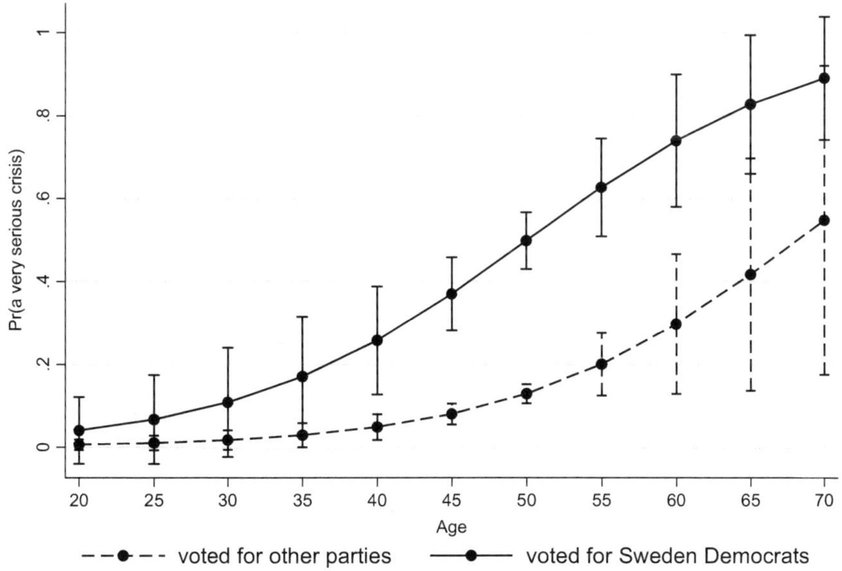

Fig. 10.3 Marginal effect of voting for Sweden Democrats on perceptions of a very serious crisis over age (with 95% confidence interval)

ceptions of crisis between the voters of Sweden Democrats and voters for the different other political parties is largest at ages of 40–60. The result is not surprising, as this is the age group which is the most vulnerable to lay-offs as results of macroeconomic changes caused by the financial crisis.

One could suggest that the strong effect of supporting an anti-immigrant populist party might be related to the political situation of the summer of 2015, and refer to the emerging refugee crisis, even though the survey's fieldwork in Sweden only lasted until June 2015. The numbers of asylum seekers increased and media attention to the issue became more intense in September 2015, but there was already a slight increase of articles mentioning the "asylum crisis" in May 2015 (in comparison with January 2015) (Ringmar 2016). The effects of this emerging "refugee crisis" probably added to the effects of the argument presented above—that partisans of the opposition have more negative perceptions of economy (Duch and Stevenson 2011). The Sweden Democrats has never been included in a national-level coalition government. Moreover, its electoral success and political statements are often framed negatively by other political parties and in the mainstream media (Hellström et al. 2012). Thus, the electorate of this party probably have less reason to trust the mainstream media when it reports the "end of the crisis". In fact, when the analysis includes a variable measuring trust in the media, the effect of voting for the Sweden Democrats decreases and trust in the media appears to have a significant negative effect on perceptions of a very serious crisis (Table 10.2, Model 5). Respondents who trust media are significantly less likely to perceive that Sweden is suffering a very serious economic crisis.

The argument about the negative attitudes of those who support oppositional parties is also reinforced by the fact that if the voters of another non-governing party—the Left Party (Vänsterparitet)—are included in the analysis, then their electorate is also slightly more likely to perceive a serious crisis in Sweden. The Left Party has been accepted as an important actor in the Swedish political arena, but it has not been part of the so-called red-green governing coalition of the Social Democratic Party and the Green Party because the Left Party is sometimes seen as "too radical". This result clearly demonstrates that it is not the ideology of the party but rather its non-mainstream, or oppositional, character that explains why the supporters of the Sweden Democrats (and those of the Left Party) are more likely to perceive that Sweden is suffering a very serious crisis.[4]

The third hypothesis focused on employment status; the results in Model 3 show that unemployment has no significant effect on an individual's economic mood. The effect is not present even if party support or reduced consumption is omitted from the analysis. There might be several reasons for such a result. First, there are relatively few unemployed people in this sample—only 5% are unemployed in the sample, versus the official 7% as recorded by the Swedish Statistics Bureau (SCB 2016). This makes it more difficult to find significant effects. On the other hand, the effect of unemployment on crisis perception might not be evident because the retrenchments in the unemployment policies in 2006 did not cancel out the "cushioning effect". Hence, those who became unemployed during the crisis years, or those who have been unemployed for some time, have not experienced a radical worsening of their living conditions as a result of the crisis.

Similar to unemployment, a status of public-sector employee has no significant effect on individuals' economic mood. Again, the lack of a real crisis in Sweden (since the crisis did not lead to retrenchments in the public sector, as it did in Southern European countries) might be the reason for this null effect. Although some private-sector workers, mainly in the automobile industry, suffered directly from the consequences of the crisis, this is not reflected in the data.

Finally, gender and age were expected to play an important role in explaining the varying perceptions of crisis in Sweden. Young people and women were expected to be more pessimistic because of their probable vulnerability to economic downturn and to retrenchments in the welfare state (unemployment and health insurance policies). None of these expectations are supported by the results, which show the effects of gender and age to be exactly the opposite of what was expected, with the effect of age actually being very small.

While on basis of Model 1 we can say that male respondents of age 40–50 had more pessimistic views than female respondents, at the age of 20 or 60, there was no clear gender difference in respondents' perception of crisis. In Model 5, after including the variables which account for the voting for Sweden Democrats, unemployment, and trust in media, the effect of gender over age disappears.

Although the gender effect in average is strong and significant, it is opposite to expectations. Even though the effect decreases somewhat after party support is included in the analysis (compare Models 2 and 3), women are significantly less likely than men to say that the Swedish economy is suffering a very serious crisis. The predicted probability of perceiving a

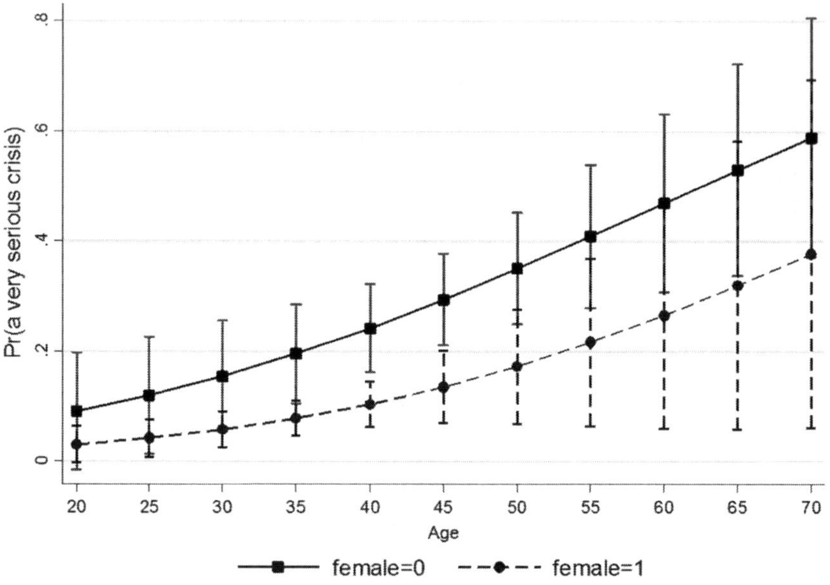

Fig. 10.4 Marginal effect of gender on perceptions of a very serious crisis over age gender (with a 95% confidence interval)

crisis is 13% for women and almost two times more (22%) for men, holding all other variables at their mean. This difference varies slightly across age (see Fig. 10.4), as there is little gender difference among young people and a significant difference for those between the ages of 40 and 60. These results are interesting because prior studies tend to show women as being more vulnerable to crisis and, as shown in Table 10.1, women in all other examined countries were more pessimistic than men. On the other hand, one recent study on risk perception and economic crisis in the US found no statistically significant gender differences in perceived risk during times of crisis (Burns et al. 2012). Considering that the difference between male and female respondents in my analysis appears mainly in the group of middle-aged people, it is likely that there are some specific characteristics of this age group that explain the difference. The analysis in this chapter controlled for the effects of education, income, news readership, and employment status. Further studies are needed to better understand this gender difference.

Conclusion

This chapter examined individuals' perception of Sweden as suffering a very serious economic crisis in June 2015, at a time when many objective economic measures, as well as the mainstream media, appeared to argue the opposite. Although Sweden was hit by the Great Recession of 2008, it was much less affected than countries such as Greece or Spain, and it recovered quickly. Hence, it is particularly interesting to set the Swedish case into the context of studies that examine changes and variation in individuals' economic mood, especially as a result of economic crisis. This issue is often seen as important for literature about economic voting. However, instead of examining the government's crisis response or individuals' satisfaction with the government, the main interest in this analysis was to examine the variation in individuals' perceptions of the national economic situation. Two different approaches were tested: one that suggested that there is little difference between the crisis perceptions of different socioeconomic groups, but that party support has a strong effect on crisis perception; and another that predicted the importance of income and socioeconomic situation in explaining variations in people's economic moods. In addition to these hypotheses, I added a third that emphasized the role of age and gender, because retrenchments in unemployment policies were expected to make young people more vulnerable to crisis, and because prior studies reported negative experiences of women in previous economic crises.

None of the approaches found clear support in the analysis of Swedish data. Reduction of consumption and income had a small effect on crisis perception. People who had to reduce their consumption during the last five years were more likely to perceive the presence of a very serious economic crisis, and the same applied for people from lower-level income groups. The effects were small, and when these findings are combined with the finding that unemployment had no significant effect on individuals' economic mood, it is not fully clear whether different socioeconomic groups in Sweden perceive the presence of economic crisis differently or not.

This lack of clarity could be explained by the fact that the Swedish welfare state has balanced or "cushioned" some negative effects of the (eventually) small crisis. For example, Sweden's public expenditures increased by 22% during 2008–2013, while those of Germany increased by 13% and those of Greece decreased by 9% (Cylus and Pearson 2015). Hence, the results of the Swedish case should not be seen as refuting the argument that different socioeconomic groups experience a crisis differently and therefore have diverse perceptions of crisis several years after the crisis.

On the other hand, similar to the results presented in the chapter about Germany, the lack of a real economic crisis brings other factors, which are important for explaining individuals' economic perceptions, into focus. Support of the populist anti-immigrant Sweden Democrats party had the strongest positive correlation with the perception of a very serious crisis. Considering the idea that the formation of individuals' perceptions of economic situation is based on media consumption, and the fact that the Swedish media mainly reported about the crisis elsewhere, I also tested the effect of trust in the media. The effect of support for the Sweden Democrats party remained strong and significant, but the results also showed that distrust of the media is strongly related to the perception of an economic crisis. The results of the analysis provide evidence for the argument that supporters of oppositional or less-mainstream parties are more likely to perceive the economic situation negatively. In fact, this appears to occur regardless of the ideological leaning of the supported parties.

Finally, the chapter demonstrated that, in Sweden, female respondents were clearly more optimistic about the status of the economy than male respondents; this division is unique in comparison with the other countries examined in this book. The high level of gender equality in Sweden and the relative strength of its welfare state might be the reasons behind this exceptional situation. Still, further comparative studies are needed to establish a better understanding of this phenomenon. The gender effect remained strong even when I examined the effects of other factors that are often related to gender: income, working in the public sector, and supporting the populist anti-immigration party. The predicted probability of saying that Sweden is suffering a very serious economic crisis was almost two times higher for men than for women. Further studies could examine whether this situation was specific to 2015, or if the pattern changes over time and was different the last time Sweden suffered a real economic crisis, in the early 1990s. This result also encourages a search for factors other than economic ones for explaining individuals' economic mood.

Notes

1. It should be recalled that the Swedish economy was restructured considerably during the 1990s, when the country experienced a truly serious economic crisis (Jensen and Davidsen 2016).

2. In the case of media coverage, there is some dispute, as Shehata and Falasca (2014) demonstrate that negative crisis-priming in the media had no effect on public approval of the government in Sweden.
3. One could also use a measure related to worsened job conditions, but issues like reduction of pay, unpaid overwork, increased workload, and so forth, apply only to employed respondents and thereby reduce the sample. The question wording used here was as follows: "In the past 5 years, have you or anyone else in your household had to take any of the following measures for financial/economic reasons?"
4. Prior studies also note that SD supporters have little political trust and tend to have a more authoritarian than libertarian value position and that the left-right ideology plays much less of a role in their identity than trust and authoritarian values do (Oskarson and Demker 2015).

References

Anderson, C. J. (2007). The End of Economic Voting? Contingency Dilemmas and the Limits of Democratic Accountability. *Annual Review of Political Science, 10*, 271–296.

Anderson, C. J., & Hecht, J. D. (2014). Crisis of Confidence? Dynamics of Economic Opinions During the Great Recession. In N. Bermeo & L. Bartels (Eds.), *Mass Politics in Tough Times: Opinions, Votes and Protest in the Great Recession* (pp. 40–72). Oxford: Oxford University Press.

Asp, K. (2011). *Mediernas prestationer och betydelse: Valet 2010.* Göteborg: Institutionen för journalistik, medier och kommunikation, Göteborgs universitet.

Berg, L., & Oscarsson, H. (2015). The Swedish General Election 2014. *Electoral Studies, 38*, 82–136.

Blomqvist, S., Burström, B., & Backhans, M. C. (2014). Increasing Health Inequalities Between Women in and Out of Work—The Impact of Recession or Policy Change? A Repeated Cross-Sectional Study in Stockholm County, 2006 and 2010. *International Journal for Equity in Health, 13*(1), 1.

Burns, W. J., Peters, E., & Slovic, P. (2012). Risk Perception and the Economic Crisis: A Longitudinal Study of the Trajectory of Perceived Risk. *Risk Analysis, 32*(4), 659–677.

Burström, B., Nylen, L., Barr, B., Clayton, S., Holland, P., & Whitehead, M. (2012). Delayed and Differential Effects of the Economic Crisis in Sweden in the 1990s on Health-Related Exclusion from the Labour Market: A Health Equity Assessment. *Social Science & Medicine, 75*(12), 2431–2436.

Cylus, J., & Pearson, M. (2015). *The Crisis and Its Implications for Household Financial Security, Government Resources and Health Expenditure. Economic Crisis, Health Systems and Health in Europe. Impact and Implications for Policy* (pp. 17–50). Maidenhead: Open University Press.

Duch, R. M., & Stevenson, R. (2010). The Global Economy, Competency, and the Economic Vote. *The Journal of Politics, 72*(01), 105–123.

Duch, R. M., Palmer, H. D., & Anderson, C. J. (2000). Heterogeneity in Perceptions of National Economic Conditions. *American Journal of Political Science, 44*, 635–652.

Duch, R. M., & Sagarzazu, I. (2014). Crisis Perceptions and Economic Voting Among the Rich and the Poor. In N. Bermeo & L. Bartels (Eds.), *Mass Politics in Tough Times: Opinions, Votes and Protest in the Great Recession* (pp. 224–260). Oxford: Oxford University Press.

Färm, K.-A., Jendel, L., & Nord, L. (2012). Bilden av finanskrisen. En studie av svenska mediers nyhetsrapportering hösten 2008. *Demicom nr 9*. Mittuniversitetet, Sundsvall. ISBN: 978-91-87103-54-4.

Financial Times. (2011, November 22). 2011 FT Ranking of European Finance Ministers—Anders Borg.

Fraile, M., & Pardos-Prado, S. (2014). Correspondence Between the Objective and Subjective Economies: The Role of Personal Economic Circumstances. *Political Studies, 62*(4), 895–912.

Hammarström, A., Gustafsson, P. E., Strandh, M., Virtanen, P., & Janlert, U. (2011). It's No Surprise! Men Are Not Hit More Than Women by the Health Consequences of Unemployment in the Northern Swedish Cohort. *Scandinavian Journal of Public Health, 39*, 187–193.

Hellström, A., Nilsson, T., & Stoltz, P. (2012). Nationalism Vs. Nationalism: The Challenge of the Sweden Democrats in the Swedish Public Debate. *Government and Opposition, 47*(2), 186–205.

Jensen, L., & Davidsen, S. (2016). The Global Financial Crisis in Denmark and Sweden: A Case of Crisis Management 'Lite'. In John Wanna, Evert A. Lindquist, & Jouke de Vries (eds.) *The Global Financial Crisis and Its Budget Impacts in OECD Nations: Fiscal Responses and Future Challenges* (p. 174–204). Edward Elgar Publishing.

Kalogeropoulos, A., Albæk, E., de Vreese, C. H., & van Dalen, A. (2017). News Priming and the Changing Economy: How Economic News Influences Government Evaluations. *International Journal of Public Opinion Research, 29*(2):269–290.

Lewis-Beck, M. S., & Paldam, M. (2000). Economic Voting: An Introduction. *Electoral Studies, 19*(2), 113–121.

Livewhat D1.2. (2014). *Working Paper on Definition and Identification of Crises*. Accessible at: http://www.livewhat.unige.ch/wp-content/uploads/2014/02/LIVEWHAT_D1.2.pdf

Livewhat D2.3. (2014). *Integrated Report on Policy Responses to Crises*. Accessible at: http://www.livewhat.unige.ch/wp-content/uploads/2014/02/LIVEWHAT_D2.3.pdf

Livewhat D2.4. (2014). *Integrated Report on Policy Responses to Crises*. Accessible at: http://www.livewhat.unige.ch/wp-content/uploads/2014/02/LIVEWHAT_D2.4.pdf

Lorentzen, T., Angelin, A., Dahl, E., Kauppinen, T., Moisio, P., & Salonen, T. (2014). Unemployment and Economic Security for Young Adults in Finland, Norway and Sweden: From Unemployment Protection to Poverty Relief. *International Journal of Social Welfare, 23*(1), 41–51.

Mailand, M., & Hansen, N. W. (2016). 9 Denmark and Sweden: The Consequences of Reform and Economic Crisis for Public Service Employment Relations. In *Public Service Management and Employment Relations in Europe: Emerging from the Crisis* (p. 218). New York: Routledge.

Niemi, R. G., Bremer, J., & Heel, M. (1999). Determinants of State Economic Perceptions. *Political Behavior, 21*(2), 175–193.

Nord, L., & Shehata, A. (2013). Finanskrisen, förväntningarna och förtroendet. *DEMICOM Report*.

Novo, M., Hammarström, A., & Janlert, U. (2001). Do High Levels of Unemployment Influence the Health of Those Who Are Not Unemployed? A Gendered Comparison of Young Men and Women During Boom and Recession. *Social Science & Medicine, 53*(3), 293–303.

Oskarson, M., & Demker, M. (2015). Room for Realignment: The Working-Class Sympathy for Sweden Democrats. *Government and Opposition, 50*(04), 629–651.

Pardos-Prado, S., & Sagarzazu, I. (2014). The Political Conditioning of Subjective Economic Evaluations: The Role of Party Discourse. *British Journal of Political Science, 46*(4), 799–823.

Ragnarsdóttir, B. H., Bernburg, J. G., & Ólafsdóttir, S. (2013). The Global Financial Crisis and Individual Distress: The Role of Subjective Comparisons After the Collapse of the Icelandic Economy. *Sociology, 47*(4), 755–775.

Ringmar, E. (2016). *Flyktingkris i den svenska dagspressen. En analys av 2015 års viktigaste begreppsförskjutning* (MA Thesis at Lund University). Accessible at: http://lup.lub.lu.se/luur/download?func=downloadFile&recordOId=8873153&fileOId=8873169

Sargent-Cox, K., Butterworth, P., & Anstey, K. J. (2011). The Global Financial Crisis and Psychological Health in a Sample of Australian Older Adults: A Longitudinal Study. *Social Science & Medicine, 73*(7), 1105–1112.

SCB. (2016). *Arbetslöshet tog fart under finanskrisen*. Accessible at: http://www.sverigeisiffror.scb.se/hitta-statistik/sverige-i-siffror/samhallets-ekonomi/arbetslosheten/

Shehata, A., & Falasca, K. (2014). Priming Effects During the Financial Crisis: Accessibility and Applicability Mechanisms Behind Government Approval. *European Political Science Review, 6*(04), 597–620.

Singer, M. (2011). When Do Voters Actually Think 'It's the Economy'? Evidence from the 2008 Presidential Campaign. *Electoral Studies, 30*(4), 621–632.

Smith, H. J., & Huo, Y. J. (2014). Relative Deprivation How Subjective Experiences of Inequality Influence Social Behavior and Health. *Policy Insights from the Behavioral and Brain Sciences, 1*(1), 231–238.

Svenska Dagbladet. (2011, March 04). Leif Petersen. *Borg har gott hopp om arbetsmarknaden*.

CHAPTER 11

Citizens and the Crisis: The Great Recession as Constraint and Opportunity

Marco Giugni and Maria T. Grasso

Resilient Europeans?

European countries have gone through various periods of economic downturn since at least the mid-1970s, when the first oil crisis put an end to three decades of post-war economic growth and wealth. However, the crisis of end of the 2000s became an unprecedentedly severe global economic crisis, hence the terminology of the Great Recession. The new conditions can be seen to have had profound consequences on people's perceptions of the economy—whether their own or that of the country in which they live—as well as on their situation more generally (see also Giugni and Grasso 2017, Temple and Grasso 2017). Furthermore, in one way or another, all have experienced the Great Recession, whether most directly, for example, due to loss of employment or reductions in consumption or indirectly by living in an economically deteriorating environment. Most

M. Giugni (✉)
Department of Political Science and International Relations, University of Geneva, Geneva, Switzerland

M.T. Grasso
Department of Politics, University of Sheffield, Sheffield, UK

M. Giugni, M.T. Grasso (eds.), *Citizens and the Crisis*,
Palgrave Studies in European Political Sociology,
https://doi.org/10.1007/978-3-319-68960-9_11

importantly, European citizens had to learn how to make sense of this new situation and, in particular for some, how to develop coping strategies and ways to respond to the challenges. In brief, they had to show a capacity for resilience, often implemented in the private sphere and in everyday life, for example, in terms of changes in production and consumption patterns at the household level, coping strategies including informal work, migration, family, or neighborhood self-help.

One possible negative effect of economic hardship is the decline of political participation and civic engagement. If citizens need to struggle with the array of difficulties produced by economic hardship, they will have less time and resources to engage in political action. Especially when they related to job loss, this may also imply the loss or absence of social networks and personal contacts which facilitate the spread of information and solidarity and motivate people to engage in political action. However, while the experience of economic difficulty may drain resources from political participation, tough economic conditions may as well generate grievances which people may seek to redress through political participation, including through recourse to protest (Giugni and Grasso 2015a; Grasso and Giugni 2016a). Using Hirschman's (1970) terminology, one might argue that those hardest hit by economic recession are also those most likely to "exit" the political sphere and withdraw from political engagement. Only those who are relatively insulated from financial hardship may have the resources needed to "voice" their concerns and engage in political action. Others still will choose "loyalty" even with the economic crisis because they are not exposed to its negative effects or because other factors lead them to support the current economic system notwithstanding unraveling economic problems.

The wide range of the consequences of crises on citizens' resilience, however, is not limited to the choice between retreating from public life and various forms of participation, on one hand, and political engagement, on the other. There is a range of other possible responses to crises and their negative consequences. Thus, the "voice" side also refers to citizens who choose different channels and strategies to make their voice heard as an active reaction to crises. Not only can they engage in political action and protest, but they may seek access to justice at various levels and take part in the associational life of their community. Economic crises may also open up new opportunities for political parties—in particular, right-wing populist parties—which voters might consider as providing attractive solutions to cope with the negative consequences of the crisis.

As regards the "exit" side, citizens might develop new attitudes and practices toward the economic system, society at large, and their own place within it, such as "alternative forms of resilience" such as barter networks, food banks, free medical services, soup kitchens, new cooperatives, and free legal advice. In addition, trust which is built in networks by social support and personal contact is vital to engaging in alternative economic practices. Studies show the existence of a wide repertoire of non-capitalist practices that involve citizens lowering their cost of living, connecting to other communities and assisting others (Kousis 1999). Alternative forms of resilience include the strengthening of social and family networks and community practices to foster solidarity in the face of crises, change of lifestyles toward more sustainable forms of consumption and production, developing new artistic expressions, and moving abroad for short or long durations (or on the contrary reducing mobility). Put simply, major dissatisfaction with the economic system may enhance the strength and resources of those who set out to engage in alternative ways of dealing with it (Giugni and Grasso 2015a). These transformations in citizen practices (from adapted to alternative) under the culture of austerity are decisive for their future survival.

The theoretical framework that has informed the research project upon which this book rests allowed for studying resilience along the analytical continuum between the individual level of single citizens who learn how to "bounce back" and downplay the costs of crises and the far-reaching forms of collective resilience aimed at entering the public domain so as to challenge inequities and foster common empowerment. In other words, individual and collective responses should not be considered as mutually exclusive strategies, but rather as a range of possible ways in which citizens may respond to economic crises as well as their social and political consequences. Such strategies may be pursued singularly or in various combined forms.

Attention was thus placed on the broad range of coping strategies which European citizens might develop under the influence of a number of factors such as the scope of the crisis, policy responses to the crisis, public discourses about the crisis, and the individual characteristics of those who are hit by the crisis. The analysis of these factors is essential for understanding how crises affect people's life and, as a result, to develop sound policies aimed at avoiding or alleviating their negative consequences. Of course, crises threaten the everyday life of most deprived sectors of the population in particular. Yet, especially intense crises are also likely to affect those who are not exposed to insecurity during ordinary times, such as certain sectors of the middle class.

As regards the scope of the economic crisis, the chapters in this volume have highlighted the relevant experiences of the crisis in each country. This is an important step since we can observe great variation across the nine countries included in our study, considering both macro-level factors such as unemployment, underemployment, inflation and GDP, and this is in turn likely to have an impact on the micro-level assessment of the conditions of individual citizens. In some cases, the crisis hit harshly, compared to cases where it is considered to have been weaker, and those cases that might be placed somewhere in between. As such, the present volume goes beyond analyses that only consider the similar ubiquitous exogenous impact of global crises. The analyses provided in the previous chapters show the specific ways in which the Great Recession has been perceived and experienced across this group of countries as well as the manner in which different groups of citizens of those countries have responded to it. At the same time, they suggest that economic crises might produce hardship and constraints, especially for certain groups of citizens, but—as any other kind of crisis—they might also open up opportunities, for example, for a new start in one's life or a renewal of the political landscape.

The Economic Crisis as Constraint

To say that people suffered from the deep and long-lasting economic crisis that struck Europe in the past ten year is to state the obvious. The analyses in the previous chapters of this book confirm that European citizens have felt the negative consequences of the crisis deeply. To begin with, many have had a clear perception that they were experiencing a period of economic downturn, and this even in those countries, such as Germany, Sweden, and Switzerland, that have largely been spared the most dramatic consequences of the crisis. Even there, citizens were sensing that Europe, if not specifically their country, was undergoing a profound economic downturn. This might have occurred later in the course of the crisis but by 2015, when we conducted our survey, it was clear to most people, if not to all, that Europe was undergoing a phase of deep recession.

Such awareness of the situation of the country's economy was accompanied by the perception that the crisis has impacted on the living and work conditions of many Europeans, sometimes profoundly so. The Great Recession has indeed created a number of constraints on European citizens, including a massive loss of jobs, especially in certain countries such as Greece, Italy, and Spain. Many had to reduce their levels of consumption and to give up, for example, going on holidays. Others were forced to take out loans or ask family and friends for financial support. Some have fallen below the poverty line during the years of the crisis, among them many who would have never imagined being in such a situation. The austerity policies enacted by governments—a blend of cuts in social expenditures and raised taxes—have certainly not improved things. Quite the contrary, they have most likely further contributed to exacerbating existent problems and inequalities.

The chapters in this book have shown that Europeans have variously experienced the extent of the economic crisis of the past ten years. This has created feelings of deprivation or exacerbated them among certain groups. More generally, the Great Recession has had heavy consequences on one's own personal life, particularly on health and well-being, although research sometimes points to contradictory results (see Burgard and Kalousova 2015 for a review). It may lead to negative views of oneself, loss of confidence, and a diminishing self-esteem, resulting in a lower level of well-being and sometimes leading to depression. Furthermore, economic hardship may also have important social consequences for citizens, in particular regarding their social life. Particularly for those who lose their job as a result of the crisis, the risk of social isolation is behind the corner. Indeed, since the seminal study by Jahoda et al. (1933), the sociological literature on unemployment has pointed to a range of negative social consequences of job loss, including a destructuration of everyday life. Unemployment, especially when it is prolonged in time, is not only associated with financial hardship, but it may also lead to social isolation due to the loss of work-related contacts and difficulties in maintaining social relations with friends and acquaintances, leading to a reduction in one's social capital (Lahusen and Giugni 2016). Furthermore, losing one's job may multiply the negative psychological effects of economic hardship.

Under certain conditions, economic hardship may also create constraints for the political behavior of citizens, both in the institutional sphere (voting) and in the extra-institutional sphere (protest). As we mentioned earlier, many a citizen, especially those hardest hit by the economic crisis, might have been tempted to withdraw from political engagement (Grasso 2018). When this occurs, the private sphere takes over from the political sphere in the importance attributed to it by people (Grasso 2016). While this process of political disaffection might have been underway well before the crisis (Grasso 2011, 2014), the latter might have accelerated and further deteriorated the situation. Economic hardship may lead to diminishing levels of political interest, trust, and efficacy, which are all attitudes and predispositions that favor political participation, hence leading to political disengagement.

Perceptions and experiences of the economic crisis, however, have not been evenly distributed across the population. In other words, not everyone has suffered to the same extent from the constraints created by the economic crisis. This was clearly shown in the analyses presented in the three chapters in the Part III of the book. One of the main goals of this book was indeed to show the differential impact of the Great Recession on European citizens. Some groups have suffered to a large extent, while others have been largely spared the negative consequences of the crisis. Needless to say, as shown by the three chapters in Part III of the book and in spite of assessments stressing the impact of the crisis on the middle class—especially in the USA and the "middle-class squeeze" thesis—the poorest and the more underprivileged have paid the higher price of both the crisis and the austerity policies enacted by governments to fight against it. Paradoxically, this is perhaps best seen precisely in those countries where the crisis was less serious, as the difference between the "winners" and the "losers" of the Great Recession becomes more visible here. In contrast, in those countries that have been more strongly hit by the crisis, the largest part of the population have suffered from its consequences and therefore differences are less marked.

The chapters in Part I have addressed specifically which social groups have been especially sensitive to the crisis. The ways in which European citizens have perceived and above all experienced the Great Recession have been shown to depend on their sociodemographic profile to a large extent. Thus, we see, for example, in the chapter on Germany has stressed the role of social class for the perception and experience of the crisis. Similarly, the chapter on Switzerland has shown that manual workers, lower income, and jobless people have suffered more from the economic crisis than other groups, but at the same time, these groups have often proved to be more resilient to it. Likewise, the chapter on Sweden has stressed that the perception of the crisis varies according to gender, income, own experience of the crisis, and political ideology or orientation.

The Economic Crisis as Opportunity

The Great Recession has put many Europeans in a difficult position. At the same time, as we have stressed earlier, European citizens have often proven themselves particularly resilient. They found ways to react to the changing economic and social conditions, whether privately and individually or publicly and collectively. More often than not, reactions have likely remained confined to the private sphere and have only covered individual needs. For example, as we already hinted above, some people might have changed their everyday-life habits as a result of the economic hardship caused by the crisis. This may include changing consumption patterns, avoiding superfluous expenses, giving up on holidays, and so forth. Their entire lifestyle may have become altered as a result of these forced changes, temporarily—until the family finances get better—but also in a more durable ways lasting beyond the crisis. Especially in the latter case, the economic crisis might in fact become an opportunity to restructure one's own life. While we are all ready to admit that the economic crisis has posed constraints upon many European citizens, we are perhaps less inclined to think that, as any other kind of crisis, it may also have opened up new opportunities for some of them, insofar as they are able to seize such opportunities.

This kind of response has little, if any, political coloring. Beyond ways to cope with economic hardship through forms of adaptation and resilience in the private sphere, the crisis has also had an impact on the political sphere of European citizens. This book, however, has focused on the political dimension. The chapters in Part I and Part II all address the political ramifications of economic crisis, including citizen's political responses to it. Such responses may relate to the institutional as well as the extra-institutional arena.

Perhaps the most straightforward response in the institutional realm is through voting. This may take the form of moving from abstention to participation or voting for a different party than was done in previous elections. One such response is well-known by students of voting behavior: not voting for the party in government. Following the economic voting literature, citizens tend to punish incumbents in times of economic downturn for what they see as their poor economic performances (see Lewis-Beck and Stegmeier 2000 for a review). Recent studies suggest that such an effect of economic voting may be stronger in times of crisis, that is, when the economy goes bad (Hernández and Kriesi 2016). Critics of economic voting theory, however, have questioned such a centrality of the economy in determining the vote choice, suggesting that not all follow economic considerations and showing that the salience of the economy varies across individuals and contexts (Singer 2011). As the chapter on the UK shows, this country is a case in point at least in part supporting the latter view, as the governing party, which moreover, implemented the austerity measures, was reelected in the 2015 general election. Thus, it appears as though a combination of factors is at work, including the salience of the issues debated during an election campaign and one's wider ideological positioning, which means individuals do not simply switch sides in bad economic times.

A related response to the Great Recession in the form of vote choice could consist in the increasing support for parties that have put anti-austerity at center stage and, more generally, are critical of the European Union. We can mention the resounding electoral breakthrough of Alexis Tsipras and *Syriza* in Greece in 2015, the thunderous success of *Podemos* in Spain in the same year, or the perhaps less well-known but equally important electoral gains of the *Movimento 5 Stelle* in Italy in 2013. These are only the most well-known examples of parties—whether on the left or on the right of the political spectrum— critical of the European Union and especially of the austerity policies it supported during the economic crisis which were able to exploit the opportunities provided by the economic crisis. Some of these parties—in particular, the three mentioned above—have been depicted as movement parties insofar as they are based on new organizational models influenced both by party and movement characteristics (della Porta et al. 2017). As the chapter on Spain has illustrated on the example of *Podemos*, these parties owe their success to their populist stance, therefore capitalizing on the rise of populist attitudes among the electorate during and partly as a result of the economic crisis. Populism seems indeed one of the most peculiar traits characterizing electoral politics during the Great Recession (Kriesi and Pappas 2015). In addition to these new parties, more traditional radical right parties have also taken advantage of the hardship produced by the economic crisis as well as of the rise of populist attitudes among the citizenry to make electoral gains, often focusing on the immigration issue and linking it to the failure of facing the negative consequences of the economic crisis.

The increasing support given to populist parties often goes hand in hand with a diminished support to established parties and, more broadly, to the political system as a whole. The chapter on Poland perhaps offered an extreme example of this. The country has witnessed a political legitimation crisis during the years of the crisis. While the roots of such a legitimation crisis are antecedent, it led to a withdrawal of support from the political system as well as to a legitimization divide within Polish society which was triggered by neoliberal policies which were supposed to protect the economy from the effects of the crisis, but in fact produced such a legitimation crisis. Yet, going beyond the specific case at hand, while political crises of this kind are never desirable, they might also contain the seeds for a reshuffling of a political system hence providing an opportunity for change. This is in line with studies stressing that events like crises allow for adopting and implementing significant changes that otherwise might be unlikely (Jones and Baumgartner 2012; Keeler 1993; Vis and van Kersbergen 2007).

In addition to influencing individual political attitudes and behaviors, as seen, for example, changing voting patterns, giving rise to populist attitudes, or eroding system support, often citizens' responses to the economic crisis have entered the public sphere and taken on a collective dimension (Giugni and Grasso 2016; Grasso and Giugni 2013; Grasso and Giugni 2016a, Grasso and Giugni 2016b). To be sure, individual political attitudes and behaviors have collective consequences such as favoring a party rather than another. However, such collective consequences are simply by-products of individual behaviors, while participation in various forms of collective action has an inherently collective nature from the start. Protest is one of the most visible such responses. The idea that economic or other kinds of hardship create grievances that lead to protest behavior is an old one in social movement theory. So-called grievance or breakdown theories have very much stressed this aspect at least since the 1950s (see Buechler 2004 for a review). These theories were largely dismissed starting from the late 1970s, when resource mobilization and political process theory took over, but have been revamped especially since the advent of the Great Recession. In spite of the existence of many different variants of this theory, they all stress the role of social stress as well as the direct impact of grievances, hardship, and deprivation on the propensity of people to get engaged in protest activities. While it is uncertain whether the economic crisis has led to an overall increase in protest rather than simply reflecting preexisting national trends (Cinalli and Giugni 2016), it is undeniable that there are a number of large-scale protests, most notably in those countries most seriously affected by the crisis such as Greece, Italy, and Spain.

In some cases, such reactions have been creative, like in the myriad of local initiatives variably known as social economy (Moulaert and Ailenei 2005), solidarity (or solidary) economy (Laville 2010), or alternative forms of resilience (Kousis 2017), referring broadly to alternative economic practices initiated by citizen groups and networks. These initiatives include a wide range of actions ranging from solidarity bartering, trading schemes, local and alternative currencies, ethical banks, local market cooperatives, cooperatives for the supply of social services such as in health and education, alternative forms of production, critical consumption, and spontaneous actions of resistance and reclaim to the reproduction of cultural knowledge via oral and artistic expression (Kousis and Paschou 2017). As such, they can be seen as being located between political and non-political actions (see also Giugni and Grasso 2015b). From the perspective of social movement analysis, such initiatives often see the involvement of "sustainable community movement organizations" (Graziano and Forno 2014), new collective initiatives which empower consumer and producer networks on a smaller scale.

As the chapter on France illustrates, the Great Recession has brought itself a transformation of action repertoires of contention that has opened up the space for new forms of participation, in particular forms requiring a lower level of time commitment, such as online activism and non-institutional forms of political participation. The economic crisis has also favored citizens' involvement in certain forms of political participation. Volunteering in social solidarity networks is one example of this, as the chapter on Greece shows. Political consumerism is another example, whereby the crisis has led or at least strengthened a transformation of the constituency of economic activism and favored the involvement of less politicized citizens, as the chapter on Italy illustrates.

Thus, in addition to posing strong constraints for the citizenry, economic crises may also open up new opportunities, not only in personal lives but also in the political realm. We should, however, refrain from assigning a normative connotation to such opportunities, as they do not necessarily lead to positive outcomes. Economic crises may broaden the political offer by favoring the rise of new parties, bring people to political participation, lead to a renewal in the forms of collective action, or empower citizens, but they may also give rise to populist attitudes, parties, and movements, generate political apathy, and lead to political crises and stalemate. In other words, the Great Recession has arguably opened up opportunities for certain political actors to increase their presence and for European citizens to get involved in political or "near political" activities. However, the direction of such trends remains an open question.

The Intertwining of the Economy and Politics

One of the main lessons that we can draw from the analyses presented in the previous chapters is that economy and politics intertwine in a number of ways. At the system level, economic crises might provoke political crises or worsen preexisting ones. To be sure, political crises may be independent from economic considerations and concerns, and stem from example from corruption, unapplied rule of law, as well as more generally from government ineffectiveness. While political and institutional crises often have their internal and independent origin, however, they might interact with economic crises in various, sometimes unexpected, ways. The most likely scenario is probably that economic downturn exacerbates preexisting political crises. Yet, political crises may also be a result of economic crises. The circumstances under which this occurs are complex and multifaceted. In terms of social movements' literature, they are likely to rest upon dynamics involving a combination of grievances, organization, and opportunity as well as a range of institutional and non-institutional actors (Kriesi 2015).

Most importantly in this context, the economy and politics also link together when it comes to the impact of economic crises on citizens. As Bermeo and Bartels (2014: 4; emphasis in original) have maintained "*dramatic political reactions to the Great Recession were associated less with the direct economic repercussions of the crisis than with government initiative to cope with those repercussions.*" Thus, citizens' perceptions, experiences, and responses stem above all (indirectly) from political consideration rather than (directly) from the impact of economic hardship. From the perspective of social movement analysis, this calls into question the so-called grievance or breakdown theories of collective action. What really matters for economic hardship to impinge upon political behavior, it appears, is the way in which grievances are politically framed and subjectively understood within the wider context of political opportunities. In the context of the Great Recession, for example, we were able to show by means of political claims data that, at the aggregate level, the effect of material deprivation depends on the perceptions of the political environment and, more specifically, that it is moderated by perceptions of political stability and of the effectiveness of government (Giugni and Grasso 2016). As such, perceptions of political stability and government effectiveness act as signals leading material deprivation to become politicized as a grievance. Furthermore, individual-level grievances interact with macro-level factors to impact on protest behavior. Our own analysis of the survey data upon which this book is based in fact shows that the impact of individual subjective feelings of deprivation is conditional on contextual macroeconomic and policy factors (Grasso and Giugni 2016a). More specifically, we found that, while individual-level deprivation has a direct effect on the propensity to have protested in the last year, this effect is greater under certain macroeconomic and political conditions. We have interpreted these interactions terms of their role for opening up political opportunities for protest among those who feel they have been most deprived in the current crisis.

The chapters in this book offer numerous examples of the intertwining of economic and political factors in accounting for the impact of economic downturn on citizens. In particular, the chapters in Part I and Part II examine the impact of the economic crisis on citizens' political attitudes and behaviors, respectively, in the institutional and extra-institutional domain. As such, they all show how the economy and politics relate to each other. This can be seen, for example, in the chapter on the UK, which shows the relationship between the economic crisis, political, and partisanship (see also English et al. 2016; Grasso et al. 2017; Temple et al. 2016), but it is perhaps most obvious in the chapter on Spain, which shows the impact of the crisis on the development of populist attitudes and more specifically on the emergence of the leftist populist party *Podemos*, and in the chapter on Poland, which examines how neoliberal policies and privatization measures led to a legitimation crisis in the context of the Great Recession.

The linkages between economic and political factors, furthermore, are also visible in the three chapters that have examined the transformation of political participation in the shadow of the Great Recessions. In this vein, the chapter on France has documented a "post-contentious" turning point in French politics whereby new forms of political participation have been strengthened, the chapter on Italy has witnessed a shift in the composition of the Italian political consumerism community during the crisis, and the chapter on Greece has shown how the economic crisis has spurred political participation in the form of volunteering within the Greek social solidarity networks.

Finally, while best seen in the chapters in Part I and Part II, the intermeshing of the economic and the political to some extent also appears from the chapters in Part III. For example, the chapter on Germany shows that populism and dissatisfaction with the government enhanced the awareness of the economic crisis. Furthermore, the chapter on Switzerland—perhaps the one in which the political dimension is less present—still points to the existence of a linkage between economic and political factors, as the citizens' capacity for resilience is positively associated with their satisfaction with the way government is dealing with economy. Finally, the chapter on Sweden suggests that the perception that a serious crisis was going on depended on the level of distrust that citizens have toward the authorities. In brief, one cannot fully understand the social impact of economic crises without taking into account the intermeshing of the economy with politics.

Beyond the Great Recession

The analyses presented in this book suggest a number of avenues for further research on the impact of economic crises on citizens. Let us mention four such strands, all in turn linked to each other. The first suggestion is very simple: to examine different periods of economic downturn. This book has dealt with a specific historical period and geographical area: the early 2000s and early 2010s in Europe. We found a strong impact of that crisis on European citizens, albeit not necessarily a direct and homogeneously distributed one, but rather an impact that is mediated by political factors and is unevenly distributed across different sectors of the society. Yet, nothing guarantees us that the same—or even similar—effects would be found in other places and in other times. In the end, each crisis has its own peculiarities and it is characterized by specific interactive dynamics of players and arenas (Jasper and Duyvendak 2015). Only by multiplying the comparisons across countries and across time will we be able to make valid and reliable empirical generalizations about the impact of economic crises on citizens' attitudes and behaviors.

A second avenue for further research relates to what we said earlier concerning one of the main lessons to be learned from the analyses presented in the previous chapters, namely, the intertwining of the economic and political dimensions. This applies to both the origins and the consequences of economic crisis. On the one hand, the latter might have their origin in financial dynamics, as the Great Recession had, but they are often spurred or at least accelerated by certain political decisions. For example, many observers today agree that the austerity policies adopted by many European countries and encouraged—to say the least—by the so-called Troika of the European Commission, the Central European Bank, and the International Monetary Fund have done little to cushion the negative impact of the Great Recession. Quite on the contrary, most of us today are ready to maintain that these policies have only worsened the situation. On the other hand, economic crises often result in political crises. Such an intertwining of economic and political factors is famously at the heart of certain accounts of social revolutions (Skocpol 1979), but it often also applies at a lower scale, in everyday politics. Spelling out when and how these conditions link to radical social reorganizations remains a major task for social scientists in the future.

Relatedly, a third path for future investigation lies in exploring the interaction of the contextual and individual levels and how they combine to lead citizens to respond, especially in political terms, to economic hardship. Studying the micro-macro link is a long-standing concern in sociology and the social sciences more generally (Alexander et al. 1987; Turner and Markovsky 2007). Research on political participation has paid increasing attention to the interplay between micro-level and macro-level factors in accounts of protest behavior as well as political participation more generally (Dalton et al. 2010; Grasso and Giugni 2016a; Kern et al. 2015; Quaranta 2015, 2016). Further work should follow this path and continue to examine how micro-macro dynamics help explain the impact of economic crises on citizens' attitudes and behaviors. Micro-level economic hardship has been shown to impinge on citizens' attitudes and behaviors to the extent that certain macro-level conditions are present (Grasso and Giugni 2016a). The latter include broader economic and political developments as well as political opportunities for translating individual grievances into protest behavior, but other contextual factors—for example, prevailing discourses about the crisis—might matter as well.

A fourth and final possible line of inquiry which we would like to suggest for future work consists in comparing citizens' attitudes and behaviors in periods of economic downturn and in period of economic expansion. We should not forget that certain developments we tend to link to the crisis may well have been underway before it. For example, populism is not a creation of the Great Recession, but took on a new strength during the crisis. Similarly, alternative forms of resilience have not been invented during the economic crisis, but probably multiplied in these years. Ultimately, whether economic crises have a specific impact on citizens' attitudes and behaviors can only be determined by comparing situations of profound economic downturn with more standard situations. To be sure, one can compare countries that have been seriously hit by the crisis and others that have been spared its worse effects. Moreover, one can compare groups that have been affected to different extents by economic hardship, as some of the chapters in this book have done. However, there are many different variables involved in such cross-country or cross-group comparisons that it would become difficult to isolate the effect of the crisis. A stronger test would be to compare the same country during and outside phases of deep economic downturn. To do so, of course, one needs clear criteria to determine when a country is in times of crisis and longitudinal data to analyze patterns over time. We hope that future research will heed this call and deepen further our understandings of the effects of crises on the various social and political factors outlined in this volume.

References

Alexander, J. C., Giesen, B., Münch, R., & Smelser, N. J. (1987). *The Micro-Macro Link*. Berkeley: University of California Press.

Bermeo, N., & Bartels, L. M. (2014). Mass Politics in Tough Times. In N. Bermeo & L. M. Bartels (Eds.), *Mass Politics in Tough Times: Opinions, Votes and Protest in the Great Recession* (pp. 1–39). Oxford: Oxford University Press.

Buechler, S. M. (2004). The Strange Career of Strain and Breakdown Theories of Collection Action. In D. A. Snow, S. A. Soule, & H. Kriesi (Eds.), *The Blackwell Companion to Social Movements* (pp. 47–66). Malden: Blackwell.

Burgard, S. A., & Klousova, L. (2015). Effects of the Great Recession: Health and Well-Being. *Annual Review of Sociology, 41*, 181–201.

Cinalli, M., & Giugni, M. (2016). Collective Responses to the Economic Crisis in the Public Domain: Myth or Reality? *Politics and Policy, 44*, 427–446.

Dalton, R., Sickle, A. V., & Weldon, S. (2010). The Individual–Institutional Nexus of Protest Behaviour. *British Journal of Political Science, 40*, 51–73.

English, P., Grasso, M. T., Buraczynska, B., Karampampas, S., & Temple, L. (2016). Convergence on Crisis? Comparing Labour and Conservative Party Framing of the Economic Crisis in Britain, 2008–2014. *Politics & Policy, 44*(3), 577–603.

Forno, F., & Graziano, P. R. (2014). Sustainable Community Movement Organisations. *Journal of Consumer Culture, 14*, 139–157.

Giugni, M., & Grasso, M. T. (Eds). (2015a). *Austerity and Protest: Popular Contention in Times of Economic Crisis*. London: Routledge.

Giugni, M., & Grasso, M. T. (2015b). Environmental Movements in Advanced Industrial Democracies: Heterogeneity, Transformation, and Institutionalization. *Annual Review of Environment and Resources, 40*, 337–361.

Giugni, M., & Grasso, M. T. (2016). How Civil Society Actors Responded to the Economic Crisis: The Interaction of Material Deprivation and Perceptions of Political Opportunity Structures. *Politics and Policy, 44*, 447–472.

Giugni, M., & Grasso, M. T. (2017). Citizens and the Crisis: Perceptions, Experiences, and Responses to the Great Recession in Nine Democracies. In M. Giugni & M. T. Grasso (Eds.), *Citizens and the Crisis: Perceptions, Experiences, and Responses to the Great Recession in Europe*. London: Palgrave Macmillan.

Grasso, M. T. (2011). *Political Participation in Western Europe*. D.Phil. Thesis, Nuffield College, University of Oxford.

Grasso, M. T. (2014). Age-Period-Cohort Analysis in a Comparative Context: Political Generations and Political Participation Repertoires. *Electoral Studies, 33*, 63–76.

Grasso, M. T. (2016). *Generations, Political Participation and Social Change in Western Europe*. London: Routledge.

Grasso, M. T. (2018). Young People's Political Participation in Times of Crisis. In S. Pickard & J. Bessant (Eds.), *Young People Regenerating Politics in Times of Crisis*. London: Palgrave.

Grasso, M. T., & Giugni, M. (2013, September 12–14). Anti-austerity Movements: Old Wine in New Vessels? In *XXVII Meeting of the Italian Political Science Association (SISP)*, University of Florence, Florence.

Grasso, M. T., & Giugni, M. (2016a). Protest Participation and Economic Crisis: The Conditioning Role of Political Opportunities. *European Journal of Political Research, 55*(4), 663–680.

Grasso, M. T., & Giugni, M. (2016b). Do Issues Matter? Anti-Austerity Protests' Composition, Values, and Action Repertoires Compared. *Research in Social Movements, Conflicts and Change 39*, 31–58.

Grasso, M. T., Farrall, S., Gray, E., Hay, C., & Jennings, W. (2017). Thatcher's Children, Blair's Babies, Political Socialisation and Trickle-Down Value-Change: An Age, Period and Cohort Analysis. *British Journal of Political Science*. https://doi.org/10.1017/S0007123416000375.

Hernández, E., & Kriesi, H. (2016). The Electoral Consequences of the Financial and Economic Crisis in Europe. *European Journal of Political Research, 55*, 203–224.

Hirschman, A. O. (1970). *Exit, Voice, and Loyalty: Responses to Decline in Firms, Organizations, and States*. Cambridge, MA: Harvard University Press.

Jahoda, M., Lazarsfeld, P. F., & Zeisel, H. (1933). *Marienthal: The Sociography of an Unemployed Community*. Brunswick: Transaction Publishers.

Jasper, J. M., & Duyvendak, J. W. (2015). *Players and Arenas: The Interactive Dynamics of Protest*. Amsterdam: Amsterdam University Press.

Jones, B. D., & Baumgartner, F. R. (2012). From There to Here: Punctuated Equilibrium to the General Punctuation Thesis to a Theory of Government Information Processing. *Policy Studies Journal, 40*, 1–20.

Keeler, J. T. S. (1993). Opening the Window for Reform: Mandates, Crises, and Extraordinary Policy-Making. *Comparative Political Studies, 25*, 433–486.

Kern, A., Marien, S., & Hooghe, M. (2015). Economic Crisis and Levels of Political Participation in Europe (2002–2010): The Role of Resources and Grievances. *West European Politics, 38*, 465–490.

Kousis, M. (1999). Sustaining Local Environmental Mobilisations: Groups, Actions and Claims in Southern Europe. In C. Rootes (Ed.), *Environmental Movements: Local, National and Global* (pp. 172–198). London: Frank Cass.

Kousis, M. (2017). Alternative Forms of Resilience Confronting Hard Economic Times: A South European Perspective. *Partecipazione e Conflitto, 10*, 119–135.

Kousis, M., & Paschou, M. (2017). Alternative Forms of Resilience: A Typology of Approaches for the Study of Citizen Collective Responses in Hard Economic Times. *Partecipazione e Conflitto, 10*, 136–168.

Kriesi, H. (2015). Political Mobilization in Times of Crises: The Relationship Between Economic and Political Crises. In M. Giugni & M. T. Grasso (Eds.), *Austerity and Protest: Popular Contention in Times of Economic Crisis* (pp. 19–33). Farnham: Ashgate.

Kriesi, H., & Pappas, T. S. (Eds.). (2015). *European Populism in the Shadow of the Great Recession*. Colchester: ECPR Press.

Lahusen, C., & Giugni, M. (2016). Experiencing Long-Term Unemployment in Europe: An Introduction. In C. Lahusen & M. Giugni (Eds.), *Experiencing Long-Term Unemployment in Europe: Youth on the Edge* (pp. 1–16). Houndmills: Palgrave.

Laville, J.-L. (2010). Solidarity Economy. In K. Hart, J.-L. Laville, & A. D. Cattani (Eds.), *The Human Economy* (pp. 225–235). Cambridge: Polity Press.

Lewis-Beck, M. S., & Stegmaier, M. (2000). Economic Determinants of Electoral Outcomes. *Annual Review of Political Science, 3*, 183–219.

Moulaert, F., & Ailenei, O. (2005). Social Economy, Third Sector and Solidarity Relations: A Conceptual Synthesis from History to Present. *Urban Studies, 42*, 2037–2053.

della Porta, D., Fernández, J., Kouki, H., & Mosca, L. (2017). *Movement Parties Against Austerity*. Cambridge: Polity.

Quaranta, M. (2015). *Political Protest in Western Europe: Exploring the Role of Context in Political Action*. Heidelberg/New York: Springer.

Quaranta, M. (2016). Protesting in 'Hard Times': Evidence from a Comparative Analysis of Europe, 2000–2014. *Current Sociology, 64*, 736–756.

Singer, M. M. (2011). Who Says 'It's the Economy'? Cross-National and Cross-Individual Variation in the Salience of Economic Performance. *Comparative Political Studies, 44*, 284–312.

Skocpol, T. (1979). *States and Social Revolutions: A Comparative Analysis of France, Russia and China*. Cambridge: Cambridge University Press.

Temple, L., & Grasso, M. T. (2017). Austerity, Politics, and Partisanship in the UK. In M. Giugni & M. T. Grasso (Eds.), *Citizens and the Crisis: Perceptions, Experiences, and Responses to the Great Recession in Europe*. London: Palgrave Macmillan.

Temple, L., Grasso, M. T., Buraczynska, B., Karampampas, S., & English, P. (2016). Neoliberal Narrative in Times of Economic Crisis: A Political Claims Analysis of the UK Press, 2007–2014. *Politics & Policy, 44*(3), 553–576.

Turner, J., & Markovsky, B. (2007). Micro-Macro Links. In G. Ritzer (Ed.), *The Blackwell Encyclopedia of Sociology* (pp. 2997–3004). Malden: Blackwell.

Vis, B., & van Kersbergen, K. (2007). Why and How Do Political Actors Pursue Risky Reforms? *Journal of Theoretical Politics, 19*, 153–172.

Appendix

Chapter 2

Table A.2.1 Descriptive statistics

Variable	*n*	*Mean*	*Std. Dev.*	*Min*	*Max*
Age	1547	51.64124	14.77078	18	86
Male (ref = Female)	1547	0.4899806	0.5000613	0	1
Low education (ref = Higher)	1547	0.2527473	0.4347278	0	1
Unemployed (ref = Employed)	1547	0.0420168	0.2006924	0	1
Blue collar (ref = White collar)	1547	0.1848739	0.3883208	0	1
Working class (ref = Middle/upper)	1547	0.3671622	0.4821871	0	1
Left-right scale	1547	4.87999	1.540182	0	10
Political interest (ref = Not interested)	1547	0.7724628	0.4193777	0	1
Crisis (ref = No crisis)	1547	0.3962508	0.4892758	0	1
Gov. assessment: Economy	1547	4.982547	2.881727	0	10
Gov. assessment: Poverty	1547	3.565611	2.65528	0	10
Gov. assessment: Unemployment	1547	4.383969	2.691552	0	10
Gov. assessment: Immigration	1547	2.69554	2.371892	0	10
Reduced items	1547	1.99095	2.354961	0	10
Deprived	1547	3.826115	2.029891	0	10
Struggling bills (ref = Not struggling)	1547	0.1797027	0.3840637	0	1
Claiming benefits (ref = Not claiming)	1547	0.2236587	0.4168307	0	1

M. Giugni, M.T. Grasso (eds.), *Citizens and the Crisis*,
Palgrave Studies in European Political Sociology,
https://doi.org/10.1007/978-3-319-68960-9

Calculating Country Outlook and Household Outlook

These variables were coded using the variables in Fig. 2.1. "Country Outlook" used county compared to one year ago and country in next year. Those who thought it the same across both instances were classed as "no change". If respondent answered better-better, better-no change, no change-better, they were classed as optimistic. If respondent answered worse-worse, worse-no change, no change-worse, they were classed as pessimistic. The same principle applied to "Household Outlook" across the three household level variables (in order: compared to five years ago, compared to one year ago, in the future). The comparison to parent variables was not used. The descriptive statistics for the categories can be seen below:

Table A.2.2 Percentages optimistic, pessimistic, and no change (country and household level)

	Freq.	%
Country level		
Optimistic	802	51.8
No change	394	25.5
Pessimistic	351	22.7
Household level		
Optimistic	773	50.0
No change	154	10.0
Pessimistic	620	40.0

Table A.2.3 Voting in 2015 General Election (odds ratios) [Models—(1), (3), and (5) control for past party support, reference category is the party of the predicted vote]

	(1) *Lab 2015*	*(2)* *Lab 2015*	*(3)* *Con 2015*	*(4)* *Con 2015*	*(5)* *UKIP 2015*	*(6)* *UKIP 2015*
Age	1.02	1.02	0.97	0.98	1.01	1.01
	(0.03)	(0.03)	(0.03)	(0.03)	(0.04)	(0.04)
Age^2	1.00	1.00	1.00	1.00	1.00	1.00
	(0.00)	(0.00)	(0.00)	(0.00)	(0.00)	(0.00)
Male (ref = Female)	0.84	0.80	0.52^{***}	0.57^{***}	1.59^{*}	1.63^{**}
	(0.13)	(0.11)	(0.09)	(0.09)	(0.31)	(0.30)
Low education (ref = Higher)	0.95	0.94	0.91	1.12	1.39	1.70^{**}
	(0.20)	(0.16)	(0.19)	(0.20)	(0.31)	(0.35)

(*continued*)

Table A.2.3 (continued)

	(1) Lab 2015	*(2) Lab 2015*	*(3) Con 2015*	*(4) Con 2015*	*(5) UKIP 2015*	*(6) UKIP 2015*
Unemployed (ref = Employed)	0.76	0.80	1.51	1.38	0.89	1.03
	(0.27)	(0.24)	(0.66)	(0.53)	(0.40)	(0.42)
Blue collar (= White collar)	0.64*	0.94	0.98	0.72	0.85	0.82
	(0.14)	(0.17)	(0.24)	(0.15)	(0.22)	(0.19)
Working class (ref = Middle/upper)	1.43*	1.35*	0.67*	0.66*	1.43	1.30
	(0.25)	(0.19)	(0.13)	(0.11)	(0.30)	(0.25)
Left-right scale (0–10)	0.81**	0.69***	1.59***	1.95***	1.22*	1.40***
	(0.06)	(0.05)	(0.15)	(0.16)	(0.12)	(0.12)
Political interest (ref = Not interested)	1.15	1.23	0.68	0.72	1.28	1.29
	(0.22)	(0.20)	(0.13)	(0.12)	(0.30)	(0.28)
Crisis (ref = No crisis)	1.00	0.89	0.90	0.98	1.23	1.31
	(0.17)	(0.13)	(0.17)	(0.16)	(0.26)	(0.25)
Country outlook						
Optimistic (ref = No change)	0.64*	0.59**	1.52	1.44	0.80	0.74
	(0.13)	(0.10)	(0.34)	(0.27)	(0.20)	(0.18)
Pessimistic (ref = No change)	0.85	0.73	0.83	0.74	0.66	0.62
	(0.18)	(0.13)	(0.30)	(0.23)	(0.19)	(0.17)
Household outlook						
Optimistic (ref = No change)	0.59	0.71	1.11	1.42	1.05	0.97
	(0.17)	(0.16)	(0.33)	(0.35)	(0.36)	(0.30)
Pessimistic (ref = No change)	0.61	0.75	0.91	1.24	1.39	1.27
	(0.17)	(0.17)	(0.29)	(0.33)	(0.48)	(0.40)
Government assessment (0 Extremely dissatisfied, 10 Extremely satisfied)						
Economy	0.94	0.89**	1.28***	1.34***	0.90	0.91
	(0.05)	(0.04)	(0.07)	(0.06)	(0.05)	(0.05)
Poverty	0.92	0.88**	0.98	1.08	1.17**	1.17**
	(0.05)	(0.04)	(0.05)	(0.05)	(0.06)	(0.06)
Unemployment	1.01	1.01	0.98	1.03	1.04	1.02
	(0.05)	(0.04)	(0.05)	(0.05)	(0.05)	(0.05)
Immigration	1.04	1.08*	1.16***	1.06	0.60***	0.58***
	(0.04)	(0.03)	(0.05)	(0.04)	(0.04)	(0.04)

(continued)

Table A.2.3 (continued)

	(1) Lab 2015	*(2) Lab 2015*	*(3) Con 2015*	*(4) Con 2015*	*(5) UKIP 2015*	*(6) UKIP 2015*
Material deprivation						
Reduced items (0–10)	0.98	0.96	1.04	1.02	0.98	1.00
	(0.04)	(0.03)	(0.05)	(0.04)	(0.05)	(0.05)
Deprived (0–10)	0.99	1.00	0.97	0.98	1.12*	1.12*
	(0.05)	(0.04)	(0.05)	(0.04)	(0.06)	(0.06)
Struggling bills (ref = Not struggling	0.73	0.80	1.17	1.12	0.99	0.99
	(0.16)	(0.15)	(0.32)	(0.27)	(0.28)	(0.26)
Claiming benefits (ref = Not claiming)	1.31	1.10	0.87	0.94	0.80	0.87
	(0.25)	(0.17)	(0.19)	(0.18)	(0.20)	(0.20)
Existing support						
Labor	*Ref*		0.04***		0.05***	
			(0.01)		(0.02)	
Conservative	0.02***		*Ref*		0.11***	
	(0.01)				(0.04)	
Liberal democrat	0.17***		0.08***		0.07***	
	(0.03)		(0.02)		(0.03)	
Green	0.02***		0.07***		N/A	
	(0.02)		(0.05)		–	
UKIP	0.05***		0.06***		*Ref*	
	(0.02)		(0.03)			
Others	0.01***		0.03***		0.03***	
	(0.01)		(0.02)		(0.02)	
Don't know	0.13***		0.13***		0.08***	
	(0.03)		(0.03)		(0.03)	
N	1547	1547	1547	1547	1523[a]	1547
Pseudo-R^2	0.40	0.17	0.49	0.35	0.29	0.21
Log lik.	−545.80	−753.80	−494.67	−637.77	−404.27	−449.30

Exponentiated coefficients, standard errors in parentheses

*$p < 0.05$; **$p < 0.01$; ***$p < 0.001$

[a]The *n* changes in model (5) as no UKIP voters in 2015 previously supported the Green party; therefore this category predicted failure (0) perfectly and had to be omitted from the model

Chapter 3

Variable Operationalization

Occupation
"Please tell us which one of the following options best describes the sort of paid work you do. If you are not in paid work now, please tell us what you did in your last paid employment." Respondents answering "Skilled Manual Work (e.g. plumber, electrician, fitter)" or "Semi-Skilled or Unskilled Manual Work (e.g. machine operator, assembler, postman, waitress, cleaner, laborer, driver, bar-worker, call-center worker)" are coded as manual workers. The occupation of the household's chief income earner was used when the respondent's was not available.

Occupational Status
Is coded as 1 if the individual is employed, 2 if unemployed, or 3 if not active.

Household Income
"What is your household's MONTHLY income, after tax and compulsory deductions, from all sources? If you don't know the exact figure, please give your best estimate." Coded in deciles of the income distribution in the given country, and adjusted for the size of the household using the OECD-modified equivalence scale.

Reduced Consumption
"In the past 5 years, have you or anyone else in your household had to take any of the following measures for financial/ economic reasons?" The listed items were (1) reduced consumption of staple foods; (2) reduced recreational activities; (3) reduced use of own car; (4) delayed payments on utilities; (5) moved home; (6) delayed or defaulted on a loan installment; (7) sold an asset; (8) cut TV/phone/internet service; (9) did not go on holiday; (10) reduced or postponed buying medicines/visiting the doctor. Additive index (alpha = 0.86).

Worsened Job Conditions
"Please select those of the following has happened to you in the last five years." The listed items were (1) I took a reduction in pay; (2) I had to take a job for which I was overqualified; (3) I had to work extra unpaid

overtime hours; (4) I had to work shorter hours; (5) I had to take or look for an additional job; (6) My work load increased; (7) The working environment deteriorated; (8) I had less security in her job; (9) I had to accept less convenient working hours; (10) Employees were dismissed in the organization for which I work; (11) I was forced to take undeclared payments. These questions were asked only to those that are employed or have been in the past; all other respondents are assigned the lowest value in the resulting scale. Additive index (alpha = 0.83).

Perceptions of the National Economic Situation

Responses to two questions were combined: (i) "Would you say that over the past year the state of the economy in [respondent's country] has become…?" (ii) "Would you say that over the next year the state of the economy in [respondent's country] will become…? Both measured on an 11-point scale from 0 ("Much worse") to 10 ("Much better"). Additive index (alpha = 0.85).

Political Knowledge

An additive index based on four items was used: (i) "Can you tell who is the person in this picture?" [Picture of Jean Claude Junker] (1) José Manuel Durão Barroso, former President of the European Commission; (2) Thorbjørn Jagland, Secretary General of the Council of Europe; (3) Donald Tusk, President of the European Council; (4) Jean Claude Juncker, current President of the European Commission. (ii) "What does public deficit mean?" (1) The lack of public service provision; (2) The money the government owes to its creditors; (3) The money the government fails to collect due to tax fraud; (4) The difference between government receipts and government spending. (iii) "Who sets the interest rates applicable in [respondent's country]?" (1) The government of [respondent's country]; (2) The International Monetary Fund; (3) The European Central Bank; (4) The Central Bank of [respondent's country]. (iv) "As a percentage, what do you think is the current unemployment rate in [country of respondent]?" Responses within a ±1% of the official rate were considered correct. A Don't Know option was offered and people could also skip the question.

Closeness to the Incumbent

Responses to two questions were combined: (i) "Which of the following parties do you feel closest to?" Eight parties were listed, plus options for "other party", "no party", and "don't know". [If party name is chosen]

(ii) "How close do you feel to [party]?" (1) not very close; (2) quite close; (3) very close. Based on the party or parties in each of the country's government at the time of the survey, the resulting scale was coded to take on four possible values: not close to a party in government; not very close; quite close; very close.

Left–Right Identification
"People sometimes talk about the Left and the Right in politics. Where would you place yourself on the following scale where 0 means 'Left' and 10 means 'Right'?" Measured on an 11-point scale.

Attitudes Toward Immigrants
Responses to two questions were combined: (i) "Would you say it is generally bad or good for the [respondent's country]'s economy that people come to live here from other countries? Please state your answer on this scale where 0 means 'Bad' and 10 means 'Good'". (ii) Would you say that the [respondent's country]'s cultural life is generally undermined or enriched by people coming to live here from other countries? Please state your answer on this scale where 0 means "Undermined" and 10 means "Enriched." Both measured on 11-point scales. Additive index (alpha = 0.86).

Interest in Politics
"How interested, if at all, would you say you are in politics?" Response options are not at all, not very, quite, very interested.

Retrospective Evaluations of the National Economic Situation
"Would you say that over the past year the state of the economy in [respondent's country] has become…?" Measured on an 11-point scale from 0 ("Much worse") to 10 ("Much better").

Education
Highest completed level of education in nine categories from primary school or less to postgraduate education. Low education refers to less than secondary education.

Religiosity
"Regardless of whether you belong to a particular religion, how religious would you say you are on a scale from 0 to 10 where 0 means not at all religious and 10 means extremely religious?"

Table A.3.1 Correlates of populist attitudes

	Model 1
Female	−0.042
	(0.032)
Age	0.009
	(0.007)
Age squared	−0.000
	(0.000)
Non-national	−0.120
	(0.088)
Low education	−0.022
	(0.035)
Manual occupation	0.050
	(0.038)
Unemployed	0.007
	(0.043)
Income	−0.248*
	(0.097)
Reduced consumption	0.021
	(0.071)
Worsened job conditions	0.041
	(0.060)
National economy	−0.927**
	(0.088)
Political knowledge	0.185**
	(0.059)
Attachment to incumbent	−0.167*
	(0.068)
Left-right placement	−0.311**
	(0.075)
Attitudes toward immigrants	0.041
	(0.068)
N	1580

Standard errors in parentheses $+p<0.1$; $*p<0.05$; $**p<0.01$

Table A.3.2 Populism and vote intention in the 2015 general elections *[Abstention: reference category]*

	PP	*PSOE*	*Podemos*	*C's*
Populist attitudes	−0.089	−0.073	0.903***	0.383+
	(0.219)	(0.199)	(0.203)	(0.201)
Ideology	6.837***	−3.752***	−4.298***	2.507***
	(0.793)	(0.720)	(0.708)	(0.712)
Political sophistication	1.583**	1.571**	0.987+	1.390*
	(0.579)	(0.545)	(0.537)	(0.540)
Economic situation	3.974***	−0.246	−1.143+	1.220+
	(0.748)	(0.657)	(0.641)	(0.661)
Education	0.931+	0.295	0.894+	0.861
	(0.564)	(0.537)	(0.529)	(0.529)
Ocupp: Employed	[REF.]	[REF.]	[REF.]	[REF.]
Ocupp: Unemployed	0.463	−0.109	−0.007	0.084
	(0.396)	(0.358)	(0.348)	(0.359)
Ocupp: Not active	−0.766*	−0.732*	−0.622+	−0.701*
	(0.356)	(0.326)	(0.320)	(0.324)
Age	0.030**	0.008	−0.020+	0.002
	(0.012)	(0.011)	(0.011)	(0.011)
Female	0.512+	0.232	0.153	0.120
	(0.294)	(0.274)	(0.270)	(0.272)
Religiosity	0.852	0.411	−0.758	−0.291
	(0.526)	(0.489)	(0.485)	(0.486)
Interest	2.044***	2.824***	3.397***	2.714***
	(0.605)	(0.556)	(0.546)	(0.557)
Constant	−7.971***	0.516	−0.441	−3.680***
	(1.061)	(0.899)	(0.910)	(0.925)
N	1564	1564	1564	1564
R^2	0.228	0.228	0.228	0.228

+p<0.1; *p<0.05; **p<0.01; ***p<0.001

Table A.3.3 Populism and vote recall in the 2011 general election *[Abstention: reference category]*

	PP	*PSOE*
Populist attitudes	0.394**	−0.036
	(0.141)	(0.134)
Ideology	5.306***	−3.346***
	(0.495)	(0.456)
Political sophistication	−0.188	0.004
	(0.342)	(0.326)
Economic situation	1.751***	0.074
	(0.446)	(0.421)
Education	0.027	0.013
	(0.323)	(0.312)
Ocupp: Employed	[REF.]	[REF.]
Ocupp: Unemployed	−0.064	−0.418+
	(0.237)	(0.225)
Ocupp: Not active	−0.794***	−0.649**
	(0.221)	(0.206)
Age	0.046***	0.036***
	(0.007)	(0.007)
Female	0.210	0.173
	(0.179)	(0.172)
Religiosity	0.576+	0.041
	(0.312)	(0.303)
Interest	1.325***	1.246***
	(0.352)	(0.326)
Constant	−6.662***	−0.238
	(0.701)	(0.619)
N	1724	1724
R^2	0.173	0.173

Notes: Standard errors in parentheses. The baseline category is abstention. Results for IU, UPyD, non-state-wide parties and other parties are omitted. All variables are coded between 0 and 1.

+p<0.1; *p<0.05, **p<0.01, ***p<0.001

Chapter 8

Table A.8.1 List of variables

Variable	*Original question(s)*	*Recoding*
Occupational class	Comprehensive list of occupations	Four groups: higher service class (28.9%), lower service class (48.1%), skilled manual workers (13%), unskilled workers (9.9%); dichotomized
Income class	Ten income groups from below € 750 to more than € 4200	Four groups: higher class 3.160 € (17.5%), middle incomes between 2.160 and 3.160 € (20.7%), lower middle incomes between 1.240 and 2.160 € (31%), and lower incomes below 1.240 € (30.9%); dichotomized
Educational class	ISCED compatible list of education degrees	Three groups: more than secondary education (27.6%), secondary education (55.3%), lower than secondary education (17.1%); dichotomized
Perceived class	Please tell us which one of the following options best describes the sort of paid work you do. If you are not in paid work now, please tell us what you did in your last paid employment	Four groups: higher class (10.8%), middle class (47.5%), lower middle class (24.3%), lower class (17.4%); dichotomized
Relative deprivation	Five items	Scale (r^2 = 0.75); higher score = less deprived; standardized
Living alone	Single item, dummy	1 = Living alone
Social trust	Generally speaking, would you say that most people can be trusted, or that you can't be too careful in dealing with people? Please state your answer on a scale of 0 to 10, where 0 means "You can't be too careful" and 10 means that "Most people can be trusted"	Recoded 1–11 to 0–10, 12 = missing; standardized
Meeting friends regularly	During the past month, how often have you met socially with friends not living in your household? (please provide a rough estimate); four answers possible	Dichotomized: 0 = less than twice a month; 1 = every week or more often

(continued)

Table A.8.1 (continued)

Variable	*Original question (s)*	*Recoding*
Life satisfaction	All things considered and using the scale on where 0 means "Completely dissatisfied" and 10 means "Completely satisfied," how satisfied or dissatisfied are you with your life as a whole these days?	Recoded 1–11 to 0–10, 12 = missing; standardized
Confident in assistance	"If I have difficulties, someone could take care of me"; dummy	0 = yes; 1 = no
Confident in financial assistance	"If I have difficulties, someone could take care of me financially"; dummy	0 = yes; 1 = no
Left-right scale	People sometimes talk about the left and the right in politics. Where would you place yourself on the following scale where 0 means "Left" and 10 means "Right"?	Standardized
Political trust	Ten items on trust in political institutions, 0 = no trust; 10 complete trust	Scale (r^2 = 0.96); higher score = higher political trust; standardized
Satisfaction with democracy	On the whole, how satisfied or dissatisfied are you with the way democracy works in Germany? 0 = extremely dissatisfied; 10 extremely satisfied	Standardized
Support for democracy	Four items	Scale (r^2 = 0.75); higher score = less support; standardized
Cultural right left	Five items	Index; higher score = the more left
Economic left right	Five items	Scale (r^2 = 0.67), higher score = more right; standardized
Populims_s	Eight items	Scale (r^2 = 0.88), higher score = more populist; standardized
Polint_d	How interested, if at all, would you say you are in politics?; not at all, not very, quite, very, don't know	0 = not interested; 1 = interested
Internal political efficacy	Three items	Scale (r^2 = 0.85), higher score = higher efficacy; standardized

(*continued*)

Table A.8.1 (continued)

Variable	*Original question(s)*	*Recoding*
External political efficacy	Three items	Scale (r^2 = 0.55), higher score = higher efficacy; standardized
Political knowledge	Comprised of three political knowledge questions	0 = all wrong; 1 = one correct; 2 = two correct; 3 = all answers correct; standardized
Gov_economy	How satisfied or dissatisfied are you with the way in which your country's government is dealing with the following on a scale from 0 to 10, where 0 means "extremely dissatisfied" and 10 means "extremely satisfied"?	Standardized
Gov_poverty		Standardized
Gov-education		Standardized
Gov_unemployme		Standardized
Gov_healthcare		Standardized
Gov_precemploym		Standardized
Gov_immigration		Standardized
Gov_childcare		Standardized
Education_father2	See educational class	See educational class
Gender	Dummy	0 = male; 1 = female
Age	Ranging from 18 to 88	Standardized
East	List of German Bundesländer	0 = West Germany, 1 = East Germany
Living in rural area	Which of the following best describes the area in which you live? Answers: A big city; Suburbs or outskirts of big city; Town or small city; Country village; Farm or home in the country side	Dichotomized, 1 = big city or suburbs, 0 = small city or rural
Migrant background	Country of birth of respondent, of mother, and of father	Migrant = 1 if one of the three is born abroad
Religiosity	Regardless of whether you belong to a particular religion, how religious would you say you are on a scale from 0 to 10 where 0 means "Not at all religious" and 10 means "Extremely religious"?	Standardized
Member of a religion	List of religious affiliations	0 = no religion or atheist; 1 = all religions

Chapter 10

Table A.10.1 Descriptive data for the variables used in the analysis ($N = 1375$)

Variable	*Mean*	*Standard deviation*	*Min.*	*Max.*
Crisis	0.194	0.396	0	1
Age	48.52	15.56	18	88
Female	0.481	0.499	0	1
Reduced consumption	1.531	2.232	0	10
Voted for Sweden Democrats	0.195	0.397	0	1
Unemployed	0.046	0.210	0	1
Public sector	0.343	0.474	0	1
Trust in media	3.212	2.408	0	10
Education			1	3
University	37%			
Completed secondary	37%			
Less than secondary	26%			
Income (groups)	6.261	2.90	1	10
Newspaper readership (index)	1.256	1.060	0	5

Notes: *N* for public-sector employees is 1311, as the unemployed cannot simultaneously work in the public sector

Index[1]

[1] Please note: page numbers in bold type indicate figures or illustrations, those in italics indicate tables.

M. Giugni, M.T. Grasso (eds.), *Citizens and the Crisis*, Palgrave Studies in European Political Sociology, https://doi.org/10.1007/978-3-319-68960-9

R

S

T

U